Supreme Court of JudicatureOntario

The Rules of Practice and Procedure of the Supreme Court of

Judicature

For Ontario, Revised, Classified and Consolidated

Supreme Court of JudicatureOntario

The Rules of Practice and Procedure of the Supreme Court of Judicature
For Ontario, Revised, Classified and Consolidated

ISBN/EAN: 9783337157838

Printed in Europe, USA, Canada, Australia, Japan

Cover: Foto ©Suzi / pixelio.de

More available books at **www.hansebooks.com**

THE RULES OF

PRACTICE AND PROCEDURE

OF THE

SUPREME COURT OF JUDICATURE

FOR ONTARIO.

REVISED, CLASSIFIED AND CONSOLIDATED.

UNDER THE AUTHORITY OF CHAPTER 8 OF THE ACTS PASSED IN THE 50TH
YEAR OF THE REIGN OF HER MAJESTY QUEEN VICTORIA.

TORONTO:
PRINTED BY WARWICK & SONS, 26 AND 28 FRONT STREET WEST.
1888.

TABLE OF CONTENTS.

CHAPTER I.

CHAPTER II.

OFFICERS AND OFFICES.

CHAPTER III.

SITTINGS OF THE COURTS.

CHAPTER IV.

ACTIONS—COMMENCEMENT OF ACTIONS, ETC.

CHAPTER V.

PLEADINGS.

CHAPTER VI.

MISCELLANEOUS PROCEEDINGS IN AN ACTION.

CHAPTER VII.

JUDGMENTS, MOTIONS FOR JUDGMENT, ETC.

CHAPTER VIII.

APPEALS.

CHAPTER IX.

ENFORCEMENT OF JUDGMENTS AND ORDERS.

CHAPTER X.

CHAPTER XI.

PROCEEDINGS WITHOUT WRIT.

CHAPTER XII.

EXTRAORDINARY REMEDIES.

CHAPTER XIII.

COSTS.

CHAPTER XIV.

THE

CONSOLIDATED RULES OF PRACTICE

OF THE

SUPREME COURT OF JUDICATURE
FOR ONTARIO.

CHAPTER I.

INTERPRETATION.

1. Nothing in these Rules shall be construed as intended to affect Criminal matters not the practice or procedure in criminal proceedings, or proceedings on the affected. Crown or Revenue side of the Queen's Bench or Common Pleas Divisions. J. A. Rule 484.

2. A "Judge" in these Rules means a Judge of the Supreme Court, or "Judge" a Judge having the authority for the time being of a Judge of the High meaning of Court unless there is something in the context indicating a different meaning. J. A. Rule 491.

3. All rules and orders heretofore passed by any of the Superior Courts Former of Law or Equity in Ontario or Upper Canada and not included in these practice superrules are rescinded, save and except those mentioned in the schedule hereseded. to, and these rules shall take effect on and after the 1st day of March, 1888. All practice inconsistent therewith is superseded. As to all matters not provided for in these rules, the practice is, as far as may be, to be regulated by analogy thereto.

(*a*) Rules 210, 211 and 537, are not to come into force until on and after the 1st September, 1888, and in the meantime the existing practice as to the weekly sittings of the Court shall be continued.

4. The interpretation clauses of the Judicature Act shall apply to these Interpretarules unless there is anything in the subject or context repugnant thereto. tion.

5. The division of these rules into chapters, titles and headings is for Division of convenience only, and is not to affect their construction. rules.

6. Every rule hereafter made shall be construed as intended to come Promulgation into force on the seventh day after the day of its publication in the On- of rules. tario *Gazette*, unless such prior publication is expressly dispensed with in or by the rule.

CHAPTER II.

OFFICERS AND OFFICES.

1. OFFICE HOURS. ETC.

Office hours to be observed in offices of the Court.

7. Except during Vacations, and excepting Sundays, Christmas Day, Good Friday, Easter Monday, New Year's Day, the birthday of the Sovereign, and any day appointed for the celebration of the birthday of the Sovereign, Dominion Day, and any day appointed by proclamation of the Governor General, or Lieutenant Governor, as a public holiday, or for a General Fast, or Thanksgiving, the offices of the Supreme Court, Court of Appeal, and of the High Court of Justice for Ontario and its Divisions, shall be kept open from 10 a.m. to 4 p.m. during the sittings of the respective Divisional Courts, and at other times from 10 a.m. until 3 p.m.   J. A. Rules 537 and 545.

Office hours of offices of High Court during vacation.

8. The offices of the High Court of Justice, and of the Divisions thereof, and of the Court of Appeal, shall be kept open during the Long Vacation, and the Christmas Vacation, from 10 of the clock in the forenoon until 12 o'clock noon.   J. A. Rule 535.

No business to be transacted except upon attendance of party, or his attorney, or the clerk or agent of attorney.

9. No business shall be transacted in any of the offices of the Courts, either in procuring or suing out process, or in entering judgments or taking any proceeding whatever in a cause, unless upon the personal attendance of the party on whose behalf such business is required to be transacted, or of the counsel or solicitor of such party, or the clerk or agent of the solicitor, or the clerk of the agent.   Rules T. T. 1856, 145.

Officers to be auxiliary to one another.

10. All officers shall be auxiliary to one another for promoting the correct, convenient, and speedy administration of business.   J. A. Rule 415.

2. CLERK OF THE PROCESS.

Clerk of Process to issue writs for commencement of actions.

11. The Clerk of the Process shall, on receiving a certified copy of the writ to be filed by him, issue any writ of summons required for the commencement of an action.   Rule T. T. 1856, 150.

12. The Clerk of the Process shall have a seal for sealing writs, to be approved by the Judges of the Supreme Court of Judicature, and he shall seal therewith and sign all writs and process issued by him. *See* R. S. O. 1877, c. 39, s. 43.

13. All other writs required to be issued by the Clerk of the Process to Issue of writs. the parties or their solicitors, shall be issued according to the established practice. Rules T. T. 1856, 152.

14. The Clerk of the Process shall attend in his office at all times when Attendance at the Registrars are required to attend in their respective offices, and shall office. permit all necessary searches respecting writs so issued by him. Rules T. T. 1856, 153.

15. The Clerk of the Process shall, on the opening of the respective Copies of writs offices each morning, or as soon thereafter as may be, deliver to the to be sent to Registrars of the Queen's Bench and Common Pleas Divisions and to the Registrars. Clerk of Records and Writs for the Chancery Division, the copies of writs of summons issued in such Divisions respectively on the preceding day, that the same may be filed with the papers in the respective actions to which such writs belong. Rules of 19 Feb. 1859. *See* J. A. Rule 547.

16. The Clerk of the Process shall deliver to each of the Registrars of Quarterly the respective Divisions on the first day of January, the first day of April, returns of the first day of July, and the first day of October, if not a Sunday or legal writs. holiday, and if so then on the first day thereafter not being a Sunday or legal holiday, in each and every year, quarterly returns of all writs issued by him during the preceding quarter to the respective Divisions, naming each description of writ, and the dates on which the same were issued, to each of the Registrars requiring the same. Rule of 19 Feb., 1859.

3. REGISTRARS, LOCAL REGISTRARS, ETC.

17. The Registrars or Assistant-Registrars or such other officers as the Attending Judges of the Supreme Court shall approve of, shall attend the Weekly court. Sittings of the High Court in rotation. *New.*

18. Local and Deputy Registrars are to perform the duties of their Rules and offices in the same manner, and under the same regulations, as the like regulations duties are performed by the Clerk of Records and Writs ; and all orders, relating to rules, and regulations in force respecting the Clerk of Records and W., to apply Writs, and respecting the regulation of his office, are to be in force and to Local applicable to the Local and Deputy Registrars in relation to such duties and Dep. as they are hereby required to perform ; and the like sums and fees pay- Registrars. able to the Clerk of Records and Writs, are to be payable to the Local and Deputy Registrars, in relation to similar matters. Chy. O. 34.

19. Where the offices of Deputy Clerk of the Crown and Deputy Deputy Clerks Registrar in any county are not held by the same person, the Deputy of the Crown Clerk of the Crown shall in actions in the Queen's Bench and Common and Deputy Pleas Divisions have the powers and duties of a Deputy Registrar (not Registrars. Local Master), in addition to the powers and duties heretofore belonging to a Deputy Clerk of the Crown ; and the Deputy Registrar shall in actions in the Chancery Division have the powers and duties of a Deputy Clerk of the Crown, in addition to the powers and duties heretofore belonging to a Deputy Registrar. In counties where there is a Local Registrar, every reference in these Rules to the said two offices, or either of them, shall be deemed to apply to the Local Registrar. Rules 417, 545. *See* J. A. s. 125 (5).)

Entry of orders.

20. (Subject to the foregoing Rules, where an action is commenced in the office of a Deputy Registrar or Deputy Clerk of the Crown or Local Registrar, those officers respectively shall have all such powers and authorities in relation to the action as the Clerk of Records and Writs has in the case of an action where appearance is to be entered in his office, all such orders) in the action as require to be entered (except orders made by the Local Judge or the Local Master of the county under the authority and jurisdiction vested in them under these Rules) shall be entered in the office of such Deputy Registrar or Deputy Clerk or Local Registrar. Rules 418, 509 ; Chy. O. 35.

List of judgments entered in outer offices to be forwarded to head office of Division in Toronto.

21. Every Deputy Clerk of the Crown, Deputy Registrar, and Local Registrar, shall once in every three months transmit to the Registrar of each Division at Toronto, a list, in the form No. 215 in the Appendix, of all judgments which have been entered by him in such Division during such period ; and from the said lists the Registrars of the several Divisions shall prepare and from time to time keep up, a general index or list of judgments, which shall be open to inspection by all persons interested, upon payment of the usual fee.   J. A. Rule 517.

4. JUDGMENT CLERKS.

Judgment clerks.

22. Two of the officers of the High Court shall, in addition to their other duties, be Judgment Clerks of the High Court, for the purpose of settling the form and terms of special judgments and orders.   *See* J. A. Rule 416.

5. CLERK OF RECORDS AND WRITS.

Clerk of Records and Writs, duties of.

23. The Clerk of Records and Writs is to perform in the Chancery Division the same duties as heretofore in relation to the several matters hereinafter mentioned, that is to say :

1. Receiving, filing, and custody of, pleadings, petitions, reports, depositions, affidavits, bonds, and other papers and proceedings, and making entries thereof in the proper books.

2. Amending pleadings.

3. Entering consents, and notes of default in pleading, and giving certificates thereof.

4. Certifying proceedings.

5. Examining and authenticating office copies of pleadings and other proceedings.

6. Preparing and issuing writs other than those required to be issued by the Clerk of the Process, commissions and orders of course.

7. Preparing and signing certificates for registration, and issuing the same.

8. Attending on the opening of commissions.

10. The care and custody of all documents ordered to be deposited for safe keeping, or produced under any order of Court.

11. The care and custody of the books kept under the Act for Quieting Titles, and making the necessary entries therein.

12. Preparing and signing certificates of the filing of petitions, under said Act, and issuing the same.

13. Transmitting such petitions to the proper Referee.

14. Entering and issuing certificates of title and conveyances, granted under the said Act. Chy. O. 23.

15. Attending with records and exhibits on the Judges of the Court or elsewhere.

16. Setting down actions for trial, and motions for the Divisional Court.

17. Setting down all motions, appeals, demurrers and special cases in all Divisions of the High Court for the weekly Sittings and all appeals in Chambers.

24. The Clerk of Records and Writs shall make out and transmit to the proper Registrar a list of all actions and matters set down for trial or argument as soon as the time for setting the same down has elapsed. *See* Chy. O. 26.

25. All orders of course, or which by the English practice, prior to the first day of Trinity Term, 1856, might be had as a matter of course upon signature of counsel at side bar, or were given by the Master, Clerk of the Papers, or Clerk of the Rules, in England, whether in Term time or in Vacation are to be issued on præcipe at any time, by the Registrars of the Queen's Bench and Common Pleas Divisions, Clerk of Records and Writs, or the Deputy Clerk of the Crown. Deputy or Local Registrar as the case may require. *See* Rules T. T. 1856, 120 ; Chy. O. 25, 595. *Rules which by English practice were granted, of course, to be granted by in same manner.*

6. MARSHALS AND CLERKS OF ASSIZE.

26. The Deputy Clerks of the Crown and Local Registrars in the several Counties and Unions of Counties, except the County in which the City of Toronto is situated, shall *ex officio* be and act as Marshals and Clerks of Assize at the Circuit Sittings of the High Court for the trial of causes, matters and issues, and of criminal matters or proceedings, and at any Courts of Assize and Nisi Prius, Oyer and Terminer, and General Gaol Delivery, appointed to be holden by commission in their respective Counties or Unions of Counties, and shall have all the powers and perform all the functions incident to the same as such Marshals and Clerks of Assize. R. S. O. 1877, c. 41, s. 13. *Who to officiate as Clerks of Assize.*

27. The said Deputy Clerks of the Crown and Local Registrars respectively shall, immediately after each sitting of such Courts, forward by post to the Registrar of the Queen's Bench Division at Toronto, every recognizance, indictment, paper or proceeding in any criminal matter, in their custody as such officers respectively, and also the usual and proper returns as such Marshals and Clerks of Assize. R. S. O. 1877, c. 41, s. 14. *To make return of proceedings and transmit indictments, &c., to the Registrar to Queen's Bench Division.*

(a) The Deputy Clerks of the Crown and the Local Registrars shall pay the postage on the transmission to Toronto of the indictments and other proceedings in criminal cases, and the same is to be repaid out of the Consolidated Revenue Fund. R. S. O. 1877, c. 41, s. 15. *And to pay the postage thereon &c.*

28. The Marshal and Clerk of Assize for the County of York, shall perform the duties of Marshal and Clerk of Assize at the Sittings of the High Court for the trial of causes and issues and of criminal matters or proceedings, and at any Courts of Assize and Nisi Prius, Oyer and Terminer and General Gaol Delivery holden for the County of York, and shall be subject to all the provisions of this Act, in reference to records, exhibits and other documents ; and he shall also perform such other duties as he may from time to time be directed, by rules of the Judges of the Supreme Court, or High Court under section 105 of *The Judicature Act* to perform ; and subject to such duties and rules, he shall be a Clerk in the office of the Registrar of the Queen's Bench Division. *Marshal and Clerk of Assize for County of York. Duties.*

(b) The person so appointed shall take and receive the same fees only as other Marshals and Clerks of Assize ; and such fees shall be by him accounted for, paid over and applied in the manner provided by law ; and he shall not take for his own use or benefit, directly or indirectly, any fee or emolument save the salary to which he may be entitled by law. *Fees.*

Clerk of Courts for criminal trials when held in County of York at same time as Courts for civil trials.

(c) When the Circuit Sittings of the High Court at the County Town of the County of York for the trial of civil and criminal proceedings are held separately, or when any Court of Assize and Nisi Prius by commission in the County of York is held separate and apart from any Court of Oyer and Terminer and General Gaol Delivery held by commission in the said County, and at the same time, the Registrars of the Queen's Bench and Common Pleas Divisions of the High Court shall alternately, personally or by Deputy, act as Clerks of the Sittings for criminal proceedings or of such Courts of Oyer and Terminer and General Gaol Delivery, only as long as such separate Sittings or such Courts are being held at the same time, and shall, while so acting, have all the powers and exercise all the functions that are by law had and exercised by Marshals and Clerks of Assize. R. S. O. 1877, c. 41, s. 16.

To return records and exhibits to registrars of different divisions.

(d) The Marshal and Clerk of Assize for the County of York shall forthwith, after the close of each Assize, or earlier if required, return to the Clerk of Records and Writs, and the Registrars of the Queen's Bench and Common Pleas Divi-ions, all records in their respective Divisions, together with all exhibits and other documents appertaining thereto. Rule of 16th May, 1876.

Absence of Clerk of Assize provided for.

29. In the event of any Marshal or Clerk of Assize or Registrar being absent, or being prevented by illness or other cause from performing his duties as such Marshal or Clerk or Registrar, the presiding Judge at such Sitting or Courts may authorize some person to act as Marshal or Clerk of Assize, and the person so authorized to act shall receive the remuneration payable for the performance of the duties. R. S. O. 1877, c. 41, s. 17.

7. MASTER IN CHAMBERS.

Master in Chambers.

30. The Master in Chambers, in regard to all actions and matters in the High Court, including proceedings in the nature of a *quo warranto* under *The Municipal Act*, shall be and hereby is empowered and required to do all such things, transact all such business, and exercise all such authority and jurisdiction in respect to the same as by virtue of any statute or custom, or by the rules of practice of the Superior Courts, or any of them, respectively, were at the time of the passing of the Acts 33 Vict. (O.) cap. 11, 37 Vict. (O.)c. 7 and *The Ontario Judicature Act, 1881*— or are now done, transacted, or exercised by any Judge of the said Courts sitting at Chambers, save and except in respect to the matters following : -

Criminal matters, etc.

1. All matters relating to criminal proceedings, or the liberty of the subject ;

Appeals.

2. Appeals and appplications in the nature of Appeals ;

Lunacy.

3. Proceedings as to Lunatics under the Revised Statutes of Ontario, chapter 54, sections 5, 6, 7, 8, 9, 17 and 18, and chapter 44, section 140.

Arrest

4. Applications to arrest ;

Petitions by trustees for advice.

5. Petitions for advice under the Revised Statutes, chapter 110, section 37 ;

Custody of infants.

6. Applications as to the custody of infants under the Revised Statutes, chapter 137, section 1 ;

Leases and sales of settled estates. Settlements by infants, etc. Special cases.

7. Applications as to leases and sales of settled estates ; to enable minors, with the approbation of the Court, to make binding settlements of their real and personal estate on marriage ; and in regard to questions submitted for the opinion of the Court in the form of special cases on the part of such persons as may by themselves, their committees, or guardians, or otherwise, concur therein ;

8. Opposed applications for Administration Orders ; Administration, or

9. Opposed applications respecting the Guardianship of the person and property of Infants ; respecting infants or their estates.

10. Applications for Prohibition, Mandamus or Injunction. Mandamus and injunctions.

11. Proceedings as to Partition and sale of Real Estate, under the Revised Statutes, chapter 104. Partition.

12. Applications for leave to appeal after the time limited for that purpose has elapsed. Application to appeal.

13. Appeals from Judges of County Courts or Local Masters, or in respect of any other matter which by these Rules is expressly required to be done by a Judge of the High Court. Appeals

14. The payment of money out of Court, or dispensing with payment of money into Court, in administration and partition matters, Payment out of court

and except (unless by consent of the parties) in respect of the following proceedings and matters, that is to say:— In certain matters jurisdiction by consent.

The removal of causes from Inferior Courts, other than the removal of judgments for the purpose of having execution.

The referring of causes.

Reviewing taxation of costs, except as provided in Rule 854.

Staying proceedings after verdict or judgment.

J. A. Rules 420, 548 ; Chy. O. 560 ; C. L. Rules of 9th Feb., 1870.

31. Any official Referee, upon request of the Master in Chambers, or of a Judge of the High Court, may sit with or for such Master ; and while sitting for him shall have all the authority and power of such Master, but shall not be entitled to any fees. J. A. Rule 421. Official Referees may sit in Chamber for M. in C.

32. The Master in Chambers, or Referee sitting for him, may refer any matter pending before him to a Judge of the High Court for decision, and the Judge may dispose of the same in whole or in part, or refer back the whole or a part. M. C. may refer to Judge

33. The Master in Chambers, or other officer holding chambers, shall sign all orders made by him, and shall cause such as require entry to be entered in a book to be kept for that purpose. See Chy. O. 565. M. C. to sign orders

8. REFEREES.

34. Where any cause or matter, or any question in any cause or matter, is referred to a referee, he may, subject to the order of the Court or a Judge, hold the trial or reference at, or adjourn it to, any place which he may deem most convenient, and have any inspection or view, either by himself or with his assessors if any, which he may deem expedient for the better disposal of the controversy before him. He shall, unless otherwise directed by the Court or a Judge, proceed with the trial *de die in diem* in a similar manner as in actions tried by a jury. J. A. Rule 276. Trial before referee.

35. Where matters of the nature of those commonly referred to the Master are referred to a Referee, the practice and procedure, including the procuring of the attendance of witnesses, shall be the same as nearly as may be as the practice and procedure in the Master's office. Procedure before Referee

36. When matters in the nature of the trial of an issue are referred to a Referee, the practice and procedure, including the procuring of the Procedure before Referee.

8

OFFICERS AND OFFICES.

attendance of witnesses, shall be as nearly as may be, the same as the
practice and procedure at a trial, but not so as to make the tribunal of the
Referee a public Court of Justice. *See* J. A. Rule 277.

Authority of Referee **37.** Subject to any order to be made by the Court or Judge the Referee
shall have the same authority in the conduct of any reference or trial as a
Judge of the High Court when presiding at any trial. J. A. Rule 278.

Not to commit to prison. **38.** Nothing in these Rules contained shall authorize a referee to
commit any person to prison or to enforce an order by attachment or
otherwise. J. A. Rule 279.

Referee may submit questions to the Court. **39.** The referee may, before the conclusion of any trial before him, or
by his report under the reference made to him, submit any question
arising therein for the decision of the Court, or state any facts specially
with power to the Court to draw inferences therefrom, and in any such
case the order to be made on the submission or statement shall be entered
as the Court may direct. J. A. Rule 280.

Court may remit case, or decide on evidence taken. **40.** The Court shall have power to require any explanations or reasons
from the referee, and to remit the cause or matter, or any part thereof,
for re-trial or further consideration, to the same or any other referee ; or
the Court may decide the question referred to a referee on the evidence
taken before him, either with or without additional evidence, as the Court
may direct. J. A. Rule 281

9. LOCAL JUDGES.

Jurisdiction in Chambers of Local Judges. **41.** The Judge of every County Court other than the County Court
of York, shall in all actions brought in their County have concurrent
jurisdiction with and the same power and authority as the Master in
Chambers in all proceedings now determined in Chambers at Toronto
except that the authority of such Judge shall not extend to proceedings
in the nature of a *quo warranto* under *The Municipal Act* or to the payment
of money out of Court, or dispensing with payment of money into Court,
in any action or matter, or to appeals from the Taxing Officers in Toronto
pending taxation, or to making an order for the sale of infants' estate.
48 V. c. 13, s. 21. J. A. Rule 584.

Power to refer to Judge of High Court. **42.** Every Local Judge may refer any matter pending before him in
Chambers to a Judge of the High Court for decision, and the Judge may
dispose of the same in whole or in part, or refer back the whole or a part
See J. A. Rule 426.

10. MASTER'S OFFICE.

(i) *General Rules.*

Interpretation **43.** In the following rules from 44 to 137 inclusive, the word
"Master" shall include Local Master and Official or other Referee, as well
as the Master in ordinary of the Supreme Court.

Court may dispose of matters without reference. **44.** In all cases where a reference might be directed, the Court may
dispose of all matters itself without a reference, and may direct the pro-
ceedings to be taken in Court, or in Chambers, as it finds expedient. Chy.
O. 540.

Order to be carried into M. O. within 14 days. **45.** Every order of reference is to be brought into the proper office
for prosecution within 14 days after the order is drawn up, or after the
same should have been drawn up, by the party having the carriage of the
same ; otherwise any other party to the cause, or any party having an
interest in the reference, may assume the carriage of the order. Chy.
O. 211.

ery half-hour from 12.85 to 2.35 a.n
Belt Line and Yonge street cars w
leave the same point every twen
minutes during the same hours. The
will be no change in the King east ca
which will leave King and Yon
streets at 12.35, 1.35 and 2.35 a.m.

WANT UNION WAGES.

On Friday night last the Executi
Committee of the Dominion Trad
Congress, accompanied by Mr. Robe
Glockling, as representative of t
Bookbinders' Union, waited on Ho
Geo. W. Ross, Minister of Educatio
in reference to a clause in all Gover
ment contracts guaranteeing the uni
rate of wages. Mr. Ross express
sympathy with the object the deput
tion had in view, but pointed out th
there were difficulties in the way

...der ...
...pect ... which ...
...e situate in his co...y, ha...
...it jurisdiction with, and...
...wer and authority as, the...
...ambers in all proceedings...
...mined in Chambers at Tor...
...t that the authority of suc...
...il not (except as provided b...
...facilitate the local administ...
...tice in certain cases (57 Vic...
...rule 1,164) extend to the pay...
...ney into court in any ac...
...tter, or to appeals from the...
...cers in Toronto pending taxa...
...making an order for the sal...

46. When in proceedings before the Master, it appears to him that some persons not already parties ought to be made parties, and ought to attend, or be enabled to attend the proceedings before him, he may direct an office-copy of the judgment or order to be served upon such parties; and upon due service thereof, such parties are to be treated and named as parties to the action, and are to be bound by the judgment or order in the same manner as if they had been originally made parties. Chy. O. 244. *Master may add parties in his office.*

47. The office-copy of a judgment or order directed to be served under Rule 46 is to be endorsed with a notice to the effect set forth in Form No. 33 in the Appendix, with such variations as circumstances require. Chy. O. 245. *Office-copy of judgment to be served on parties added in M. O.*

48. A party served with an office-copy of a judgment or order under Rule 46, may apply to the Court, at any time within 14 days from the date of such service, to discharge the judgment or order, or to add to, vary, or set aside the same. Chy. O. 246. *Parties added in M. O. may move against judgment.*

49. Where, at any time during the prosecution of a reference, it appears to the Master, with respect to the whole or any portion of the proceedings, that the interests of the parties can be classified, he may require the parties constituting each or any class, to be represented by the same solicitor; and where the parties, constituting such class, cannot agree upon the solicitor to represent them, the Master may nominate such solicitor for the purpose of the proceedings before him. Chy. O. 218, *first part.* *Master may classify, and appoint solicitors to represent different classes.*

50. ... prosecuting a reference, does not proceed with due ..., the Master is to be at liberty, upon the application of any other interested, either as a party to the suit, or as one who has come under ... his claim under the judgment or order, to commit to ... prosecution of the reference; and from thenceforth neither the ... defendant nor his solicitor is to be at liberty to attend the ... the prosecutor of the judgment or order. Chy. O. 212. *Master may change conduct of reference.*

51. Where there is undue delay in prosecuting a reference in the ... of a Master, he may issue his warrant to the solicitors or parties ..., which may be transmitted by post, calling upon them to show ... why the reference should not be duly proceeded with. In default ... cause being shewn to excuse the delay, or upon default being ... attending upon the return of the warrant, the Master is to certify ... Court the circumstances of the case; and thereupon the reference ... office is to be deemed closed, and is not to be resumed until further ... Chy. O. 584. *Where there is undue delay in prosecuting a reference, Master may close it.*

52. Unless the Master in his discretion thinks fit to postpone the same, every reference is to be called on and proceeded with at the day and time fixed; and so de die in diem, without interruption, and without a fresh warrant, unless he is of opinion that an adjournment other than de die in diem would be proper, and conducive to the ends of justice; and when an adjournment is ordered, the Master is to note in his book the time and reason thereof. Chy. O. 213, 214. *Reference to be proceeded with on day fixed and de die in diem.*

53. In no case is any matter to be discontinued or adjourned for the mere purpose of proceeding with any other matter, unless that course becomes necessary. Chy. O. 215. *References not to be adjourned to take up other cases.*

54. Upon the bringing in of a judgment or order, the solicitor bringing in the same is to take out a warrant (unless the Master dispenses therewith) appointing a time, which is to be settled by the Master, for the purpose of taking into consideration the matters referred by the judgment or order, and is to serve the same upon the parties, or their solicitors, unless the Master dispenses therewith. Chy. O. 216. *Warrant to consider to be taken unless dispensed with by Master.*

Warrant to consider, proceedings on return.

55. Upon the return of the warrant to consider, or upon the bringing in of the reference where the warrant is dispensed with, the Master is to fix a time at which to proceed to the hearing and determining of the reference, and is to regulate in all other respects the manner of proceeding with the reference, and is to give any special directions, he thinks fit as to :—

(1.) The parties who are to attend on the several accounts and enquiries ;

(2.) The time at which, or within which, each proceeding is to be taken ;

(3.) The mode in which any accounts referred to him are to be taken or vouched ;

(4.) The evidence to be adduced in support thereof ;

(5.) The manner in which each of the accounts and enquiries is to be prosecuted ;

And such directions may be afterwards varied or added to, as may be found necessary. Chy. O. 217.

No statement in pleading, or evidence at trial necessary to enable Master to exercise his powers.

56. To enable the Master to exercise all or any of the powers conferred upon him by, or to take the accounts and make the enquiries referred to in, the following Rules, it shall not be necessary that any of the matters therein mentioned, shall have been stated in the pleadings, or that evidence thereof shall have been given before the judgment or order of reference, or that the judgment or order shall contain any specific direction in respect thereof. Chy. O. 219.

Powers of Master to take accounts.

57. Under a judgment or order of reference, the Master shall have power:

With rests.

(1.) To take the accounts with rests or otherwise ;

To enquire as to wilful neglect and default.

(2.) To take account of rents and profits received or which, but for wilful neglect or default, might have been received ;

To set occupation rent.

(3.) To set occupation rent ;

To allow for improvements

(4.) To take into account necessary repairs, and lasting improvements, and costs and other expenses properly incurred otherwise, or claimed to be so ;

To make just allowances.

(5.) To make all just allowances.

To report special circumstances.

(6.) To report special circumstances ;

And to enquire as to all matters relating to accounts.

(7.) And generally, in taking the accounts, to enquire, adjudge, and report as to all matters relating thereto, as fully as if the same had been specially referred. Chy. O. 220.

Master may order witnesses to be examined before

58. Under a judgment or order of reference, witnesses may be examined before any Examiner of the Court. Chy. 221, *part.*

Master may cause parties to be examined, and may order production of documents.

59. The Master may cause parties to be examined, and to produce books, papers and writings, as he thinks fit, and may determine what books, papers and writings are to be produced, and when and how long they are to be left in his office ; or in case he does not deem it necessary that such books and papers or writings should be left or deposited in his office, he may give directions for the inspection thereof, by the parties requiring the same, at such time and in such manner as he deems expedient. Chy. O. 222.

60. The Master may cause advertisements for creditors, and if he thinks it necessary, but not otherwise, for heirs or next of kin, or other unascertained persons, and the representatives of such as are dead, to be published as the circumstances of the case require ; and in such advertisements he is to appoint a time within which such persons are to come in and prove their claims, and within which time, unless they so come in, they are to be excluded from the benefit of the judgment or order. Chy. O. 223 Master may advertise for creditors, heirs or next of kin, etc. Time to be limited for coming in.

61. The Master is to proceed on the claims brought in before him pursuant to such advertisement, without further notice, and may examine witnesses in relation thereto at the time appointed in the advertisement, or thereafter as he sees fit ; and he is to allow or disallow, or adjourn the claims as to him seems just. Chy. O. 224. Master to proceed on claims brought in.

62. Under every order whereby the delivery of deeds or execution of conveyances is directed, the Master is to give directions as to delivery of such deeds, and to settle conveyances where the parties differ, and to give directions as to the parties to the conveyances, and as to the execution thereof. Chy. O. 226. Master's powe as to settlement of conveyances.

63. Where any account is to be taken, the accounting party is, unless the Master otherwise directs, to bring in the same in the form of debtor and creditor, verified by affidavit. The items on each side of the account are to be numbered consecutively, and the account is to be referred to by the affidavit as an exhibit, and not to be annexed thereto. Chy. O. 227. Form of accounts to be brought in by accounting party.

64. The Master, if he thinks fit, may direct that in taking accounts, the books of account, in which the accounts required to be taken have been kept, or any of them, be taken as *prima facie* evidence of the truth of the matters therein contained, with liberty to the parties interested to take such objection thereto as they may be advised. Chy. O. 228. Master may direct books of account to be taken as *prima facie* evidence.

65. No state of facts, charges, or discharges are to be brought into the Master's office ; and where original deeds or documents can be brought in, no copies are to be made without special direction. Chy. O. 229. No state of facts, etc. to be brought in.

66. Where directed, copies, abstracts of, or extracts from accounts, deeds, or other documents and pedigrees, and concise statements, are to be supplied ; and where so directed, copies are to be delivered as the Master may direct. Chy. O. 230. Copies, abstracts, etc., to be supplied as Master directs.

67. A party directed by the Master to bring in an account, or do any other act, is to be held bound to do the same in pursuance of the direction of the Master, without any warrant or written direction being served for that purpose. Chy. O. 231. Parties bound by Master's direction without warrant.

68. Before proceeding to the hearing and determining of a reference, the Master may appoint a day in the meantime, if he thinks fit, for the purpose of entering into the accounts and enquiries, with a view to ascertaining what is admitted and what is contested between the parties. Chy. O. 232. Warrant to appoint a day to ascertain what is admitted and what contested.

69. Where the Master has omitted to appoint a day for the purposes mentioned in Rule 68, he may grant to the party bringing in accounts a warrant to proceed on the same, for the purposes aforesaid ; such warrant to be underwritten, as follows : "On leaving the accounts of, &c., and take notice that you are required to admit the same, or such parts thereof as you can properly admit." Chy. O. 233. When day not previously appointed, warrant may issue to ascertain what admitted.

Party seeking to charge accounting party must give notice of particulars.

70. A party seeking to charge an accounting party beyond what he has in his account admitted to have received, is to give notice thereof to the accounting party, stating so far as he is able, the amount so sought to be charged, and the particulars thereof in a short and succinct manner. Chy. O. 237.

Master's Book, how to be kept.

71. The Master is to keep in his office a book, to be called the "Master's Book," in which, upon the bringing in of a judgment or order of reference, are to be entered, the style of the cause, the name of the solicitor prosecuting the reference, the date of the judgment or order being brought in, and the proceedings then taken ; and the Master is also to enter therein, from time to time, the proceedings taken before him, and the directions which he gives in relation to the prosecution of the reference, or otherwise. Chy. O. 238.

Master to certify proceedings in his office.

72. Upon the application of any person, the Master is to certify, as shortly as he conveniently can, the several proceedings had in his office in any cause or matter, and the dates thereof. Chy. O. 239.

Master to devise simplest and speediest method of prosecuting references.

73. In giving directions, and in regulating the manner of proceeding before him, the Master is to devise and adopt the simplest, most speedy, and least expensive method of prosecuting the reference, and every part thereof ; and with that view, to dispense with any proceedings ordinarily taken, but which he conceives to be unnecessary and to shorten the periods for taking any proceedings ; or to substitute a different course of proceedings for that ordinarily taken. Chy. O. 240.

Appointments for several days may be included in one warrant.

74. Where the Master directs parties not in attendance before him to be notified to attend at some future day, or for different purposes at different future days it shall not be necessary to issue separate warrants, but the parties shall be notified by one appointment, signed, by the Master, of the proceedings to be taken, and of the times by him appointed for the taking of the same. Chy. O. 241.

Parties notified by Master not to be served with warrant.

75. Where parties are notified by appointment from the Master, of proceedings to be taken before him, no warrants are to be issued as to such parties, in relation to the same proceedings. Chy. O. 242.

Parties notified, liable for default, as if served with warrant.

76. Parties making default upon such appointments, are to be subject to the same consequences as if warrants had been served upon them. Chy. O. 243.

Master to notify parties when hearing concluded, and to note it in his book. Thereafter no evidence to be given except by leave.

77. As soon as the hearing of any matter pending before the Master is completed, he shall so inform the parties to the reference then in attendance, and make a note to that effect in his book ; and after such entry no further evidence is to be received, or proceedings had, without the special permission of the Master ; and the Master may proceed to prepare his report or certificate without further warrant, except the warrant to settle which is to be served on the parties as the Master directs. Chy. O. 247.

Points intended to be raised on appeal to be taken before Master.

78. Parties are to raise before the Master, in respect of any matters presented in his office, for his decision, all points which may afterwards be raised upon appeal. Chy. O. 248.

Accounts, charges, affidavits, etc., not to be set out in report.

79. In the Master's report no part of any account, charge, affidavit, deposition, examination, or answer, brought in or used in the Master's office, is to be stated or recited, but instead thereof the same may be referred to by date or otherwise, so as to inform the Court as to the paper or document so brought in or used. Chy. O. 249.

Schedule to be attached as to moneys in

80. Reports affecting money in Court, or to be paid into Court, are to set forth in figures in a schedule a brief summary of the sums found by

Rule 63 (10) (1) rescinded, and
owing substituted therefor :—
Where he acts as Master in
's in a matter within his jur-
as Master in Ordinary, the
able in stamps shall, in re-
such business, be the same as

the report, and which may be paid or payable into or out of Court, and **Court, or pay-**
the funds or shares to which the sums of money are respectively charge- **able into**
able. Chy. O. 250.   **Court.**

81. As soon as the Master's report or certificate is prepared, it is to be **Report to be**
delivered out to the party prosecuting the reference, or in case he declines **issued to party**
to take the same, then, in the discretion of the Master, to any other party **prosecuting**
applying therefor; and a common attendance is to be allowed to the party **reference, or if**
taking the same. Chy. O. 251.   **he decline it,**
                                                                           then to any
                                                                           other party.

82. No written objections or exceptions need be taken before the **Without pre-**
Master previously to an appeal. See Chy. O. 253.   **vious excep-**
                                                                      tions before
                                                                      Master.

83. Any party affected by a report may file the same, or a duplicate **Any party may**
thereof, and the filing of a duplicate shall have the same effect as the **file report, or**
filing of the report. Chy. O. 254.   **duplicate.**

84. In cases of references to Local Masters the report shall be filed in **Reports where**
the office of such Local Master, but may, at the request of any party to **to be filed.**
the proceedings, after having been so filed, be forwarded to (the office of
the Clerk of Records and Writs.) In all other cases the report shall be
filed in (the proper office in Toronto of the Division to which the action or
proceeding is assigned.) See J. A. Rule 599.

85. Where the Master is directed to appoint money to be paid at **Payment of**
some time and place, he is to appoint the same to be paid into some Bank **money into**
at its head office, or at some branch or agency office of such Bank, to the **bank, how to**
joint credit of the party to whom the same is made payable, and of the **be directed in**
Accountant ; the party to whom the same is made payable to name the **report.**
Bank into which he desires the same to be paid, and the Master to name
the place for such payment. Chy. O. 255.

86. Where money is paid into a bank, in pursuance of such ap- **Party may pay**
pointment, the party paying may pay the same either to the credit of **money in to the**
the party to whom the same is made payable, or to the joint credit of the **sole credit of**
party and the Accountant ; and if the same be paid to the sole credit of the **the party**
party, such party shall be entitled to receive the same without the order **entitled thereto**
of the Court. Chy. O. 256.   **or to the joint**
                                                                       credit of such
                                                                       party and the
                                                                       Accountant.

87. In administration suits reports are, as far as possible, o be in the **Reports in ad-**
form No. 42 in the Appendix. Chy. O. 589.   **ministration**
                                                                        suits.

88. The Master in Ordinary shall have the same power, authority, and **Master in Ordi-**
jurisdiction, as the Master in Chambers, in respect of all causes and matters **nary, jurisdic-**
referred to him, or which may arise in his office. J. A. Rule 541 (a). **tion of, in**
                                                                        Chambers.

Where he acts as Master in Chambers in a matter within his juris- **Fees.**
tion as Master in Ordinary, the fees payable in stamps shall be the
as if he were acting as Master in Ordinary.

Any Official Referee, upon the request of the Master in Ordinary, or **Official Referee**
Judge of the High Court, may sit with or for the Master ; and while **may sit for**
for him shall have all the authority and power of such Master, but **Master and**
shall not be entitled to any fees. J. A. Rule 541 (b).   **have like**
                                                                    powers.

(ii) *Sales.*

89. Where a sale is ordered, the Master may cause the property, or a **General pro-**
competent part thereof, to be sold either by public auction, private **visions were a**
contract, or tender, or part by one mode and part by another, as he may **sale is ordered.**
think best for the interest of all parties. J. A. Rule 331.

Conduct of sale under trusts of will or settlement.   **90.** Where the trusts of any will or settlement are being administered, and a sale is ordered of any property vested in the trustees of such will or settlement upon trust for sale or with power of sale by the trustees, the conduct of the sale shall be given to the trustees, unless the Court or, a Judge otherwise directs.   J. A. Rule 403.

Copy of order directing sale, is not to be brought into M. O. unless required by the Master.   **91.** Where a sale is to take place under a judgment or order of the Court, no copy of the judgment or order, or any part thereof, is to be brought into Chambers, or the Master's office, but the original judgment or order is to be used, unless the Judge or Master requires a copy.   Chy. O. 374.

Appointment to settle advertisement.   **92.** An appointment or warrant in respect of the sale is to be obtained from the Judge or Master, and served, upon all necessary parties.   Chy. O. 375.

Draft advertisement to be brought in, but no particulars or conditions.   **93.** At the time appointed thereby, the party having the conduct of the sale, is to bring into Chambers, or the Master's office, a draft advertisement, but no particulars or conditions of the sale, or any draft or copy thereof.   Chy. O. 376.

Advertisements of sale to contain.   **94.** The advertisement is to contain the following particulars :—

Style of cause.   (1.) The short style of cause ;

Recital of order.   (2.) That the sale is in pursuance of a judgment or order of the Court ;

Time and place of sale.   (3.) The time and place of sale ;

Description of property.   (4.) A short and true description of the property to be sold ;

Manner of sale.   (5.) The manner in which the property is to be sold, whether in one lot or several, and if in several, in how many, and what lots ;

Terms of payment of purchase money.   (6.) What proportion of the purchase money is to be paid down by way of deposit, and at what time or times, and whether the residue of such purchase money is to be paid with, or without interest ;

Any special conditions.   (7.) Any particulars, in which the proposed conditions of sale differ from the standing conditions.   Chy. O. 377.

Master on return of warrant, to settle advertisement to appoint auctioneer, and fix time, and place, of sale etc.   **95.** At the time named in the appointment or warrant, the Judge or Master is to settle the advertisement ; to fix the time and place of sale ; to name an auctioneer, where one is to be employed ; and to make every other necessary arrangement preparatory to the sale, so that nothing may remain to be done but to insert the advertisement ; and all the before mentioned matters must be done at one meeting, namely, upon the return of the appointment or warrant where it is practicable, and no adjournment of such meeting is to take place, and no new meeting is to be appointed for the aforesaid purposes, unless it is unavoidable.   Chy. O. 378.

Standing conditions of sale.   **96.** The standing conditions of sale are to be those set forth in Form No. 43 in the Appendix.   Chy. O. 379.

Master may fix upset price, or reserved bidding.   **97.** The Judge or Master may, without further order, fix an upset price, or reserved bidding, where it is thought expedient ; but this must be done at the meeting held for the purpose of settling the advertisement and making the other arrangements preparatory to the sale, and it must be notified in the conditions of sale.   Chy. O. 380 ; J. A. Rule 331 *part*.

All parties may bid, except party   **98.** All parties may bid, without taking out an order for the purpose, except the party having the conduct of the sale, and except any trustees, agents, and other persons in a fiduciary situation ; and where any parties having con-are to be at liberty to bid, it must be notified in the conditions of sale. duct of sale, Chy. O. 381.

99. The advertisement is to be inserted by the party conducting the Party having sale, at such times and in such manner as the Judge or Master appointed conduct of sale to advertise it at the meeting before mentioned. Chy. O. 382. as directed.

100. The Master or his Clerk is to conduct the sale where no auctioneer Master, clerk, is employed. Chy. O. 383. or auctioneer may conduct sale.

101. Biddings need not be in writing, but a written agreement is to Biddings. be signed by the purchaser at the time of sale. Chy. O. 384.

102. The deposit is to be paid to the vendor, if present, or if not, to Deposit at sale his solicitor, at the time of sale, and is forthwith to be paid by him into how to be paid. Court. Chy. O. 385.

103. After the sale is concluded, the auctioneer, where one is employed Affidavit of is to make the usual affidavit, and where no auctioneer is employed, the auctioneer, or certificate of Master or his Clerk is to certify to the same effect. Chy. O. 386. Master, of re-sult of sale.

104. The report on sale is to be in the form No. 44 in the Appendix, or Report on sale as near thereto as circumstances permit. Chy. O. 387. form of.

105. A sale must be objected to by motion to the Court or a Judge to Sale may be set aside the same ; and notice of the motion must be served upon the objected to on purchaser, and on the other parties to the cause ; but the biddings are only motion. to be opened on special grounds, whether the application is made before or after the report stands confirmed. Chy. O. 388.

106. At any time after the confirmation of the sale the purchaser may After confirm-pay his purchase money and interest, if any, or the balance thereof, into ation of report Court without further order, upon notice to the party having the conduct purchaser may of the sale ; and when he is entitled to be let into possession of the estate, chase money he may, if possession is wrongfully withheld from him, proceed at his own into Court. expense to obtain an order against the party in possession for the delivery How obtain thereof to him, or may call upon the vendor to cause possession to be de-possession. livered to him. Chy. O. 389

107. The Master is to settle all necessary conveyances for the purpose Settlement of of carrying out the sale in case the parties differ, or in case there are any conveyance. persons under any disability (other than coverture) interested in such sale. J. A. Rule 331.

108. After a sale under an order is confirmed, the vendor is, forthwith Delivery of upon demand, to deliver an abstract of title to the purchaser ; and if the abstract. purchaser does not serve objections within 7 days, he is to be deemed If no object-to have accepted the abstract as sufficient. If objections are served, the stract to be vendor is to answer them within 14 days ; and if the purchaser is deemed suffi-still dissatisfied, and if the parties cannot otherwise agree, either party cient. may obtain from the Master a warrant to consider the abstract. Chy. O. Objections to 390. abstract, how disposed of.

109. The Master is to determine all questions upon the abstract and Master to de-the sufficiency thereof ; and, if desired by the purchaser, may require the termine ques-vendor to make the same as perfect as he can ; and if the vendor neglects ficiency of ab-or refuses to do so, he may permit the purchaser to supply defects therein, stract. at the vendor's expense. Chy. O. 391.

Master is not to make a report, but is to mark objections allowed, or disallowed.   **110.** The Master is not to make a report on the abstract, but is to mark the objections as allowed or disallowed, as the case may be ; and when he finds the abstract perfect, or as perfect as the vendor can make it, he is to certify to that effect at the foot or on the back ; and such finding is to be final without filing, unless appealed from in the same manner as from a Master's report. Chy. O. 392

After abstract confirmed, no further objection allowed.   **111.** After an abstract is confirmed, or is accepted by the purchaser as sufficient, no objection to the abstract is to be allowed. Chy. O. 393.

Verification of abstract.
Notice to deliver objections and requisitions.   **112.** After acceptance or confirmation of the abstract, the verification is to be proceeded with, and the vendor is with all diligence to afford the purchaser all the means of verification in his power, in the manner, and according to the practice usual with conveyancers ; and after having done so, he may serve a notice on the purchaser to make the objections or requisitions, if any, within 7 days, or that otherwise he will be deemed to have accepted the title. Chy. O. 394.

Objections, and requisitions, to whom to be delivered   **113.** Upon being served with such notice, the purchaser, if dissatisfied, is to serve his objections or requisitions within the time thereby limited ; and the like course is to be followed upon such objections or requisitions as is prescribed by Rules 108, 109, and 110, in relation to the abstract. Chy. O. 395.

On refusal of vendor to verify abstract Master may authorize purchaser to do so.   **114.** In case of the refusal or neglect of the vendor to verify any portion of the abstract to the best of his ability, or to furnish any necessary proof or documents in his power, the Master may authorize the purchaser to do so at the vendor's expense. Chy. O. 396.

Rules 108-114 apply to all references as to title   **115.** The foregoing Rules 108 to 114 inclusive, are to apply to all cases of reference to the Master as to title, as well as to sales by the Court. Chy. O. 397.

(iii) Receivers, Committees, etc.

Warrant for appointment of receiver, to name receiver and sureties.   **116.** The party prosecuting the order for a receiver is to obtain an appointment or a warrant from the Master, and to serve the same on all the necessary parties, naming in the copy thereof served, the proposed receiver and his sureties. See Chy. O. 278.

On return of warrant, bond to be brought in.   **117.** At the time appointed, the party prosecuting the order is to bring into the Master's office the bond or recognizance proposed as security. See Chy. O. 279 ; J. A. Rule 519.

Party desiring to propose another person as receiver, to give notice.   **118.** Any other party desirous of proposing another person as receiver, is to serve notice of his intention so to do upon the other parties, naming in the notice the person proposed by him as receiver, and his sureties, and is then in like manner to bring into the Master's office the bond or recognizance proposed by him as security. See Chy. O. 280.

Master to appoint receiver and settle, and approve, security.   **119.** At the time named in the appointment or warrant the Master is, in the presence of the parties, or those who attend, to consider the appointment of the receiver, and to determine respecting the same ; and to settle and approve of the proposed security. See Chy. O. 281.

Master not to make report appointing a receiver; but to sign appointment.   **120.** The Master is to make no report approving of or appointing the receiver, but is to appoint such receiver by signing a written appointment to the following effect, viz : "IN THE HIGH COURT OF JUSTICE, DIVISION, [style of cause]—I hereby appoint [receiver's name] receiver in this action, [signature of Master] ;" which appointment is to be signed without any warrant or attendance for that purpose. See Chy. O. 282.

121. After the execution and filing of the securities settled and approved by the Master, the appointment is to be filed by the party who has procured the person named by him as receiver to be appointed, and may be moved against within seven days by any party interested. *See* Chy. O. 283.

Master's appointment of receiver to be filed.

122. Committees of the persons and estates of lunatics, idiots, and persons of unsound mind, and guardians, excepting guardians *ad litem*, are to be appointed in the same manner as receivers, as nearly as circumstances will permit. Chy. O. 557.

Committees of lunatics to be appointed in same manner as receivers.

123. Where an order directs the appointment of a receiver, committee of the person and estate of a lunatic, idiot, or person of unsound mind, or a guardian other than a guardian *ad litem*, and does not regulate the matter herein provided for, the Master is to fix the time or times in each year when the person appointed is to pass his accounts and pay his balances into Court ; and in default of compliance with such direction, the person appointed may, on the passing of his accounts, be disallowed any salary or compensation for his services, and may be charged with interest upon his balances. Chy. O. 588.

Master to appoint time for Receivers, and Committees, to pass accounts where not fixed by Court.

(iv) *Foreclosure, Sale and Redemption.*

124. Upon a reference under a judgment for foreclosure or sale the Master is to enquire and state, whether any person or persons, and who other than the plaintiff, has or have any lien, charge, or incumbrance upon the land and premises embraced in the mortgage security of the plaintiff, in the writ or pleadings mentioned, subsequent thereto. Chy. O. 442.

Master to inquire as to incumbrances.

125. The plaintiff is to bring into the Master's Office certificates from the Registrar and Sheriff of the County wherein the lands lie, setting forth all the incumbrances which affect the property in the writ or pleadings mentioned, and such other evidence as he may be advised. Chy. O. 443.

Plaintiff to bring into M. O. Sheriff's and Registrar's certificates.

126. The Master is to direct all such persons as appear to him to have any lien, charge or incumbrance upon the estate in question, to be made parties to the action, and to be served with a notice in the form No. 34 in the Appendix. Chy. O. 444.

Master is to add parties.

127. Any party served with a notice under Rule 126 may apply to the Court at any time within 14 days from the date of the service, to discharge the order making him a party, or to add to, vary, or set aside the judgment. Chy. O. 445.

Parties added may move against order.

128. The Master, before he proceeds to hear and determine, is to require an appointment to the effect set forth in form No. 35 in the Appendix, to be served upon incumbrancers made parties before the judgment. Chy. O. 446.

Incumbrancers to be served with appointment.

129. Where any person who has been duly served with a notice under Rule 126 or with an appointment under Rule 128, neglects to attend at the time appointed; the Master is to treat such non-attendance as a disclaimer by the party so making default ; and the claim of such party is to be thereby foreclosed, unless the Court orders otherwise, upon application duly made for that purpose. Chy. O. 447.

Parties not attending, who have been duly served to be foreclosed

130. When all parties have been duly served, the Master is to take an account of what is due to the plaintiff, and to such other incumbrancer or incumbrancers (if any), for principal money and interest; and to tax to them their costs, and settle their priorities : and also to appoint a time and place, or times and places, for payment according to the practice of the Court. Chy. O. 448.

Master to take accounts of plaintiff and incumbrancers

2

Master's re-
port, contents
of.

131. The Master's report must state the names of all persons who have been made parties in his office, and who have been served with the notice or appointment hereinbefore provided, and the names of such as have made default, and must settle the priorities, &c., of such as have attended, and these latter are to be certified as the only incumbrancers upon the estate. Chy. O. 449.

Subsequent ac-
counts to be
taken by Mas-
ter.

132. All subsequent accounts are, from time to time, to be taken, subsequent costs taxed, and necessary proceedings had, for redemption by, or foreclosure of, the other party or parties entitled to redeem the mortgaged premises, as if specific directions for all these purposes had been contained in the judgment. Chy. O. 452.

Sale,—pro-
ceedings on.

133. If the judgment directs a sale instead of foreclosure on default in payment, then on default being made, and an order for sale obtained, the premises are to be sold, with the approbation of the Master, and he is to settle the conveyance to the purchaser in case the parties differ about the same ; and the purchaser is to pay his purchase money into Court, to the credit of the action, subject to the further order of the Court. Chy. O. 453.

Purchase
money, appli-
cation of.

134. The purchase money, when so paid, is to be applied in payment of what has been found due to the plaintiff and the other incumbrancer or incumbrancers (if any), according to their priorities, together with subsequent interest, and subsequent costs. Chy. O. 454.

Master to take
account in re-
demption suits

135. Upon a reference under a judgment for redemption, the Master is, without any special direction, to take an account of what is due to the defendant for principal money and interest, and his costs are to be taxed, and a time and place or times and places appointed for payment according to the present practice of the Court in that behalf. J. A. Rule 332.

Procedure
where order is
for redemp-
tion, etc.

136. Where the order is for redemption or foreclosure, or redemption or sale, such proceedings are in such case to be thereupon had, and with the same effect as in an action for foreclosure or sale, and in such case the last incumbrancer is to be treated as the owner of the equity of redemption. J. A. Rule 335.

Assignment of
property and
delivery of
documents.

137. In an action for foreclosure or sale upon payment by the defendant, or in an action for redemption upon payment by the plaintiff, of the amount found due, the plaintiff or defendant shall, unless the judgment otherwise directs, assign and convey the mortgaged premises in question to the defendant, (or plaintiff, as the case may be,) making the payment, or to whom he may appoint, free and clear of all incumbrances done by him, and deliver up all deeds and writings in his custody or power relating thereto, upon oath, and in case of a corporation the affidavit shall be made by the officer thereof having the custody of such deeds and writings. J. A. Rule 336.

11. LOCAL MASTERS.

138. Every Local Master who does not practise as a Barrister or Solicitor and who has not taken out certificates to practice, shall, in addition to his other powers as Local Master, have in all actions brought in his County concurrent jurisdiction with and the same power and authority as the Master in Chambers in all proceedings now taken in Chambers at Toronto, except that the authority of such Local Masters shall not extend to proceedings in the nature of a *quo warranto* under *The Municipal Act*, or to payment of money out of Court, or dispensing with payment into Court, or to appeals from the taxing officers at Toronto pending taxation ; or to making an order for sale of infants' estate. *See* 48 V. c. 13, s. 21; J. Rules 22, 584.

12. ACCOUNTANT'S OFFICE.

(i) *General Rules.*

139. The Suitors' Accounts in the Court of Appeal, and the High Suitors' Court shall be in charge of the "The Accountant of the Supreme Court of accounts. Judicature for Ontario." J. A. Rule 475.

140. In the following Rules the word "Accountant" shall mean "The "Accountant" Accountant of the Supreme Court of Judicature for Ontario." J. A. Rule defined. 550.

141. The following books are to be kept by the Accountant:—   Books to be kept.

1. A Book of Directions to the Bank to receive money.

2. A Book of Cheques.

3. A Journal.

4. A General Ledger.

5. A Stock Journal.

6. A Stock Ledger.

7. A Balance Book.

8. A Book of Investments.

9. A Bond Index.

10. A Deposit Index.

11. A Private Ledger. J. A. Rule 551.

142. The *Directions* and *Cheques* are to be in the form approved of by Directions and the Judges of the Chancery Division, and are to be numbered consecu- cheques. tively. J. A. Rule 552.

143. The *Journal* is to show the several sums daily paid into and out Journal. of Court, and is to be so kept, that at the foot of the account for each month will appear the total amount paid into, and out of Court during such month, and the amounts to the debit and credit of the said account are to be transferred each month to the Private Ledger. J. A. Rule 553.

144. The *General Ledger* is to contain a separate account for every General action or matter, in which there is money in Court; and also, "The Ledger. Suitors' Fee Fund Account," and "The Suspense Account" for each Division of the High Court, and for the Court of Appeal, each of which accounts is to show correctly the state and condition thereof for the time being. J. A. Rule 554.

145. In each of the suitor's accounts there are from time to time to be Form of entered, the date, purport, or material contents, of all orders, judgments, accounts. reports, pleadings, affidavits, or other documents affecting the payment, into or out of Court, of money therein; also, every sum paid into Court, and by whom, and for what purpose paid in, and under what authority; and also every sum paid out, to whom, and on what account paid out, and under what authority. J. A. Rule 555.

146. Each account opened in the Ledger is from time to time until the Crediting same shall be closed, to be credited with the bank interest which shall Bank interest. from time to time accrue in respect of such account and a corresponding transfer of interest is to be made at the bank by cheque signed and countersigned as in other cases, and there is also to be entered in each account any statement or memorandum of any other matters material to be recorded for the information of the Court or its officers, or any of the parties. J. A. Rule 556.

Compound interest.

147. Compound interest is not to be credited to any action or matter, or allowed or paid to any suitor in respect of any fund which has not been in Court for at least five years. J. A. Rule 557.

Balances under $10 standing for 2 years carried to Suspense Account.

148. Whenever the balance remaining to the credit of any action or matter to which an adult party is entitled does not exceed $10, and 2 years elapses without the balance being claimed, the account in such action or matter shall be closed by the transfer of the balance to "The Suspense Account" of the proper Division of the High Court, or of the Court of Appeal, but such transfer shall not in anywise prejudice the claim of any suitor entitled to the balance to its payment. J. A. Rule 558.

Stock Journal and Ledger.

149. In the *Stock Journal* and *Stock Ledger* are to be entered all transactions relating to Dominion stock held or purchased by the Court for suitors, other than such orders, reports and other particulars as to the said stock as are entered in the General Ledger. J. A. Rule 559.

Balance Book.

150. The *Balance Book* is to contain a statement to be entered therein quarterly of the balances at the credit of the various accounts in the three Ledgers at the date of such statement ; such balances are to be made up to the 31st of March, 30th of June, 30th of September, and 31st of December of every year. J. A. Rule 560.

Book of Investments.

151. In the *Book of Investments* are to be entered under the heading of the action or matter in which any mortgage or other security other than Dominion stock has been taken by the order of the Court, the date, and a concise statement of the material contents of the mortgage or other security, and of all subsequent orders and proceedings in relation thereto until the mortgage or other security is discharged by the order of the Court. J. A. Rule 561.

Bond Index.

152. In the *Bond Index* shall be entered under the heading of the action or matter in which the same may be entitled, a memorandum of all bonds, or recognizances, filed or deposited with the Accountant, and also receipts for all bonds, or recognizances delivered out pursuant to any order. J. A. Rule 562.

Deposit Index.

153. In the *Deposit Index* shall be entered under the heading of the action or matter in which the same may be ordered to be deposited, a memorandum of all securities for money, or other documents, books, papers, or other things which may at any time be ordered to be deposited with the Accountant for safe custody, and also receipts for all such documents, books, papers, or other things so deposited as may be delivered out pursuant to any order. J. A. Rule 563.

Private Ledger.

154. In the *Private Ledger* is to be entered "The General Interest Account," "The Toronto General Trust Company Account," the "Bank Account," and "The Account of Official Guardian *ad litem*." J. A. Rule 564.

Books to be open to inspection.

155. The books kept under these Rules, except the Private Ledger, are to be open to inspection by any person interested in any account entered therein, or his solicitor or agent. The Accountant is to give a certificate of the state of any account, or an extract therefrom, or of any entry in such books, at the desire of any person interested, or his solicitor or agent, and all such certificates shall be signed by the Accountant, or the Chief Clerk in the Accountant's office. J. A. Rule 565.

Securities to be taken in name of Accountant.

156. All mortgages and other securities taken under an order or judgment of the Court and all bonds, recognizanc.s and other instruments requir-d by the practice of the Court for the purpose of security are to be taken in the name of the Accountant, his successors and assigns, unless it is expressly directed that the same are to be taken in the name of some other person or persons. J. A. Rules 566, 519.

157. One Auditor or more shall be appointed to the Supreme Court. Audit of It shall be the duty of the Auditor in each year to examine the several Accounts. account books in the Accountant's office and to compare the balances entered in the *Balance Book* with the balances entered in the Ledgers, and with the Bank Account, and to certify such balances if found to be correct, and to make such further and other examination of the said book as he may think necessary for the proper audit thereof, and to report forthwith, after making such examination, the result thereof to the Judges of the Chancery Division, and from time to time to make such suggestions to the said Judges as may appear to be desirable for the efficient keeping of the accounts in the said Accountant's office. J. A. Rule 567.

158. The remuneration of each Auditor is hereby fixed at the sum of Auditors' re $100 per annum, for which sum a cheque is to be issued payable out of the muneration. General Interest Account, upon the fiat of any Judge of the High Court. J. A. Rule 568.

159. During the month of January in each year the Accountant shall Salaries and present to the Judges a statement of the amounts paid for salaries and ex expenses of penses of the Accountant's office during the previous year, and the names of office. the persons to whom such amounts were respectively paid, and also an estimate of the salaries and expenses of the Accountant's office for the cur rent year, and such estimates shall be examined by the Judges who shall be be at liberty to make such variations therein as they may think necessary, and when approved of by them, a fiat shall be endorsed thereon or appended thereto which shall be signed by one or more of such Judges, authorizing the payment from time to time as may be requisite of such sums as shall be necessary, not exceeding in the aggregate the amounts specified in the said estimates, for the services and purposes mentioned in the said estimates. J. A. Rule 569.

160. Cheques for the salaries and expenses included in such estimates Cheques for as shall be so approved of as aforesaid may from time to time as occasion salaries. may require, be signed, countersigned, and issued to the parties entitled, without further order. J. A Rule 570.

161. The Accountant shall prepare in the month of January in every Accountant to year a statement of all moneys paid into Court and withdrawn respectively, render state and a statement of the condition of the various accounts upon the 31st day ments yearly. of the preceding December, and shall transmit one copy to the Provincial Secretary and one to the President of the High Court of Justice. with a declaration thereto annexed, made before a Justice of the Peace or Com missioner for taking affidavits, in the form No. 216 in the Appendix. J. A. Rule 476.

162. A list signed by the Accountant of all the mortgages and List of mort securities, other than Dominion Stock, outstanding on the 1st January and gages and 1st July in each year is to be delivered to, and left with, the President securities to be of the High Court within 10 days thereafter, and such list is to set forth with Judges. in convenient form :

1. The short style of the cause or matter ;
2. Date of order under which mortgage or other security executed ;
3. Date thereof ;
4. Amount ;
5. When payable ;
6. For whose benefit ;
7. What sums, if any, overdue for principal or interest ;
8. Name of mortgagor or party giving security ;
9. Locality (not description) of mortgaged property ;
10. Remarks. Chy. O. 367.

(ii) *Mode of paying into Court.*

Excepted towns.   **163.** The next seven Rules as to the mode of paying money into Court shall not apply to moneys so payable at L'Orignal, Cayuga, or Sault Ste. Marie, until further order. New.

Bank of Commerce.   **164.** A person desiring to pay money into Court shall pay the same into the Canadian Bank of Commerce at Toronto or at some branch or agency thereof, or as mentioned in Rule 165 and in no other way. New.

Other Banks.   **165.** Money required to be paid into Court in any of the following places (so long as the Canadian Bank of Commerce shall have no branch office thereat) shall be paid into the branch or agency office of the Bank set opposite the said places respectively.

St. Thomas	The Merchants Bank
Kingston	The Bank of Montreal
Owen Sound	The Merchants Bank
Milton	The Bank of Hamilton
Perth	The Bank of Montreal
Brockville	The Bank of Montreal
Napanee	The Merchants Bank
Cobourg	The Bank of Montreal
Whitby	The Dominion Bank
Brampton	The Merchants Bank
Picton	The Bank of Montreal
Pembroke	The Bank of Ottawa
Cornwall	The Bank of Montreal
Lindsay	The Bank of Montreal
Welland	The Imperial Bank
Port Arthur	The Ontario Bank

New.

Direction.   **166.** The person paying money into Court shall first obtain from the Accountant, Local Registrar, Deputy Registrar, or Deputy Clerk of the Crown, a direction to the Bank to receive the money. Chy O. 352 altered.

Præcipe and order to be left.   **167.** The person applying for the direction is to file a præcipe therefor in the form No. 112 in the Appendix and is to leave with the officer issuing the direction, the judgment, order, writ, or pleading or copy thereof, under which the money is payable, and in case the direction is obtained elsewhere than in Toronto he shall also leave the necessary postage for the transmission of the documents to the Accountant and a further copy of the pleading for transmission. Chy O. 353 altered.

Outside towns.   **168.** Where the direction is issued elsewhere than in Toronto, the officer issuing the same shall forthwith transmit to the Accountant by post the præcipe for such direction together with the papers left on the application therefor. New.

Date of crediting money.   **169.** The person paying money into Court elsewhere than in Toronto shall be entitled to credit therefor as of the date on which the same was deposited in the bank, but the party entitled thereto shall not be entitled to receive bank interest thereon until the money shall have been received by the Canadian Bank of Commerce at Toronto. New.

Receipt to be given in duplicate by Bank.   **170.** The Bank, on receiving money to the credit of any cause or matter, is to give a receipt therefor in duplicate ; and one copy is to be delivered to the party making the deposit, and the other is to be posted or delivered the same day to the Accountant. Chy. O. 354.

Payment with defence in certain towns.   **171.** Money paid into Court with a defence at L'Orignal, Cayuga or Sault Ste. Marie, shall be paid to the proper officer of the Court, who, for receiving the same, may exact a sum not exceeding one per cent. on the sum so paid in, and shall sign a receipt for the amount in the margin of the pleading, for signing which receipt he shall be entitled to twenty cents, and the sum so paid in may be paid out to the plaintiff, or to his solicitor upon a written authority from the plaintiff. R.S.O. 1877, c. 50, s. 109.

(iii) Payment out of Court, Investments, etc.

172. Money is to be paid out of Court upon the cheque of the Accountant, countersigned by any one of the Registrars. J. A. Rule 477.

Payment out of Court. Amended Rule 1421

173. Money paid in with a de'ence at L'Orignal, Cayuga, or Sault Ste. Marie, is to be paid out with the privity of the officer who received the same.

174. No cheque shall be issued prior to the long vacation in any year unless the precipe therefor is lodged in the Accountant's office on or prior to the twentieth day of June, unless otherwise ordered by a Judge. J. A. Rule 606.

See Rule 1422

174 a
175. Every cheque is to be initialed by the chief Clerk in the Accountant's office before the same is presented for the signature of the Accountant or other officer. J. A. Rule 478.

Cheques to be initialed by Chief Clerk.

176. The person entitled to a cheque is to produce and leave with the Accountant the orders and reports entitling such person to the money, and is to file a precipe in the form No. 113 in the Appendix. Chy. O. 356.

On application for payment out, orders and reports to be produced.

177. Copies of orders dispensing with payment of money into Court are in all cases to be left with the Accountant forthwith after entry thereof. J. A. Rule 504.

Copies of orders.

178. The orders and reports produced as aforesaid are to be re-delivered to the party entitled thereto, with the cheque. Chy. O. 358.

Orders and. reports, to be returned.

179. Where money or stock, or securities in Court are directed by an order to be paid or transferred to an unmarried woman, and she marries before payment of the money or transfer of such stock or securities, the Accountant, if the same do not in the whole exceed $600 of principal money, or $50 in annual instalments, may draw for the money or make or execute a transfer of such stock or securities, in favour of such woman, upon an affidavit of herself and her husband that no settlement or agreement for a settlement has been made or entered into before, upon or since their marriage ; or in case any settlement or agreement for a settlement has been entered into, then upon an affidavit by the woman and her husband, identifying the settlement or agreement for a settlement, and stating that no other settlement or agreement for a settlement has been made or entered into as aforesaid, and an affidavit of the solicitor of the woman and her husband, that such solicitor has carefully perused such settlement or agreement for a settlement, and that according to the best of his judgment, such money, stock or securities are not, nor is any part thereof, subject to the trusts of the settlement or agreement for a settlement, or in any manner comprised therein or affected thereby. J. A. Rule 571.

Stock, how transferred to a married woman.

180. Where moneys or stock, or securities in Court are directed to be paid out of Court or transferred to the legal personal representative of any person, or to persons to be named in an order or report, and such moneys, stocks, or securities are reported or found to be due to any persons as legal personal representatives, the same or any portion thereof for the time being remaining unpaid or untransferred, may, upon proof, to the satisfaction of the officers signing and countersigning the cheque, of the death of any of them whether before, on, or after the day of the date of the order, be paid to the survivors or survivor of them. J. A. Rule 572.

Transfer of stock to representatives of person entitled.

181. Where moneys, stock or securities in Court are directed to be paid out or transferred by the Accountant to any person named in the order or judgment, or named, or to be named in any report, the same or any portion thereof for the time being remaining unpaid or untransferred,

Money, etc., payable to representatives may be paid to survivor of them.

may, on proof, to the satisfaction of the officers signing and countersigning the cheque, of the death of such person, whether before, on, or after the date of the order or judgment, and that his legal personal representatives are entitled thereto, be paid or transferred to the legal personal representatives of such deceased person or the survivors or survivor of them. J. A. Rule 573.

Principal money, etc., not to be paid to representatives after 6 years.

182. No principal sum of money, nor any stocks, funds, shares or securities shall, under Rules 180 and 181, be paid, transferred or delivered out of Court to the legal personal representatives of any person under any probate, or letters of administration, purported to be granted at any time subsequent to the expiration of 6 years from the day of the date of the order, or judgment, directing such payment, transfer or delivery. J. A. Rule 574.

Interest in like manner not to be paid after 6 years.

183. No interest or dividends shall under Rule 181 be paid out of Court to the legal personal representatives of any person under any probate, or letters of administration, purported to be granted at any time subsequent to the expiration of 6 years after the day of the date of the order or judgment directing such payment, or after the last receipt of such interest or dividends under such order or judgment, whichever shall last happen. J. A. Rule 575.

Payments to partners.

184. Where money is directed to be paid out of Court to any persons named or to be named in an order or report, and the money is, by the order or report, found to be due to them as partners, the same may be paid to any one or more of the partners by cheque payable to the firm. J. A. Rule 576.

Investment of funds in Court in Dom. Stock.

185. Persons entitled to money in Court may have a sufficient amount of the unappropriated Dominion Stock standing in the name of the Accountant appropriated as an investment of such money, or of part thereof, at par value. J. A. Rule 577.

Appropriation made without order.

186. If all parties interested consent in writing, the consent is to be filed with the Accountant, and he is to make the appropriation without an order being drawn for the purpose, and is to enter the consent in the Stock Ledger under the heading of the cause or matter, with the material contents of all orders, judgments and reports necessary to show who are interested in such account and the shares in which they are respectively interested therein, which may not be entered in the General Ledger. J. A. Rule 578.

Purchase of Stock if none held for investment.

187. If there is no unappropriated stock applicable to the purpose, a direction signed and countersigned in the same manner as a cheque, is to be delivered to the bank for the purchase, to be made in the name of the Accountant, and when the purchase is made a cheque is to be drawn for the amount and the brokerage charges, signed and countersigned as aforesaid, and like entries are to be made in the Stock Ledger. J. A. Rule 579.

Crediting interest on stock.

188. The interest on stock so appropriated or purchased, is, each half year, to be credited to the various accounts entitled thereto; and wherever interest is ordered to be paid from time to time to any person in respect of the moneys which shall have been so invested he is to be entitled to receive a cheque therefor without further order. J. A. Rule 580.

Stock may be purchased from time to time under one order.

189. Where an order or judgment directing the investment from time to time of any interest or dividends accruing upon any stock, funds, shares or securities standing in the name of the Accountant in trust in or to the credit of any action, matter or account, or upon any stocks, funds, shares or securities which may be directed to be transferred into the name of the Accountant, or to be carried over from one account to another, or upon any stocks, funds, shares or securities which may be directed to be pur-

nt Changes in the Court Pr
cedure.

ng of the judges of the Court of Jur
held in Osgoode Hall Saturday fo
nsider certain anomalies in the rul
re. Chief Justice Hagarty preside
were present :—Sir Thomas Ga
r Boyd and Mr. Justice Osler, M
ec. Mr. Justice Ferguson and M
icMahon.

was amended so as to read, " T
Court of the Chancery Division sh
ngs commencing on the first Mond
he first Thursday in December a
Thursday in February of each year
olution was passed :—

as, Under rule 191 it is provided th
ent of moneys in court by the
al Trusts Company shall be subje
val of the official guardian of t
of Justice for Ontario; and where
icial guardian has expressed his
relieved of the duty in question p
sections 114 and 115, Judicature A
ered that James S. Cartwright, E
rar of the Queen's Bench Division
High Court of Justice, be appoint
of the said official guardian
the said duty, and that the se
eneral Trusts Company is to satis
gistrar of the Queen's Bench Di
ecurity as to value; and that
same to the court before chequ
ach investment ; and the said co
to pay into court to the credit of
iterest funds the fees heretofore p
l official guardian by the said co
espect of said services."

urther decided that no order for
ation of an infant estate shall
il such infant is represented by
iardian of the High Court of Justi
be duly notified of the intended

N. Others foll
val makers is the
'DAISY." T
better.
ion, testimonials
Department, I

NG &

REAL.

DA

itire Retail Stock

PAF

o per cent

chased with any cash in Court, or with any cash to be paid into Court, with his privity, is brought to the Accountant for the purpose of having such direction for investment carried into effect, the Accountant may from time to time until he receives notice of an order or judgment to the contrary without any further request invest the interest or dividends so directed to be invested, together with all accumulations of interest or dividends thereon, as soon as conveniently may be after they accrue due and have been received, in the purchase of the particular description of stocks, funds, shares or securities named in the order or judgment directing such investment, and place such stocks, funds, shares or securities when purchased to the credit of the action, matter or account respectively, as may be directed by such order or judgment. J. A. Rule 581.

190. It shall be the duty of the Official Guardian to see that moneys payable on mortgages held by the Accountant, in which persons for whom the said Guardian has acted are interested, are promptly paid, and that the mortgaged premises are kept properly insured, and that the taxes thereon are duly paid. J. A. Rule 507.

Official Guardian to see to payment of mortgages in which moneys of parties for whom he has acted are invested.

(a) There shall be paid quarterly to the Official Guardian out of the surplus interest fund for services rendered by him under this Rule the sum of $200 per annum ; and in the event of the fund to the credit of the account of the Official Guardian exceeding the sum requisite to meet the other charges thereon, the moneys so to be paid out of the said surplus interest fund, shall be recouped out of the funds to the credit of the said account of the said Official Guardian. J. A. Rules 507, 536.

Remuneration of Guardian.

191. The Judges may arrange with the Toronto General Trusts Company to make investments, and to take the securities in the name of the Accountant of the Supreme Court of Judicature, of moneys in Court, upon first mortgages of lands, and may direct the issue of cheques therefor upon condition that the said Company do, by proper instrument, guarantee the sufficiency of such securities, and the due payment of interest at the rate of 4½ per cent. per annum, half-yearly, on the moneys so invested from the date of the receipt by the Company of the money for each investment, and also the due repayment of the principal moneys so invested ; and upon further condition that in case the said Company makes an investment as aforesaid at a higher rate than 6 per cent., then the said Company is to pay interest thereon to the Court at the rate of 4¾ per cent.; and upon further condition that the said Company is to satisfy the Official Guardian of the said High Court of the sufficiency of the security as to value, and he is to certify the same to the Court before the cheque issues for each investment. J. A. Rule 521.

Toronto General Trusts Co. empowered to make investments of funds in Court.

(iv) Stop Orders.

192. Where any stock, debentures, funds, securities, or moneys, are standing in Court to the credit of any action, or to the account of any class of persons, or are invested in the name of the Accountant, or other officer of the Court, and an order is made to prevent the transfer or payment of such stock, debentures, funds, securities or moneys, or any part thereof, without notice to the assignee of any person entitled in expectancy or otherwise to any share or portion of such stock, debentures, funds, securities, or moneys, the person by whom any such order is obtained, or the share of such stock, debentures, funds, securities, or moneys affected by such order, shall be liable at the discretion of the Court or a Judge, as the case may be, to pay any costs, charges and expenses which by reason of any such order having been obtained, shall be occasioned to any party to the action or matter, or any person interested in any such stock, debentures, funds, securities, or moneys. Chy. O. 286.

Liability of person obtaining Stop Order to pay costs and expenses occasioned thereby

Notice of Stop Order need not be served on parties not sought to be affected thereby.   **193.** A person applying for such order, shall not be required to serve notice thereof upon the parties to the cause, or upon the persons interested in such parts of the stock, debentures, funds, securities, or moneys, as are not sought to be affected by the order. Chy. O. 287.

193 A   *See Rule 14 28*

13. TAXING OFFICERS.

Taxing Officers.   **194.** There shall be two or more Taxing Officers of the Supreme Court at Toronto. *See* J. A. Rule 438.

Local taxing Officers.   **195.** Every Local Registrar, Local Master, Deputy Registrar and Deputy Clerk of the Crown, is a Local Taxing Officer.

Powers of local taxing Officers   **196.** Every Local Taxing Officer, shall, subject to the provisions of rules 1207 to 1211 inclusive, in actions begun or pending in his office, be entitled to tax all bills of costs, including counsel fees, subject only to appeal to a Judge of the High Court. This Rule shall not apply to cases in which infants are concerned, unless the official guardian is the guardian *ad litem* for the infants. 48 V. c. 13, s. 22.

Powers of taxing Officers.   **197.** All Taxing Officers, shall, for the purpose of any taxation, have power to administer oaths and take evidence, direct production of books and documents, make certificates, and give general directions for the conduct of taxations before them. *See* J. A. Rule 438.

14. BARRISTERS AND SOLICITORS.

Solicitors' Roll   **198.** There shall be one Roll of Solicitors of the Supreme Court of Judicature for Ontario, and all persons who shall be admitted as Solicitors shall sign the same upon taking the prescribed oaths. J. A. Rule 602.

Registrar of C. P. D. to have custody of roll.   **199.** The Registrar of the Common Pleas Division shall have the custody of such Roll and of all former Rolls of Attorneys and Solicitors, and he shall on the request of the Registrar of any other Division of the High Court, or of the Court of Appeal, transmit such Roll to such officer, who shall forthwith return the same to the Registrar of the Common Pleas Division when the purpose for which the same may be required shall have been accomplished. J. A. Rule 603.

Repealed
Rule 1560

Barristers' Rolls.   **200.** *Mutatis mutandis*, the Roll and Rolls for Barristers shall be in the same form and custody as the Solicitors' Roll and Rolls. J. A. Rule 604

Striking solicitor off roll.   **201.** Where a case appears justifying or requiring by the practice hitherto an order against a Solicitor that he be struck off the Roll of Solicitors, unless he shall, before a time therein limited, show unto the Court good cause to the contrary, it shall be competent for the Court, in lieu thereof, to issue an order calling upon the Solicitor to answer the matters appearing on affidavit or otherwise. Chy. O. 52.

Book to be kept by Registrar, in which addresses of solicitors practising in Toronto to be entered.

Repealed Rule 1423 (A)

Change of residence to be entered.   **202.** A book to be called "The Solicitors' and Agents' Book" shall be kept by the Registrars of the Queen's Bench and Common Pleas Divisions of the High Court in Toronto and the Clerk of Records and Writs, at their respective offices, to be there inspected by any solicitor or his clerk without fee or reward ; and every solicitor practising in said Court and residing within the city of Toronto or having an office and carrying on his business within the said city, shall enter in such book (in alphabetical order) his name and place of business or some other proper place within the city where he may be served with pleadings, notices, orders, and other proceedings ; and as often as any such solicitor changes his place of business or the place where he may be so served as aforesaid, he shall make the like entry thereof in the said book. Rules T. T. 1856, 136. Chy. O. 24.

203. Every other solicitor practising in the said Court shall enter in the said books (in like alphabetical order) his name and place of business, and also in an opposite column the name of some solicitor having an office and carrying on business in the city of Toronto as his agent. Rules T. T. 1856, 137. Chy. O. 24.

Book to be kept by Registrars in which names and addresses of Toronto agents to be entered.

204. Every Deputy or Local Registrar is to keep in his office a book to be called "The Solicitors' and Agents' Book," in which each solicitor residing elsewhere than in the County in which such Deputy or Local Registrar's office is, may specify the name of an agent, being a solicitor of this Court, and having an office in the city or town where the office of such Deputy or Local Registrar is situated, upon whom all writs, pleadings, notices, orders, warrants, and other documents, and written communications in relation to proceedings conducted in the office of the Local Master, Deputy Clerk, Deputy or Local Registrar of such County, may be served. Chy. O. 33.

Deputy Registrars. Solicitors and Agents' book.

15. SHORTHAND WRITERS.

205. All moneys received by a short-hand writer for copies of evidence shall, when the short-hand writer is paid by salary, be accounted for by him to the Clerk of the proper Court, and shall be by the Clerk of such Court deposited in the Bank for the time being, where moneys of the Province are deposited, to the credit of an account to be called "The Short-hand Writers' Fund." C. L. Rules, 10th March, 1876, 5.

Money received by short-hand writer how applicable.

206. When the short-hand writer is not paid by salary, the said moneys shall belong to and be the property of the said short-hand writer. C. L. Rules, 10th March, 1876, 6.

Short-hand writers not paid by salary, entitled to fees.

16. EXPERTS.

207. The Court may obtain the assistance of accountants, merchants, engineers, actuaries, or other scientific persons, in such way as it thinks fit, the better to enable it to determine any matter in evidence in any cause or proceeding, and may act on the certificate of such persons. Chy. O. 541.

Court may obtain services of experts.

CHAPTER III.

SITTINGS OF THE COURTS.

1. COURT OF APPEAL.

208. There shall be five sittings of the Court of Appeal in the year for the hearing of arguments, commencing on the second Tuesday in January, the first Tuesday in March, the second Tuesday in May, the first Tuesday in September, and the second Tuesday in November, or in case any of these days shall be a legal holiday, then on the following day. App. O. 53.

Sittings of Court of Appeal.

209. In case of sittings at any other time being deemed necessary, or convenient, for the despatch of business, due notice of the time of holding the same will be given. App. O. 54.

Extra sittings may be appointed.

. 2. HIGH C

(i) *Weekly S*

Weekly
sittings of
High Court.

210. A Judge shall sit at Osgoode
the vacations, for the purpose of dispos
which may be transacted by a single Jud

Order of
business.

211. The business of the weekly si
unless the Judge otherwise orders :—
Appeals ; Wednesday—Court ; Thursda
(a) *all documents d*

Cases to be
called in
order entered
on list.

212. All cases entered for argumen
and disposed of in the order in which
unless the Judge otherwise orders. Ru

(ii) *Sittings fo*

Sittings for
trials.

213. The High Court shall sit for th
may be fixed from time to time.

(iii) *Vacation*

Vacation
Judges.

214. One or more of the Judges of the High Court shall be selected
at the commencement of each Long Vacation, for the hearing in Toronto
during vacation of all such applications as may require to be immediately
or promptly heard. Such Judge or Judges shall act as vacation Judge or
Judges for one year from appointment. In the absence of arrangement
between the Judges, the vacation Judge or Judges shall be the Judge or
Judges last appointed (whether as Judge or Judges of the said High Court
or of any Court whose jurisdiction is by the Act vested in the said High
Court) who have not already served as vacation Judges of any such Court ;
and if there shall not be any Judge or Judges for the time being of the said
High Court who shall not have so served, then the vacation Judge or
Judges shall be the Judge or Judges (if any) who has or have not so served
and the senior Judge or Judges who has or have so served once only
according seniority of appointment whether in the said High Court or
such other Court as aforesaid. J. A. Rule 481.

amended
Rule 142 8

Jurisdiction of
vacation
Judges.

215. The vacation Judges may sit either separately, or together as a
Divisional Court, as occasion shall require, and may hear and dispose of all
actions, matters, and other business ~~to whatever Division the same may~~
~~be assigned.~~ No order made by a vacation Judge shall be reversed or
varied except by a Divisional Court or the Court of Appeal, or the Judge
who made the order. Any other Judge of the High Court may sit in
vacation for any vacation Judge. J. A. Rule 482.

amended
Rule 142 8 (2)

(iv) *Divisional Courts.*

Sittings of
Divisional
Courts of Q.
B. and C. P.
Divisions.

216. The sittings of the Divisional Courts shall be three in every
year, viz , the Michaelmas sittings, the Hilary sittings, and the Easter
sittings.

(Rules 216—218 inc.)
Repealed 1860

(a) The Michaelmas sittings shall begin on the third Monday in
November, and end on Saturday of the second week there-
after ; the Hilary sittings shall begin on the first Monday in
February and end on the Saturday of the following week ; ther
Easter sittings shall begin on the third Monday in May and
end on the Saturday of the second week thereafter ;

Judges of any Division of the said Court, or ▓▓▓▓ that the number of days so provided for ▓▓ any sitting ▓ not required, or is insufficient, for the ▓ despatch of the business to be transacted by the Court in ▓▓h sittings, such Judges may from time to time, shorten ▓▓ period for holding the sittings to such period, not less than 2 weeks, or increase the length of the same to any period, as the case may require ;

(c) The preceding provisions of this Rule are not to apply to the Chancery Division except when the Judges thereof shall be of opinion that the business of the said Division is such as to render the said provisions necessary or convenient for the due despatch of business, and shall give notice to that effect ;

last Monday *may*

217. The Divisional Court of the Chancery Division shall hold sittings commencing on the ~~first Thursday~~ in ~~September~~, the first Thursday in December, and third Thursday in February in each year. J. A. Rule 524.   *Sittings of Divisional Court in Ch'y Div.*   *amended 1890*

218. Divisional Courts of the High Court are to sit at such further or other times as may be directed by the High Court or as, in the opinion of the Judges of the Division, may be necessary for the due despatch of business. J. A. Rule 524.   *Repealed '1884 Rule 1429*

219. The following proceedings and matters shall be heard and determined before the Divisional Court ; but nothing herein contained shall be construed so as to take away or limit the power of a single Judge to hear and determine any such proceedings or matters in any case in which he has heretofore had power to do so, or so as to require any interlocutory proceeding therein, heretofore taken before a single Judge, to be taken before a Divisional Court :   *Proceedings to be taken before Divisional Courts. amended R Rule 1430 " 1431*

~~Appeals from orders of a Judge in Chambers.~~

Proceedings directed by any Statute to be taken before the Court, and in which the decision of the Court is final.

Cases of Habeas Corpus, in which a Judge directs that a motion for the writ, or the writ be made returnable before a Divisional Court.

Other cases where all parties agree that the same be heard before a Divisional Court.

Applications for new trials in the said Divisions where the action has been tried with a jury. J. A. Rule 471.

220. Six cases, in the order of their priority, on the general list of a Divisional Court, shall be set down by the Registrar in the peremptory list for argument, on each day of the Sittings of the Divisional Court, excepting upon the last day, and, except by consent and by leave of the Court, no argument shall be heard in any other case, until the cases in the peremptory list for the day are disposed of. C. L. Rules 17 Nov. 1875, 9, 10 ; 27 Nov. 1880.   *Peremptory list.*

221. Any case entered on the peremptory list for any day, and postponed by order, or default, shall be placed at the foot of the general list, unless, for sufficient cause, it is otherwise specially ordered by the Court. C. L. Rules 17 Nov. 1875, 11.   *Postponed cases.*

222. If either party to a case on the peremptory list, is prepared to be heard and the other party is not prepared, and it is not duly postponed as aforesaid, the Court may hear the party so prepared, whereupon the   *Party ready to proceed with case on peremptory list,*

may be heard, though other side not ready, or cause may be enlarged. case shall stand for judgment; or the Court may extend the time on sufficient cause being shown by affidavit, to enable the other party to be heard, on payment of the costs of the day, if the Court shall so order. If neither party to a case on the peremptory list is ready, the Court may, if it sees fit, strike the case out of the list.   C. L. Rules 17 Nov. 1875, 12.

Causes on peremptory list not disposed of, to be entered first for next day.   **223.** If all the cases on the peremptory list for any day, are not disposed of on that day, such cases shall be entered by the Registrar first on the peremptory list for the next day as part of the 6 cases for such next day.   C. L. Rule 17 Nov. 1875, 13; 27 Nov. 1880.

CHAPTER IV.

ACTIONS—COMMENCEMENT OF ACTIONS, ETC.

---

1. FORM AND COMMENCEMENT OF ACTION.

(i) *Writ of Summons.*

All actions commenced by writ of summons.   **224.** All actions which prior to *The Ontario Judicature Act, 1881,* were commenced by any form of writ, and all suits which were commenced by bill or information shall be commenced by the issue of a writ of summons, which shall be prepared by the plaintiff, and shall contain ~~the name of the Division from which it is issued~~, the names of the parties and the characters in which they sue and are sued, and the office in which and the time within which the defendant is to enter his appearance, and shall be indorsed with a short statement of the nature of the plaintiff's claim.   *See* R. S. O. 1877, c. 50, s. 14 ; c. 52, s. 4.   J. A. Rules 1, 5, 13, 22, 23.

amended Rule 1438

Proceedings to be assigned to a Div. of the H. C.   **225.** Every matter or proceeding not commenced by writ of summons shall be assigned to one of the Divisions of the High Court, by marking the document by which the same is commenced with the name of the Division.   *See* 44 V. c. 5, s. 25.

Repealed Rule 1434

Writs to issue in rotation.   **226.** Writs of summons shall be issued in rotation from the Queen's Bench, Chancery, and Common Pleas Divisions ; and in the County of York shall be issued by the Clerk of the Process, and in other counties

Repealed Rule 1435

or union of counties for judicial purposes, by the Deputy Clerk of the Crown or Local Registrar, as the case may be.

(*a*) Writs issued by a Deputy Clerk or a Local Registrar need not be signed or sealed by the Clerk of the Process. *See* J. A. Rule 545 ; R. S. O 1877, c. 50, ss. 5, 6. *Repealed Rule 1486*

227. The Clerks of the County Courts shall issue all similar writs in the County courts. County Courts respectively. R, S. O., 1877, c. 50, s. 6.

The officer issuing a writ of summons.

228. ~~The Clerk of the Process and each Deputy Clerk of the Crown~~, ~~Local Registrar and Clerk of each County Court~~, shall note in the margin of every writ issued by him, from what office and in what County the writ issued, and shall subscribe his name thereto. *See* R. S. O. 1877, c. 50, s. 9. Office from which issued to be noted in the margin.

229. Every writ of summons shall be signed and sealed by the officer issuing the same, and shall thereupon be deemed to be issued. J. A. Rule 24. Sealing and issue of writ.

230. A plaintiff may issue his writ of summons in any County. *See* J. A. Rule 20 ; R. S. O. 1877, c. 50, s. 10. Writ may issue in any county.

231. Where the service is to be made in Ontario, the writ of summons for the commencement of an action shall be in Form No. 1 in the Appendix hereto, with such variations as circumstances may require. J. A. Rule 7. Writ for service in Ontario.

232. Where there is jurisdiction to proceed with an action on a service out of Ontario, the writ of summons to be so served shall be in Form No. 2, in the Appendix hereto, with such variations as circumstances may require and shall bear the indorsement contained in said form purporting that such writ is for service out of Ontario. Where a defendant is not a British subject, and is not in British Dominions, notice of the writ of summons is to be served in lieu of service of the writ, and such notice shall be in Form No. 3 in the Appendix with such variations as circumstances may require. J. A. Rule 8 ; R. S. O. 1877, c. 50, s. 48. Writ and notice for service out of jurisdiction.

233. Every writ of summons and every other writ shall bear date on the day on which the same is issued, and shall be tested in the name of the President of the High Court of Justice, and shall require the defendant to appear thereto in 'ten days after service, including the day of service, if the service is to be made in Ontario. J. A. Rule 9. Date and teste of Writ.

234. The plaintiff or his solicitor shall, on presenting any writ of summons for sealing, leave with the officer a copy of such writ, and of all the indorsements thereon, signed by or for the solicitor leaving the same, or by the plaintiff himself if he sues in person. J. A. Rule 547, *first part*. Copy to be filed.

235. The officer issuing the writ shall make an entry of every writ of summons issued by him in a book to be called the Process Book, which is to be kept in the manner in which process books have heretofore been kept ; and the action shall be distinguished by a number in the manner in which actions are now distinguished in such last mentioned books ; and in case of any further proceeding in the action, an entry thereof shall be made in another book to be called the Procedure Book, which is to be kept in the manner in which Procedure Books have heretofore been kept. J. A. Rule 26. Process Book.

236. The plaintiff in any action may, at the time of, or at any time during twelve months after the issuing of the original writ of summons, issue one or more concurrent writ or writs, each concurrent writ to bear teste of the same day as the original writ, and to be marked by the officer issuing the same with the word " concurrent" in the margin, and the date of issuing the concurrent writ : Provided always, that such concurrent writ or writs shall only be in force for the period during which the original writ in such action is in force. J. A. Rule 27. Concurrent writs for service within and without the jurisdiction.

Concurrent writs.

237. A writ for service within the jurisdiction may be issued and marked as a concurrent writ with one for service, or whereof notice in lieu of service is to be given, out of the jurisdiction ; and a writ for service, or whereof notice in lieu of service is to be given, out of the jurisdiction, may be issued and marked as a concurrent writ with one for service within the jurisdiction. J. A. Rule 28.

(ii) *Renewal of Writ.*

Currency of writ.

238. No original writ of summons shall be in force for more than twelve months from the day of the date thereof, including the day of such date ; but if any defendant therein named shall not have been served therewith, the plaintiff may, before the expiration of the twelve months, apply to a Judge for leave to serve the writ after, and notwithstanding the lapse of, the said period.

(*a*) The Judge, if satisfied that reasonable efforts have been made to serve such defendant, or for other good reason, may order that the service shall be good if made within twelve months from the date of the order ; and so from time to time during the currency of the further period allowed.

(*b*) The writ shall in such case be renewed by being marked with the date of the day, month and year of such renewal ; such renewal to be so marked by the proper officer, upon delivery to him by the plaintiff or his solicitor of a memorandum in Form No. 92, in the Appendix.

(*c*) In such case the original writ shall be available to prevent the operation of any statute whereby the time for the commencement of the action is limited and for all other purposes, from the date of the original issue of the writ. J. A. Rule 31.

Evidence of renewal.

239. The production of a writ of summons purporting to have been renewed in manner aforesaid shall be sufficient *primâ facie* evidence for all purposes of the writ having been so renewed, and of the commencement of the action as of the date of the issue of the writ in manner provided as aforesaid. J. A. Rule 32.

(iii) *Indorsement of Address.*

Address of plaintiff and of solicitor.

240. Where a plaintiff sues by a solicitor, the writ of summons or notice in lieu of service of a writ of summons, shall be indorsed with the solicitor's name or firm and place of business, where writs, notices, petitions, orders, warrants and other documents, proceedings, and written communications may be left for him.

(*a*) Where any such solicitor is only agent of another solicitor, there shall be added to his name or firm and place of business the name or firm and place of business of the principal solicitor. J. A. Rule 18.

Address of plaintiff in person.

241. Where a plaintiff sues in person, there shall be indorsed upon the writ of summons, or notice in lieu of service of a writ of summons, his place of residence and occupation.

(*a*) If his place of residence is more than two miles from the office in which the appearance of defendant is to be entered there shall be indorsed also another proper place, to be called his address for service, which shall not be more than two miles from such office, where writs, notices, petitions orders, warrants and other documents. proceedings, and written communications not requiring personal service may be left for him.

(*b*) If the writ or notice is not so indorsed, or if such address or place be more than two miles from the office aforesaid, then the opposite party shall be at liberty to proceed by posting up in such office all notices, petitions, orders, warrants and other documents, proceedings and written communications requiring service. J. A. Rule 19.

242. Indorsements similar to those mentioned in the two next preceding Rules shall also be made upon every writ sued out and upon every document by which proceedings are commenced in cases where proceedings are commenced otherwise than by writ of summons. See Chy. O. 40, 41 ; R. S. O. 1877, c. 50, ss. 30, 31.

Indorsements on other proceedings.

(iv) *Indorsement of Claim.*

243. In the indorsement required by Rule 224, it shall not be essential to set forth the precise ground of complaint, or the precise remedy or relief to which the plaintiff considers himself entitled. J. A. Rule 11.

Precise statement not essential.

244. The indorsement of claim may be to the effect of such of the forms in Part II. of the Appendix hereto as shall be applicable to the case, or if none be found applicable then of such other similarly concise form as the nature of the case may require. J. A. Rule 12.

Form of indorsement.

245. In all actions where the plaintiff seeks only to recover a debt or liquidated demand in money payable by the defendant, with or without interest, arising (*a.*) upon a contract, express or implied, (as, for instance, on a bill of exchange, promissory note, or cheque, or other simple contract debt) ; or (*b.*) on a bond or contract under seal for payment of a liquidated amount of money ; or (*c.*) on a statute where the sum sought to be recovered is a fixed sum of money or in the nature of a debt other than a penalty ; or (*d.*) on a guaranty, whether under seal or not, where the claim against the principal is in respect of a debt or liquidated demand only ; or (*e.*) on a trust : or (*f.*) in actions for the recovery of land, with or without a claim for rent or mesne profits, by a landlord against a tenant whose term has expired or has been duly determined by notice to quit, or against persons claiming under such tenant ; the writ of summons may, at the option of the plaintiff, be specially indorsed with a statement of his claim, or of the remedy or relief to which he claims to be entitled. Such special indorsement shall be to the effect of such of the Forms in sec. IV. of Part II. of the Appendix as shall be applicable to the case. Eng. R. 1883

Debt or liquidated demand.

(2) Where a writ has been so indorsed the indorsement shall be considered as particulars of demand, and no further or other particulars need be delivered unless ordered by the Court or a Judge. R. S. O. 1877, c. 50, s. 19.

246. Where the plaintiff's claim is for a debt or liquidated demand only, the indorsement, besides stating the nature of the claim, shall state the amount claimed for debt, or in respect of such demand, and for costs, respectively, and shall further state that upon payment thereof within eight days after service, or, in case of a writ not for service within the jurisdiction, within the time allowed for appearance, further proceedings will be stayed. Such statement may be in the form in the Appendix Part II., sec. II. The defendant may, notwithstanding such payment, have the costs taxed, and if more than one-sixth shall be disallowed, the plaintiff's solicitor shall pay the costs of taxation. J. A. Rule 15.

Indorsement in cases of debt or liquidated demand.

247. In all cases of ordinary account, as, for instance, in the case of a partnership, or executorship, or ordinary trust account, where the plaintiff desires to have an account taken in the first instance, the writ of summons shall be indorsed with a claim that such account be taken. This Rule does not apply to proceedings under Rules 965 to 988. J. A. Rule 16.

Indorsement of claim for account.

3

amended Rule 14.28

Indorsement in mortgage actions where immediate possession or payment desired.

248. Where the claim is for the foreclosure of a mortgage or the sale of mortgaged property, and the plaintiff desires an order against a defendant for the immediate delivery of possession, or for immediate payment, the writ must, in addition to the ordinary notice, be indorsed with a further notice to the effect of such of the forms in the Appendix hereto, Part II., sec. VI., as are applicable to the case. J. A. Rule 17.

Indorsement in action of dower.

249. In case the plaintiff in an action of dower claims damages for detention of her dower, the indorsement on the writ of summons shall contain a statement that the plaintiff claims damages for the detention of her dower, from some day to be stated in the notice. *See* R. S. O. 1877, c. 55, ss. 9, 10.

2. Disclosure by Solicitors and Plaintiffs.

Whether writ issued by his authority.

250. Every solicitor whose name is signed to or indorsed on any writ of summons shall, on demand in writing made by or on behalf of any defendant who has been served therewith or has appeared thereto, declare forthwith in writing whether the writ has been issued by him or with his authority or privity.

(*a*) If he answers in the affirmative, then he shall also, in case the Court or a Judge so directs, disclose in writing within a time to be limited by the Court or Judge, the profession or occupation, and place of abode of the plaintiff, on pain of being guilty of a contempt of the Court from which the writ appears to have issued.

(*b*) If the solicitor declares that the writ was not issued by him or with his authority or privity, all proceedings upon the same shall be stayed, and no further proceedings shall be taken thereupon without leave of the Court or a Judge. J. A. Rule 29

Names and addresses of members of firm suing as partners.

251. Where a writ is sued out by partners in the name of their firm, the plaintiffs or their solicitor, shall, on demand in writing by or on behalf of any defendant, declare forthwith in writing the names and places of residence of all the persons constituting the firm.

(*a*) If the plaintiffs or their solicitor fail to comply with such demand, all proceedings in the action may, upon an application for that purpose, be stayed upon such terms as the Court or a Judge may direct.

(*b*) Where the names of the partners are so declared, the action shall proceed in the same manner, and the same consequences in all respects shall follow, as if they had been named as the plaintiffs in the writ; but all proceedings shall, nevertheless, continue in the name of the firm. J. A. Rule 30.

3. Service of Writ of Summons.

(i) *Mode of Service.*

Undertaking to accept service.

252. No service of a writ of summons or other document by which an action or proceeding may be commenced shall be required where the defendant by his solicitor accepts service, and undertakes to appear thereto. J. A. Rule 33. Chy. O. 47.

Personal and substituted service.

253. Where service is required, the writ of summons may be served in any County in Ontario and the service thereof, whenever practicable, shall be personal; but if it be made to appear to the Court or Judge on affidavit that the plaintiff is from any cause unable to effect prompt personal service, the Court or Judge may make such order for substituted or other service, or for the substitution for service of notice by advertisement or otherwise, as may seem just. R. S. O. 1877, c. 50, s. 20; c. 55, s. 11. J. A. Rule 34.

251. Upon the delivery of a writ of summons at the office of a Sheriff, *Indorsement* to be served by him, he, his Deputy or Clerk, shall indorse thereon the *of receipt of* time when it was so delivered ; and in case the writ is not fully and com- *process, etc. ;* pletely served within ten days after such delivery, the plaintiff, his *non-service,* solicitor or agent, shall be entitled to receive back the same ; and the *plaintiff; costs* Sheriff, Deputy Sheriff or Clerk shall indorse thereon the time of the *of service.* delivery ; and the costs of the mileage and service of the writ by any literate person afterwards, shall, in case the person to be served was at any time during such ten days within the County, be allowed in the taxation of costs, as if the service had been by the Sheriff or his officer.   R. S. O. 1877, c. 50, s. 23 ; c. 40, s. 95.

255. If the Sheriff, being applied to, neglects or refuses to return the *Failure by* writ, after the expiration of the ten days, the plaintiff may issue a dupli- *Sheriff to re-* cate or concurrent writ on the *præcipe* already filed, and the costs of the *deliver.* first or other writ not returned may be charged against and recovered from the Sheriff by the plaintiff or his solicitor.   R. S. O. 1877, c. 50, s. 24 ; c. 40, s. 96.

256. The person serving a writ of summons shall, within three days at *Indorsement* most after the service, indorse on the writ the day of the month and *of service.* week of the service thereof ; otherwise the plaintiff shall not be at liberty, in case of non-appearance, to proceed by default without the leave of a Judge, such leave to be obtained at the cost of the plaintiff, and such cost to be in no event charged against the defendant.

(a) Every affidavit of service of such writ shall mention the day on which such indorsement was made.   J. A. Rule 44.

(a) *Married Women, Infants, Lunatics.*

257. A married woman shall be served in the same manner as a party to *Married* an action or matter not under any disability ; and the like proceedings may *Woman.* be had on such service and with the like effect, as if the married woman were a *feme sole.*   J. A. Rule 35.

258. Where the action is in respect of an estate in which an infant is *Service on* interested, service on the official guardian shall be good service on the *official guar-* infant defendant.   *dian.*

(a) If in such case there are more than one infant defendant, for whom service is to be made on the official guardian, one copy only need be so served.

(b) From the time of such service the official guardian shall become and be the guardian *ad litem* of the infant, unless and until the Court other-wise orders ; and it shall be his duty forthwith to attend actively to the interests of the infant in the action, and for that purpose to communicate with all proper parties, including the father or guardian (if any) of the infant, and also the person with whom or under whose care the infant resides, in case such person is not the infant's father or guardian ; and the guardian is to make such other inquiries and to take such other proceed-ings as the interests of the infant may require.   J. A. Rule 36, *first part.*

259. Where an action is brought against an infant defendant for the *Service on* recovery of lands, goods, or chattels of which he is personally in posses- *infant* sion, service shall be made on the infant personally, and one copy of the *personally.* writ shall also be posted (prepaid) to, or delivered at the office of the official guardian.   J. A. Rule 37.

Torts.

260. When the action is against an infant in respect of a personal tort or for the mere recovery of money, the infant shall be served as in the case of an adult defendant.

Guardian other than official guardian.

261. When the infant is personally served and is not represented by the official guardian, there may be a guardian appointed for the infant as in actions at common law before the Judicature Act.

Motion for guardian.

262. Any person interested may move before a Judge in Chambers, on such material as he may think proper, for an order appointing a guardian other than the official guardian ; whereupon such order as may be considered most conducive to the interests of the infant shall be made. J. A. Rule 36, *last part.*

Lunatics.

263. Where a lunatic, or where a person of unsound mind not so found by inquisition or judicial declaration, is a defendant to the action, service on the committee of the lunatic, or on the person with whom the person of unsound mind resides, or under whose care he or she is, shall, unless the Court or a Judge otherwise orders, be deemed good service on such defendant. J. A. Rule 38.

Guardian *ad litem.*

264. No further proceedings are to be taken against such a defendant who has no committee, until a guardian *ad litem* is appointed. J. A. Rule 39.

(b) *Partners.*

Partners.

265. Where partners are sued in the name of their firm, the writ shall be served either upon any one or more of the partners, or at the principal place within Ontario of the business of the partnership, upon any person having at the time of service the control or management of the partnership business there ; and, subject to the Rules hereinafter contained, such service shall be deemed good service upon the firm. J. A. Rule 40.

Person doing business under name of firm.

266. Where one person carrying on business in the name of a firm apparently consisting of more than one person, is sued in the firm name, the writ may be served at the principal place within Ontario of the business so carried on, upon any person having at the time of service the control or management of the business there ; and, subject to any Rules of Court, such service shall be deemed good service on the person so sued. J. A. Rule 41.

(c) *Corporations.*

Service on corporations, how effected.

267. A writ of summons issued against a corporation aggregate, and, in the absence of its appearance by solicitor, all papers and proceedings in the action before final judgment, may be served on the Mayor, Warden, Reeve, President, or other head officer, or on the Township, Town, City or County Clerk, or on the Cashier, Treasurer or Secretary, Clerk or Agent of such corporation, or of any branch or agency thereof in Ontario ; and every person who, within Ontario, transacts or carries on any of the business of, or any business for, any corporation whose chief place of business is without the limits of Ontario, shall, for the purpose of being served with a writ of summons issued against such corporation, be deemed the agent thereof. R. S. O. 1877, c. 50, s. 21. *See* Chy. O. 91, 92.

Services of papers on certain corporations.

268. A writ of summons issued against a railway, telegraph, or express corporation, and all subsequent papers and proceedings, in the event of an appearance not having been duly entered, may be served on the agent of such corporation, at any branch or agency thereof, or on any station master of any railway company, or on any telegraph operator, or express agent having charge of any telegraph or express office belonging to such corporation ; and any such station master, operator or express agent

shall, for the purpose of being served with a writ of summons issued
against such corporation, or any paper or proceeding as aforesaid, in the
event of non-appearance, be deemed the agent thereof. R. S. O. 1877, c.
50, s. 22.

269. Where, by any statute, provision is made for service of any Service as pro-
writ of summons, bill, petition, or other process upon any corporation, or vided by any
any society or fellowship, or any body or number of persons, whether special statute
corporate or otherwise, every writ of summons may be served in the
manner so provided. J. A. Rule 42.

270. In case an action against a corporation is brought in Ontario on a
judgment, or decree obtained in the Province of Quebec, service of process
on the officer or officers thereof named in the Act incorporating such corporation, or in case there be no officer named in the said Act, then service
of process according to the law of the Province of Quebec, shall be held to
be personal service. R. S. O. 1877, c. 50, s. 147.

(ii) *Service out of Ontario.*

271. Service out of the jurisdiction of a writ of summons or notice Service out of
of a writ of summons or other document by which a matter or proceeding jurisdiction.
is commenced may be allowed by the Court or a Judge whenever—[Eng.
R. 1883, 64, (a), (b), (c), (d), (e), (f), (g)]

(a) The whole subject-matter of the action is land situate within
Ontario (with or without rents or profits) ; or

(b) Any act, deed, will, contract, obligation, or liability affecting land
or hereditaments situate within Ontario, is sought to be construed, rectified,
set aside, or enforced in the action ; or [Ont. R. 45 (a), altered].

(c) Any relief is sought against any person domiciled or ordinarily
resident within Ontario ; or

(d) The action is for the administration of the personal estate of any
deceased person, who at the time of his death was domiciled within the
jurisdiction, or for the execution (as to property situate within the jurisdiction) of the trusts of any written instrument, of which the person to
be served is a trustee, which ought to be executed according to the law of
Ontario ; or [New.]

(e) The action is founded on any breach or alleged breach within
Ontario of any contract wherever made, which, according to the
terms thereof, ought to be performed within Ontario ; or [Ont. R. 45 (b).]

(f) Any injunction is sought as to anything to be done within Ontario,
or any nuisance within Ontario is sought to be prevented or removed,
whether damages are or are not also sought in respect thereof ; or [Ont.
R. 45 (c), (d).]

(g) Any person out of the jurisdiction is a necessary or proper party to an
action properly brought against some other person duly served within the
jurisdiction. *New.*

272. Notice in lieu of a writ of summons shall be served in the same Service of
manner as writs of summons are served. J. A. Rule 49. notice in lieu
of writ.

273. Where a party to any action or matter is absent from the Pro- Other modes of
vince or cannot be found therein to be served, the Court may authorize proceeding
proceedings to be taken against him according to the practice of the against absent
Court in the case of a defendant whose residence is unknown, or in defendant.
any other manner that may be provided or ordered, if the Court, under
the circumstances of the case, deems such mode of proceeding conducive
to the ends of justice. R. S. O. 1877, c. 40, s. 94.

Service made without previous order may be allowed.

274. It shall not be necessary before serving a writ, or notice of a writ, or copy of any other document by which a matter or proceeding is commenced to apply to the Court or a Judge to allow the service ; but in case proof is given to the satisfaction of the Court or Judge that the service was duly made and that the case was a proper one for service out of the Province under the preceding Rules, the service shall be allowed. J. A. Rule 48. R. S. O. 1877. c. 40, s. 93.

Rescinded 29th Sep 1854 —

4. APPEARANCE, ETC.

(i) *General Rules.*

Service in Ontario.

275. When a defendant is served within Ontario, and not in Algoma or Thunder Bay, he shall appear within ten days, including the day of service.

Algoma or Thunder Bay.

(*a*) If served within Algoma or Thunder Bay he is to have thirty days in an action for the recovery of land, and twenty days in other actions, after the service, except where he is served between the first day of November and the 30th day of June or on either of said days, in which case he shall have an additional period of ten days. 47 V. c. 14, s. 7.

Time for entering appearance and delivering defence.

276. Where a defendant is served out of Ontario he shall have the time following for entering his appearance and delivering his defence and both proceedings shall be taken within the time named.

See Rule 1811

(*a*) If the defendant is served within any part of the Dominion of Canada (other than Ontario, Manitoba, Keewatin or the North-West Territories, or British Columbia,) or within the United States of America, he is to have six weeks after the service.

(*b*) If served within any part of the United Kingdom (including the Isle of Man and the Channel Islands), or of Manitoba, Keewatin or the North-West Territories, British Columbia or Newfoundland, he is to have eight weeks after the service.

(*c*) If served elsewhere than within the limits above designated, he is to have twelve weeks after the service.

(*d*) The writ of summons in such case may be in the form No. 2 in the Appendix, and the statement of claim is to be served therewith. J. A. Rule 46.

How entered.

277. A defendant shall enter his appearance to a writ of summons by delivering a memorandum in writing, dated on the day of delivering the same, and containing the name of the defendant's solicitor, or stating that the defendant defends in person, to the proper officer in that office in the same County where the writ of summons was issued, in which, by the memorandum subscribed on the writ or by the notice of the writ, the appearance is required to be entered, except where by any Rule of Court it may be otherwise provided, or where the Court or a Judge otherwise directs. *See* J. A. Rules 51, 546.

Two or more defendants, etc.

278. If two or more defendants in the same action appear by the same solicitor and at the same time, the names of all the defendants so appearing shall be inserted in one memorandum. J. A. Rule 59.

Appearance, where entered.

279. All proceedings in actions to final judgment shall be carried on in the office in which the appearance is to be entered. J. A. Rule 546.

Issue to be filed.

280. When an issue is directed to be tried it shall ~~be filed~~ as soon as settled, ~~and may~~ be filed in the county in which it is directed to be tried, and thereafter the proceedings in the issue shall be carried on in the said

amended Rule 1442

county in the same manner as the proceedings in an action commenced in such county. But the Court or a Judge may order otherwise, and may change the place of trial in the same manner and subject to the same rules as in an action.

281. A defendant may appear at any time before judgment. If he appears at any time after the time limited for appearance he shall, on the same day, give notice thereof to the plaintiff's solicitor, or to the plaintiff himself if he sues in person, and he shall not, unless the Court or a Judge otherwise orders, be entitled to any further time for delivering his defence, or for any other purpose, than if he had appeared according to the writ ; and if the defendant appears after the time appointed by the writ, and omits to give such notice of his appearance, the plaintiff may proceed as in case of non-appearance. J. A. Rule 61. *When appearance may be entered and when notice is to be given.*

282. The solicitor of a defendant appearing by a solicitor shall state in the memorandum his place of business. J. A. Rule 52. *Address of Solicitor.*

283. A solicitor not entering an appearance in pursuance of his written undertaking so to do on behalf of any defendant, shall be liable to an attachment. J. A. Rule 60. *Solicitor's undertaking*

284. A defendant appearing in person shall state in the memorandum his address; and if he resides more than two miles from the office from which the writ of summons was issued, he shall state in such memorandum a place to be called his address for service, which shall not be more than two miles from such office. J. A. Rule 53. *Address of defendant in person.*

285. If the memorandum does not contain the address of the solicitor or the defendant (as the case may be) as required by the preceding Rules, the memorandum shall not be received ; and if such address is illusory or fictitious, the appearance may be set aside by the Court or a Judge, on the application of the plaintiff ; and the plaintiff may be permitted, by the Court or a Judge, to proceed by posting up the proceedings in the office where the appearance is required to be entered. J. A. Rule 54. *Where no address or improper address given.*

286. The Memorandum of Appearance may be in the Form No. 93, in the Appendix, with such variations as the circumstances of the case may require. *Form of memorandum.*

(a) In case a defendant does not require the plaintiff to deliver a statement of claim he shall so state in his memorandum of appearance, and in that case shall serve a copy of such appearance on the plaintiff. J. A. Rule 55.

287 Upon receipt of a Memorandum of Appearance, the officer shall forthwith enter the appearance n the Procedure Book. J. A. Rule 56. *Entry of memorandum.*

(ii) *Partners.*

288. Where partners are sued in the name of their firm, they shall appear individually in their own names, but all subsequent proceedings shall, nevertheless, continue in the name of the firm. J. A. Rule 57. *Partners.*

289. Where any person carrying on business in the name of a firm apparently consisting of more than one person is sued in the name of the firm, he shall appear in his own name ; but all subsequent proceedings shall, nevertheless, continue in the name of the firm. J. A. Rule 58. *Appearance by person sued under firm name.*

(iii) *Dower.*

Defendant may file appearance and acknowledge tenancy.

290. Any defendant named in the writ, in an action for dower, may, within the time appointed, file an appearance and acknowledgment that he is tenant of the freehold of the land named in the writ, together with his consent that the plaintiff may have judgment for her dower therein and may take the proceedings authorized by *The Act respecting Dower* to have the same assigned to her, unless the parties otherwise agree, and he shall forthwith serve the plaintiff or her solicitor with a copy of such appearance, acknowledgment and consent, together with an affidavit of the day of the entering and filing the same in the proper office ; and in every such case when the defendant so admits the right to recover, the plaintiff may enter judgment of seisin forthwith, and may obtain a writ of assignment of dower, but shall not be entitled to tax or recover the costs of suit or of entering such judgment against the defendant. R. S. O. 1877, c. 55, s. 20.

Judgment of seisin and writ of assignment thereon.

(a) In case the plaintiff claims arrears of dower or damages for detention of her dower, neither the entry of a judgment of seisin nor the taking of proceedings for the assignment of her dower thereunder shall prevent her from proceeding with the action for the recovery of such arrears or damages. *New.*

Case wherein defendant may sue out execution, if plaintiff does not.

291. In case the defendant has filed and served an acknowledgment and consent under the preceding Rule, and the plaintiff does not within 3 months thereafter sue out and cause to be executed a writ of assignment of dower, the defendant may, by leave of the Court or a Judge, sue out such writ ; and the writ shall be, as nearly as may be, in the same form as a writ sued out by the plaintiff, and the like proceedings shall be had thereon. R. S. O. 1877, c. 55, s. 21.

Landlord be substituted as defendant.

292. In an action for dower the landlord or other person under whom a tenant in possession, who is not also tenant of the freehold, holds or entered into possession, may, if he has not been served with the writ, without leave, appear and defend, by filing with his appearance an affidavit that he is tenant of the freehold, and is advised and believes that there is good ground for disputing the plaintiff's claim to dower. *See* R. S. O. 1877, c. 55, s. 14.

(iv) *Recovery of Land.*

Appearance without leave by person not named as a defendant.

293. Any person not named as a defendant in a writ of summons for the recovery of land, may, without leave, appear and defend, by filing with his appearance an affidavit stating that he is in possession of the land either by himself or his tenant (as the case may be), and stating further, in case the possession is by his tenant, that the defendant named in the writ is his tenant. The affidavit may be in the form of affidavit numbered 47, in the Appendix. J. A. Rule 62.

Appearance by landlord in action for land.

294. Where such affidavit is not filed, any person not named as a defendant in a writ of summons for the recovery of land, may, by leave of the Court or Judge, appear and defend, on filing an affidavit shewing that he is in possession of the land, either by himself or his tenant. J. A. Rule 63.

Form of appearance by landlord.

295. Any person appearing to defend an action for the recovery of land as landlord, in respect of property whereof he is in possession in person or by his tenant, shall state in his appearance that he appears as landlord. J. A. Rule 64.

Notice of appearance by person not named as a defendant in writ.

296. Where a person not named as defendant in a writ of summons for the recovery of land enters an appearance according to either of the foregoing Rules, the appearance shall be entitled in the action against the party or parties named in the writ as defendant or defendants ; and the person so entering an appearance shall forthwith give notice thereof to the plaintiff's solicitor, or to the plaintiff if he sues in person, and shall in all subsequent proceedings be named as a party defendant to the action ; and if such person appears and omits to give notice of his appearance, the plaintiff may proceed as in case of non-appearance. **J. A.** Rule 65.

297. Any person appearing to a writ of summons for the recovery of Limited ap-land shall be at liberty to limit his defence to a part only of the property pearance in mentioned in the writ, describing that part with reasonable certainty in action for land. his memorandum of appearance, or in a notice intituled in the cause and signed by him or his solicitor, such notice to be served within four days Notice. after appearance upon the solicitor whose name is indorsed on the writ, if any ; and if none, then filed in the proper office ; and an appearance where the defence is not so limited shall be deemed an appearance to defend for the whole. **J. A.** Rule 66.

298. The notice to be served as mentioned in the last preceding Rule Form of no-may be in the Form No. 14 in the Appendix, with such variations as cir- tice. cumstances may require. **J. A.** Rule 67.

(v) *Limited defence.*

299. Any person appearing to a writ of summons in other cases may Limitation of limit his defence to the question of the amount to which the plaintiff is defence to entitled, and in that case may in his appearance, or, by notice served question of with n four days thereafter, state that he disputes only the amount amount only. claimed by the plaintiff; and he need not file any further defence for the purpose of disputing such amount ; and the plaintiff is to proceed as if the d fendant had filed a defence disputing the amount of the claim. The notice disputing the amount of the claim may be in the Form No. 15, in the Appendix, with such variations as circumstances may require. J. A. Rule 68.

5. PARTIES.

(i) *Generally.*

300. All persons may be joined as plaintiffs in whom the right to any Who may be relief claimed is alleged to exist, whether jointly, severally, or in the joined as alternative. And, without any amendment, judgment may be given for plaintiffs. such one or more of the plaintiffs as may be found to be entitled to relief, for such relief as he or they may be entitled to. J. A. Rule 89, part.

301. All persons may be joined as defendants against whom the right to Who may be any relief is alleged to exist, whether jointly, severally, or in the alterna- joined as tive. And, without any amendment, judgment may be given against such defendants. one or more of the defendants as may be found to be liable, according to their respective liabilities. J. A. Rule 91.

302. It shall not be necessary that every defendant to an action shall Where defen-be interested as to all the relief thereby prayed for, or as to every cause dant not inter-of action included therein ; but the Court or a Judge may make such order ested in all the as may appear just, to prevent any defendant from being embarrassed or relief prayed. put to expense by being required to attend any proceedings in the action in which he may have no interest. J. A. Rule 92.

303. The plaintiff may, at his option, join as parties to the same action All or any all or any of the persons severally, or jointly and severally, liable on any parties liable one contract, including parties to bills of exchange and promissory notes. on one con-J. A. Rule 93. tract may be joined.

304. Where any person is surety for the payment of a mortgage debt, joined with such person may be made a party to an action for the sale of the mortgaged mortgagor, property. Chy. O. 427. and relief ob-tained against both.

Surety may be

Where relief is sought subject to prior mortgage, prior mortgagee an unnecessary party.

305. Where the plaintiff prays a sale or foreclosure, subject to a prior mortgage, the prior mortgagee is not to be made a party either originally or in the Master's office, except under special circumstances to be alleged in the statement of claim. Chy. O. 440.

Parties interested in equity of redemption may be allowed to be added in the Master's office

306. Where it appears conducive to the ends of justice that parties interested in the equity of redemption should be allowed to be made parties in the Master's Office, by reason of the parties so interested being numerous or otherwise, the Court may direct that parties so interested be made parties in the Master's Office, upon such terms as to the Court or a Judge seems fit; such order to be made only where one or more parties interested in the equity of redemption are already before the Court. Chy. O. 438.

Officers of corporations not to be made defendants merely for discovery.

307. Where an action is brought against a corporation aggregate, no officer of the corporation is to be made a defendant for discovery only. Chy. O. 63.

Several defendants in cases of doubt.

308. Where in any action the plaintiff is in doubt as to the person from whom he is entitled to redress, he may, in such manner as hereinafter mentioned, or as may be prescribed by any special order, join two or more defendants, to the intent that in such action the question as to which, if any, of the defendants is liable, and to what extent, may be determined as between all parties to the action. J. A. Rule 94.

Trustees, executors and administrators.

309. Trustees, executors, and administrators may sue and be sued on behalf of, or as representing, the property or estate of which they are trustees or representatives, without joining any of the parties beneficially interested in the trust or estate, and shall be considered as representing such parties in the action; but the Court or a Judge may, at any stage of the proceedings, order any of such parties to be made parties to the action, either in addition to, or in lieu of, the previously existing parties thereto. J. A. Rule 95.

If a deceased person has no personal representative, proceedings may go on, or the Court may appoint a representative.

310. Where, in any action or other proceeding, it is made to appear that a deceased person who was interested in the matters in question has no legal personal representative, the Court or a Judge may either proceed in the absence of any person representing the estate of the deceased person, or may appoint some person to represent such estate for all the purposes of the action or other proceeding, on such notice to such person or persons, if any, as the Court thinks fit, either specially or by public advertisement, and notwithstanding that the estate in question may have a substantial interest in the matters, or that there may be active duties to be performed by the person so appointed, or that he may represent interests adverse to the plaintiff, or that there may be embraced in the matter an administration of the estate whereof representation is sought; and the order so made and any orders consequent thereon, shall bind the estate of such deceased person in the same manner in every respect as if there had been a duly appointed legal personal representative of such person, and such legal personal representative had been a party to the action or proceeding, and had duly appeared and had submitted his rights and interests to the protection of the Court. R. S. O. 1877, c. 49, s. 9.

Appointment of Administrator to represent estate in proceedings in High Court.

311. Where no probate of the will of a deceased person, or letters of administration to his estate, have been granted by a Surrogate Court, and representation of such estate is required in any action or proceeding in the High Court, the Court may appoint some person administrator or administrator *ad litem* (according as the case may require) to the estate ; and the person so appointed shall give the security required from, and have the rights, authority, and responsibility of, an administrator or administrator *pendente lite* (as the case may be), appointed by the Surrogate Court, but the Court may dispense with such security.

(*a*) Where a general administrator is appointed under this Rule, the same fees shall be payable in stamps as would be payable to the Crown, or to the Judge of the Surrogate Court, under any Act then in force, upon the grant of administration of an estate of the same value made by the Surrogate Court.

(*b*) Where administration is granted by the High Court under this Rule, the Registrar shall forthwith transmit by mail to the Surrogate Clerk, a certified copy of the grant ; and in case the grant is with will annexed, he shall, at the same time, also transmit to the said Clerk a certified copy of the will ; and the Surrogate Clerk shall make similar entries in respect of the documents so transmitted as he makes in respect of particulars furnished to him under section 14 of *The Revised Statute respecting the Surrogate Courts.* 48 V. c. 13, s. 11.

312. Where no order for general administration is asked or required, Order for account against or where it is shewn that an executor *de son tort* has taken possession of executor *de son* the bulk of the personal assets belonging to the estate of a deceased *tort.* person, such executor *de son tort* may on the application of any one interested in the estate of the deceased, and, without the appointment of any other personal representative of the estate, be required to account for any assets of the estate which have come to his hands ; and where a proper case is made for the appointment by the High Court of a receiver of the estate of a deceased person who has no legally appointed personal representative, the estate may be administered under the direction of the Court without the appointment of any person other than the receiver to represent the estate. 48 V. c. 13, s. 12.

313. An infant may sue as plaintiff by his next friend ; and may defend Infants. any action by his guardian appointed for that purpose, or by the official guardian as the case may be. J. A. Rule 96.

314. A married woman may sue for alimony without a next friend. Married women.

(*a*) In cases not provided for by *The Married Women's Property Act*, a married woman may sue as plaintiff by her next friend. J. A. Rule 97 ; 47 V. c. 19, s. 11.

315. Where there are numerous parties having the same interest in Where parties one action, one or more of such parties may sue or be sued, or may be are numerous. authorized by the Court to defend, in such action, on behalf of, or for the benefit of, all parties so interested. J. A. Rule 98.

316. In any case in which the right of an heir-at-law or of the next of Persons appointed kin, or of a class depends upon the construction which the Court may pointed to represent put upon an instrument, and it is not known or is difficult to ascertain who is or are such heir-at-law or next of kin or class, and the Court considers that in order to save expense or for some other reason it will be convenient to have the question or questions of construction determined before such heir-at-law, next of kin or class, shall have been ascertained by means of inquiry or otherwise, the Court may appoint some one or more person or persons to represent such heir-at-law, next of kin or class, and the judgment of the Court in the presence of such person or persons shall be binding upon the party or parties or class so represented. J. A. Rule 99.

317. Any two or more persons claiming or being liable as co-partners Partners may may sue or be sued in the name of the respective firms, if any, of which sue in firm such persons were co-partners at the time of the accruing of the cause of name.

action ; and any party to an action may in such case apply to the Court or a Judge for a statement of the names of the persons who were, at the time of the accruing of the cause of action, co-partners in any such firm, to be furnished in such manner, and verified on oath or otherwise, as the Judge may direct. Provided that, in the case of a co-partnership which has been dissolved, to the knowledge of the plaintiff, before the commencement of the action, the writ of summons shall be served upon every person sought to be made liable. J. A. Rules 100, 501 and Eng. R. 1883, 136.

Person trading under firm name.

318. Any person carrying on business in the name of a firm, apparently consisting of more than one person, may be sued in the name of such firm. J. A. Rule 101.

Court may proceed though some of the parties interested are not before it.

319. Where questions arise between parties, who are some only of those interested in the property respecting which the question arises ; or where the property in question is comprised with other property in the same settlement, will, or other instrument, or is the property of an intestate, the Court may adjudicate on the questions arising between such parties without making the other parties interested in the property respecting which the question arises, or interested under the settlement, will, or other instrument, parties to the action ; and without requiring the whole trusts and purposes of the settlement, will, or instrument, or the whole estate of the intestate, to be executed or administered under the direction of the Court, and without taking the accounts of the trustees or other accounting parties, or ascertaining the particulars or amount of the property touching which the question or questions have arisen, or of the whole estate or assets ; but where the Court is of opinion that the application is fraudulent, or collusive, or that for some other reason the application ought not to be entertained, it may refuse to make the order asked. Chy. O. 57.

Cases where one of a class may sue without joining others.

320. It shall not be competent to a defendant to take an objection for want of parties in any case to which the seven sub-clauses next hereinafter set forth apply.

Residuary legatee, etc.

1.—A residuary legatee, or next of kin, may have a judgment for the administration of the personal estate of a deceased person without serving the remaining residuary legatees or next of kin.

Legatee whose legacy is charged on realty.

2.—A legatee interested in a legacy charged upon real estate ; or a person interested in the proceeds of real estate directed to be sold, may have a judgment for the administration of the estate of a deceased person, without serving any other legatee or person interested in the proceeds of the estate.

Residuary devisee or heir.

3.—A residuary devisee, or heir, may have the like judgment, without serving any co-residuary devisee, or co-heir.

One of several c. q. t.

4.—One of several *cestuis que trustent*, under a deed or instrument, may have a judgment for the execution of the trusts of the deed or instrument, without serving any other of such *cestuis que trustent*.

In actions for protection of property.

5.—In all cases of actions for the protection of property pending litigation, and in all cases in the nature of waste, one person may move on behalf of himself, and of all persons having the same interest.

Administration against one c. q. t.

6.—An executor, administrator, or trustee, may obtain a judgment against any one legatee, next of kin or *cestui que trust*, for the administration of the estate or the execution of the trusts.

Assignee of chose in action may sue without joining assignor.

7.—An assignee of a chose in action may institute an action in respect thereof without making the assignor a party thereto. Chy. O. 58 ; J. A. Rule 102. (See *Imp. Act* 15 & 16, c. 86, s. 42.)

321. In all the above cases the Court, if it sees fit, may require any other person to be made a party to the action, and may, if it sees fit, give the conduct of the action to such person as it deems proper; and may make such order in any particular case as it deems just for placing the defendant on the record on the same footing in regard to costs as other parties having a common interest with him in the matter in question. Chy. O. 59. *In such cases Court may require persons to be joined as parties.*

322. In all the above cases the persons who, but for Rule 320, would have been necessary parties to the action, are to be served with an office-copy of the judgment (unless the Court or Master dispenses with such service) indorsed with the notice set forth in Form No. 33 in the Appendix, and after such service, they shall be bound by the proceedings in the same manner as if they had been originally made parties to the action; and upon service of notice upon the plaintiff they may attend the proceedings under the judgment. Any party so served may apply to the Court to add to, vary, or set aside the judgment within fourteen days from the date of such service. Chy. O. 60, 587. *Persons who would be necessary parties except for Rule 320 must be served with judgment.*

323. Where a defendant, at the trial or on motion for judgment, objects that an action is defective for want of parties, the Court, if it thinks fit, may pronounce a judgment saving the rights of the absent parties. Chy. O. 65. *Objection to nonjoinder at hearing, judgment saving rights of absentees.*

324. No action shall be defeated by reason of the misjoinder of parties, and the Court may in every action deal with the matter in controversy so far as regards the rights and interests of the parties actually before it. *Misjoinder.*

(*a*) The Court or a Judge may, at any stage of the proceedings, either upon or without the application of either party, and upon such terms as may appear to the Court or Judge to be just, order that the name of any party, whether as plaintiff or defendant improperly joined, be struck out, and that the name of any party, whether plaintiff or defendant, who ought to have been joined, or whose presence before the Court may be necessary in order to enable the Court effectually and completely to adjudicate upon and settle all the questions involved in the action, be added. *Adding and striking out parties.*

(*b*) No person shall be added or substituted as a plaintiff suing without a next friend, or as the next friend of a plaintiff under any disability, without his own consent in writing thereto to be filed.

(*c*) All parties whose names are so added or substituted as defendants shall be served with a writ of summons or notice in manner hereinafter mentioned, or in such manner as may be prescribed by any special order, and the proceedings as against them shall be deemed to have begun only on the service of such writ of summons or notice. J. A. Rule 103.

325. Any application to add, or strike out, or substitute a plaintiff or defendant may be made to the Court or a Judge at any time before trial by motion, or at the trial of the action in a summary manner. J. A. Rule 104. *How application is to be made.*

326. Where a defendant is added or substituted, unless otherwise ordered by the Court or Judge, the plaintiff shall sue out an amended writ of summons, and serve the new defendant with such writ, or notice in lieu of service thereof, in the same manner as original defendants are served. J. A. Rule 105. *Amended writ where new defendant added.*

327. If a statement of claim has been delivered previously to such defendant being added, the same shall, unless otherwise ordered by the Court or Judge, be amended in such manner as the making of the new defendant a party may render desirable; and a copy of the amended *Amended statement of claim.*

statement of claim shall be delivered to the new defendant at the time when he is served with the writ of summons or notice, or afterwards within 4 days after his appearance. J. A. Rule 106.

Contribution or indemnity between defendants and other persons.   **328.** Where a defendant is, or claims to be, entitled to contribution or indemnity, or any other remedy or relief ov███████████ ▓▓▓▓ person, or where from any other cause it appears to ████████████████ question in the action should be determin██████████████ plaintiff and defendant, but as between the ████████████ other person, or between any or either of th█████████████ on notice being given to such last-mentioned█████████████ may be proper for having the question so de██████████████

Notice to persons not already parties.   **329.** Where a defendant is entitled to contribution, indemnity, or other remedy or relief over against any person not a party to the action, he may serve a notice to that effect ;

(a) A copy of such notice shall be filed with the proper officer, and served on such person, according to the rules relating to the service of writs of summons ;

(b) The notice shall state the nature and grounds of the claim, and shall, unless otherwise ordered by the Court or a Judge, be served within the time limited for delivering his statement of defence ;

(c) Such notice may be in the form or to the effect of the Form No. 18 in the Appendix, with such variations as circumstances may require and therewith shall be served a copy of the statement of claim, or if there be no statement of claim, then a copy of the writ of summons in the action. J. A. Rule 108.

Court may direct notice to be given.   **330.** Where, under Rule 328, it is made to appear to the Court or a Judge, at any time before or at the trial, that a question in the action should be determined, not only as between the plaintiff and defendant, but as between the plaintiff and defendant and any other person, or between any or either of them, the Court or Judge, before or at the time of making the order for having such question determined, shall direct such notice to be given by the plaintiff at such time and to such person and in such manner as may be thought proper ; and if made at the trial, the Judge may postpone such trial as he may think fit. J. A. Rule 109.

Appearance by third party.   **331.** If a person not a party to the action, who is served as mentioned in Rule 329, desires to dispute the plaintiff's claim in the action as against the defendant on whose behalf the notice has been given, he must enter an appearance in the action within 8 days from the service of the notice ; in default of his so doing, he shall be deemed to admit the validity of the judgment obtained against such defendant, whether obtained by consent or otherwise ; provided always, that a person so served and failing to appear within the said period of 8 days, may apply to the Court or a Judge for leave to appear, and such leave may be given upon such terms, if any, as the Court or Judge shall think fit. J. A. Rule 110.

Direction as to mode of determining questions in action.   **332.** If a person not a party to the action served under these Rules appears pursuant to the notice, the party giving the notice may apply to the Court or a Judge for directions as to the mode of having the question in the action determined ;

(a) The Court or Judge, upon the hearing of such application, may, if it shall appear desirable so to do, give to the person so served liberty to defend the action upon such terms as shall seem just, and may direct such pleadings to be delivered, or such amendments in any pleadings to be made, and generally may direct such proceedings to be taken, and give such directions, as to the Court or Judge shall appear proper for having the question most conveniently determined, and with respect to the mode and extent in or to which the person so served shall be bound or made liable by the decision of the question, and as to the costs of the proceedings. J. A. Rule 111.

333. A plaintiff is not to be unnecessarily delayed in recovering his ~~claim by reason~~ of questions between defendants in which the plaintiff is not ~~interested~~ ; and the Court or Judge is to give such direction as may ~~be necessary~~ to prevent such delay of the plaintiff, where this can be done, on ~~terms or~~ otherwise, without injustice to the defendants.   J. A. Rule 112. *Plaintiff not to be delayed by questions between defendants.*

334. In any cause or matter for the administration of the estate of a deceased person, no party other than the executor or administrator shall, unless by leave, be entitled to appear either in Court or in Chambers, or in a Master's office, on the claim of any person not a party to the cause against the estate of the deceased in respect of any debt or liability.   The Court, Judge or Master as the case may be, may direct any other party to the cause to appear, either in addition to or in the place of the executor or administrator, upon such terms as to costs or otherwise as he shall think fit.   J. A. Rules 114, 518. *Parties to administration proceeding.*

(ii) Guardians.

335. In all cases in which lunatics and persons of unsound mind, not so found by inquisition or judicial declaration, might respectively before the passing of *The Ontario Judicature Act. 1881,* have sued as plaintiffs, or would have been liable to be sued as defendants, in any action or suit, they may respectively sue as plaintiffs in any action by their committees or next friends in manner practised in the Court of Chancery before the passing of the said Act, and may in a like manner defend any action by their committees or guardians appointed for that purpose.   J. A. Rule 124. *Insane persons.*

336. Where no appearance has been entered to a writ of summons for a defendant who is a person of unsound mind not so found by inquisition or judicial declaration in lieu of an inquisition, the plaintiff may apply to the Court or a Judge for an order that a guardian of such defendant be appointed, by whom he may appear and defend the action. *No appearance by person of unsound mind.*

(a) But no such order shall be made unless it appears on the hearing of such application that the writ of summons was duly served, and that notice of the application was. after the expiration of the time allowed for appearance, and at least six clear days before the day in the notice named for hearing the application, served upon, or left at the dwelling-house of, the person with whom or under whose care such defendant was staying at time of serving such writ of summons.   J. A. Rule 69.

(b) Upon such application the Official Guardian shall be so appointed, unless a Judge otherwise orders.   J. A. Rule 588.

337. Where infants, or persons of unsound mind not so found by inquisition, are served with any office copy of a judgment or order in any proceedings, or are made parties to actions after judgment, guardians *ad litem* are to be appointed for them in like manner as before judgment. Chy. O. 522, 525. *Appointment of guardian ad litem to infants, or lunatics added after judgment.*

338. Where a person required to be served with an office-copy of a judgment or order is an infant, or a person of unsound mind not so found by inquisition, the service is to be effected upon such person or persons, and in such manner, as the Master, before whom the reference under the judgment or order is being prosecuted, directs. Chy. O. 523. *Service of infant or lunatic with judgment, how effected.*

Person desiring to have a guardian ad litem.
appointed to himself, may attend Judge with proposed guardian.
Evidence required on application.

339. A person desirous of appointing a guardian for himself other than the official guardian to defend an action or matter, may go before a Judge or Master with the proposed guardian if he thinks fit to do so. But he must satisfy the Judge or Master by affidavit that the proposed guardian is a fit person, and has no interest adverse to that of the person of whom he is to be the guardian in the matter in question ; and if the affidavit is not sufficient for this purpose, the Judge or Master may examine the proposed guardian, or the person making the affidavit, *vira voce*, or require further evidence to be adduced until he is satisfied of the propriety of the appointment. Chy. O. 526.

6. JOINDER OF CAUSES OF ACTION.

What causes of action may be joined.
340. Subject to the following Rules, the plaintiff may unite, in the same action and in the same statement of claim, several causes of actione J. A. Rule 115 *first part.*

Action for recovery of land.
341. No cause of action shall, unless by leave of the Court or a Judge, be joined with an action for the recovery of land, except claims in respect of mesne profits or arrears of rent or double value in respect of the premises claimed, or any part thereof, and damages for breach of any contract under which the same or any part thereof are or is held, or for any wrong or injury to the premises claimed. J. A. Rule 116.

(a) Nothing in these Rules contained shall prevent any plaintiff in an action of foreclosure or redemption, or for the immediate payment of the mortgage moneys, from asking for or obtaining a judgment or order against the defendant for delivery of the possession of the mortgaged property to the plaintiff, either forthwith or on or after a final order for foreclosure or redemption, as the case may be, and such an action shall not be deemed an action for the recovery of land within these meaning of the Rules. *See* Chy. O. 464.

Claims by assignee in insolvency.
342. Claims by an assignee in insolvency as such shall not unless by leave of the Court or a Judge, be joined with any claim by him in any other capacity. J. A Rule 117.

Claims by or against husband and wife
343. Claims by or against husband and wife may be joined with claims by or against either of them separately. J. A. Rule 118.

Claims by or against executor.
344. Claims by or against an executor or administrator as such may be joined with claims by or against him personally, provided the last mentioned claims are alleged to arise with reference to the estate in respect of which the plaintiff or defendant sues or is sued as executor or administrator. J. A. Rule 119.

Joint and several claims.
345. Claims by plaintiffs jointly may be joined with claims by them or any of them separately against the same defendant. J. A. Rule 120.

Order for separate issues.
346. If it be made to appear to the Court or a Judge that several causes of action joined in the same action are such as cannot all be conveniently disposed of in one action, the Court or a Judge may order any of such causes of action to be excluded, or may direct the issues respecting the separate causes of action to be tried separately, and may direct the statement of claim, or, if no statement of claim has been delivered, the copy of the writ of summons and the indorsement of claim on the writ of summons, to be amended accordingly, and may make such order as to costs as may be just. J. A. Rules 115, 121, 122, 123.

7. MORTGAGE ACTIONS.

347. Instead of a foreclosure, a mortgagee may pray for a sale of the mortgaged premises, and that any balance of the mortgage debt remaining due after such sale may be paid by the mortgagor, or any surety for payment of the mortgage debt who is a party to the action, and the same may be adjudged accordingly. Chy. O. 426. *(margin: Mortgagee may have sale instead of foreclosure.)*

348. The Court may direct a sale of the property, instead of a foreclosure of the equity of redemption, on such terms as the Court thinks fit; and, if the Court thinks fit, without previously determining the priorities of incumbrancers, or giving the usual or any time to redeem. Chy. O. 428. *(margin: Sale may be ordered, instead of foreclosure.)*

349. If the request for a sale is made by a subsequent incumbrancer, or by the mortgagor, or by any person claiming under them respectively, the party making the request is to deposit in Court the sum of $80 for the purpose of covering expenses unless otherwise ordered by the Court or a Judge. *See* Chy. O. 429. *(margin: Where sale is asked by the mortgagor or incumbrancer, deposit to be made.)*

350. An incumbrancer made a party in the Master's office, and entitled to, and desiring a sale of the mortgaged premises, is to make the necessary deposit therefor before the Master's report is settled, whereupon an order may be issued on *præcipe* directing a sale of the mortgaged premises instead of a foreclosure, and thereupon the Master is to compute subsequent interest, and appoint a time and place, or times and places, for payment ; and all subsequent proceedings are to be taken and had as if the judgment had been in the first instance a judgment for sale. Chy. O. 456. *(margin: Incumbrancer made a party to a foreclosure suit, in the M. O., may apply for a sale.)*

351. If before or upon the deposit to obtain a sale being made, the plaintiff prefers that the sale be conducted by the defendant desiring the sale, he may so elect ; and he is thereupon to notify the defendant of such election. The notice may be to the effect set forth in Form No. 32 in the Appendix. Chy. O. 430. *(margin: Plaintiff may require defendant asking sale to conduct it.)*

352. Upon the plaintiff's filing in the office in which appearance is required to be entered a note of such election, and proof of service of such notice, the defendant making the deposit is to be entitled to a return thereof. Chy. O. 431. *(margin: On filing notice, deposit to be returned to defendant.)*

353. In default of payment being made according to the report in a foreclosure or redemption action, a final order of foreclosure may be granted against the party making default on an *ex parte* application. Chy. O. 451. *(margin: In default of redemption final order may be granted in Chambers.)*

354. In the event of the purchase money being insufficient to pay what has been found due to the plaintiff for principal, interest, and costs, subsequent interest, and subsequent costs in an action for sale, the plaintiff is to be entitled (where the mortgagor is a defendant, and such relief is prayed for), to an order *ex parte* for the payment of the deficiency. Chy. O. 455. *(margin: Order for payment of deficiency may be obtained, when.)*

355. Where the state of the account ascertained by an order, or by the report of the Master, is changed by payment of money, by receipt of rents and profits, by occupation rent, or otherwise, before the final order for foreclosure or sale is obtained, the plaintiff, or other party to whom the mortgage money is payable, may give notice to the party by whom the same is payable, that he gives him credit for a sum certain, to be named in the notice, and that he claims that there remains due in respect of such mortgage money a sum certain, to be also named in the notice. Chy. O. 457. *(margin: Where account changed after order, or, report, notice of credit may be given.)*

356. Upon the final order for foreclosure or sale being applied for, if the Judge thinks the sums named in the notice proper to be allowed and paid under the circumstances, the order for final foreclosure is to go without further notice, unless the Judge directs notice to be given. Chy. O. 458. *(margin: Final order may be granted.)*

4

Party receiving sums after report, etc., may apply for new day for payment.

357. The party to whom the mortgage money is payable, may apply in Chambers for a reference to a Master, or for an appointment, to fix such sums respectively ; and in the latter case either upon notice, or *ex parte,* as the Judge thinks fit ; and the order to be made thereupon is to be served, or service thereof to be dispensed with, as the Judge directs. Chy. O. 459.

Party served with notice of credit, may apply.

358. The party to whom such notice is given may apply in Chambers for an appointment to ascertain and fix the amounts proper to be allowed and paid, instead of the amounts mentioned in such notice ; or for a reference to a Master for the like purpose ; and in case the Judge thinks a reference to a Master proper, the same may be made *ex parte* unless the Judge otherwise directs.   Chy. O. 460.

Action brought for default in payment of instalment of principal, or interest may be dismissed on payment of arrears and costs.

359. In an action for the foreclosure or sale of the equity of redemption in any mortgaged property, or for recovery of possession thereof, for default in the payment of interest, or of an instalment of the principal, the defendant may, before judgment, move to dismiss the action upon paying into Court the amount then due for principal, interest and costs. Chy. O. 461; R. S. O. 1877, c. 51, s. 71.

After judgment proceedings may be stayed on payment of arrears, and costs.

360. In an action for the purpose and under the circumstances specified in the last Rule, a defendant may move to stay the proceedings in the action, after judgment, but before sale or final foreclosure, or recovery of possession of the mortgaged property by the plaintiff, upon paying into Court the amount then due for principal, interest, and costs.   Chy. O. 462.

On subsequent default decree may be enforced.

361. Where an application is made to stay the proceedings under Rule 360, the judgment may afterwards be enforced, by order of the Court, upon subsequent default in the payment of a further instalment of the principal, or of the interest.   Chy. O. 463.

Order on default.

362. In a redemption action, in default of payment being made according to the report, the defendant is to be entitled on an *ex parte* application in Chambers to a final order of foreclosure against the plaintiff, or to an order dismissing the action with costs to be paid by the plaintiff to the defendant, forthwith after taxation thereof.   J. A. Rule 333.

Directions where plaintiff in redemption suit is foreclosed.

363. In a redemption action where the plaintiff is declared foreclosed, directions may be given either by the final order foreclosing the plaintiff, or by subsequent orders, that all necessary inquiries be made, accounts taken and proceedings had for redemption or foreclosure, or redemption or sale, as against any subsequent incumbrancers, or for the adjustment of the relative rights and liabilities of the original defendants as among themselves, and such order shall have the same force and effect as a judgment obtained by the original defendant.   J. A. Rule 334.

8. Crown Actions.

Forms and procedure in Crown actions.

364. The procedure and forms which are from time to time in force for the prosecution of rights, claims or demands, or for the recovery of the possession of any lands, deeds or personal property between subject and subject, shall be used in the like cases for the prosecution of rights, claims or demands which Her Majesty may have against any person or persons, body or bodies corporate, or for the recovery of the possession of any lands, deeds or personal property whereto Her Majesty claims to be entitled, but the right of reply shall be always allowed to the Attorney-General, and to any Queen's Counsel having written authority from him for that purpose.   R. S. O. 1877, c. 58, ss. 6, 8.

Costs in revenue cases.

365. In case in any action, or other proceeding before any Court or tribunal in Ontario, by or on behalf of the Crown, against any

corporation or person, in respect of any lands, tenements or hereditaments, or of any goods or chattels belonging to or accruing to the Crown,
or standing or being in the name of Her Majesty, or in respect of any sum
of money due and owing to Her Majesty by virtue of any vote of the
Legislature for the service of the Crown, or by virtue of any statute relating to the public revenue, or in any manner whatsoever, judgment is given
for the Crown, Her Majesty's Attorney-General may recover costs in the
same manner as and under the same rules, regulations and provisions that
apply to the payment or receipt of costs in proceedings between subject
and subject. R. S. O. 1877, c. 58, s. 9.

366. If in any information, action, or other proceeding, judgment Defendant
is given against the Crown, the defendant is entitled to costs, subject to may recover costs in re-
the same rules as though such proceeding had been had between subject venue cases.
and subject. R. S. O. 1877, c. 58, s. 10.

367. Notwithstanding the want of enrolment, writs of summons to High Court
repeal letters patent, grants or other matter of record under the Great may issue writs of
Seal, shall be issued in the same cases and under the same restrictions, summons
as nearly as may be, as writs of *scire facias* were on the 5th day of in the same
December, 1859, issuable from the Court of Chancery in England ; and cases as *sci. fa.*
all the proceedings thereafter shall be the same as the proceedings in formerly
an ordinary actio ; but before the issue of any such writ, the party mak- issued.
ing application for the same shall, in addition to the *fiat* of the Attorney-
General, file in the Court from which the writ is to be issued, an exempli-
fication under the Great Seal of the Province of the letters patent, grant
or other matter of record with respect to which the said writ is to be
issued. *See* R. S. O. 1877, c. 58, ss. 11, 12.

CHAPTER V.

PLEADINGS.

1. STATEMENT OF CLAIM.

368. The plaintiff shall state the nature of his claim and the relief
sought in a pleading to be called the Statement of Claim.

369. The delivery of the statement of claim shall be regulated as fol- Time within
lows:— which to be
delivered.

(*a*) If the defendant does not state that he does not require the delivery
of a statement of claim, the plaintiff shall, unless otherwise ordered by
the Court or a Judge, deliver it within three months from the time of the
defendant's entering his appearance.

(*b*) If the defendant states that he does not require the delivery of
a statement of claim, the plaintiff shall file a copy of the summons with
all indorsements thereon within the same time.

(*c*) The plaintiff may, if he thinks fit, deliver a statement of claim, with
the writ of summons, or notice in lieu of writ of summons, or at any time

afterwards, either before or after appearance, and although the defendant may have appeared and stated that he does not require the delivery of a statement of claim : Provided that in no case where a defendant has appeared shall a statement be delivered more than 3 months after the appearance has been entered, unless otherwise ordered by the Court or a Judge. J. A. Rule 158. *See* J. A. Rule 126.

Notice in lieu of statement of claim.

370. Where the writ is specially indorsed and the defendant has not dispensed with a statement of claim, it shall be sufficient for the plaintiff to file a copy of the writ, with a copy of the special indorsement thereon, if not filed already, and deliver as his statement of claim a notice to the effect that his claim is that which appears by the indorsement upon the writ, unless the Court or a Judge orders him to deliver a further statement.

(*a*) Such notice may be either written or printed, or partly written and partly printed, and may be in the Form No. 16 in the Appendix, and shall be marked on the face in the same manner as is required in the case of an ordinary statement of claim.

(*b*) When the plaintiff is ordered to deliver such further statement it shall be delivered within such time as by the order is directed ; and if no time is so limited then within the time prescribed by Rule 369. J. A. Rule 159.

2. DEFENCE AND COUNTERCLAIM.

When defence must be delivered.

371. Where a statement of claim is delivered to a defendant he shall deliver his defence, counter-claim or demurrer within 8 days from the delivery of the statement of claim, or from the time limited for appearance, whichever shall be last, unless such time is extended by the Court or a Judge. J. A. Rule 160. *See* J. A. Rule 126.

Where no statement of claim.

372. A defendant who has appeared in an action and stated that he does not require the delivery of a statement of claim and to whom a statement of claim is not delivered, may deliver a defence, counter-claim or demurrer at any time within 8 days after his appearance, unless such time is extended by the Court or a Judge. J. A. Rule 161.

Set-off and counter-claim.

373. A defendant in an action may set up by way of counter-claim, against the claim of the plaintiff, any right or claim whether the same sound in damages or not.

(*a*) A counterclaim shall have the same effect as a statement of claim in a cross action, so as to enable the Court to pronounce a final judgment in the same action, both on the original and on the cross claim. J. A. Rule 127 (*a*).

Striking out counter-claim.

374. Where a defendant sets up a counter-claim, if the plaintiff, or any other person named in manner aforesaid as party to such counter-claim, contends that the claim thereby raised ought not to be disposed of by way of counter-claim, but in an independent action, he may at any time before trial apply to the Court or a Judge for an order that such counter-claim may be excluded ; and the Court or a Judge may on the hearing of such application, make such order as shall be just. J. A. Rule 168.

Judgment for balance of counter-claim.

375. Where in any action a counter-claim is established against the plaintiff's claim, the Court may, if the balance is in favour of the defendant, give judgment for the defendant for such balance, or may otherwise adjudge to the defendant such relief as he may be entitled to upon the merits of the case. J. A. Rule 169.

Where counter-claim affects third persons.

376. Where a defendant sets up any counter-claim which raises questions between himself and the plaintiff along with any other person or persons, he shall entitle it as a statement of claim, setting forth the names of all the persons who, if such counter-claim were to be enforced by cross-action, would be defendants to such cross-action, and shall deliver his counter-claim to such of them as are parties to the action within the period within which he is required to deliver it to the plaintiff. J. A. Rule 164.

377. Where any such person as in the last preceding Rule mentioned is not a party to the action, he shall be summoned to appear by being served with a copy of the counter-claim, and such service shall be regulated by the same rules as are hereinbefore contained with respect to the service of a writ of summons, and every counterclaim so served shall be indorsed in the Form No. 19 in the Appendix or to the like effect. J. A. Rule 165. *Service of counter-claim on third party.*

378. Any person not a defendant to the action, who is served with a counter-claim as aforesaid, must appear thereto as if he had been served with a writ of summons to appear in an action. J. A. Rule 166. *Appearance by third party.*

379. Any person, including the plaintiff, named as a party to a counter-claim, may deliver a defence thereto as if it were a statement of claim. J. A. Rule 167. *Defence by third party.*

380. The plaintiff shall deliver his defence to the counter-claim within 8 days from service thereof on him. *Time for delivery.*

381. A plaintiff shall deliver his reply, if any, within 3 weeks after the defence or the last of the defences shall have been delivered, unless the time shall be extended by the Court or a Judge. J. A. Rule 173. *Delivery of reply.*

382. No pleading subsequent to reply other than a joinder of issue shall be pleaded without leave of the Court or a Judge, and then upon such terms as the Court or Judge thinks fit. J. A. Rule 174. *Leave for subsequent pleadings.*

383. Subject to the last preceding Rule, every pleading subsequent to reply shall be delivered within 4 days after the delivery of the previous pleading, unless the time is extended by the Court or a Judge. J. A. Rule 175. *Time for delivery.*

3 DEMURRER.

384. Any party may demur to any pleading of the opposite party, or to any part of a pleading setting up a distinct cause of action, ground of defence, counterclaim, reply, or as the case may be, on the ground that the facts alleged therein do not shew any cause, of action or ground of defence to a claim or any part thereof, or counter-claim, or reply, or as the case may be, to which effect can be given by the Court as against the party demurring. J. A. Rule 189. *Demurrer when allowed.*

385. A demurrer shall state specifically whether it is to the whole or to part, and if to part only, to what part, of the pleading of the opposite party. It shall state some ground in law for the demurrer, but the party demurring shall not, on the argument of the demurrer, be limited to the ground so stated. A demurrer may be in the Form No. 89 in the Appendix. If no ground, or only a frivolous ground of demurrer is stated, the Court or a Judge may set aside such demurrer, with costs. J. A. Rule 190. *Form of demurrer.*

386. A demurrer shall be delivered in the same manner and within the same time as any other pleading in the action. J. A. Rule 191. *Delivery of demurrer.*

387. A defendant desiring to demur to part of a statement of claim, and to put in a defence to the other part, shall combine such demurrer and defence in one pleading. And so in every case where a party entitled to put in a further pleading desires to demur to part of the last pleading of the opposite party, he shall combine such demurrer and other pleading. J. A. Rule 192. *Demurrer and defence to be combined.*

Plea and demurrer to same pleading without leave. **388.** Either party may without leave plead and demur to the same pleading at the same time, by filing an affidavit by the party distinctly denying some one or more material statement or statements in the pleading ; or stating that the several matters sought to be pleaded by way of confession and avoidance are respectively true in substance and in fact ; and that he is further advised and believes that the objections raised by such demurrer are good and valid objections in law. The affidavit is to be annexed to and filed with the plea and demurrer, and a copy of the affidavit is to be served with the plea and demurrer. J. A. Rule 193:

Leave to demur and plead to the same matter. **389.** If the party demurring desires to be at liberty to plead as well as to demur to the matter demurred to without filing such affidavit, he may, before demurring, apply to the Court or a Judge for an order giving him leave to so plead-and demur ; and the Court or Judge, if satisfied that there is reasonable ground for the demurrer, may make an order accordingly, or may reserve leave to the party to plead after the demurrer is overruled, and may direct which issue shall be first disposed of ; or may make such other order and upon such terms as may be just. J. A. Rule 194 ; C. L. Rule May 21, 1877. R. S. O. 1877, c. 50, s. 118.

Amending. **390.** The party whose pleading is demurred to may, at any time within four days from delivery of the demurrer or before the demurrer is set down, on payment of $5 to the party demurring, obtain an order on præcipe to amend the pleading or that portion of it which is demurred to.

Pleadings after demurrer is overruled. **391.** Where a demurrer is overruled, the Court may make such order, and upon such terms as to the Court shall seem right, for allowing the demurring party to raise by pleading any case he may be desirous to set up in opposition to the matter demurred to. J. A. Rule 201.

4. Close of Pleadings.

When pleadings closed. **392.** As soon as either party has joined issue upon any pleading of the opposite party simply, without adding any further or other pleading thereto, or as soon as the time for amending the pleadings under these Rules or under any order made in the action or for delivering a reply or subsequent pleading or demurrer, has expired, the pleadings as between such parties shall be deemed to be closed without any joinder of issue being pleaded by any or either party. J. A. Rule 176.

Note may be entered of default. **393.** Where any party makes default in delivering a statement of defence, demurrer, or subsequent pleading, within the time limited therefor, in cases where interlocutory or final judgment cannot be signed, the opposite party may, at any time before the pleading is filed, upon proof of the default, by *præcipe* to the officer with whom the pleadings are filed, require him to note that the pleadings in the action are closed as to the party in default ; and thereupon the officer shall enter such note in the pleadings book accordingly, and thereafter no pleading by the party in default shall be received or filed without the order of a Judge. J. A. Rule 596.

5. Pleading Generally.

Old rules abolished. **394.** The following Rules of pleading substituted for those used in the Court of Chancery and in the Courts of Common Law, prior to *The Ontario Judicature Act 1881*, shall continue to be used. J. A. Rule 125.

Copies of pleadings. **395.** Every pleading may be either printed or written, or partly printed and partly written, but no more than four copies of any pleading or other document are to be allowed to any party in a cause or matter, exclusive of the draft, but inclusive of all other copies that may be required or made, in the progress of the cause. J. A. Rule 129.'

396. If more than three copies exclusive of the draft, are required of *Printing*
any pleading or other document, the party may have the pleading or *pleadings.*
document printed for the purposes of the cause or matter, and in that
case he shall in lieu of all charges for copies be allowed thirty cents per
folio of the pleading or document, and his reasonable disbursements of
procuring the same to be printed.   J. A. Rule 130.

397. Every pleading in an action shall be delivered between parties, *How plead-*
and shall be marked on the face with the date of the day on which it is *ings delivered*
filed, and with the reference to the Division to which the action is assigned, *should be*
the title of the action, the description of the pleading, and the name and *marked.*
place of business of the solicitor and agent (if any) of the party filing the
same, or the name and address of the party filing the same if he does not
act by a solicitor.   J. A. Rule 132.

398. Delivering a statement of claim or defence or other pleading in- *Delivery in-*
cludes filing.   J. A. Rule 150. *cludes filing.*

399 Pleadings shall contain a concise statement of the material facts *Form of*
upon which the party pleading relies, but not the evidence by which they *pleadings.*
are to be proved ; dates, sums and numbers shall be expressed in figures ;
the signature of counsel shall not be necessary ; forms similar to those in
Part VI. of the Appendix may be used.   J. A. Rule 128, *part.*

400. Each party is to admit such of the material allegations contained *Admission of*
in the statement of claim or defence of the opposite party as are true ; or he *statements of*
may give notice, by his own statement or otherwise, that he admits for *opponent.*
the purposes of the action the truth of the case generally, or of any part
of the case, stated or referred to in the statement of claim or defence of
the opposite or any other party.   J. A. Rule 240.

401. Admissions are, in all cases where it is practicable, to be by refer- *Manner of*
ence to the numbers of the paragraphs in the pleading to which they *making ad-*
relate, with such qualifications as may be necessary or proper for protect- *missions.*
ing the interests of the party making such admissions : thus—"the defendant admits the allegations made in the first, second and third paragraphs
of the plaintiff's claim."   J. A. Rule 146.

402. Each party in any pleading must allege all such facts not *What facts*
appearing in the previous pleading (if any), as he means to rely on, and *must be*
must raise all such grounds of defence or reply, as the case may be, as if *pleaded.*
not so raised on the pleadings would be likely to take the opposite party
by surprise, or would raise new issues of fact not arising out of the
pleadings, as (for instance) fraud, or that any claim has been barred by
a Statute of Limitations, or has been released.   J. A. Rule 147.

403. Save as otherwise provided, the silence of a pleading as to any *Silence of*
allegations contained in the previous pleading of the opposite party is *pleading no*
not to be construed into an implied admission of the truth of such allega- *admission.*
tion ; and any allegation introduced for the purpose of preventing such
implied admission, and not for the purpose of making intelligible the
grounds of defence, is to be considered impertinent.   J. A. Rule 148.

404. Every statement of claim shall state specifically the relief which *Relief claimed*
the plaintiff claims, either simply or in the alternative, and may also ask *to be stated*
for general relief.   And the same rule shall apply to any counter-claim *specifically.*
made, or relief claimed by the defendant, in his statement of defence.
If the plaintiff's claim be for discovery only, the statement of claim shall
shew it.   J A. Rule 133.

Distinct claims or defences.   **405.** Where the plaintiff seeks relief in respect of several distinct claims or causes of complaint founded upon separate and distinct facts, they shall be stated, as far as may be, separately and distinctly. And the same rule shall apply where the defendant relies upon several distinct grounds of defence, or counter-claim founded upon separate and distinct facts. J. A. Rule 134.

Effect of document may be stated.   **406.** Where the contents of any document are material, it shall be sufficient in any pleading to state the effect thereof as briefly as possible, without setting out the whole or any part thereof unless the precise words of the document or any part thereof are material. J. A. Rule 135.

Allegation of malice, etc.   **407.** Where it is material to allege malice, fraudulent intention, knowledge or other condition of the mind of any person, it shall be sufficient to allege the same as a fact, without setting out the circumstances from which the same is to be inferred. J. A. Rule 136.

Allegation of notice.   **408.** Where it is material to allege notice to any person of any fact, matter or thing, it shall be sufficient to allege such notice as a fact unless the form or precise terms of the notice is or are material. J. A. Rule 137.

Implied contract.   **409.** Where any contract or any relation between any persons does not arise from any express agreement, but is to be implied from a series of letters or conversations, or otherwise from a number of circumstances, it shall be sufficient to allege the contract or relation as a fact, and to refer generally to the letters, conversations, or circumstances without setting them out in detail ; and if in such a case, the person so pleading desires to rely in the alternative upon more contracts or relations than one, as to be implied from such circumstances, he may state the same in the alternative. J. A. Rule 138.

Facts presumed need not be stated.   **410.** Neither party need in any pleading allege any matter of fact which the law presumes in his favour, or as to which the burden of proof lies upon the other side, unless the same has first been specifically denied.

[*E.g.*—Consideration for a bill of exchange where the plaintiff sues only on the bill, and not for the consideration as a substantive ground of claim.] J. A. Rule 139.

Denial of representative capacity.   **411.** If either party wishes to deny the right of any other party to claim as executor, or as trustee, or as assignee in insolvency, or in any representative or other alleged capacity, or the alleged constitution of any partnership firm, he shall deny the same specifically, or the same will be taken to be admitted. J. A. Rule 140.

Incorporation.   **412.** Unless the incorporation of a corporate party to an action is specifically denied in the pleadings, it shall not be necessary to prove it.

Bare denial of contract only denial of the making.   **413.** Where a contract is alleged in any pleading, a bare denial of the contract by the opposite party shall be construed only as a denial of the making of the contract in fact, and not of its legality or its sufficiency in law, whether with reference to the Statute of Frauds or otherwise. J. A. Rule 141.

No plea in abatement.   **414.** No plea or defence shall be pleaded in abatement. J. A. Rule 142.

No new assignment.   **415.** No new assignment shall be necessary or used. But everything which was formerly alleged by way of new assignment is to be introduced by amendment of the statement of claim. J. A. Rule 143.

Defence to action for recovery of land.   **416.** No defendant in an action for the recovery of land who is in possession by himself or his tenant need plead his title, unless his defence depends on an equitable estate or right, or he claims relief upon any equitable ground against any right or title asserted by the plaintiff. But, except in the cases hereinbefore mentioned, it shall be sufficient to state by way of defence that he is so in possession. And he may nevertheless rely upon any ground of defence which he can prove, except as hereinbefore mentioned. J. A. Rule 144.

117. Nothing in these Rules contained shall affect the right of a defendant to plead not guilty by statute. And every defence of not guilty by statute shall have the same effect as a plea of not guilty by statute has heretofore had. But if the defendant so pleads he shall not plead any other defence without the leave of the Court or a Judge. J. A. Rule 145. *Plea of not guilty by statute.*

118. Where a defendant pleads not guilty by statute, intending to give the special matter in evidence, by virtue of an Act of Parliament, he shall insert in the margin of the paragraph of the statement of defence containing the plea the words "By Statute," together with the year or years of the reign in which the Act or Acts of Parliament upon which he relies for that purpose were passed, and also the chapter and section of each of such Acts, and shall specify whether such Acts are public or otherwise, otherwise the plea shall be taken not to have been pleaded by virtue of an Act of Parliament. Rules of pleading T. T. 1856, 21. *Plea of "Not guilty by Statute," to contain reference to Statute relied on.*

119. No pleading shall, except by way of amendment, raise any new ground of claim or contain any allegation of fact inconsistent with the previous pleadings of the party pleading the same. J. A. Rule 149. *Inconsistent pleadings.*

6. ISSUES.

120. Where in any action it appears to a Judge that the pleadings do not sufficiently define the issues of fact in dispute between the parties, he may direct the parties to prepare issues, and such issues shall, if the parties differ, be settled by the Judge. J. A. Rule 177. *Settlement of issues.*

7. STRIKING OUT, AMENDING PLEADINGS, ETC.

121. If upon the hearing of a cause or matter, the Court is of opinion that any pleading, petition or affidavit, or any part of a pleading, petition or affidavit is scandalous, the Court may order the pleading, petition or affidavit to be taken off the file, or may direct the scandalous matter to be expunged, and is to give such directions as to costs as it may think right. Chy. O. 69. *Court may order scandalous matter to be expunged.*

122. A motion to have any pleading, petition or affidavit taken off the file for scandal, or to have the scandalous matter expunged, may be made to the Court or a Judge at any time before the hearing of the cause or matter. Chy. O. 70. *Motion may be made at any time before hearing.*

123. The Court or a Judge may, at any stage of the proceedings, order to be struck out or amended any matter in the pleadings respectively which may be scandalous, or which may tend to prejudice, embarrass, or delay the fair trial of the action. J. A. Rule 178. *Amendment with leave.*

124. The plaintiff may, without any leave, amend his statement of claim once at any time before the expiration of the time limited for reply and before replying, or, where no defence is delivered, at any time before the expiration of 4 weeks from the appearance of the defendant who last appears. J. A. Rule 179. *Amendment by plaintiff without leave.*

125. A defendant who has set up any set-off or counter-claim may, without any leave, amend such set-off or counter-claim at any time before the expiration of the time allowed him for pleading to the reply, and before pleading thereto, or in case there be no reply, then within 28 days from the filing of his defence or counter-claim. J. A. Rule 180. *Amendment by defendant without leave.*

Disallowance of amendment. **426.** Where any party has amended his pleadings under either of the last 2 preceding Rules, the opposite party, may, within 8 days after the delivery to him of the amended pleading, apply to the Court or a Judge, to disallow the amendment, or any part thereof, and the Court or Judge may, if satisfied that the justice of the case requires it, disallow the same, or allow it, subject to such terms as to costs or otherwise as may seem just. J. A. Rule 181.

Leave to plead or amend after amendment. **427.** Where any party has amended his pleading under Rules 424 or 425, the other party may without leave amend his former pleading within 4 days after the delivery of the pleading so amended : or he may apply to the Court or a Judge for leave to amend his former pleading within such further time and upon such terms as may seem just. J. A. Rule 182.

Amendment by consent. **428.** Either party may amend his pleading at any time without order on filing the written consent of the opposite party or his solicitor. J. A. Rule 183

Application for leave to amend. **429.** In all cases not provided for by the preceding Rules numbered from 424 to 428, application for leave to amend any pleading may be made by either party to the Court or a Judge in Chambers, or to the Judge at the trial of the action, and such amendment may be allowed upon such terms as to costs or otherwise, as may seem just. J. A. Rule 184.

Time limited for amendment. **430.** If a party who has obtained an order for leave to amend a pleading delivered by him does not amend the same within the time limited for that purpose by the order, or if no time is thereby limited, then within 14 days from the date of the order, such order to amend shall, on the expiration of the time limited as aforesaid, or of the 14 days, as the case may be, become *ipso facto* void, unless the time is extended by the Court or a Judge. J. A. Rule 185.

How alterations to be made. **431.** A pleading may be amended by written alterations in the copies filed and served and by additions on paper to be interleaved therewith if necessary ; unless the amendments require the insertion of more than 200 words in any one place, or are so numerous or of such a nature that making them in the copies filed and served would render the same difficult or inconvenient to read ; in either of which cases the amendment must be made by delivering a re-print or fresh copy of the pleading as amended. J. A. Rule 186.

Marking of amended pleadings. **432.** Where any pleading is amended, such pleading when amended shall be marked with the date of the order, if any, under which the same is so amended, and of the day on which such amendment is made, in manner following, viz : " Amended　　　　day of　　　　under order dated　　　　day of　　　　."

(a) Where a pleading is amended, the amendment shall be written in ink of a different colour from that used in the original pleading. J. A. Rule 187.

Delivery of amended pleadings. **433.** Where a pleading is amended, such amended pleading shall be delivered to the opposite party within the time allowed for amending the same. J. A. Rule 188.

8. Pleading Matters arising pending the Action.

Before delivery of defence. **434.** Any ground of defence or counter-claim which has arisen after action brought, but before the defendant has delivered his statement of defence, may be pleaded by the defendant in his statement of defence or counter-claim, either alone or together with other grounds of defence. J. A. Rule 151.

435. If, after a counter-claim has been delivered, any ground of defence arises to anything alleged therein by the defendant, it may be pleaded by the plaintiff thereto, or be introduced by amendment into the statement of claim, within three weeks after the counter-claim or the last of the counter-claims has been delivered, unless the time is extended by the Court or a Judge. J. A. Rule 152. *Before delivery of defence to counter-claim.*

436. Where any ground of defence or counter-claim arises after the defendant has delivered his statement of defence, he may within 8 days after such ground of defence or counter-claim has arisen, deliver a further defence or counter-claim setting forth the same, or introduce the same by amendment into his statement of defence or counter-claim. J. A. Rule 153. *After delivery of defence.*

437. Where a ground of defence to any counter-claim arises after the expiration of three weeks from the time of delivering the counter-claim or the last of the counter-claims, the plaintiff, within 8 days after such ground of defence has arisen, may deliver a further pleading setting forth the same. or may introduce such new ground of defence into his statement of claim by amendment. J. A. Rule 154. *After delivery of reply.*

438. In any such case the amendment of the pleading filed may be made without an order, on filing a *precipe* and an affidavit that the matter of the amendment arose within 8 days next before the day of the making of such amendment. J. A. Rule 155. *Amendment on præcipe.*

439. In cases not provided for by the preceding Rules, the leave of the Court or a Judge to amend the statement of claim or defence or counter claim, or to deliver a further defence or counter claim or reply, is to be obtained on notice supported by affidavit. J. A. Rule 156. *Amendment by leave.*

440. Where any defendant, in his statement of defence or counter-claim, whether by way of amendment or otherwise, alleges any ground of defence or counter-claim which has arisen after the commencement of the action, the plaintiff may deliver a confession of such defence ; which confession may be in the Form No. 17 in the Appendix with such variations as circumstances may require ; and he may thereupon sign judgment for his costs up to the time of the pleading of such defence unless the Court or a Judge shall, either before or after the delivery of such confession, otherwise order. J. A. Rule 157. *Plaintiff may deliver confession of defence.*

CHAPTER VI.

MISCELLANEOUS PROCEEDINGS IN AN ACTION.

1. Effect of Non-compliance and Errors.

Formal objections. **441.** No proceeding shall be defeated by any formal objection. R.S. O. 1877, c. 49, s. 7.

Non-compliance with Rules. **442.** Non-compliance with any of these Rules shall not render the writ or any other proceeding in any action or matter void unless the Court or a Judge so directs, but such proceedings may be set aside either wholly or in part as irregular, or amended, or otherwise dealt with in such manner and upon such terms as the Court or Judge thinks fit. J. A. Rule 473.

Irregularity, motion to set aside proceedings to be made promptly. **443.** No application to set aside process or proceedings for irregularity shall be allowed, unless made within a reasonable time, nor if the party applying has taken a fresh step after knowledge of the irregularity. Rules T. T. 1856, 106.

2. Amendments.

Amendment of defects or errors. **444.** The Court or a Judge may at any time, and on such terms as to costs or otherwise as to the Court or Judge may seem just, amend any defect or error in any proceedings ; and all such amendments may be made as may be necessary for the advancement of justice, determining the real question or issue raised by or depending on the proceedings, and best calculated to secure the giving of judgment according to the very right and justice of the case. J. A. Rules 10, 474.

nd by direction of the Pre
e High Court, in future
cords, affidavits and pape
in the several offices of t
of Justice for Ontario, sh
length and width of half
olscap paper, and shall
alf lengthwise. —M. B. Juc

445. Where an action has been commenced in the name of the wrong person as plaintiff, or where it is doubtful whether it has been commenced in the name of the right plaintiff or plaintiffs, the Court or a Judge, if satisfied that it has been so commenced through a *bona fide* mistake, and that it is necessary for the determination of the real matter in dispute so to do, may order any other person or persons to be substituted or added as plaintiff or plaintiffs, upon such terms as may seem just. J. A. Rule 90.

446. In case an amendment is directed or allowed to be made at the trial, it shall not be necessary to draw up or issue an order therefor. The amendment may be at once made on the record, or a minute of the amendment to be made may be entered in the book of the Registrar, Deputy or Local Registrar, Clerk or Marshal, and the amendment may be formally made at any time afterwards.

3. PAPER, NOTICES AND WRITTEN PROCEEDINGS GENERALLY.

447. All notices required by these Rules or the practice of the Court shall be in manuscript or print, or partly in manuscript and partly in print, unless expressly authorized by the Court or a Judge or by these Rules to be given orally. J. A. Rule 451 ; Rules T. T. 1856, 131.

448. Proceedings, if printed, shall be printed with pica type leaded, on good paper, of foolscap size. J. A. Rule 452.

449. Every petition, issue, special case, affidavit and other proceeding of a like nature, shall be divided into numbered paragraphs, and shall state concisely such matters and facts as may be necessary to truly inform the Court. *See* J. A. Rule 128, *part.*

450. All rolls and records shall be upon parchment, or paper, of such width and length as the Registrars shall prescribe by written notice, to be put up in some conspicuous place in their respective offices and in the offices of the several Deputy Clerks of the Crown, and none of these officers shall be bound to receive any roll or record not made up in conformity to such notice, and such rolls and records shall not exceed, when folded, 14 inches in length and 4 inches in breadth, written upon at least a sheet of paper and folded accordingly. Rules T. T. 1856, 147.

451. In all proceedings in a cause or matter, except pleadings, petitions in the nature of pleadings, judgments and decretal orders, the following short style of cause shall be sufficient :

" *Between John Smith and others,— Plaintiffs,*
and
Richard Roe and others,—Defendants."

In case of proceedings which it has been the practice to entitle more shortly thus : " *Smith* v. *Roe,*" such practice is to continue. Chy. O. 597.

452. The word folio shall mean one hundred words. Rules T. T. 1856, 167.

4. COPIES OF PAPERS—FORMS.

453. Office-copies of affidavits, and other proceedings for service are dispensed with ; and where service is required, true copies, instead of office-copies, are to be served ; but this order is not to apply to judgments or orders of which office-copies are by the practice of the Court required to be served. Chy. O. 402.

454. Office copies of judgments to be served on persons made parties in the Master's office, may be certified by the Deputy Clerk of the Crown, Deputy or Local Registrar, as the case may require, at the place where the reference is being prosecuted. Chy. O. 547.

Copies of documents to be demanded in writing.

455. A party requiring a copy of any pleading, affidavit, exhibit, or document not directed to be served is to make a written application for the same to the solicitor of the party by whom it has been filed, or on whose behalf it is to be used ; and where the party has no solicitor, then to the party himself. Chy. O. 548.

Where copy of document demanded, it is to be furnished within 48 hours.

456. Where an application is made for a copy of any pleading, affidavit, exhibit or document, it is to be delivered within 48 hours from the time of the demand ; and any further time which may elapse before the delivery is not to be computed against the party demanding the same. Chy. O. 549.

Copies of documents in possession of another party.

457. As to taking copies of documents in possession of another party, or extracts therefrom, under Rules of Court or any special order, the party entitled to take the copy or extract is to pay the solicitor of the party producing the document for such copy or extract as he may, by writing, require, at the rate of 10 cents per folio ; and if the solicitor of the party producing the document refuses or neglects to supply the same, the solicitor requiring the copy or extract is to be at liberty to make it, and the solicitor for the party producing is not to be entitled to any fee in respect thereof. J. A. Rule 433.

Forms to be used.

458. The forms contained in the Appendices hereto are to be used with such variations or modifications as circumstances may require ; but any variance therefrom, not being in matter of substance, shall not affect their regularity. Rules T. T. 1856, 169 ; J. A. Rule 485.

5. SERVICE OF PAPERS.

Pleadings, etc., may be served in any County.

459. Unless otherwise provided by Statute or Rule of Court, pleadings and notices required to be served in any action, whether in the Supreme Court of Judicature or County Courts, may be served in any County. R. S. O. 1877, c. 50, s. 59.

Solicitor's acceptance need not be verified

460. Admissions and acceptances of the service of an order, notice of motion or other paper, upon the opposite solicitor, need not be verified by affidavit. Chy. O. 48.

Country agent, when to be served.

amended Rule 1448

461. All writs, pleadings, notices, orders, appointments, warrants, and other documents, and written communications, which do not require personal service upon the party to be affected thereby, shall be served upon his solicitor when residing in Toronto, or if his solicitor does not reside in Toronto then either upon his solicitor, or, if such solicitor does not reside in the county where such proceedings are conducted then upon the agent, if any, named in the "Solicitors and Agents' Book," provided for by Rule 204, or upon the Toronto agent of such solicitor named in the "Solicitors and Agent's Book," provided for by Rule 203, unless the Court, or a Judge, or a Master, before whom any such proceeding is had, shall give any direction as to the solicitor upon whom any such

Service, where solicitor neglects to enter name of agent.

notice, appointment, warrant, or other document or written communication is to be served. Where any solicitor has not caused such entry to be made in either of the "Solicitors and Agents' Books," provided for by Rules 203 or 204, then the posting up of a copy of any such notice, appointment, warrant, or other document, or written communication, for such solicitor in the office in which the proceedings are being conducted, is to be deemed sufficient service, unless the Court, or Judge, or Master, as the case may be, directs otherwise. Chy. O. 42, 43 ; R. S. O. 1877, c. 50, s. 57 ; Rules T. T. 1856, 136, 137.

Consequence of omission of indorsement.

462. Where a party sues or defends in person, and no address for service of such party is written or printed pursuant to the directions of Rules 238 to 240, or where a party has ceased to have a solicitor, all writs, notices, orders, appointments, warrants, and other documents, proceedings, and written communications, not requiring personal service upon the party to be affected thereby, shall, unless the Court otherwise directs, be deemed to be sufficiently served upon such party, by posting up a copy in the office in which the proceedings are being conducted. But if an address for service is written or printed as aforesaid, then all such writs, notices, orders, warrants and other documents, proceedings, and written communications, shall be deemed sufficiently served upon such party if left for him at such address for service. Chy. O. 45.

463. A party suing or defending by a solicitor shall not be at liberty to change his solicitor in any action or matter without an order of the Court for that purpose, which may be obtained on *præcipe;* and until such order is obtained and served, and notice thereof given to the officer with whom the pleadings are filed, the former solicitor shall be considered the solicitor of the party. Chy. O. 49. Rules T. T. 1856, 4. *Change of solicitor.*

464. In all cases where a plaintiff has sued out a writ in person, or a defendant has appeared in person, and either party by a solicitor gives notice in writing to the opposite party, or the solicitor or agent of such party, of the solicitor being authorized to act as solicitor for the party on whose behalf the notice is given, all pleadings, notices, orders, and other proceedings, which according to the practice of the Court are to be delivered to, or served upon, the party on whose behalf such notice is given, shall thereafter be delivered to, or served upon such solicitor. Rules T. T. 1856, 139. *Where party has acted in person, and notice given by solicitor that he is authorized to act, subsequent proceedings to be served on solicitor.*

465. In any action instituted by a mortgagee or other person having a charge on real property, for the foreclosure or sale of property, and to which action any judgment creditor of the mortgagor, or of the person liable to the charge, is a defendant, personal service on such defendant shall not be necessary, and it shall be sufficient to serve his solicitor in the action in which the judgment has been recovered, with the process of the Court, whether the same be an office copy of the judgment or decretal order, or any other order or notice which by order of Court may be directed, and whether the same be issued by the Court or by any officer thereof ; but the plaintiff in any such action may elect to serve the judgment creditor personally instead of serving the solicitor. R. S. O. 1877, c. 40, s. 92. *Service of proceedings for foreclosure or sale may be on solicitor in certain cases.*

466. It shall not be necessary to the regular service of an order, that the original shall be shown, except in cases of arrest or attachment. Rules T. T. 1856, 134. *Original or need not be shown except in cases of attachment.*

467. Where it appears, upon the hearing of any matter, that by reason of absence, or for any other sufficient cause, the service of notice of the application or of the appointment, cannot be made, or ought to be dispensed with, such service may be dispensed with, or any substituted service, or notice, by advertisement, or otherwise, may be ordered. Chy. O. 199. *Service of notice of motion in Chambers may be dispensed with. Or substituted service ordered.*

6 **TRANSMISSION OF PAPERS.**

468. Every Deputy Clerk of the Crown, Deputy or Local Registrar, shall, within 24 hours after notice in writing delivered to him in his office, for that purpose, and payment of the necessary postage enclose, seal up, and transmit by post to the office of the proper Division at Toronto, addressed to the Registrar thereof, any record in his custody mentioned in the notice, together with all exhibits filed at the trial, and in default thereof he may be adjudged guilty of a contempt of Court, and be dealt with in the discretion of the Court accordingly ; and if, after such notice, the record is not in Court at the time of making any motion requiring a reference thereto, the party moving may, on filing an affidavit of the service of notice and that the record, on search, has not been found in the said Registrar's office, be allowed by the Court to make the motion without the production of such record. R. S. O. 1877, c. 50, s. 279. *On receiving notice, Deputy Clerks to transmit record to Toronto, sealed up, etc Failure to be a contempt.*

Transmission of documents from one officer of the Court to another. **409.** Where pleadings or other documents, filed with an officer of the Court, are required by any other officer, the officer with whom the pleadings or other documents are filed, is, upon production of a request signed by the officer requiring the pleadings or other documents, that the same are required for some proceeding before him, to transmit the pleadings or other documents upon payment of postage or express charges and return. *See* Chy. O. 542, 544.

Documents, how transmitted **470.** Documents shall be transmitted by post or express, and not otherwise, and with the documents shall be transmitted the necessary postage or express charges for the return of the same, unless they are to be delivered by one officer to another in the same town, when they shall be transmitted by delivering the same to the officer requiring them, or his clerk. *See* Chy. O. 543, 544. Rules T. T. 1856, 148.

Documents to be returned. **471.** As soon as the purpose for which any such documents are required is completed, the officer to whom they have been sent is to re-transmit them to the office from which they were sent. Chy. O. 545.

7. TIME.

Months shall mean calendar months. **472.** Where by these Rules, or by any judgment or order, time for doing any act or taking any proceeding is limited by months, not expressed to be lunar months, such time shall be computed by calendar months. J. A. Rule 454.

Period of less than 6 days. **473.** Where any limited time less than 6 days from or after any date or event is appointed or allowed for doing any act or taking any proceeding, holidays, as defined by *The Interpretation Act*, shall not be reckoned in the computation of such limited time. J. A. Rule 455.

Days, how computed. **474.** In all cases in which any particular number of days not expressed to be clear days, is prescribed by the Rules or practice of the Court, the same shall be reckoned exclusively of the first day, and inclusively of the last day. J. A. Rule 456.

Clear days. **475.** In all cases expressed to be clear days, or where the term "at least" is added, both days shall be excluded. App. O. 60.

Where last day is Sunday. **476.** Where the time for doing any act or taking any proceeding expires on a Sunday, or other day on which the offices are closed, and by reason thereof such act or proceeding cannot be done or taken on that day, such act or proceeding shall, so far as regards the time of doing or taking the same, be held to be duly done or taken on the next day on which the offices are open. J. A. Rule 457.

amended Rule 1450

Computation of period of stay of proceedings. **477.** The day on which an order that the plaintiff do give security for costs is served, and the time thenceforward until and including the day on which the security is given, is not to be reckoned in the computation of time allowed to a defendant to appear or deliver a defence. Chy. O. 409.

Enlargement of time by consent. **478.** The time for delivering or amending any pleading may be enlarged by consent in writing, without application to the Court or Judge. J. A. Rule 458.

2 clear days' notice. **479.** Unless the Court or Judge gives special leave to the contrary, there must be at least 2 clear days between the service of a notice of motion or petition and the day for hearing the motion or petition ; and in the computation of such 2 clear days, Sundays, and days on which the offices are closed are not to be reckoned. Chy. O. 264. J. A. Rule 407.

Time for service of pleadings, etc. **480.** Unless otherwise specially ordered in the particular case, service of pleadings, notices, orders, and other proceedings, shall be effected before the hour of four o'clock in the afternoon ; except on Saturday, when it shall be effected before the hour of two o'clock in the afternoon. Service effected after four o'clock in the afternoon on any week day except Saturday, shall be deemed to have been effected on the following day. Service effected after two o'clock on Saturday shall be deemed to have been effected on the following Monday. J. A. Rule 540.

481. An attendance on a motion in Chambers, or on an appointment Half an hour's before a Master, Registrar, or other officer, for half an hour next attendance on immediately following the return thereof, shall be deemed a sufficient a summons, or attendance. Rules T. T. 1856, 124. appointment, is sufficient.

482. On every appointment the party on whom the same is served One appoint-shall attend such appointment without waiting for a second, or in ment sufficient default thereof the officer before whom the appointment is may proceed *ex parte* on the first appointment. Rules T. T. 1856, 144.

483. No pleadings shall be amended or delivered in the long vacation, Pleading in except by consent or unless directed by the Court or a Judge. J. A. vacation. Rule 460.

484. The time of the long vacation shall not be reckoned in the Long vacation nted or allowed by these Rules for filing, when not com-leading, or in the times allowed for the puted. wise directed by the Court or a Judge : *amended*

Rule 1451

ng absolute ;

order under Rule 622 ;

, or set aside a Judgment by any party J. A. Rule 461 ; Chy. O. 408.

any proceeding in appealing to the Court County Court appeals. App. O. 57.

all have power to enlarge or abridge the Enlargement or any Rules relating to time, or fixed by or abridgment doing any act or taking any proceeding, of time. e justice of the case may require ; and any d although the application for the same is on of the time appointed or allowed. J.

observed by the High Court of Justice Time for vaca-be as follows : tions in the High Court of t of the months of July and August. Justice, and Court of onsist of the period from the 24th day of Appeal. he following January, both days inclusive.

ATION FOR DISCOVERY.

or issue whether plaintiff or defendant, or Examination te, any one who is or has been one of the of parties for e, may without any special order for the discovery. before the trial touching the matters in arty adverse in point of interest ; and may estify in the same manner, upon the same me rules of examination, as any witness d. *See* Chy. O. 138 ; R. S. O. c. 50,

Party benefitted.   **488.** A person for whose immediate benefit an action is prosecuted or defended is to be regarded as a party for the purpose of examination. J. A. Rule 224.

Time when examination may be had.   **489.** The examination on the part of a plaintiff may take place at any time after the statement of defence of the party to be examined has been delivered or after the time for delivering the same has expired ; and the examination on the part of a defendant may take place at any time after such defendant has delivered his statement of defence ; and the examination of a party to an issue, at any time after the issue has been filed. *See* Chy. O. 140.

Subpœna and appointment.   **490.** Whenever a party is entitled to examine another party he may procure an appointment therefor from the Local Registrar, Local Master, Deputy Clerk of the Crown, or a special examiner, in the County where the party to be examined resides, and the party to be examined, upon being served with a copy of the appointment and a subpœna, and upon payment of the proper fees, shall attend thereon and submit to examination. *See* J. A. Rule 598.

Service of appointment.   **491.** The party examining shall serve a copy of the appointment upon the solicitor of the party to be examined, if he has a solicitor in the cause, at least forty-eight hours before the examination. *See* J. A. Rule 598.

See Rule 1452

Order to examine.   **492.** Upon application to the Court or a Judge, an order may be made for the examination of any party liable to be examined as aforesaid before any other person or in any other county than those before mentioned, and upon service of a copy of the appointment of the person before whom the examination is to take place and a copy of the order upon the party to be examined, and upon payment of the proper fees he is to attend and submit to examination. A copy of the appointment shall be served upon the solicitor of the party at least forty-eight hours before the examination.

Production of papers.   **493.** The party or person to be examined shall, if so required by notice, produce on the examination all books, papers and documents which he would be bound to produce at the trial under a *subpœna duces tecum.* R. S. O. 1877, c. 50, s. 161 part.

Parties and others may be examined on their own behalf.   **494.** Any party or officer so examined, may be further examined on his own behalf, or on behalf of the body corporate of which he is or has been an officer, in relation to any matter respecting which he has been examined in chief ; and when one of several plaintiffs or defendants has been examined, any other plaintiff or defendant united in interest may be examined on his own behalf or on behalf of those united with him in interest, to the same extent as the party examined. R. S. O. 1877, c. 50, s. 156 (1). Chy. O. 141, 142.

When explanatory examination to take place.   **495.** Such explanatory examination shall be proceeded with immediately after the examination in chief, and not at any future period, except by leave of the Court or a Judge ; and for the purposes of this and the preceding Rule, when the officer of a body corporate has been so examined as aforesaid on behalf of the body corporate, the body corporate shall be deemed to be fully represented by such officer. R. S. O. 1877, c. 50, s. 156 (2).

Mode of conducting examination.   **496.** Any party or person examined orally under the preceding Rules shall be subject to cross-examination and re-examination ; and the examination, cross-examination and re-examination shall be conducted as nearly as may be in the mode in use on a trial. R. S. O. 1877, c. 50, s. 161.

497. A party to the action who admits, upon his examination, that he A party admitting the possession of documents may be ordered to produce them.
has in his custody or power any deed, paper, writing, or document relating
to the matters in question in the cause, is to produce the same for the inspection of the party examining him upon the order of the Court or a
Judge, or of the Deputy Clerk, Local Registrar, Special Examiner, or
Local Master, before whom he is examined, and for that purpose a reasonable time is to be allowed. But no party shall be obliged to produce any
deed, paper, writing, or document, which is privileged or protected
from production. Chy. O. 147.

498. Either party may appeal from the order of the Deputy Clerk, Master's and Examiner's order for production appealable.
Local Registrar, Master, or Examiner; and thereupon the Deputy
Clerk, Local Registrar, Master, or Examiner, is to certify under his hand
the question raised and the order made thereon. Chy. O. 148.

499. Any party or person refusing or neglecting to attend at the time Penalty on witness refusing to attend or answer, etc.
and place appointed for his examination, or refusing to be sworn or to
answer any lawful question put to him by the examiner or by any party
entitled so to do, or his counsel, solicitor or agent, shall be deemed guilty
of a contempt of Court and proceedings may be forthwith had by attachment. If a defendant, he shall be liable to have his defence, if any,
struck out, and to be placed in the same position as if he had not defended ;
and the party examining may apply to the Court or a Judge for an order
to that effect, and an order may be made accordingly. R. S. O. 1877, c.
50, s. 162 ; J. A. Rule 236 ; Chy. O. 144 ; 41 V. c. 8, s. 9.

500. If the party or person under examination demurs or objects to Demurrer to questions.
any question or questions put to him, the question or questions so put,
and the demurrer or objection of the witness thereto, shall be taken down
by the examiner and transmitted by him to the office of the Court where
the pleadings are filed to be there filed ; and the validity of such
demurrer or objection shall be decided by the Court or a Judge ; and the
costs of and occasioned by such demurrer or objection shall be in the
discretion of the Court or Judge. R. S. O. 1877, c. 50, s. 163.

501. Subject to the 2 next following Rules the depositions taken upon Depositions how to be taken down.
any such oral examination as aforesaid shall be taken down in writing by
the examiner, not ordinarily by question and answer, but in the form of
a narrative, expressed in the first person ; and when completed shall be
read over to the party examined, and shall be signed by him in the
presence of the parties, or of such of them as may think fit to attend.

(a) In case the party or person examined refuses or is unable to sign the Signing depositions.
depositions, then the examiner shall sign the same ; and the examiner
may upon every examination state any special matter to the Court if he
thinks fit.

(b) It shall be in the discretion of the examiner to put down any par- Taking down questions.
ticular question or answer, if there appears to be any special reason for so
doing, and any question or questions objected to shall at the request of
either party be noticed or referred to by the examiner in or upon the
depositions ; and he shall state his opinion thereon to the counsel,
solicitors, agents or parties, and if requested by either party, he shall on
the face of the depositions refer to such statement. R. S. O. 1877, c. 50,
s. 164.

502. In case of an examination before the trial, or otherwise than at Shorthand.
the trial of an action, if the examining party desires to have such examination taken in shorthand, he shall be entitled to have it so taken at the
place of examination except where the Court or a Judge sees fit to order
otherwise. J. A. Rule 219.

503. Where an examination in a cause or proceeding in any court is Question and answer.
taken by the examiner, or any other duly authorized person, in shorthand, the examination may be taken down by question and answer ; and
in such case it shall not be necessary for the depositions to be read over

to, or signed by, the person examined, unless the Judge so directs where the examination is taken before a Judge, or in other cases unless any of the parties so desires.

Certified copy to have effect of original depositions.   (a) A copy of the depositions so taken, certified by the person taking the same as correct, shall for all purposes have the same effect as the original depositions in ordinary cases. 41 V. c. 8, s. 8.

Depositions to be returned to Court.   **504.** Wherever, by virtue of these Rules, an examination of any party or witness has been taken before a Judge of the High Court or of any County Court, or before any officer or other person authorized or appointed to take the same, the depositions-taken down by the examiner shall, at the request of any party interested and upon payment of his fees, be returned to and kept in the office of the Court in which the proceedings are carried on ; and office copies of such depositions may be given out, and the examinations and depositions certified **Office copies.**   under the hand of the Judge or other officer or person taking the same, or a copy thereof certified under the hand of the proper officer, shall, without proof of the signature, be received and read in evidence, saving all just exceptions. R. S. O. 1877, c. 50, s. 165.

Examiners may make a special report to the Court.   **505.** Every Judge, officer or other person taking examinations under these Rules, may, and if need be shall, make a special report to the Court in which such proceedings are pending, touching such examination and the conduct or absence of any witness or other person thereon or relating thereto ; and the Court shall institute such proceedings and make such order upon such report as justice may require, and as may be instituted and made in any case of contempt of the Court. R. S. O. 1877, c. 50, s. 166.

Part of examination to be evidence.   **506.** Any party may, at the trial of an action or issue, use in evidence any part of the examination of the opposite parties ; provided always, that in such case the Judge may look at the whole of the examination, and if he is of opinion that any other part is so connected with the part to be so used that the last mentioned part ought not to be used without such other part, he may direct such other part to be put in evidence. J. A. Rule 239.

9. PRODUCTION AND INSPECTION OF DOCUMENTS.

Discovery before and after close of pleadings.   **507.** It shall be lawful for the Court or a Judge at any time pending any action or proceeding, to order the production by any party thereto, upon oath, of such of the documents in his possession or power relating to any matter in question in such action or proceeding, as the Court or Judge thinks right ; and the Court may deal with such documents, when produced, in such manner as appears just. J. A. Rule 221.

Order for production of documents.   **508.** Any party may, after the defence is delivered, or a plaintiff may, after the time for delivering the defence has expired, and any party to an issue may, after the issue has been filed, obtain an order of course upon præcipe, directing the adverse party within 10 days after the service thereof, to make discovery on oath of the documents which are or have been n his possession or power, relating to any matters in question in the action ; and to produce and deposit the same with the proper officer for the usual purposes, and such party shall make discovery and produce and deposit the documents accordingly, without further notice. J. A. Rules 222 and 513.

Position of a third party served by a defendant.   **509.** A third party who has been served by a defendant under ~~Rule 329~~, and has entered an appearance, shall, for all purposes of and incident to the production of documents, and examination, be as

Rules 328. & 332 (c)

between him and such defendant in the same situation as a defendant, and the defendant serving him shall, for the same purposes, be in the same situation as a plaintiff; the time for taking out an order for production or for examining shall be after the party so served has delivered a defence, or where the application is on behalf of the defendant so serving such third party, the time shall be after the time for delivering the defence has expired. J. A. Rule 223.

510. A person for whose immediate benefit an action is prosecuted or defended is to be regarded as a party for the purpose of production of documents. J. A. Rule 224.
Person benefitted, a party for certain purposes.

511. Where the party required to produce documents is a corporation aggregate, the affidavit shall be made by one of the officers of the corporation, and his affidavit shall have the same effect (as nearly as may be) as the affidavit of a party, unless where the Court or Judge sees reason for holding otherwise. J. A. Rules 225, 226.
Affidavit on production by a corporation.

512. The deponent in every affidavit on production shall be subject to cross-examination.
Cross-examination of deponent.

513. The affidavit to be made by a party against whom an order for production has been made, shall specify which, if any, of the documents therein mentioned he objects to produce, and said affidavit may be in the Form No. 48 in the Appendix with such variations as circumstances may require. J. A. Rule 228.
Affidavit on production, form of.

514. Every party to an action or other proceeding shall be entitled, at any time before or at the hearing thereof, to give notice in writing to any other party, in whose pleadings or affidavits reference is made to any document, to produce such document for the inspection of the party giving the notice, or of his solicitor, and to permit him to take copies thereof; and any party not complying with such notice shall not afterwards be at liberty to put any such document in evidence on his behalf in the action or proceeding, unless he satisfies the Court that the document relates only to his own title, he being a defendant to the action, or that he had some other sufficient cause for not complying with the notice. J. A. Rule 229.
Notice to produce documents referred to in pleading or affidavits.

515. Notice to any party to produce any documents referred to in his pleading or affidavits may be in the Form No. 23 in the Appendix, or to the same effect. J. A. Rule 231.
Form of notice to produce.

516. The party to whom such notice is given shall, within 2 days from the receipt of the notice, if all the documents therein referred to have been set forth by him in such affidavit as is mentioned in Rule 513, or if any of the documents referred to in the notice have not been set forth by him in any such affidavit, then within 4 days from the receipt of the notice, deliver to the party giving the same a notice stating a time within 3 days from the delivery thereof at which the documents, or such of them as he does not object to produce, may be inspected at the office of his solicitor, and stating which (if any) of the documents he objects to produce and on what ground. Such notice may be in the Form No. 25, in the Appendix, with such variations as circumstances may require. J. A. Rule 232.
Notice to inspect.

517. If the party served with notice under Rule 516 omits to give such notice of a time for inspection, or objects to give inspection, the party desiring it may apply to a Judge for an order for inspection. J. A. Rule 233.
Order for inspection on default.

518. Every application for an order for inspection of documents shall be to a Judge. And, except in the case of documents referred to in the pleadings or affidavits of the party against whom the application is made,
Application for order.

or disclosed in his affidavit of documents, such application shall be founded upon an affidavit shewing of what documents inspection is sought, that the party applying is entitled to inspect them, and that they are in the possession or power of the other party. J. A. Rule 234.

When inspection objected to.

519. If the party from whom discovery of any kind or inspection is sought objects to the same, or any part thereof, the Court or a Judge, if satisfied that the right to the discovery or inspection sought depends on the determination of any issue or question in dispute in the action, or that for any other reason it is desirable that any issue or question in dispute in the action should be determined before deciding upon the right to the discovery or inspection, may order that such issue or question be determined first, and reserve the question as to the discovery or inspection. J. A. Rule 235.

Consequences of disobeying an order for discovery.

520. If any party fails to comply with any order for production or inspection of documents, he shall be liable to attachment. If a defendant, he shall be liable to have his defence, if any, struck out, and to be placed in the same position as if he had not defended ; and the party who obtained the order for production or inspection may apply to the Court or a Judge for an order to that effect, and an order may be made accordingly. J. A. Rule 236 ; Chy. O. 144 ; 41 V. c. 8, s. 9.

Service of notice on solicitor when sufficient.

521. Where the application for such last mentioned order is made by reason of default in production of books and papers in the Master's office, or pursuant to an order to produce, or in carrying in accounts, service of the notice of motion upon the solicitor of the party required to obey the same, is to be sufficient service. Chy. O. 296.

Service of order on solicitor when sufficient.

522. Service of an order for discovery or inspection made against any party on his solicitor shall be sufficient service to found an application for an attachment for disobedience to the order. But the party against whom the application for an attachment is made may shew in answer to the application that he has had no notice or knowledge of the order. J. A. Rule 237.

Attachment of solicitor.

523. A solicitor upon whom an order against any party for discovery or inspection is served under the last Rule, who neglects without reasonable excuse to give notice thereof to his client shall be liable to an attachment. J. A. Rule 238.

Rules as to examination, discovery and inspection to apply to parties residing out of Ontario.

524. The preceding Rules as to preliminary examination of parties, and discovery and inspection of documents, shall, so far as practicable, apply to parties residing out of Ontario, and in such cases the Court or Judge may order the examination of the parties to be taken at such place and in such manner as may seem just and convenient, and service of the order for examination, discovery, or inspection, and of all other papers necessary to obtain the benefit of the provisions of the said Rules shall be sufficient if made on the solicitor of the party in the action, in the same manner as other papers in the action are served on the solicitor therein ; unless the Court or Judge makes other order to the contrary : and if there is no such solicitor, or he cannot for any reason be served. the Court or Judge may order the service in any other manner to be mentioned in the order in that behalf. 41 V. c. 8, s. 9.

to
1463

10. MOTIONS AND OTHER APPLICATIONS.

(i) *Generally.*

Application to Court or Judge to be by motion.

525. Where any application is authorized to be made to the Court or a Judge in an action or proceeding, such application shall be made by motion. J. A. Rule 404.

No rule or order nisi.

526. No summons, rule or order to shew cause shall be granted in any action or matter ; but when any person other than the applicant is entitled to be heard thereon, he shall be served with a notice of the motion. *See* J. A. Rules 405, 412.

527. The Court or Judge, if satisfied that the delay caused by pro- Notice of motion. When ceeding by notice of motion, would or might entail irreparable or serious orders *ex parte* mischief, may make any order *ex parte*, upon such terms as to costs or can be made. otherwise, and subject to such undertaking, if any, as the Court or Judge may think just ; and any party affected by such order may move to set aside or vary the same. J. A. Rule 406.

528. Where infants are concerned, no order dispensing with payment When guar of money into Court is to be made without notice to the guardian *ad litem* dian to be notified. of the infants. J. A. Rule 505.

529. If on the hearing of a motion or other application, the Court or All proper Judge is of opinion that any person to whom notice has not been parties not served. given ought to have had notice, the Court or Judge may either dismiss the motion or application, or adjourn the hearing thereof in order that notice may be given, upon such terms, if any, as the Court or Judge may think fit to impose. J. A. Rule 408.

530. No application for interim alimony shall be made until the time for Interim delivering the defence has expired. Chy. O. 489. alimony.

531. The hearing of any motion or application may from time to time Adjournment. be adjourned upon such terms, if any, as the Court or Judge shall think fit. J. A. Rule 409.

532. The plaintiff shall, without any special leave, be at liberty to Service before serve any notice of motion or other notice, or any petition upon any appearance. defendant, who, having been duly served with a writ of summons to appear in the action, has not appeared within the time limited for that purpose. J. A. Rule 410.

533. The plaintiff may also, without any special leave, serve a notice of Service with motion for an injunction, and may, by leave of the Court or a Judge to be writ or before obtained *ex parte*, serve any other notice of motion, upon any defendant pearance. along with the writ of summons, or at any time after service of the writ of summons and before the time limited for the appearance of such defendant. J. A. Rule 411

534. A notice of motion to set aside any proceeding for irregularity Irregularity must specify clearly the irregularity complained of and the several to be stated in objections intended to be insisted on. Chy. O. 277. Rules T. T. 1856, notice. 107.

535. Every notice of motion by way of appeal from or to set aside an Motion award shall specify the grounds intended to be insisted upon. *See* Rules against award. T. T. 1856, 141.

536. Any party affected by an *ex parte* order, except the party issuing *Ex parte* the same, may move to rescind or vary the same before the Judge or officer orders may be who made the order, or any Judge or officer having jurisdiction, within four against. days from the time of its coming to his notice, or within such further time as the Court or Judge may allow, and whether it has been acted upon by the party issuing the order or not. ˉ*New.*ˉˉ

537. All motions, demurrers, special cases, appeals and other matters Setting down to be heard in Court at the weekly sittings, except *ex parte* applications, motions. shall be set down for argument in the office of the Clerk of Records and Writs, who shall post up in a convenient place a list of the cases so set down not later than the day before the day for which the same are so set down, and shall furnish a copy of such list to the Registrar or other officer who is to attend the sittings of the Court. *See* J. A. Rule 600.

538. All motions and applications to the Court required to be set down Mode of set- for argument, and all appeals, demurrers and special cases shall be set down ting down by delivering to the proper officer a precipe specifying the matter to be motions.

set down and the day for argument thereof, and requiring him to set the same down. When a married woman, infant, or person of unsound mind is a party to the action, a copy of the order giving leave to enter a special case for argument shall also be produced. J. A. Rules, 202, 252.

Setting down demurrer.

539. Where a demurrer either to the whole or part of a pleading is delivered, either party may enter the demurrer for argument immediately, and the party so entering such demurrer shall, on the same day, give notice thereof to the other party.

Setting down demurrers and special cases. Copy of demurrer book or case to be left for Judge.

540. Demurrers and special cases shall be set down to be heard, and notice thereof given to the opposite party, 6 clear days before the day on which they are to be heard ; and a copy of the demurrer book, or of the special case, shall be left at the office of the Clerk of Records and Writs, for the use of the Judge before whom the demurrer, or special case, is to be heard, 2 days before the day appointed for the hearing. Rules H. C. J., v., vi.

Time for setting down.

541. All other motions and applications to the Court, except *ex parte* applications, are to be set down at latest on the day before the day of argument, unless the Court otherwise orders.

(ii) *Applications at Chambers.*

Business to be transacted in Chambers.

542. The following business shall be disposed of in Chambers, together with such other matters as the Court from time to time thinks may be more conveniently disposed of there than in Court, viz :—

1. For the sale of the estates of infants, under the Revised Statutes of Ontario.

2. As to the guardianship, maintenance, and advancement of infants ;

3. For the administration of estates upon motion, without action ;

4. Relating to the conduct of actions or matters ;

5. As to matters connected with the management of property ;

6. For the payment into Court of moneys, by parties desiring on their own behalf to pay in the same. Chy. O. 197.

Form of order.

543. An order shall be in the Form No. 120 in the Appendix hereto, with such variations as circumstances require. It shall be marked with the name of the Judge or officer by whom it is made. J. A. Rule 413.

Clerk to sign orders in Judge's Chambers.

544. All orders made by a Judge of the High Court in Chambers in Toronto shall be signed by the Clerk in Chambers, whose duty it shall be to see that such orders are in due form before signing the same. J. A. Rule 582.

Appeals.

545. Every appeal to be heard in Chambers shall be set down for argument with the Clerk of Records and Writs at latest on the day before the day of argument, and a list of cases to be heard on any day shall be prepared and exposed as soon as the time expires for setting down cases for that day.

Certain orders to be entered in full.

546. All orders for administration, or partition, made in Chambers shall be drawn up as judgments and entered in like manner as other judgments are required to be entered. All orders declaring persons lunatics, or for the sale of infants' estates, or for payment of money into, or out of, Court, or for continuing proceedings upon the death or transmission of interest of any party to an action, and all final orders of sale or foreclosure, and all vesting orders, shall be entered in full in a book to be provided for the purpose, before the same shall be issued or acted on. J. A. Rule 583.

547. Where an account is taken in Chambers, special directions may be given with respect to the mode in which the account is to be taken and vouched ; and the proceedings shall be as nearly as may be the same as upon a reference to a Master under Rules 63 to 66 and 46 to 48. *See* Chy. O. 200. *Where account taken in Chambers.*

548. The Court may adjourn for consideration in Chambers any matter which, in the opinion of the Court, may be disposed of more conveniently in Chambers ; and any matter pending in Chambers may be adjourned to open Court ; and such matter may be so adjourned at the request of either party, subject to such order as to costs or otherwise as the Court thinks right to impose. Chy. O. 208. *Matters may be adjourned from Court to Chambers, or vice versa.*

549. A Judge sitting in Chambers may exercise the same power and jurisdiction, in respect of the business brought before him, as is exercised by the Court ; all orders made by a Judge in Chambers are to have the force and effect of orders of the Court ; and all or any of the powers, authorities, and jurisdictions, given to the Master by any Act or Acts now in force, or by any Rule of the Court, may be exercised by a Judge in Chambers. Chy. O. 210. *Judge in Chambers may exercise powers of Court, and also powers of the Master.*

· •

11. INQUIRIES AND ACCOUNTS.

550. The Court will not refer to arbitration. *Arbitration.*

551. The Court or a Judge may, at any stage of the proceedings in a cause or matter, direct any necessary inquiries or accounts to be made or taken, notwithstanding that it may appear that there is some special or further relief sought for, or some special issue to be tried, as to which it may be proper that the cause or matter should proceed in the ordinary manner. J. A. Rule 244. *Reference at any stage.*

552. Where a reference is made to any official or other referee under the Judicature Act, the referee shall have all the powers as to certifying and amending of a Judge of the High Court of Justice, and shall make his report of and concerning the matters ordered to be tried pursuant to the statute ; *Provisions of reference to official or other referee.*

(*a*) The referee may, if he thinks fit, examine the parties to the action, and their respective witnesses, upon oath or affirmation, and the parties shall produce before the referee all books, deeds, papers and writings in their or either of their custody or power relating to the matters ordered to be tried ;

(*b*) Neither the plaintiff nor the defendant shall bring or prosecute any action against the referee, or against each other, of or concerning the matters ordered to be tried, and if either party by affected delay or otherwise wilfully prevents the referee from making his report, he or they shall pay such costs to the other as the High Court, or any Judge thereof, may think reasonable and just :

(*c*) In the event of the referee declining to act, or dying before he has made his report, the parties may, or if they cannot agree, one of the Judges of the High Court may, upon application by either party, appoint a new referee. J. A. Rule 245.

553. An order under the next preceding Rule shall be read as if it contained the provisions set forth in the said Rule, and shall not set forth the said provisions, but may contain any variation therefrom, and any other directions which the Court or Judge sees fit to make. J. A. Rule 247. *Order to be read as containing above provisions.*

12. Special Cases.

Parties may concur in stating special case.   **554.** The parties may after the writ of summons has been issued in any action, or in any pending matter not commenced by writ, concur in stating the questions of law arising in the action or matter in the form of a special case for the opinion of the Court ;

(a) The parties to a special case may, if they think fit, enter into an agreement in writing, that on the judgment of the Court being given in the affirmative or negative of the question or questions of law raised by the special case, a sum of money, fixed by the parties, or to be ascertained by the Court or in such manner as the Court may direct, shall be paid by one of the parties to the other of them, either with or without costs of the action or matter ; and the judgment of the Court may be entered for the sum so agreed or ascertained, with or without costs, as the case may be, and execution may issue upon such judgment forthwith, unless otherwise agreed, or unless stayed on appeal ;

(c) Upon the argument of such case the Court and the parties shall be at liberty to refer to the whole contents of the documents referred to, and the Court shall be at liberty to draw from the facts and documents stated in any such special case any inference, whether of fact or law, which might have been drawn therefrom if proved at a trial. J. A. Rule 248.

Preliminary question of law.   **555.** If it appears to the Court or a Judge, either from the statement of claim or defence or reply, or otherwise, that there is in any action or matter a question of law which it would be convenient to have decided before any evidence is given or any question or issue of fact is tried, or before any reference is made to a referee or an arbitrator, the Court or Judge may make an order accordingly, and may direct such question of law to be raised either by special case or in such other manner as the Court or Judge may deem expedient ; and all such further proceedings as the decision of such question of law may render unnecessary may thereupon be stayed. J. A. Rule 249.

Preparing case.   **556.** Every special case shall be signed by the several parties or their solicitors, and shall be filed by the plaintiff. Copies for the use of the Judges shall be delivered by the plaintiff. J. A. Rule 250.

Persons under disability.   **557.** No special case in an action to which a married woman, not being a party thereto in respect of her separate property, or of any separate right of action by or against her, or an infant, or person of unsound mind not so found by inquisition, is a party shall be set down for argument without leave of the Court or a Judge, the application for which must be supported by sufficient evidence that the statements contained in such special case, so far as the same affect the interest of such married woman, infant, or person of unsound mind, are true. J. A. Rule 251.

Application of rules.   **558.** The 4 next preceding Rules shall apply to every special case stated in an action or matter or in any proceeding incidental to an action. J. A. Rule 253.

13. Evidence Generally.

(i) Subpœnas, etc.

Subpœnas.   **559.** All writs of subpœna may be tested, or may bear date upon the day when the same are issued. R. S. O. 1877, c. 62, s. 15.

Subpœna to produce original record not to issue without order.   **560.** No subpœna for the production of an original record, or of an original memorial from any registry office, shall be issued, unless the order of the Court or a Judge is produced to the officer issuing the same, and filed with him, and unless the writ is made conformable to the description of the document in such order. Rules T. T. 1856, 31.

561. Any number of names may be included in one *subpœna*, and no more than one subpœna shall be allowed on taxation of costs, unless a sufficient reason be established to the satisfaction of the taxing officer for issuing more than one. Rules T. T. 1856, 163.

562. Wherever any party in any civil action desires to call the opposite party as a witness at the hearing or trial he shall either subpœna such party or give him or his solicitor at least eight days notice of the intention to examine him as a witness in the cause, and if such party does not attend on such notice or subpœna, such non-attendance shall be taken as an admission *pro confesso* against him in any such action, unless otherwise ordered by the Court or Judge in which or before whom such examination is pending, and a general finding or judgment may be had against the party thereon, or the plaintiff may be non-suited, or the proceedings in the action may be postponed by the Court or Judge, on such terms as the Court or Judge sees fit to impose. R. S. O. 1877, c. 62, s. 18.

563. Upon proof to the satisfaction of the Judge presiding at the sittings of any Court of the service of a subpœna upon any witness who fails to attend or to remain in attendance in accordance with the requirements of the subpœna, and that a sufficient sum for his fees as a witness had been duly paid or tendered to him, and that the presence of such witness is material to the ends of justice, the said Judge may, by his warrant, directed to any sheriff or other officer of the Court, or to any constable, cause such witness to be apprehended and forthwith brought before him or any other Judge who may thereafter preside at such sittings, to give evidence, and in order to secure his presence as a witness, such witness may be taken on such warrant before the presiding Judge and detained in the custody of the person to whom the warrant is directed, or otherwise, as the presiding Judge may order, until his presence, as such witness, shall be required, or, in the discretion of the said Judge, he may be released on a recognizance (with or without sureties) conditioned for his appearance to give evidence.

(a) The warrant may be similar to the Form No. 202 in the Appendix, and may be executed in any part of Ontario. 44 V. c. 5, ss. 83, 84.

(ii) *Evidence at Trials and References.*

564. In the absence of any agreement between the parties, and subject to these Rules, the witnesses at the trial of an action or at an assessment of damages shall be examined viva voce and in open Court, but the Court or a Judge may at any time for sufficient reason order that any particular fact or facts may be proved by affidavit, or that the affidavit of any witness may be read at the hearing or trial, on such conditions as the Court or Judge may think reasonable, or that any witness whose attendance in Court ought for some sufficient cause to be dispensed with, be examined before an examiner ; provided that where it appears to the Court or Judge that the other party *bona fide* desires the production of a witness for cross-examination, and that such witness can be produced, an order shall not be made authorizing the evidence of the witness to be given by affidavit. J. A. Rule 282.

565. All witnesses in any matter pending before a Master, Local Master or Referee, shall give their testimony viva voce, and be subject to examination before the Master, unless it is otherwise ordered by the Master, or by the Court or a Judge, on special grounds, or with the consent of the parties in the suit or controversy to which the testimony relates. R. S. O. 1877, c. 40, s. 100.

566. The Court or a Judge may, in any cause or matter where it appears necessary for the purposes of justice, make any order for the examination upon oath before an officer of the Court, or any other person or persons, and at any place, of any witness or person, and may order any deposition so taken to be filed in the Court, and may empower any party to the cause or matter to give such deposition in evidence therein, on such terms, if any, as the Court or Judge may direct.   J. A. Rule 285.

Affidavits by consent, or by leave of the Court.

567. At the trial of an action, or of any further directions therein, affidavits of particular witnesses, or affidavits as to particular facts and circumstances, may be used by consent, or by leave of the Court ; and such consent may be given on behalf of persons under disability, with the approbation of the Court.   Chy. O. 176.

When to be filed by plaintiff.

568. In case the parties in any action consent to the evidence being taken by affidavit as between the plaintiff and the defendant, the plaintiff within 14 days after such consent has been given, or within such time as the parties may agree upon, or a Judge in Chambers may allow, shall file his affidavits and deliver to the defendant or his solicitor a list thereof. J. A. Rule 301.

When to be filed by defendant.

569. The defendant within 14 days after delivery of such list, or within such time as the parties may agree upon, or a Judge in Chambers may allow, shall file his affidavits and deliver to the plaintiff or his solicitor a list thereof.   J. A. Rule 302.

Filing affidavits in reply.

570. Within 7 days after the expiration of the said 14 days, or such other time as aforesaid, the plaintiff shall file his affidavits in reply, which affidavits shall be confined to matter strictly in reply, and shall deliver to the defendant or his solicitor a list thereof.   J. A. Rule 303.

Cross-examination on affidavit.

571. Where the evidence is taken by affidavit, any party desiring to cross-examine a deponent who has made an affidavit filed on behalf of the opposite party, may serve upon the party by whom such affidavit has been filed, a notice in writing, requiring the production of the deponent for cross-examination before the Court at the trial, such notice to be served at any time before the expiration of 14 days next after the end of the time allowed for filing affidavits in reply, or within such time as in any case the Court or a Judge may specially appoint ; and unless such deponent is produced accordingly, his affidavit shall not be used as evidence unless by the special leave of the Court. The party producing such deponent for cross-examination shall not be entitled to demand the expenses thereof in the first instance from the party requiring such production.   J. A. Rule 304.

Compelling attendance of witness.

572. The party to whom such notice as is mentioned in the last preceding Rule is given, shall be entitled to compel the attendance of the deponent for cross-examination in the same way as he might compel the attendance of a witness to be examined.   J. A. Rule 305.

Libel or slander, particulars.

573. In actions for libel or slander, in which the defendant does not by his defence assert the truth of the statement complained of, the defendant shall not be entitled on the trial to give evidence in chief, with a view to mitigation of damages, as to the circumstances under which the libel or slander was published, or as to the character of the plaintiff, without the leave of the Judge, unless seven days at least before the trial he furnishes particulars to the plaintiff of the matters as to which he intends to give evidence.   Eng. R. 1883, 461.   New.

Copies of depositions certified by person taking the same admissible in evidence.

574. Where an examination of any party or parties, witness or witnesses, has been taken before a Judge of the High Court, or of any County Court, or before any other officer or person appointed to take the same, copies of such examinations and depositions certified under the hand of the Judge, officer or other person taking the same shall, without proof of the signature, be received and read in evidence, saving all just exceptions.   42 V. c. 15, s. 3.

Evidence of service of notice to produce.

575. An affidavit of the Solicitor in the cause or his clerk, of the service of any notice to produce, and of the time when it was served, with a copy of such notice to produce, shall be sufficient evidence of the service of the notice, and of the time when it was served. R. S. O. 1877, c. 50, s. 173.

(iii) *Evidence on Motions.*

576. Upon any motion or petition, evidence may be given by affidavit. *Evidence on motion, or petition.*

577. Every person who makes an affidavit to be used in any action or *Cross-exami-* proceeding shall be liable to cross examination thereon, and may be required *nation on affi-* to attend in the same manner, and subject to the same rules, as a party *davits.* to be examined in the cause. *Mech. Rule 490 + sub*

578. A party to any action or proceeding may, by a writ of subpœna *Attendance of* *ad testificandum,* or *duces tecum,* require the attendance of a witness to be *witnesses for* examined before the Court, or before any officer having jurisdiction in the *examinations* County where the witness resides for the purpose of using his evidence *how procured.* upon any motion, petition, or other proceeding before the Court, or any Judge or judicial officer in Chambers.

(*a*) The attendance of such witness is to be secured in the same manner, and subject to the same rules, as upon the examination of a party in the cause. J. A. Rule 598.

579. Upon the hearing of any motion before the High Court or a Judge *Court or* the Court or Judge at discretion, and upon such terms as it or he thinks *Judge may, on* reasonable, may from time to time order to be produced such documents *hearing any* as it or he thinks fit, and may order such witnesses as it or he thinks *motion or sum-* necessary, to appear and be examined *viva voce* before such Court or Judge, *the production* or before a Judge of any County Court, or before any other person, and *of documents* upon reading the report of the Judge of the County Court, or other per- *or viva voce ex-* son, as the case may be, or if no such reference is made, then upon exam- *aminations.* ining such documents or hearing such witnesses by the Court or Judge, the Court or Judge may make such order as seems just; and in cases within the jurisdiction of a County Court, the Court or a Judge *And may make* therein having jurisdiction in the case, may order the production of doc- *rule or order* uments or the attendance of witnesses before such Court or Judge, or *thereon.* before the Clerk of such County Court, and upon hearing such evidence or reading the report of the Clerk, may make such order as seems just, in like manner as if the proceedings were had in the High Court. R. S. O. 1877, c. 50, s. 175.

580. The Court or Judge may, by the order, command the attendance *Power by* of the witnesses named therein for the purpose of being examined, or *order to* may command the production of any writings or other documents, to be *compel* mentioned in the rule or order, and in the case of a Judge, he may, if *attendance* necessary or convenient so to do, direct the attendance of the witness *product on of* to be at his own place of abode or elsewhere. R. S. O. 1877, c. 50, s. *documents in* 176. *such cases.*

581. If in addition to the service of the order an appointment of *Disobedience* the time and place of attendance in obedience thereto, signed by the *to be a con-* person or persons appointed to take the examination, or by one or more *tempt of Court* of such persons, is also served together with or after the service of the order, the wilful disobedience of the order shall be a contempt of Court, and proceedings may be forthwith had by attachment. But *Witnesses to* —1. Every person whose attendance is so required, shall be entitled *be paid ex-* to the like payment for attendance and expenses as if he had been sub- *penses.* pœnaed to attend upon a trial; 2. No person shall be compelled to *What docu-* produce under any such rule or order, any writing or other document which *ments need not* he would not be compellable to produce at the trial of the cause; 3. *be produced.*

Examinations may be adjourned. The Court or Judge, or person appointed to take the examination, may adjourn the same from time to time as occasion may require. R. S. O. 1877, c. 50, s. 177.

How prisoners may be brought to give evidence. **582.** The Sheriff, gaoler, or other officer having the custody of any prisoner, shall take the prisoner for any examination authorized by these Rules, when so directed by an order of the Court or Judge ; which order may be issued by the Court or Judge under such circumstances as appear to warrant the production of the prisoner. R. S. O. 1877, c. 50, s. 178.

Certified copies of proceedings may be obtained from the office where filed. **583.** Wherever any party wishes to produce to the Court or a Judge, the writ or any pleading, or other proceeding filed in any office of the Court, he may demand and receive from the officer in whose office the writ pleading or other proceeding is, a copy of the same certified by the officer to be a true copy of the original, and the copy so certified shall be admissible in evidence in all causes and matters and between all persons and parties, to the same extent as the originals would be admissible.

Default in payment, how to be proved. **584.** Where default is made in the payment of money appointed to be paid into a Bank, the certificate of the Cashier, Manager, or Agent of the Bank, where the same is made payable, or of the like Bank officer, shall be sufficient evidence of default. Where the affidavit of the party entitled to receive the same is by the present practice required, the same shall still be necessary. Chy. O. 257.

Power given to High Court to receive further evidence in all appeals, etc. **585.** In all appeals, either to the Court of Appeal or the High Court or a Judge, and on all motions to set aside or vary verdicts or judgments or hearings in the nature of appeals, the Court or Judge appealed to shall have all the powers and duties as to amendment and otherwise of the Court, Judge or officer appealed from, together with full discretionary power to receive further evidence upon questions of fact ; such evidence to be either by oral examination before the Court or Judge appealed to, or by affidavit, or by depositions taken before a special examiner or Commissioner.

(2) Such further evidence may be given without special leave upon interlocutory applications, or in any case as to matters which have occurred after the date of the decision from which the appeal is brought.

(3) Upon appeals from a judgment upon the merits at the trial or hearing of any action or matter, such further evidence (save as aforesaid) shall be admitted on special grounds only, and not without the special leave of the Court. 41 V. c. 8, s. 7. R. S. O. 1877, c. 38, s. 22.

(iv) *Commissions to examine Witnesses.*

Non-resident party. **586.** In case a party to any civil action is resident out of Ontario, and in case the opposite party requires a commission to examine such non-resident party, and states by affidavit the facts intended to be proved before such commission, and in case the Court or Judge is satisfied that such commission is applied for in good faith and not for purposes of delay, the Court in which the action has been brought, or any Judge thereof may, at the instance of the opposite party, issue a commission for the examination of such non-resident party in the same manner as a commission may be issued for the examination of witnesses. R. S. O. 1877, c. 62, s. 19.

Refusal to attend. **587.** If such party refuses to attend before the Commissioners, such refusal, being proved by affidavit or otherwise to the satisfaction of a Judge of the Court in which the action or the trial is pending, shall authorize a verdict or judgment to pass against the party, or he shall be non-suited. R. S. O. 1877, c. 62, s. 20.

Aged or infirm persons. **588.** In case the plaintiff or defendant in any action in the High Court or in any County Court, is desirous of having at the trial thereof the testimony of any aged or infirm person resident within Ontario, or of any person who is about to withdraw therefrom, or who is residing without the limits thereof, the Court in which the action is pending, or a Judge thereof, may, upon the motion of such plaintiff or defendant, and upon hearing the parties order the issue of a commission or commissions under the seal of the Court in which the action is pending, to a Commissioner or Commissioners, to take the examination of such person or persons respectively. R. S. O. 1877, c. 62, s. 21.

589. Due notice of every such commission shall be given to the adverse party, to the end that he may cause the witnesses to be cross-examined. R. S. O. 1877, c. 62, s. 22.

Notice of commission.

590. Foreign commissions for the examination of witnesses without the jurisdiction of the Court, in proceedings before a Master may, on the certificate of the Master, be issued upon præcipe. Chy. O. 221.

Commissions on Master's certificate.

591. Upon an application for a commission to take evidence the applicant is in the notice of motion to state the name of the commissioner to whom he desires the commission to be issued ; and where the opposite party desires to name another commissioner, he is, on the return of the motion, to give notice to the applicant of the name of any other commissioner. J. A. Rule 286.

Notice of motion.

592. Upon the hearing of the motion the Court or Judge (or officer before whom the motion is made) may order the issue of the commission directed to the persons so named or to such other person or persons as may seem proper. J. A. Rule 287.

Commission to whom directed.

593. The order or certificate for the issue of a commission is to state the name of the commissioner to whom it is to be directed, and whether the examination of witnesses thereunder is to be taken upon oral questions or upon written interrogatories, and also whether or not notice of the execution thereof is to be given to the opposite party ; and in case notice is to be so given, then the name and the address of the person on whom such notice is to be served are to be stated in the order. J. A. Rule 288.

Particulars to be stated in order.

594. The examination of witnesses under a commission is to be taken either orally or upon written interrogatories, or partly in one way and partly in the other, as the Court or a Judge may direct. All oral questions shall be reduced into writing and with the answers thereto returned with the commission. *See* J. A. Rule 239.

Mode of examination.

595. Where the examination is to take place upon written interrogatories, the interrogatories in chief are to be delivered to the opposite party (unless otherwise ordered) at least 8 days before the issue of the commission ; and the cross-interrogatories are to be delivered to the opposite party (unless otherwise ordered) within 4 days after the receipt of the interrogatories in chief ; and in default of cross-interrogatories being so delivered, the opposite party may send the commission without cross-interrogatories. J. A. Rule 290.

Examination on written interrogatories.

596. An commission may be executed *ex parte*, unless the opposite party shall, upon the hearing of the application for the order or Master's certificate for the issue of the commission, require notice of the execution of the commission, and give the name and place of abode of some person resident within two miles of the place where the commission is to be executed, upon whom notice may be served. J. A. Rule 291.

Examination ex parte.

597. Where notice of the execution of the commission is required to be served, 48 hours' notice shall be sufficient ; such notice is to be in writing, stating the time and place of the intended examination, and is to be addressed to the person named for that purpose in the order or certificate for the issue of the commission ; and service upon him, or upon a grown

Notice of execution of commission.

up person, at the address stated in the order or Master's certificate, shall be sufficient. If the name or address stated in such order or certificate shall prove to be illusory or fictitious, or if the party so notified fails to attend, pursuant to the notice, the commission may be executed *ex parte*. J. A. Rule 292.

Copies as evidence.

598. In the event of any witness on his examination, cross-examination or re-examination, producing any book, document, letter, paper or writing, and refusing for good cause to be stated in his deposition, to part with the original thereof, then a copy thereof, or extract therefrom, certified by the commissioners or commissioner present to be a true and correct copy or extract, shall be annexed to the witness' deposition. J. A. Rule 293.

Oath of witness.

599. Every witness to be examined under the commission shall be examined on oath, affirmation, or otherwise in accordance with his religion, by or before the said commissioners or commissioner. J. A. Rule 294.

Examination through an interpreter.

600. If any one or more of the witnesses do not understand the English language (the interrogatories, cross-interrogatories, and *vivâ voce* questions, as the case may be, being previously translated into the language with which he or they is or are conversant), then the examination shall be taken in English through the medium of an interpreter or interpreters, to be nominated by the commissioners or commissioner, and to be previously sworn according to his or their several religions by or before the said commissioners or commissioner truly to interpret the questions to be put to the witness or witnesses, and his and their answers thereto. J. A. Rule 295.

Depositions to be signed.

601. The depositions to be taken under and by virtue of the said commission shall be subscribed by the witness or witnesses, and by the commissioners or commissioner who shall have taken such depositions. J. A. Rule 296.

Return of commission and use thereof as evidence.

602. The interrogatories, cross-interrogatories, and depositions together with any documents referred to therein, or certified copies thereof or extracts therefrom, shall be sent to the Judge or officer on or before such day as may be ordered in that behalf, enclosed in a cover under the seal or seals of the said commissioners or commissioner, and office copies thereof may be given in evidence on the trial of the action, by and on behalf of the said parties respectively, saving all just exceptions, without any other proof of the absence, from this country of the witness or witnesses therein named, than an affidavit of the solicitor or agent of the party as to his belief of such absence. J. A. Rule 297.

Parties joining in commission.

603. Where, upon the application for a commission to take evidence, the opposite party desires to join in the commission and examine witnesses on his own behalf thereunder, or names a commissioner, each party is to pay the cost of the commission consequent upon the examination of his witnesses and the appointment of his commissioner, without prejudice to the question by whom such costs are ultimately to be borne ; and if for any reason the commissioner named by either party refuses to act in the execution of the commission upon receiving 48 hours' notice in writing from the other of them so to do, the commission may be executed by the commissioner giving such notice alone. J. A. Rule 298.

Order for commission to be read as including above particulars.

604. Every order for a commission shall be read as if it contained the above particulars, and shall not set forth the same, but may contain any variations therefrom, and any other directions, which the Court or Judge shall see fit to make. J. A. Rule 300.

(v) *Affidavits.*

Form of affidavits.

605. Every affidavit shall be drawn up in the first person, stating the name of the deponent at the commencement in full, and his description and true place of abode, and shall be signed by him. J. A. Rules 464, 465 ; Chy. O. 258.

606. In every affidavit made by two or more deponents the names of Affidavits
the several persons making the affidavit shall be inserted in the jurat, made by two
except that if the affidavit of all the deponents is taken at one time by _{deponents.}
the same officer, it shall be sufficient to state that it was sworn by both
(or all) of the "above-named" deponents. J. A. Rule 466.

607. The jurat may be in the form or to the effect following.   Jurat.

Sworn before me at   , in the County of   , on the
   day of   A.D. .   Chy. O. 258.

608. There shall be appended to or indorsed upon every affidavit a Indorsement.
note showing on whose behalf it is filed. J. A. Rule 467.

609. Affidavits shall be confined to such facts as the witness is able of Affidavits how
his own knowledge to prove, except on interlocutory motions, on which framed.
statements as to his belief, with the grounds thereof, may be admitted.
See J. A. Rule 284 ; Chy. O. 259.

610. Any affidavit in an action or proceeding to which a municipal or Affidavits by
other corporation is a party may be made by any officer, servant, or agent officers for
of the corporation having knowledge of the facts required to be deposed corporation.
to, and he shall state therein that he has such knowledge. J. A. Rule
595.

611. No affidavit having in the jurat or body thereof any interlineation, Alterations in
alteration, or erasure shall without leave of the Court or a Judge be read affidavits.
or made use of in any matter pending in Court unless the interlineation
or alteration (other than by erasure) is authenticated by the initials of the
officer taking the affidavit ; nor in the case of an erasure, unless the words
or figures appearing at the time of taking the affidavit to be written on the
erasure are rewritten, and signed or initialed in the margin of the affidavit
by the officer taking it. J. A. Rule 468.

612. Where an affidavit is sworn by any person who appears to the Affidavits by
officer taking the affidavit to be illiterate, the officer shall certify in the illiterate
jurat that the affidavit was read in his presence to the deponent, that the persons.
deponent seemed perfectly to understand it, and that the deponent made
his or her signature in the presence of the officer. No such affidavit shall
be used in evidence in the absence of this certificate, unless the Court or
a Judge is otherwise satisfied that the affidavit was read over to and
apparently perfectly understood by the deponent. J. A. Rule 469.

613. No affidavit shall be read or made use of for any purpose, if No affidavit to
sworn before the solicitor of the party in the cause on whose behalf the be sworn
affidavit is made, or before the clerk, or partner, of such solicitor ; but before solici-
this Rule shall not extend to affidavits to hold to bail. Rules T. T. 1856. tor of party.
114.

614. All affidavits and other papers required to be filed in any action Stamps on
or matter on motions and other matters shall, before being used, be affidavits.
stamped with a proper filing stamp, and at or before the time of using them
shall be filed in the proper office of the Division of the High Court to
which the action or matter is assigned. *See* J. A. Rule 470 ; Chy. O.
260.

615. Affidavits to be used on a motion in Chambers shall be filed with Affidavits,
the Clerk in Chambers, who shall, in cases in the Chancery Division, where filed.
transmit them to the Records and Writs office when the motion is disposed of. *See* Chy. O. 30.

G

Affidavits in chief, when to be filed.   **616.** All the affidavits upon which a notice of motion, or petition is founded, must be filed before the service of the notice of motion or petition. Chy. O. 261.

(vi) *Admissions.*

Notice to admit documents.   **617.** Either party may call upon the other party to admit any document, saving all just exceptions. J. A. Rule 241.

Form of notice.   **618.** A notice to admit documents may be in the Form No. 26, in the Appendix. J. A. Rule 242.

Proof of admissions.   **619.** The production of any written admissions purporting to be admissions in the action, and to be made in pursuance of any notice to admit documents or otherwise, and to be signed by the solicitor of the party by whom, or on whose behalf, they purport to be made, shall be sufficient *prima facie* evidence of such admissions. J. A. Rule 243.

14. TRANSMISSION OF INTEREST PENDENTE LITE.

Action not to abate by reason of marriage, age, etc., or death between verdict and judgment.   **620.** An action shall not become abated by reason of the marriage, death, or bankruptcy of any of the parties, if the cause of action survives or continues, and shall not become defective by the assignment, creation, or devolution of any estate or title *pendente lite.* And whether the cause of action survives or not, there shall be no abatement by reason of the death of either party between the verdict or finding of the issues of fact and the judgment, but judgment may in such case be entered notwithstanding the death. J. A. Rules 383, 601.

Assignment *pendente lite*   **621.** In case of an assignment, creation or devolution of any estate or title *pendente lite*, the action may be continued by or against the person to or upon whom such estate or title has come or devolved. J. A. Rule 384.

Order to add parties on change of interest how obtained.   **622.** Where by reason of marriage, death or bankruptcy, or any other event occurring after the commencement of an action and causing a change or transmission of interest or liability, or by reason of any person interested coming into existence after the commencement of the action, it becomes necessary or desirable that any person not already a party to the action should be made a party thereto, or that any person already a party thereto should be made a party thereto in another capacity, an order that the proceeding in the action shall be carried on between the continuing parties to the action and such new party, may be obtained on *præcipe*, upon an allegation of such change, or transmission of interest or liability' or of such person interested having come into existence. J. A. Rule 385'

Service of order.   **623.** An order so obtained shall, unless the Court or a Judge otherwise directs, be served upon the continuing party or parties to the action or their solicitors, and also upon each such new party (unless the person making the application be himself the only new party), and the order shall from the time of such service, subject nevertheless to the next 5 following Rules, be binding on the person served therewith. J. A. Rule 386.

Application to discharge order.   **624.** Where any person who is under no disability, or under no disability other than coverture, or being under any disability other than coverture, has a guardian *ad litem* in the action, shall be served with such order, such person may apply to the Court or a Judge to discharge or vary such order at any time within 14 days from the service thereof. J. A. Rule 387.

Indorsement on order.   **625.** Upon every copy of such order served, there shall be endorsed a memorandum in the form or to the effect set forth in Form 20 in the Appendix. J. A. Rule 388.

626. Where any person being under any disability other than cover- Application to
ture, and not having had a guardian *ad litem* appointed in the action, is discharge or-
served with any such order, such person may apply to the Court or a der by persons
Judge to discharge or vary the order, at any time within 14 days from bility.
the appointment of a guardian *ad litem* for such party, and until such
period of 14 days shall have expired the order shall have no force or
effect as against such last mentioned person. J. A. Rule 389.

627. Where the order is served out of Ontario, the party served is to Application to
have the same time to apply to discharge the order, as a defendant has to discharge
appear to a writ of summons so served ; but an application may be made served out of
for shortening the time. J. A. Rule 390. Ontario.

628. Where the Court or a Judge authorizes publication instead of Application in
service, the Court or Judge is at the same time to appoint such time for case of order
applying to discharge the order as seems proper. J. A. Rule 391. allowing ser-
vice by publi-
cation.

629. Where an action would but for these Rules have abated by reason Right of defen-
of the death of either party, and in which the proceedings may be dant in action
continued under these Rules, the defendant or person against whom the which may be
so continued.
action may be so continued, may apply on notice to compel the plaintiff,
or person entitled to proceed with the action, to proceed according to the
provisions of these Rules within such time as the Court or a Judge may
order or in default for an order dismissing the action or for payment of
the costs thereof or for such order as may be just. R. S. O. 1877, c. 50,
ss. 241, 242.

630. Wherever any judgment or order has been made for payment of Costs.
costs and the action or matter would, but for these Rules, become abated,
any person interested under the judgment or order may under these Rules
continue the proceedings and thereupon prosecute and enforce the judgment
or order. *See* R. S. O. 1877, c. 40, s. 102.

631. In case an action on a bill or note is brought against more than When execu-
one defendant, who must otherwise have been sued separately, and it tors of deceas-
happens that any defendant dies pending the action, an action may never- ed defendants
theless be brought against the executors or administrators of such deceased may be sued.
defendant. R. S. O. 1877, c. 50, s. 138.

15. Payment into Court in Satisfaction.

632. A defendant may, either before or at the time of delivering his When
defence, or afterwards by leave of the Court or a Judge, pay into Court defendant
a sum of money in satisfaction of the cause or a part of the cause of action, may pay in.
or one or more of the causes of action for which the plaintiff sues, and the
money when so paid in shall remain in Court subject to further order,
unless the plaintiff elects to take it out. But the payment of money into
Court shall not be deemed an admission of the cause of action in respect of
which it is so paid.

633. Payment into Court shall be signified in the defence and the To be signified
claim or cause of action in satisfaction of which the payment is made shall in defence.
be specified therein. Eng. order (1883), O. 22, R. 2.

634. If a defendant pays money into court before delivering his Or in notice.
defence, he shall serve upon the plaintiff a notice specifying both the fact
that he has paid in the money, and also the claim or cause of action in
respect of which the payment has been made. The notice may be in
the Form No. 21 in the Appendix, with such variations as circumstances
may require. Eng. order (1883), O. 22, R. 4.

635. If the plaintiff takes the money out of Court he shall take it in How plaintiff
satisfaction of the very cause of action for which it was paid in, and shall may take
upon applying therefor file and serve a memorandum acknowledging the money out.
cause for which he takes it out, which may be according to the Form
No. 22 in the Appendix, and shall be equivalent to a satisfaction piece.

Election.

636. The plaintiff shall make his election to take the money out of Court within four days after the day on which he receives notice of payment in if the payment is made before defence, and if the money is paid in with the defence he shall elect, either before replying or before the expiration of the time for replying, whichever first happens.

Taxing costs.

637. When the plaintiff takes out money in satisfaction of the entire cause of action he may tax his costs of the action and sign judgment therefor, unless the defendant pays them within forty-eight hours after taxation.

Consolidated actions

638. Where money is paid into Court in two or more actions which are consolidated, the money paid in and the costs in all the actions shall be dealt with in the same manner as in the action tried. Eng. order (1883), O. 22, R. 8.

When plaintiff may pay in.

639. A plaintiff may, in answer to a counter-claim, pay money into Court in satisfaction thereof, subject to the like conditions as to costs and otherwise as upon payment into Court by a defendant. Eng. order (1883), O. 22, R. 9.

Tender.

640. With a defence setting up a tender before action, the sum of money alleged to have been tendered must be brought into Court. Eng. order (1883), O. 22, R. 3.

16. DISCONTINUANCE.

Discontinuance.

641. The plaintiff may, at any time before receipt of any defendant's statement of defence, or after the receipt thereof before taking any other proceeding in the action (save any interlocutory application) by notice in writing, filed and served, wholly discontinue his action or withdraw any part or parts of his alleged cause of complaint ; and a defendant shall be entitled to the costs of the action, if wholly discontinued against him, or to the costs occasioned by the withdrawal of the matter withdrawn if not wholly discontinued.

(*a*) Such costs may be taxed upon production of the notice so served without any order, and if not paid within four days from taxation the defendant may, without any order, sign judgment therefor.

(*b*) Such discontinuance or withdrawal, as the case may be, shall not be a defence to any subsequent action.

(*c*) Save as in these Rules otherwise provided, it shall not be competent for the plaintiff to discontinue the action without leave of the Court or a Judge, but the Court or a Judge may, before, or at, or after the hearing or trial, upon such terms as to costs, and as to any other action against all or any of the defendants, and otherwise, as may seem fit, order the action to be discontinued, or any part of the alleged cause of complaint to be struck out. J. A. Rules 170, 170*b*, 172.

Withdrawal of defence.

642. A defendant may, with the leave of the Court or a Judge, but not otherwise, withdraw his defence or counterclaim, or both, or any part of either or both, upon such terms as may be imposed. J. A. Rule 170*c*.

17. COMPOUNDING PENAL ACTIONS.

Leave to compound penal actions.

643. Leave to compound a penal action shall not be given in cases where part of the penalty goes to the Crown, unless notice has been given to the proper officer, but in other cases it may. Rules T. T. 1856, 95.

Order for compounding.

644. The order for compounding any *qui tam* action shall express therein that the defendant thereby undertakes to pay the sum for which the Court has given him leave to compound such action. Rules T. T. 1856, 96.

Queen's proportion of composition.

645. Where leave is given to compound a penal action, the Queen's proportion of the composition shall be paid into the Accountant's Office, for the use of Her Majesty. Rules T. T. 1856, 97.

18. Dismissal of Actions.

646. If the plaintiff, being bound to deliver a statement of claim, does *Dismissal of* not deliver the same within the time allowed for that purpose, the defen- *action on* dant may, at the expiration of such time, apply to the Court or a Judge to *default.* dismiss the action with costs, for want of prosecution; and on the hearing of such application the Court or Judge may, if no statement of claim has been delivered, order the action to be dismissed accordingly, or may make such other order, on such terms as to the Court or Judge seems just.   J. A. Rule 203.

647. If the pleadings are closed six weeks before the commencement *When plaintiff* of any sittings of the High Court for which the plaintiff might give notice *does not give* of trial, and he does not give notice of trial therefor, the action may be *notice of trial.* dismissed for want of prosecution. *~~Incorporated~~ v Thompson 13 R.R. 267 / When within the ~~Jamieson v Murray~~ 13 P.R. 418 / ~~~~ ~~~~*

648. If a plaintiff refuses or neglects to attend at the time and place *Refusal to be* appointed for his examination, or fails to comply with any order for *examined.* discovery or production or inspection of documents, the defendant, in addition to his other remedies, may move to dismiss the action.   J. A. Rule 236; Chy. O. 145.

19. Transfer and Consolidation of Actions.

649. Actions may be transferred from one Division of the High Court *Transferring.* to another Division by order of the Presidents of such Divisions.   J. A. *actions.* Rule 392.

650. The Presidents of the Queen's Bench, Chancery and Common *Presidents of* Pleas Divisions shall, from time to time as occasion may require, meet *Divisions to* together and examine the list of motions, and other matters set down *make transfers* for argument in each Divisional Court of the High Court, and direct *equalize busi-* the transfer of such and so many of the said motions, and other mat- *ness.* ters from one Divisional Court to another as shall, as nearly as possible in their judgment, equalize the amount of business to be done by the said Courts. J. A. Rule 393.

(a) Where an order of transfer is made under the foregoing Rules, the *Transmission* proper officer of the Division to which the cause or matter was assigned, *of papers, etc.,* shall annex together all the pleadings and papers filed with him, and trans- *on order to* mit the same, together with the order of transference or a copy thereof, to *transfer.* such other office of the High Court as the order directs.   R. S. O. 1877, c. 49, s. 22; 44 V. c. 5, s. 26.

651. Where an order has been made for the administration of the *Transfer* assets of any testator or intestate, a Judge of any Division shall have power, *after admin-* without any further consent, to order the transfer to such Division of any *istration order* action pending in any other Division by or against the executors or administrators of the testator or intestate whose assets are being so administered.   J. A. Rule 394.

652. Actions ~~in any~~ Division ~~or Divisions~~ may be consolidated by order *Consolidation* of the Court or a Judge in the manner prior to "*The Ontario Judicature* *of actions.* *Act, 1881,*" in use in the Superior Courts of Common Law.   J. A. Rule 395.

20. Trial.

(i) General Rules.

653. There shall be no local venue for the trial of any action except an *Venue* action of ejectment, but the plaintiff shall in his statement of claim name *abolished.* the county town in which he proposes that the action should be tried, and the action shall, unless a Judge otherwise orders, be tried in the place so named. Any order of a Judge, as to the place of trial, may be discharged or varied by a Divisional Court of the High Court. J. A. Rule 254.

Court may alter place of trial in ejectment actions.   (a) On the application of either party, and on grounds shown by affidavit, the Court or a Judge may order that the trial of an action of ejectment shall take place at any other place than that named in the statement of claim. R. S. O. 1877, c. 51, s. 23.

Notice of trial.   **654.** After the close of the pleadings either party may give notice of trial for the next sitting of the Court which shall be not less than ten days thereafter for the place so named or ordered. J. A. Rule 255.

Trial of different questions in different modes.   **655.** Subject to the provisions of the Judicature Act and of the preceding Rules, the Court or a Judge may in any action at any time or from time to time order that different questions of fact arising therein be tried by different modes, or that one or more questions of fact be tried before the others, and may appoint the place or places for such trial or trials, and in all cases may order that one or more issues of fact be tried before any other or others. J. A. Rule 256.

Trial by jury.   **656.** Every trial of any question or issue of fact by a jury shall be held before a single Judge, unless such trial is specially ordered to be held before two or more Judges. J. A. Rule 257.

Trials at bar on the part of suitors.   **657.** The plaintiff and the defendant respectively, in any action in the High Court, may, in the Divisional Court sittings of the High Court next after issue joined, apply to the Court for a trial at bar, and the Court may, in its discretion, upon hearing the parties, grant or refuse the same. R. S. O. 1877, c. 39, s. 33.

On the part of the Crown.   **658.** In all cases in which the Crown may be actually or immediately interested, a trial at bar may be had as of right upon, and shall be regulated and governed by, the same principles as in similar cases in England. R. S. O. 1877, c. 39, s. 34.

When trial to be had.   **659.** In case any trial at bar is directed, the Judges attached to the Division of the High Court in which the action has been brought, may appoint such day or days for the trial thereof as they may think fit. R. S. O. 1877, c. 39, s. 35.

Form of notice of trial.   **660.** Notice of trial shall state whether it is for the trial of the action or of issues therein ; and the place and day for which it is to be entered for trial, and shall be given before entering the action for trial. It may be in the Form No. 27 in the Appendix, with such variations as circumstances may require. J. A. Rules 258, 260.

10 days notice.   **661.** Ten days' notice of trial shall be given, unless the party to whom it is given has consented to take short notice of trial ; and shall be sufficient in all cases, unless otherwise ordered by the Court or a Judge. Short notice of trial shall be 5 days' notice. J. A. Rule 259.

Short notice 5 days.

~~amended~~ **Notice of** *le 1464* **trial at Bar.**   **662.** Notice of a trial at bar shall be given to the ~~Registrar~~ *one of the Reg* of the Court before giving notice of trial to the party. Rules T. T. 1856, 37.

Entry for trial.   **663.** After notice of trial is given, either party may enter the action for trial. If both parties enter the action for trial, it shall be tried in the order of the plaintiff's entry. J. A. Rule 261.

Record.   **664.** On the day before the day for holding the Court at which the action is to be tried, the party entering the action for trial shall deliver to the proper officer one copy of the whole of the pleadings in the action for the use of the Judge at the trial, such copy to be certified as a true copy *amended* by the officer having charge of the pleadings filed, and to be called the *Rule 1465* Record. J. A. Rule 262.

665. Actions shall be entered for trial not later than the third day next Time of entry
before the first day of the sittings ; but the Judge may permit any for trial.
action to be entered after the time above limited, if upon facts disclosed
on affidavit, or on the consent of both parties, he sees fit to do so. J. A.
Rule 264.

666. Any action which is not to be tried by a jury, may be entered for Non-jury
trial at any Sittings appointed for the place named for the trial of such ac- actions.
tion. See J. A. Rule 590. *See Rule 1278* -

667. If both parties enter the action for trial at the same Sittings it Two entries.
shall be tried in the order of the plaintiff's entry. See J. A. Rule 591.

Add **668.** All actions to be tried by a jury, shall be entered for trial at the Jury actions.
+67 Assizes holden at the place named for trial of such action without an
order and without transferring such action to any other Division. J. A.
Rule 592.

669. The party entering an action for trial shall endorse on the copy Separate lists
of the pleadings delivered as aforesaid, whether the matter for trial is an of defended
assessment of damages, or an undefended issue, or a defended issue ; and and undefend-
the officer with whom the action is so entered shall make two lists, and ed issues.
enter each action in one of the said lists, in the order in which the actions
are entered with him ; and in the first list he shall enter all the assess-
ments and undefended issues, and in the second list all defended issues,
and the Judge at the trial may call on the actions in the first list at such
time and times as he finds most convenient for disposing of the business.
J. A. Rule 267.

670. Where an action has been entered for trial, it may be withdrawn by Withdrawal
either the plaintiff or the defendant, upon producing to the proper officer a of record by
consent in writing, signed by the parties, but not otherwise except by order. consent.
J. A. Rule 171.

RULE OF COURT. ... or disposed of after being once entered for trial Actions not
Ilula has been substituted for thereof given for any subsequent Court with- tried.
671 *by an order of the Supreme* her fee. See C. L. Rules 4th Dec. 1875, 2, 3.
Judicature for Ontario, passed on
ast :—
not tried or disposed of after being called on for trial, the plaintiff appears, and Non-appear-
for trial shall remain for trial ar, then the plaintiff may prove his claim, so ance of
the provisions of Rule 670, but shall upon him. J. A. Rule 268. defendant.
and at any subsequent sittings unless
a fresh notice of trial be given for
by one of the parties."
673. If, when an action is called on for trial, the defendant appears, Non-appear-
and the plaintiff does not appear, the defendant, if he has no counter- ance of
claim, shall be entitled to judgment dismissing the action, but if he has a plaintiff.
counter-claim he may prove such claim so far as the burden of proof lies
upon him. J. A. Rule 269.

674. The Judge at the trial shall at the request of either party cause Witnesses may
the witnesses to be removed from the Court during the trial, and also be put out of
the parties to the suit tendering themselves as witnesses, if the Judge Court.
deems necessary ; or he may instead require the party intending to give
evidence for himself to be examined before his other witnesses ; and
any such witness who returns to the Court without leave, shall be liable
to be punished in such manner as to the said Judge may seem proper ;
and the Judge may in his discretion exclude the testimony of any witness
who returns to the Court without leave of the Judge. R. S. O. 1877,
c. 50, s. 260.

675. At the trial, the addresses to the jury shall be regulated How address-
as follows :—the party who begins, or his counsel, in the event es of counsel
of his opponent not announcing at the close of the case of the party who to jury regu-
begins, his intention to adduce evidence, shall be allowed to address the lated.

jury a second time at the close of the case, for the purpose of summing up the evidence ; and the party on the other side, or his counsel, shall then be allowed to open his case, and also to sum up the evidence (if any). The right to reply shall be the same as at present. R. S. O. 1877, c. 50, s. 261.

Evidence omitted by accident or mistake, how supplied.

676. Where, through accident or mistake or other cause, a party omits or fails to prove some fact material to his case, the Judge may proceed with the trial, subject to such fact being afterwards proved at such time, and subject to such terms and conditions as to costs and otherwise, as the Judge shall direct ; and, if the case is being tried by a jury, the Judge may direct the jury to find a verdict as if such fact had been proved, and the verdict shall take effect on such fact being afterwards proved as directed ; and if not so proved, judgment is to be entered for the opposite party unless the Court or a Judge otherwise directs.   This Rule shall not apply to an action for libel. J. A. Rule 271.

Trial of equitable issues.

677. Where in any action equitable issues are raised by the pleadings, they shall be heard and tried, and the assessment or enquiry of damages, if any, incidental thereto, shall be assessed and enquired of by the Court or a Judge without the intervention of a jury ; but it shall be competent for the Court or Judge, upon the application of either party, supported by sufficient reasons, to order such issues to be tried or damages assessed by a jury. R. S. O. 1877, c. 50, s. 257.

Legal and equitable issues.

678. Where in any action or other proceeding at law both legal and equitable issues are raised, such issues shall be tried at the same time, unless the Court or a Judge, or the Judge presiding at the trial, otherwise directs. R. S. O. 1877, c. 50, s. 258.

Costs of protest recoverable.

679. In an action brought to recover the amount of any bill, draft, order or promissory note, and the damages and interest, the expenses of noting and protesting, and all other charges and postages incurred thereon, it shall not be necessary to specially claim such damages, interest, expenses and charges, but the same shall be allowed to the plaintiff at any trial, assessment of damages or reference, as if the same had been specially claimed. R. S. O. 1877, c. 50, s. 144.

Assessment of damages.

680. Damages in respect of any continuing cause of action shall be assessed down to the time of the assessment. Eng. R. 1883, 482.

Adjournment of trial.

681. The Judge if he thinks it expedient for the interest of justice, may postpone or adjourn the trial for such time, and upon such terms, if any, as he shall think fit. J. A. Rule 272.

Judge may direct entry of judgment ; or reserve judgment.

682. Upon the trial of an action, the Judge may, at or after the trial, direct that judgment be signed and entered for any or either party, or adjourn the case for further consideration. J. A. Rule 273.

Exhibits at trial, how to be marked.

amended
Rule 14 68

683. Exhibits put in at the trial are to be marked thus : " In the High Court of Justice—Div. [*short title*]. This exhibit (the property of   ,) is produced by the plaintiff (*or* defendant C., *as the case may be,*) this   day of   18
A. B.," (*Registrar, Deputy Clerk, Deputy or Local Registrar*). Chy. O. 177.

Evidence oral or document- ary cannot be withdrawn without leave.

amended
No 14 69

684. Where a party or witness is examined at the trial or a document is put in as evidence and marked by the Registrar, Deputy Clerk, Deputy or Local Registrar, the deposition of the party, or witness so examined, or the document so put in, is not to be withdrawn as evidence without the leave of the Court. Chy. O. 178.

685. Whoro judgment is reserved, the exhibits used at the trial shall be deposited with the Registrar, Deputy Clerk, Deputy or Local Registrar, for the use of the Court and shall not be delivered out without order or consent of parties. *See* Chy. O. 179.

Where judgment reserved; exhibits to be left with Registrar, etc.

686. Where, upon the trial of an action, it appears that the same cannot conveniently proceed by reason of the solicitor for any party having neglected to attend personally or by some person in his behalf, or having omitted to deliver any paper necessary for the use of the Court, and which according to its practice ought to have been delivered, such solicitor shall personally pay to the parties such costs as the Court thinks fit to award. Chy. O. 182.

When action cannot proceed in consequence of absence of solicitor, he may be ordered to pay costs.

687. The Registrar, Clerk of Assize or other officer present at the trial shall enter all such findings of fact as the Judge may at the trial direct to be entered, and the directions, if any, of the Judge as to judgment, and the certificates, if any, granted by the Judge, such entry to be made in a book to be kept for the purpose, and also to be indorsed on the Record. J. A. Rule 274.

By whom entries of findings to be made.

688. The said indorsement, or the certificate of the said officer or the certificate of the Judge, shall be a sufficient authority to the proper officer for signing judgments to sign judgment accordingly. The certificate may be in the Form No. 213 in the Appendix. J. A. Rule 275.

Certificate of Judge or officer.

689. The Registrar, Clerk of Assize or other officer present at the trial shall, after judgment has been given, or, in jury cases, after the time for the moving for a new trial has expired, deliver to the solicitor of the party entitled thereto any Record in their custody, upon getting a receipt for the same. R. S. O. 1877, c. 50, s. 280.

When and how Deputy Clerks shall deliver record or exhibits to attorney or parties.

(ii) *Trial of High Court cases in County Court and Vice Versa.*

690. In any of the cases in sections 96 and 97 of *The Judicature Act* the notice of trial or assessment of damages shall state that the cause will be tried, or the damages assessed at the Sittings of the High Court or County Court, according to the fact. R. S. O. 1877, c. 49, s. 33.

Notice of trial etc., in such cases.

691. Nothing herein contained shall prevent a Judge of the Court in which the action is brought, or, after the action is entered for trial or assessment, the Judge before whom the trial or assessment is intended to be had, from entertaining applications to postpone the trial or assessment. R. S. O. 1877, c. 49, s. 34.

Trials may be postponed

692. Where judgment is not reserved, and subject in that case to Rules made, and subject in all cases to rules to be made, judgment in any of the said cases may be entered immediately, unless the Judge who tried the cause certifies on the record, under his hand, that the case is one which, in his opinion, should stand to abide the result of a motion that may be made therein in the Divisional Court, or unless a Judge of the High Court otherwise orders. R. S. O. 1877, c. 49, s. 35.

Immediate judgment.

693. Any motion to be made, in respect to the trial, judgment, verdict or assessment of damages in a High Court case tried or assessed at the Sittings of any County Court shall be made in the High Court. R. S. O. 1877, c. 49, s. 36.

Motions against verdict in High Court cases tried in County Courts.

694. Any motion to be made in respect to the trial, judgment, verdict or assessment of damages in any County Court case had, tried or assessed at any Sittings of the High Court, shall be made, heard and determined at the sitting of such Divisional Court of the High Court, as the party moving or applying elects, and according to the practice of the High Court ; and any order made in such cause by such Court shall be final, and shall not be subject to appeal to the Court of Appeal. R. S. O. 1877, c. 49, s. 37.

Motion against verdict, etc., in County Court cases tried at High Court Sittings.

Powers of Judge as to County Court causes tried before him.

695. In any action in a County Court entered for trial at any Sittings of the High Court, the Judge presiding at the Sittings shall have the same powers as to amendment of the pleadings and proceedings, putting off the trial, reference, making the cause a *remanet*, and otherwise dealing with the cause and proceedings therein, as if the action had been commenced in the High Court. R. S. O. 1877, c. 49, s. 38.

When such Judge marks record as a remanet, etc., it may be tried at subsequent sitting or Assizes.

696. Whenever the said Judge endorses on the certified copy of pleading in any such action the word *"Remanet,"* and adds any words to the effect following : *"And the within cause may be entered and tried at any County Court, or sittings of the High Court,"* such cause may without payment of any further fee for entering the case be entered at any subsequent Sittings of the County Court, or Sittings of the High Court, for which notice of trial may be given, and the case may be tried and disposed of in the same way as any other case entered at such Sittings. R. S. O. 1877, c. 49, s. 39.

Certified copy of notes of cases.

amended
Rule 1474

697. On the application of any party, the County Court Clerk shall, at the cost of the party, forward to the Registrar at Toronto, of such Division of the High Court as the party designates, a certified copy of the Judge's notes of the trial, or assessment, together with the Record and the exhibits, to enable the High Court properly to dispose of any application made, or to be made, in or respecting such cases. R. S. O. 1877, c. 49, s. 42.

(iii) *Vexatious Defences in Actions to Recover Land.*

Vexatious defence without merits.

698. It being desirable, in actions to recover land brought against persons who are merely intruders, not to prevent plaintiffs from recovering land of which they have just claim on account of some want of technical form in their title, or some imperfection not affecting the merits of the case, and of which mere strangers to the title, having no claim or colour of legal claim to the possession, should not be permitted to take advantage ; the plaintiff or his solicitor, in any action to recover land, may serve a notice upon the defendant or his solicitor in words or to the effect following : *"Take notice that I claim the premises for which this action is brought as the bona fide purchaser thereof, from A.B. (or as the case may be),* and that you will be required to show upon the trial of this cause what legal right you have to the possession of the premises." R. S. O. 1877, c. 51, s. 26.

Formal defects in plaintiff's title.

699. If, upon the trial of such action, the evidence of title given by the plaintiff satisfies the Court (and the Jury, if the case is tried by a Jury) that he is entitled in justice to be regarded as the proprietor of the land or is entitled to the immediate possession thereof for any term of years, but that he cannot show a perfect legal title by reason of some want of legal form in some instrument produced, or by reason of the defective registration of some will or instrument produced, or from any cause not within the power of the plaintiff to remedy by using due diligence, the Judge, or the Jury, under the direction of the Court, may find a verdict for the plaintiff, unless the defendant or his counsel, upon being required by the other party so to do, gives such evidence of title as shows that he is the person legally entitled, or that he *bona fide* claims to be the person legally entitled to the land, by reason of the defect in the title of the plaintiff, or that he holds, or *bona fide* claims to hold, under the person so entitled. R. S. O. 1877, c. 51, s. 27.

Verdict to be endorsed as endered under rules.

700. Where a verdict or judgment is rendered or given under the authority of the foregoing provision, it shall be indorsed as rendered or given under Rules 698 and 699, and it shall be stated in the judgment to have been so given, and in any action thereafter brought for the *mesne* profits, such judgment shall not be evidence to entitle the plaintiff to recover. R. S. O. 1877, c. 51, s. 28.

(iv) *Inspection of Property.*

701. It shall be lawful for any Judge, by whom any cause or matter Judge may may be heard or tried with or without a jury, or before whom any cause or inspect. matter may be brought by way of appeal, to inspect any property or thing concerning which any question may arise therein. Eng. R. 1883, 660.

702. Either party in an action may apply to the Court or a Judge for Inspection of an order for the inspection by the jury or by himself or by his witnesses, real or person-of any real or personal property, the inspection of which may be material al property by to the proper determination of the question in dispute, and the Court or a witnesses. Judge may make such order upon such terms as to costs and other-wise, as the Court or Judge may think fit. R. S. O. 1877, c. 50, s. 168.

703. Upon any application for a view by a jury, there shall be an Party requir-affidavit stating the place at which the view is to be made, and the ing view, to distance thereof from the Sheriff's office. Unless the Court or Judge Sheriff sum to otherwise orders, the party obtaining the order for the view shall deposit pay expenses. with the Sheriff the sum of $25 in case of a common jury, and $34 in case of a special jury, if such distance does not exceed 5 miles ; and $31 in case of a common jury, and $43 in case of a special jury, if the distance be above 5 miles ; and if such sum shall be more than sufficient to pay the expenses of the view, the surplus shall forthwith be returned to the party who obtained the view, or his solicitor, and if such sum shall not be sufficient to pay such expenses, the deficiency shall forthwith be paid by such party or his solicitor to the Sheriff. Rules T. T., 1856, 39.

CHAPTER VII.

JUDGMENTS—MOTIONS FOR JUDGMENT, ETC.

1. DEFAULT OF APPEARANCE.

(i) *Generally.*

Proceedings in default of appearance. **704.** Where any defendant fails to appear to a writ of summons and the plaintiff is desirous of proceeding upon default of appearance he shall, before taking such proceeding upon default, file an affidavit of service, or of notice in lieu of service, or the undertaking of the defendant's solicitor accepting service and agreeing to enter an appearance, with an affidavit verifying the undertaking filed, as the case may be. J. A. Rule 71.

Where writ specially indorsed. **705.** In case of non-appearance by the defendant where the writ of summons is specially indorsed under Rule 245, the plaintiff may sign final judgment for any, sum not exceeding the sum indorsed on the writ, together with interest at the rate specified, if any, to the date of the judgment, and a sum for costs, and the plaintiff may forthwith issue execution upon such judgment ; but it shall be lawful for the Court or a Judge to set aside or vary such judgment upon such terms as may seem just. J. A. Rule 72.

Where several defendants. **706.** Where there are several defendants to a writ specially indorsed for a debt or liquidated demand in money under Rule 245, and one or more of the defendants appear to the writ and others of them do not appear, the plaintiff may enter final judgment against such as have not appeared, and may issue execution upon such judgment, without prejudice to his right to proceed with his action against such as have appeared. J. A. Rule 73.

Where writ not specially indorsed. **707.** Where the defendant fails to appear to the writ of summons and the writ is not specially indorsed, but the plaintiff's claim is for a debt or liquidated demand only, no statement of claim need afterwards be delivered, but the plaintiff may file an affidavit of service of the summons, or of notice in lieu of service, as the case may be, and file and serve a statement of the particulars of his claim in respect of the causes of action stated in the indorsement upon the writ, and may, after the expiration of eight days, enter final judgment for the amount shewn thereby, and costs to be taxed, provided that the amount shall not be more than the sum indorsed upon the writ, besides costs. J. A. Rule 74.

708. Where the defendant fails to appear to the writ of summons and Where claim the plaintiff's claim is not for a debt or liquidated demand only, but for for detention detention of goods and pecuniary damages, or either of them, no state- of goods and ment of claim need be delivered, but interlocutory judgment may be pecuniary damages or entered, and the value of the goods and the damages, or the damages either of them. only, as the case may be, in respect of the causes of action disclosed by the indorsement on the writ of summons shall be assessed at a sitting of the High Court for trials, or at the County Court of the County in which the action is brought. J. A. Rule 75.

709. Where there are several defendants, of whom one or more appear to Several the writ, and another, or others of them fail to appear, the plaintiff may defendants in sign interlocutory judgment against the defendant or defendants so action for failing to appear, and the value of the damages, or either damages. of them, as the case may be, may be assessed, as against the defendant or defendants suffering judgment by default, at the same time as the trial of the action or issue therein against the other defendant or defendants, unless the Court or a Judge shall otherwise direct. Eng. Rule, 1883, 106. *New.*

710 The Court or a Judge may order that instead of a trial or assess- Assessment of ment the value and amount of damages, or either of them, shall be ascer- damages. tained in any way which the Court or a Judge may direct. Eng. Rule, 1883, 106. *New.*

711. When the writ is indorsed with a claim for detention of goods and Damages and pecuniary damages, or either of them, and is further specially indorsed for a liquidated liquidated demand under rule 245 and any defendant fails to appear to demand. the writ, the plaintiff may enter final judgment for the debt or liquidated demand, interest and costs against the defendant or defendants failing to appear, and interlocutory judgment for the value of the goods and the damages, or the damages only, as the case may be, and proceed as men- tioned in such of the preceding rules as may be applicable. Eng. Rule, 1883, 107. *New.*

712. Notwithstanding anything in the Rules contained, the provisions Prov i of the Act of the Parliament of Great Britain passed in the Session ... Act 8 in the eighth and ninth year of the reign of King William the Third, iii. c. 1 entitled *An Act for the better preventing frivolous and vexatious suits*, as to main i n the assignment or suggestion of breaches, or as to judgment, shall con- tinue in force in Ontario. R. S. O. 1877, c. 50, s. 151. •

(ii) *Dower.*

713. In case of non-appearance by the defendant in an action for Action for dower, the plaintiff may enter judgment of seisin forthwith, and sue out dower, Judg- a writ of assignment of dower, but she shall not be entitled to tax or ment of seisin. recover the costs of suit or of entering such judgment against the defend- Execution. Costs. ant, unless the Court or a Judge so orders. R. S. O. 1877, c. 55, s. 15.

(*a*)In case the plaintiff claims arrears of dower or damages for detention of her dower, neither the entry of a judgment of seisin nor the taking of proceedings for the assignment of her dower thereunder, shall prevent her from proceeding with the action for the recovery of such arrears or dam- ages. *New.*

(iii) *Recovery of Land.*

714. In case no appearance is entered in an action for the recovery Action for of land, other than an action for dower, within the time limited for appea- land. rance, or if an appearance is entered but the defence is limited to part only, the plaintiff shall be at liberty to enter a judgment that the person whose title is asserted in the writ shall recover possession of the land, or of the part thereof to which the defence does not apply. J. A. Rule 76.

715. Where the plaintiff has indorsed a claim for mesne profits, arrears Assessment of of rent, or damages for breach of contract, upon a writ for the recovery of damages in ac- tion for land.

land, he may enter judgment as in the last preceding Rule mentioned, for the land ; and may proceed as in the other preceding Rules as to such other claim so indorsed.   J. A. Rule 77.

Costs where adverse possession. **716.** In case no appearance is entered in an action for recovery of land, other than an action of dower, and in case the plaintiff files the writ, and an affidavit showing that the writ has been properly served, and an affidavit that the party so served was at the time of the issue of the writ in actual adverse possession of the land, or instead of such affidavits obtains and files an order of the Court or a Judge allowing him to sign judgment as well for his costs as for recovery of possession of the land, the plaintiff may at once sign judgment that the person whose title is asserted in the writ shall recover and have possession of the land, and also his costs (to be taxed in the ordinary way), and the plaintiff may forthwith issue execution thereupon ; and the judgment may be in the words or to the effect of Form No. 162 in the Appendix, with the words following or words to the same effect added thereto, namely : "*and do also recover against the said C. D.* (the defendant) §   *for his cost of suit.*"   R. S. O. 1877, c. 51, s. 20 (2).

(iv) *Mortgage Actions.*

Judgment for foreclosure, or sale, where infants are defendants may be made in Chambers. **717.** In an ordinary action for redemption, foreclosure or sale where the defendants, or some of the defendants are infants and no defence is set up the action is not to be set down to be heard in Court by way of motion for judgment ; but after the statements of defence are filed, or after the time for filing the same has expired, the plaintiff is to file affidavits of the due execution of the mortgage, and of such other facts and circumstances as entitle him to a judgment and is to apply for the judgment in Chambers, upon notice to the guardian *ad litem* of the infants and the other defendants' solicitor, if any.   Chy. O. 434, 645, 646.

Judgment, when to be granted on *præcipe.* **718.** Where the defendant does not appear, or by his statement of defence admits the execution of the mortgage and other facts, if any, entitling the plaintiff to a judgment, or where the defendant disclaims any interest in the mortgaged premises, or where no statement of defence or demurrer is delivered, the plaintiff is, on *præcipe* to the Registrar, or Deputy or Local Registrar, or Deputy Clerk of the Crown in whose office the appearance of the defendant was required to be entered, to be entitled to judgment including, where prayed for, the relief for which a claim may be indorsed upon the writ under Rule 248.

amended Rule 1476

(*a*) The reference in such cases, when required by the practice, shall be to the Master in Ordinary or a Local Master.

(*b*) Such a judgment may be granted, notwithstanding that the defendant has been served by publication, or otherwise, or is a corporation ; provided always that where the writ has not been personally served, the claim of the plaintiff shall be duly verified by affidavit.

(*c*) This Rule shall apply to actions for redemption as well as to actions for foreclosure or sale. Chy. O. 435, 646, 648. J. A. Rules 78, 79, 502, 520.

.2. DEFAULT OF PLEADING.

Judgment on defendant's default in claim for debt. **719.** If the plaintiff's claim be only for a debt or liquidated demand, and the defendant does not, within the time allowed for that purpose, deliver a defence or demurrer, the plaintiff may, at the expiration of such time, enter final judgment for the amount claimed, with costs. J. A. Rule 204.

Where several defendants. **720.** Where in any such action as in the last preceding Rule mentioned there are several defendants, if one of them makes default as mentioned in the last preceding Rule, the plaintiff may enter final judgment against the defendant so making default and issue execution upon such judgment without prejudice to his right to proceed with his action against the other defendants.   J. A. Rule 205.

721. If the plaintiff's claim be for detention of goods and pecuniary damages, or either of them, and the defendant makes default as mentioned in Rule 719, the plaintiff may enter an interlocutory judgment against the defendant, and the value of the goods, and the damages, or the damages only, as the case may be, shall be assessed as hitherto. But the Court or a Judge may order that the value and amount of damages, or either of them, shall be ascertained in any other way in which any question arising in an action may be tried. J. A. Rule 206.

Interlocutory judgment on default in claim for damages.

722. Where in any such action as in Rule 721 mentioned there are several defendants, if one of them makes default as mentioned in Rule 719, the plaintiff may enter an interlocutory judgment against the defendant so making default, and proceed with his action against the others. And in such case, damages against the defendant making default shall be assessed at the same time with the trial of the action or issues therein against the other defendants, unless the Court or a Judge otherwise directs. J. A. Rule 207.

Where several defendants.

723. If the plaintiff's claim be for a debt or liquidated demand, and also for detention of goods and pecuniary damages, or pecuniary damages only, and the defendant makes default as mentioned in Rule 719, the plaintiff may enter final judgment for the debt or liquidated demand, and also enter interlocutory judgment for the value of the goods and the damages, or the damages only, as the case may be, and proceed as mentioned in Rule 721. J. A. Rule 208.

Where debt and damages claimed.

724. In an action for the recovery of land, if the defendant makes default as mentioned in Rule 719, the plaintiff may enter a judgment that the person whose title is asserted in the writ of summons shall recover possession of the land, with his costs. J. A. Rule 209

Default by defendant in action for land.

725. Where the plaintiff has indorsed a claim for mesne profits, arrears of rent, or double value in respect of the premises claimed, or any part of them, or damages for breach of contract, or wrong or injury to the premises claimed, upon a writ for the recovery of land, if the defendant makes default as mentioned in Rule 719, or if there be more than one defendant, and some or one of the defendants make such default, the plaintiff may enter judgment against the defaulting defendant or defendants, and proceed as mentioned in Rules 721 and 722. J. A. Rule 210.

Where claim for land and damages.

726. Where the action is in respect of a mortgage, and the plaintiff claims foreclosure, or sale, or redemption, and an appearance has been entered, but default has been made in delivering a defence or demurrer, the plaintiff shall be entitled to a judgment or order on *præcipe*, as provided in Rule 718. J. A. Rule 520.

Judgment in mortgage actions.

727. In all other actions than those in the six preceding Rules mentioned, if the defendant makes default in delivering a defence or demurrer, the plaintiff may set down the action on motion for judgment, and such judgment shall be given as upon the statement of claim the Court shall consider the plaintiff to be entitled to. J. A. Rule 211.

Other actions.

728. Where, in any such action as mentioned in the last preceding Rule, there are several defendants, then, if one of the defendants makes such default as aforesaid, the plaintiff may either set down the action at once on motion for judgment against the defendant so making default, or may set it down against him at the time when it is entered for trial or set down on motion for judgment against the other defendants. J. A. Rule 212.

Where several defendants, and one makes default.

729. In any case in which issues arise other than between plaintiff and defendant, if any party to any such issue makes default in delivering any pleading, the opposite party may apply to the Court or a Judge for such judgment, if any, as upon the pleadings he may appear to be entitled to. And the Court may order judgment to be entered accordingly, or may make such other order as may be necessary to do complete justice between the parties. J. A. Rule 213.

In case of issues between parties other than plaintiff and defendant.

3. CONFESSION OF ACTION OR JUDGMENT.

(i) *Generally.*

Defendants may confess action to recover land as to the whole or part of the property.
730. A sole defendant or all the defendants in an action for the recovery of land, may confess the action as to the whole or a part of the property by giving to the plaintiff a notice entitled in the Court and cause, signed by the defendant or defendants, and the signature attested by his or their solicitor and thereupon the plaintiff may forthwith sign judgment and issue execution, for the recovery of possession and costs, in the words or to the effect of Form No. 164 in the Appendix. R. S. O. 1877, c. 51, s. 52.

And so may one of several defendants defending for a part for which others do not defend.
731. In case one of several defendants who defends separately for a portion of the property for which the other defendant or defendants do not defend, desires to confess the plaintiff's title to such portion, he may give a like notice to the plaintiff, and thereupon the plaintiff may forthwith sign judgment and issue execution for the recovery of possession of such portion of the property, and for the costs occasioned by the defence relating to the same, and the action may proceed as to the residue. R. S. O. 1877, c. 51, s. 53.

And if others defend as to the same part.
732. In case one of several defendants who defends separately in respect of property for which other defendants also defend, desires to confess the plaintiff's title, he may give a like notice thereof, and thereupon the plaintiff may sign judgment against such defendant for the costs occasioned by his defence, and may proceed in the action against the other defendants to judgment and execution. R. S. O. 1877, c. 51, s. 54.

As to judgment on *cognovits*.
733. Final judgment upon a *cognovit actionem* or warrant of attorney to confess judgment given or executed before the suing out of any process, may be entered in any Division of the High Court, and in like manner and under like circumstances, final judgment may be entered on a *cognovit actionem* or warrant of attorney to confess judgment for an amount not exceeding $400, in any County Court, unless some particular office or some particular County Court for that purpose is expressly stated in the *cognovit* or warrant. R. S. O. 1877, c. 50, s. 296.

Leave to enter judgment on *cognovit*, when to be obtained.
734. Leave to enter up judgment upon any *cognovit* or warrant of attorney above 1, and under 10 years old, is to be obtained by order of a Judge, made *ex parte*, and if 10 years old or more, by motion upon notice. Rules T. T. 1856, 27.

Confessions and *cognovits* to be registered.
735. No confession of judgment or *cognovit actionem* shall be valid or effectual to support any judgment or writ of execution, unless within 1 month after the same has been given, the same, or a sworn copy thereof, is filed of record in the proper office of the Court in the County in which the person giving such confession of judgment or *cognovit actionem* resides ; and a book shall be kept in every such office, to be called the Cognovit Book, in which shall be entered the names of the plaintiff and defendant in every such confession or cognovit, the amount of the true debt or arrangement secured thereby, the time when judgment may be entered and execution issued thereon, and the day when such confession or cognovit, or copy thereof, is filed in the said office ; and such book shall be open to inspection by any person during office hours, on the payment of a fee of 20 cents. R. S. O. 1877, c 50, s. 297.

Cognovit to be executed in presence of solicitor.
736. No warrant of attorney to confess judgment in any action, or *cognovit actionem*, given by any person, shall be of any force, unless there shall be present some solicitor on behalf of such person expressly named by him, and attending at his request, to inform him of the nature and effect of such warrant or *cognovit*, before the same is executed, which

solicitor shall subscribe his name as a witness to the due execution thereof, and thereby declare himself to be solicitor for the person executing the same, and state that he subscribes as such solicitor, and in the affidavit of execution, the attendance of such solicitor, and the fact of his being a subscribing witness, shall be plainly stated, which affidavit and the warrant of attorney, or *cognovit*, shall be filed at the time of entering judgment thereon. Rules T. T. 1856, 26.

737. Every person who prepares any *cognovit* or warrant of attorney to confess judgment, which is to be subject to any defeasance, shall cause such defeasance to be written on the same paper or parchment on which the *cognovit* or warrant is written, or cause a memorandum in writing to be made on such *cognovit* or warrant containing the substance or effect of such defeasance. Rules T. T. 1856, 28.

Defeasance to which any cognovit is subject to be written on same paper.

(ii) *Interim Alimony.*

738. In an alimony action, the defendant may, at any time before the statement of defence is due, give notice in writing that he submits to pay the interim alimony, and costs, as demanded by the plaintiff in the indorsement on the writ; and in that case no order is to be taken out until there has been a default in payment; and in case of default, affidavits being filed verifying the indorsement and notice and the default, the order is to be issued on praecipe. Chy. O. 490. See J. A. App. (A.)8.

Defendant may notify plaintiff that he submits to pay interim alimony claimed.

4. LEAVE TO SIGN JUDGMENT.

739. Where the defendant appears to a writ of summons specially indorsed, under Rule 245, and the plaintiff is not entitled to a judgment or order, under the preceding Rules he may, on an affidavit made by himself, or by any other person who can swear positively to the debt or cause of action, verifying the cause of action, and stating that in his belief there is no defence to the action, serve the defendant with a notice of motion to shew cause before the Court or a Judge why the plaintiff should not be at liberty to sign final judgment for the amount so indorsed, together with interest, if any, or for the recovery of the land with or without rent or *mesne* profits as the case may be, and costs. A copy of the affidavit shall accompany the notice of motion. The Court or a Judge may thereupon, unless the defendant, by affidavit or otherwise, satisfies the Court or a Judge that he has a good defence to the action on the merits, or discloses such facts as may be deemed sufficient to entitle him to defend the action, make an order empowering the plaintiff to sign judgment accordingly. J. A. Rule 80.

Leave to sign final judgment.

740. The defendant may shew cause against such application by affidavit, or by offering to bring into Court the sum indorsed on the writ. In such affidavit he shall state whether the defence he alleges goes to the whole or to part only, and if so, to what part, of the plaintiff's claim. And the Judge may, if he thinks fit, order the defendant to attend and be examined upon oath; or to produce any books or documents or copies of or extracts therefrom. J. A. Rule 82.

How defendant to show cause.

741. In any case if it appears that the defence set up by the defendant applies only to a part of the plaintiff's claim, or that any part of his claim is admitted to be due, the plaintiff shall have judgment forthwith for such part of his claim as the defence does not apply to, or as is admitted to be due, subject to such terms, if any, as to suspending execution, or the payment of any amount levied or any part thereof into Court by the sheriff, the taxation of costs, or otherwise as the Judge may think fit. And the defendant may be allowed to defend as to the residue of the plaintiff's claim. J. A. Rule 83.

Defence as to part.

7

Where several defendants. **742.** If it appears to the Judge that any defendant has a good defence to the action, or ought to be permitted to defend the action, and that any other defendant has not such defence and ought not to be permitted to defend, the former may be permitted to defend, and the plaintiff shall be entitled to enter final judgment against the latter, and may issue execution upon such judgment without prejudice to his right to proceed with his action against the former. J. A. Rule 84.

Leave to defend may be absolute or conditional **743.** Leave to defend may be given unconditionally, or subject to such terms as to giving security, or otherwise, as the Court or Judge may think fit. J. A. Rule 85.

Motion for judgment by leave after service of writ. **744.** Where at any time after the writ of summons has been issued it is made to appear to the Court or a Judge on an *ex parte* application that it will be conducive to the ends of justice to permit a notice of motion for a judgment to be forthwith served, the Court or Judge may order the same accordingly ; and when such permission is granted, the Court or Judge is to give directions, as to the service of the notice of motion and filing of the affidavits, as may be expedient. J. A. Rule 324.

amended
Rule 1478

(*a*) Upon hearing the motion the Court may grant the application on such terms and conditions as may be thought proper, or may refuse the same ; or instead of either granting or refusing the same, may give such directions for the examination of either parties or witnesses, or for the making of further enquiries, or with respect to the further prosecution of the suit, as the circumstances of the case may require, and upon such terms as to costs as the Court thinks right.   J. A. Rule 542.

5. APPLICATION FOR ACCOUNT.

Action for account. **745.** In default of appearance to a writ indorsed under Rule 247, and after appearance in a case in which the preceding Rules do not entitle the plaintiff to a judgment or order on præcipe or otherwise, then unless the defendant, by affidavit or otherwise, satisfies the Court or a Judge that there is some preliminary question to be tried, an order for the account claimed, with all directions formerly usual in the Court of Chancery in similar cases, shall be forthwith made. J. A. Rule 86.

Application to be on notice. **746.** An application for such order as mentioned in the last preceding Rule shall be made on notice, and be supported by an affidavit filed on behalf of the plaintiff, stating concisely the grounds of his claim to an account. The application may be made at any time after the time for entering an appearance has expired. J. A. Rule 87.

Orders for administration, partition or sale. **747.** But the preceding two Rules are not to prevent orders for the administration of the estate real or personal of a deceased person, or for the partition or sale of an estate from being obtained on motion without any previous notice or other preliminary proceeding, and in the manner provided for by Rules 965 to 991 in that behalf. J. A. Rule 88.

6. MOTION FOR JUDGMENT.

How judgment obtained **748.** Unless it is elsewhere provided that judgment may be obtained in any other manner, the judgment of the Court shall be obtained by motion for judgment. J. A. Rule 315.

No judgment on true pleadings merely. **749.** At the trial of any action no party shall be entitled to judgment on the grounds of his pleading being true, if the facts proved are not sufficient in point of law to entitle him to judgment. 44 V. c. 5, s. 44.

750. In case the title of the plaintiff in an action to recover land, as alleged in the writ, existed at the time of service thereof, but had expired before the trial, the plaintiff shall, notwithstanding, be e titled to judgment, according to the fact that he was entitled at the time of serving the writ, and to his costs of the action. R. S. O. 1877, c. 51, s. 31. *If plaintiff was entitled at service of writ, but not afterwards.*

751. Where the evidence in any action is under these Rules taken by affidavit, the notice of motion for judgment thereon shall be given at the same time or times after the close of the evidence, as in other cases is by these Rules provided after the close of the pleadings. J. A. Rule 306. *Notice of motion for judgment.*

752. No action shall, except by leave of the Court or a Judge, be set down on motion for judgment after the expiration of 1 year from the time when the party seeking to set down the same first became entitled so to do. J. A Rule 320. *No motion after 1 year.*

753. Where issues have been ordered to be tried, or issues or questions of fact to be determined in any manner, and there is no direction of a Court or Judge for the entry of judgment, the plaintiff may set down the action on motion for judgment as soon as such issues or questions have been determined. If he does not so set it down, and give notice thereof to the other parties, within 14 days after his right so to do has arisen, then after the expiration of such 14 days, any defendant may set down the action on motion for judgment, and give notice thereof to the other parties. J. A. Rule 318. *After trial of issues of fact.*

754. Where issues have been ordered to be tried, or issues or questions of fact to be determined, in any manner, and some only of such issues or questions of fac: have been tried or determined, any party who considers that the result of such trial or determination renders the trial or determination of the others of them unnecessary, or renders it desirable that the trial or determination thereof should be postponed, may apply to the Court or a Judge for leave to set down the action on motion for judgment, without waiting for such trial or determination. And the Court or Judge may, if satisfied of the expediency thereof, give such leave, upon such terms, if any, as appear just, and may give any directions which may appear desirable as to postponing the trial of the other questions of fact. J. A. Rule 319. *After trial of some only of the issues of fact.*

755. Upon a motion for judgment, or for a new trial, the Court may, if satisfied that it has before it all the materials necessary for finally determining the questions in dispute, or any of them, or for awarding any relief sought, give judgment accordingly ; or may, if it is of opinion that it has not sufficient materials before i' to enable it to give judgment, direct the motion to stand over for further consideration, and direct such issues or questions to be tried or determined, and such accounts and inquiries to be taken and made as it may think fit. J. A. Rule 321. *On motion for judgment or new trial final judgment may be given by Court.*

756. Any party to an action may at any stage thereof apply to the Court or a Judge for such order as he may, upon any admissions of fact in the pleadings, or in the examination of any other party, be entitled to ; and it shall not be necessary to wait for the determination of any other question between the parties ; or he may so apply where the only evidence consists of documents and such affidavits as are necessary to prove their execution or identity without the necessity of any cross-examination ; or he may so apply where infants are concerned, and evidence is necessary so far only as they are concerned, for the purpose of proving facts which are not disputed. *Summary relief on motion upon admissions in pleadings, etc.*

(a) The foregoing Rules shall not apply to such applications, and any such application may be made by motion as soon as the right of the party applying to the relief claimed has appeared from the pleadings.

(b) The Court or a Judge may, on any such application, give such relief, subject to such terms, if any, as such Court or Judge may think fit. J. A. Rule 322

Pending application turned into motion for judgment or hearing of cause.   **757.** Where it is made to appear to the Court or a Judge, on the hearing of any application which may be pending before the Court or Judge, that it will be conducive to the ends of justice to permit it, the Court or Judge may direct the application to be turned into a motion for judgment, or a hearing of the cause or matter ; and thereupon the Court or Judge may make such order as to the time and manner of giving the evidence in the cause or matter, and with respect to the further prosecution thereof, as the circumstances of the case may require ; and upon the hearing it shall be discretionary with the Court or Judge to either pronounce a judgment or make such order as the Court or Judge deems expedient. J. A. Rule 323.

If cause not set down on F. D. within 14 days after confirmation of report any party interested may set down and give notice.   **758.** Where further directions have been reserved, if the party having the conduct of the action does not set the same down by way of motion for judgment on further directions, and serve notice thereof within 14 days after the confirmation of the Master's report, any other party affected by the report may set the same down, and serve notice of the motion. Chy. O., 419.

7. SETTLEMENT OF JUDGMENTS AND ORDERS.

Judgments where settled.   **759.** All judgments delivered in Toronto or elsewhere than at the place of trial shall be settled when necessary by a Registrar.

Registrars may confer.   **760.** The Registrars may confer together in settling minutes of judgments. *in cases tried*

When judgments settled by Dep. Reg.   **761.** All judgments delivered at the place of trial other than Toronto, shall be settled when necessary by the Deputy Registrar, Deputy Clerk or Local Registrar, at the place of trial ; subject to the right of any party affected to apply upon notice to the other parties interested to one of the Judgment Clerks, or to the Judge, to vary the minutes. *(See Rule*

Appointments to settle minutes or pass orders, how to be issued.   **762.** No notice of settling minutes, or passing a judgment or order is to be given unless by direction of the officer by whom the judgment or order is to be settled, nor until the proposed minutes of the judgment or order have been prepared by, or delivered to the officer by whom the same is to be settled ; the notice (where the officer deems a notice proper) is to be by an appointment signed by him, a copy whereof is to be served ; the proposed minutes shall remain in his office for inspection until settled or passed, and any party may take a copy thereof. Chy. O. 12, 596.

Procedure where party makes default.   **763.** Where a notice is given to settle minutes, or to pass a judgment or order, and the party served attends thereon, but the party giving the notice does not attend, or is not prepared to proceed, the officer settling the judgment or order may proceed *ex parte* to settle the minutes, or pass the judgment or order, or may in his discretion order the party giving the notice to pay to the other party the costs of his attendance ; or if a party served asks for delay, the Officer may grant the delay on such terms as he thinks reasonable as to payment of costs or otherwise. Chy. O. 13.

8. ENTRY OF JUDGMENTS AND ORDERS.

Judgment pronounced in Court.   **764.** Every judgment whether pronounced by the Court or signed by default shall be drawn up and signed by a Registrar, Local Registrar, Deputy Registrar or Deputy Clerk of the Crown, as the case may require. J. A. Rule 326, *first part.*

Date of judgment.   **765.** Every judgment pronounced by the Court shall be dated as of the day on which such judgment is pronounced, and shall take effect from that date, unless otherwise directed by the Court or a Judge, and shall also bear upon its face the date upon which it is signed. *See* J. A. Rule 326.

(a) Every judgment signed by default shall be dated on the day on which it is signed. *See* J. A. Rule 327.

101

746. The forms in Part X. of the Appendix may be used for judgments. *Forms.*
with such variations as circumstances may require. J. A. Rule 325.

747. In all cases the judgment pronounced by the Court may be signed *Immediate* judgment.
and entered forthwith, unless otherwise ordered.

748. Where it is provided that any judgment may be signed upon *Entry on affidavit, etc.*
the filing of any affidavit or production of any document, the officer
shall examine the affidavit or document produced, and if the same be
regular and contain all that is by law required, he shall enter judgment
accordingly. J. A. Rule 328.

769. Where any judgment may be signed pursuant to any order or *Entry on order or certificate.*
certificate, or return to any writ, the production of such order or certificate, ~~sealed with the seal of the Court~~, or of such return, shall be a
sufficient authority to the officer to sign judgment accordingly. J. A.
Rule 329.

770. In all cases where a person or party obtains a judgment or order *Orders obtained on condition deemed to be abandoned so far as beneficial to party obtaining unless condition performed.*
from the Court, or from a Master, upon condition, and fails to perform or
comply with the condition, he is to be considered to have waived or
abandoned the judgment or order, as far as the same is beneficial to himself, and any other party or person interested in the matter, on the breach
or non-performance of the condition, may either take such proceedings as
the judgment or order in such case may warrant, or such proceedings as
might have been taken if the judgment or order had not been made.
Chy. O. 196.

771. It shall not be necessary in any judgment or order to reserve *Liberty to apply, need not be reserved.*
liberty to apply, but any party may apply to the Court from time to time
as he may be advised; and where any judgment or order directs the
payment of money out of Court, it shall not be necessary to direct that a
cheque be drawn for the purpose. Chy. O. 186.

772. Every judgment shall be entered at full length in a book to be *Entry of judgment.*
kept for that purpose.

773. No order of course, and no order obtained *ex parte* and not being *Orders of course, and orders obtained ex parte, not to be entered unless directed.*
of a special nature, is to be entered in full unless so directed by the
Court or a Judge; but this provision is not to be construed as applying to
judgments, orders in the nature of judgments, or to final orders for sale,
or foreclosure. Chy. O. 195.

774. No orders of course, or orders made in Chambers, are to be *Orders required to be entered in Chambers.*
entered in full, except:

　　Judgments issued upon *Precipe;*
　　Judgments against Infants;
　　Orders declaring persons Lunatics;
　　　" 　for Administration;
　　　" 　for Partition;
　　　" 　for the Sale of Infants' Estates;
　　　" 　for Payment of Money into or out of Court;
　　　" 　for Foreclosure or Sale;
　　　" 　of Revivor;
　　Vesting Orders;

and such other orders as may from time to time, in any particular case or
otherwise, be directed to be entered. Chy. O. 594.

775. The Entering Clerk is to note in the margin of the judgment or *Entering.*
order book the day of entering a judgment or order, and is at the foot of
the judgment or order to note the same date, and the book in which the
entry has been made and the pages of such book. Chy. O. 32.

9. Form of Judgments and Orders, etc.

General form of judgment for foreclosure or sale.

776. Judgments for foreclosure or sale, where a reference is required, are, after the proper recitals hitherto in use, to direct, in general terms, that all necessary enquiries be made, accounts taken, costs taxed, and proceedings had for redemption or foreclosure, (or for redemption or sale, *as the case may be*) and that for these purposes the cause is referred to (*naming the Master*); and a judgment so expressed is to be read and construed as if the same set forth the particulars contained in Rules 124 to 134 and Rule 353. Chy. O. 441.

Orders to be divided into paragraphs.

777. Judgments and orders are to be divided into convenient paragraphs, and such paragraphs are to be numbered consecutively ; and where accounts are directed to be taken, or enquiries to be made, the direction in that behalf may be in the form No. 187 in the Appendix, with such variation as the circumstances of the case require. Chy. O. 187.

Sums to be stated in dollars and cents.

778. In all judgments and orders, sums are to be stated in dollars and cents. Chy. O. 188.

Form of orders.

779. Every judgment or order shall show on its face the day of the week and month on which it was given or made, and (except judgments signed by default or upon an order for leave to sign judgment and orders of course) shall show the name or names of the Judge or Judges who gave or made the same. *See* Rules H. C. J. viii.

10. Variation of Judgments and Orders.

Correction of mistakes in judgments and orders.

780. Clerical mistakes in judgments or orders, or errors arising therein from any accidental slip or omission, may at any time be corrected by the Court or a Judge on motion without an appeal. J. A. Rule 338.

Amendment as to matters on which there was no adjudication.

781. Where a judgment or order as drawn up requires amendment in any other particular on which the Court did not adjudicate, the same may be amended in open Court on petition without an appeal, if under all the circumstances the Court deems fit. Chy. O. 336.

Application by petition, to impeach judgments, etc.

782. Any party entitled to the variation or reversal of a judgment or order, upon the ground of matter arising subsequent to the making thereof, or subsequently discovered, or to impeach a judgment or order on the ground of fraud, or to suspend the operation of a judgment or order, or to carry a judgment or order into operation, is to proceed by petition in the cause, praying the relief which is sought, and stating the grounds upon which it is claimed. Chy. O. 330.

Petition to be verified and served on all parties interested.

783. The petition is to be verified by affidavit, and served upon the solicitors of all parties interested ; and in case a party has no solicitor, then upon the party. Chy. O. 331.

Notice to be endorsed on copy served.

784. Upon the copy of the petition served is to be endorsed the following memorandum or notice : "If you do not appear on the petition the Court will make such order on the petitioner's own shewing as shall appear just, in your absence ; and if this petition is served personally, you will not receive any notice of the future proceedings on the petition." Chy. O. 332.

Hearing of petition.

785. Upon the hearing of the petition, the Court may either make a final order, or direct the petition to stand over, with liberty to the parties interested in sustaining the judgment or order to file a special answer to the same ; and may make such order as to the production of further proof, and the manner thereof, and the further hearing of the petition, as the Court deems meet. Chy. O. 333.

786. Where the reversal or variation of order is sought upon new *Evidence required when reversal sought on new matter.* matter, such proof as would have been requisite upon a motion to file a bill of review must be supplied. Chy. O. 334.

11. ENTRY OF SATISFACTION.

787. In order to acknowledge satisfaction of a judgment, it shall be *Satisfaction of judgments, entry of.* requisite only to produce a satisfaction piece in form as hereinafter mentioned, and such satisfaction piece shall be signed by the party or parties acknowledging the same or their personal representatives, and their signatures shall be witnessed by some practising solicitor, expressly named by him or them, and attending at his or their request to inform him or them of the nature and effect of such satisfaction piece before the same is signed ; which solicitor shall declare himself in the attestation thereto to be the solicitor for the person so signing the same, and state he is witness as such solicitor (provided that a Judge at Chambers may make an order dispensing with such signature under special circumstances, if he thinks fit) ; and in cases where the satisfaction piece is signed by the personal representative of a party deceased, his representative character shall be proved by the production of the probate of the will, or of the letters of administration, to the officer in custody of the judgment.

788. Every satisfaction piece shall be entered in the office where the *Satisfaction piece where to be entered.* judgment is entered. Rules T. T. 1856, 65.

12. MOTIONS AGAINST VERDICTS OR JUDGMENTS.

789. Where there has been a trial by a jury, any application for a new *Application to Div. Court.* trial shall be to a Divisional Court. J. A. Rule 307.

790. In every notice of motion for a new trial the grounds upon *Grounds to be stated in order nisi for new trial.* which the motion is to be made shall be shortly stated therein ; but in case of any omission the Court may permit the notice to be amended and served again on such terms as are deemed reasonable. R. S. O. 1877, c. 50, s. 288.

791. A new trial shall not be granted on the ground of misdirection or *Restrictions on new trials.* of the improper admission or rejection of evidence, or because the verdict of the jury was not taken upon a question which the Judge at the trial was not asked to leave to them, unless in the opinion of the Court to which the application is made some substantial wrong or miscarriage has been thereby occasioned in the trial of the action ; and if it appears to such Court that such wrong or miscarriage affects part only of the matter in controversy, or some or one only of the parties, the Court may give final judgment as to part thereof or as to some or one only of the parties, and direct a new trial as to the other part only or as to the other party or parties. J. A. Rule 311 ; Eng. R. 1883, 556.

792. A new trial may be ordered on any question in an action, what- *New trial as to part.* ever be the grounds for the new trial, without interfering with the finding or decision upon any other question. J. A. Rule 312.

793. On the argument of a motion for a new trial or against a judg- *Counsel supporting application to begin and have reply.* ment, the counsel of the party making the motion shall begin, and shall state fully the grounds of the application, and shall have the reply. J. A. Rule 314.

794. When a new trial is granted to a party on condition of pay- *Rule for new trial on payment of costs, how rescinded for non-payment.* ment of costs, or other condition, no order shall be made on default in performing such condition unless a motion is made therefor upon notice. Rules T. T. 1856, 45.

Setting aside judgment by default. **795.** Any verdict or judgment obtained where one party does not appear at the trial may be set aside by a Divisional Court or by a Judge in Court or by the Judge at the s.ttings upon such terms as may seem fit. J. A Rule 270.

Judgment by default may be set aside on terms. **796.** Any judgment by default may be set aside by the Court or a Judge, upon such terms as to costs or otherwise as the Court or Judge may think fit. J. A. Rule 214.

Judgment of nonsuit. **797.** Any judgment of nonsuit, unless the Court or a Judge otherwise directs, shall have the same effect as a judgment upon the merits for the defendant ; but in any case of mistake, surprise, accident, or otherwise, any judgment of nonsuit may be set aside on such terms, as to payment of costs and otherwise, as to the Court or a Judge shall seem just. J. A. Rule 330.

Appeal from decision of a Judge, in what cases allowed. **798.** (Where at or after the trial of an action by a jury, the Judge has directed that any judgment be entered, any party may, without any leave reserved, apply to set aside such judgment and to enter any other judgment, on the ground that the judgment directed to be entered is wrong by reason of the Judge having caused the judgment to be wrongly entered, with reference to the finding of the jury upon the question, or questions, submitted to them.

Repealed Rule 1483

(*a*) Where at or after the trial of an action before a Judge, the Judge has directed that any judgment be entered, any party may, without any leave reserved, apply for a new trial, or to set aside the judgment, and to enter any other judgment, upon the ground that the judgment so directed is wrong.

(*b*) Such application may in either of the above cases be to a Divisional Court of the High Court, or to the Court of Appeal, and wh n the application is made to a Divisional Court it shall be made at the first sit ings for which the motion can be set down in due course after the judgment has been rendered, unless otherwise ordered. *See* J. A. Rules 510, 523.)

(*c*) It shall not be necessary to move separately against or with respect to the findings of the jury and the judgment directed to be entered thereon. *New.*

Motion for judgment where jury disagree. **799.** In any case where on the trial the jury disagree and find no verdict, the Court may, notwithstanding such disagreement give judgment of non-suit. See R. S. O. 1877, c. 50, s. 290.

Length of notice. **800.** Every motion against a judgment or for a new trial shall be a seven clear days' notice, and the motion shall be set down at least two days before the first day of the sittings of the Divisional Court for which the notice is given, unless otherwise ordered. *See* J. A Rule 522.

Abandoning motion. **801.** If a party who serves a notice of motion for a new trial or against a judgment, does not set the motion down, he shall be deemed to have abandoned the same.

Copies of short-hand notes to be delivered on motions for new trial etc. **802** On every application for a new trial, or to enter a different judgment, where the evidence was at the trial taken down by a short-hand writer, there shall, unless the Court otherwise orders, be filed when the motion is set down 3 copies of the evidence in words at length, each copy to be certified as correct by the short-hand writer. C. L. Rules, 10th March, 1876, 1.

CHAPTER VIII.

APPEALS.

1. APPEALS TO THE COURT OF APPEAL.

(i) *High Court Appeals.*

— 812 inclusive)
aled. Rule 1487

803. The notice of appeal required by Section 71 of *The Judicature Act* may be in the Form No. 41 in the Appendix.

Notice of appeal.

804. Upon the perfecting of the security, mentioned in section 71 of the Judicature Act, execution shall be stayed in the original cause, except in the following cases :—

When execution to be stayed.

(1) If the judgment appealed from directs the assignment or delivery of documents or personal property, execution shall not be stayed until the things directed to be assigned or delivered have been brought into the Court appealed from, or placed in the custody of such officer or receiver as that Court or a Judge appoints, nor until security has been given to the satisfaction of that Court or Judge, and in such sum as may be directed, that the appellant will obey the order of the Court of Appeal ;

Subject to certain exceptions in which partial performance is required by delivery into Court.

(2) If the judgment appealed from directs the execution of a conveyance or any other instrument, execution shall not be stayed until the instrument has been executed and deposited with the proper officer of the Court appealed from, to abide the judgment of the Court of Appeal ;

Or by executing instrument.

(3) If the judgment appealed from directs the sale or delivery of possession of real property or chattels real, execution shall not be stayed until security has been entered into to the satisfaction of the Court appealed from, and in such sum as that Court or a Judge directs, that during the possession of the property by the appellant, he will not commit or suffer to be committed any waste on the property, and that if the judgment be affirmed, he will pay the value of the use and occupation of the property from the time of the appeal until the delivery of possession thereof, and also, in case the judgment is for the sale of property and the payment of a deficiency arising upon the sale, that the appellant will pay the deficiency ;

Or by the giving of special security not to commit waste.

(4) If the judgment appealed from directs the payment of money, execution shall not be stayed until the appellant has given security, to the satisfaction of the Court appealed from or a Judge, that if the judgment, or any part thereof, be affirmed, the appellant will pay the amount thereby directed to be paid, or the part thereof as to which the judgment may be affirmed if it be affirmed only as to part, and all damages awarded against the appellant on the appeal. R. S. O. 1877, c. 38, s. 27.

Or to pay debt and costs.

When given, a fiat to stay execution to be granted.

805. When the security has been perfected and allowed, any Judge of the Court appealed from may issue his *fiat* to the Sheriff to whom any execution on the judgment has issued, to stay the execution, and the execution shall be thereby stayed, whether a levy has been made under it or not; but if the grounds of appeal appear to be frivolous, the Court appealed from, or a Judge, upon motion on notice, may order execution to issue or to be proceeded with. R. S. O. 1877, c. 38, s. 28.

Judge may order execution to issue.

Security to be by bond.

Form of bond.

806. Unless otherwise specially ordered by the Court appealed from, or a Judge thereof, the security required by section 71 of *The Judicature Act* and Rule 804 shall be personal and by bond, and may be in the form No. 209 in the Appendix, *mutatis mutandis*. Provided that in any case in which execution may be stayed on the giving of security under the preceding Rules, such security may be given by the same instrument whereby the security prescribed in section 71 is given. App. O. 2.

Appeal bond, parties to.

807. The bond shall be executed by the appellant or appellants, or one or more of them, and by two sufficient sureties, unless the Court or a Judge thinks fit to dispense with the execution thereof by the appellant. App. O. 3.

Amount of security to be given to procure stay of execution where judgment is for payment of money.

808. Where the judgment appealed from directs the payment of money, the security required by Rule 804, shall be in double the amount so directed to be paid; provided always that, in cases where the security to be given shall be in a sum above $2000, it shall be in the discretion of the Court appealed from or of a Judge thereof, to allow security to be given by a larger number of sureties apportioning the amount among them as may appear reasonable; and provided further, that, where the amount by the judgment directed to be paid exceeds $10,000, it shall be in the discretion of the Court or Judge to allow security to be given for such amount less than double as may appear reasonable. App. O. 4.

Where sale or delivery of possession of property ordered.

809. Where the judgment appealed from directs the sale, or delivery of possession, of real property, or chattels real, the security required by Rule 804, shall be taken in double the yearly value of the property in question, unless the Court appealed from, or a Judge thereof, otherwise directs. App. O. 5.

Affidavit of justification to be made by sureties.

810. The parties to every such bond as sureties shall by affidavit respectively make oath that they are resident householders or freeholders in Ontario, and severally worth the sum mentioned in the bond, over and above what will pay and satisfy all their debts; and the affidavit may be in the form No. 209 in the Appendix. App. O. 6.

Bond and affidavits to be filed. When allowed.

811. The bond, with an affidavit of the due execution thereof, and affidavit of justification, shall be deposited with the proper Registrar of the Court appealed from in Toronto, and shall be deemed to be perfected and allowed, unless within 14 days after being served with notice thereof the respondent moves for its disallowance. App. O. 7.

Special application to stay execution may be made.

812. The appellant may, after such deposit, make a special application, before the expiration of 14 days, to stay execution in any of the cases mentioned in Rule 804. App. O. 8.

Appeal to be a step in the cause and upon a case stated.

813. The appeal shall be a step in the cause or matter in which the judgment complained of was given, and shall be upon a case to be stated by the parties, or in the event of difference to be settled by the Court appealed from, or a Judge thereof, and shall set forth so much of the pleadings, evidence, affidavits, documents, and the ruling or judgment objected to, as may be necessary to raise the question for the decision of the Court of Appeal. R. S. O. 1877, c. 38. s. 31 (1).

Rules 813 — 827 inclusive) inclusive) Repealed Rule 1488

814. After the security has been perfected, the appellant shall prepare a draft of the case mentioned in the preceding Rule, and shall submit the draft to the respondent, who shall return the same within 4 days, with his modifications or suggestions, and in the event of differences, the appellant shall give 2 clear days notice of an application to the Court, or a Judge, to settle the case.   App. O. 9.
After security perfected, case to be prepared—draft to be submitted to respondent.

815. The case shall state the name or names of the Judge or Judges appealed from.
Name of Judge to be stated.

816. The appellant shall serve his reasons of appeal along with, and as part of, the draft case mentioned in the preceding Rules, and the respondent shall serve his reasons against the appeal, within 10 days from such service, or within such further time as a Judge of the Court of Appeal may allow.   App. O. 11.
Reasons of, and against appeal—to be served.

817. If the appeal is from a part only of the judgment, the reasons of appeal shall specify the part.   App. O. 12.
Part of judgment appealed from.

818. If the respondent neglects to serve reasons against the appeal, the Court may hear the appeal ex parte, and give judgment thereon without the intervention of the respondent.   App. O. 13.
Neglect of respondent to serve reasons against appeal—effect of.

819. Upon being served with the respondent's reasons against the appeal, or upon his having made default in service thereof, the appellant shall cause appeal books to be printed containing the case as settled by the parties, or the Judge, and the reasons for the appeal, and the reasons against the appeal, if such latter reasons have been served as aforesaid, and any notice given under Rule 821, and shall forthwith deliver one of such copies to the Registrar of the Court of Appeal, by whom the same shall be filed as the stated and settled case, and 10 copies for the use of the Judges and officers of the Court; and also 30 copies for the purpose of being delivered, in the event of an appeal to the Supreme Court of Canada, to the party appealing to that Court, for use upon such appeal. App. O. 14, 69.
Appeal book to be printed.

Number of copies to be delivered.

820. The respondent may, after such printed book has been delivered to the Registrar, apply to a Judge of the Court of Appeal for leave to serve his reasons, upon affidavit accounting for the delay, and such leave may be given upon such terms as the Judge may think proper.   App. O. 15.
Leave to deliver reasons against appeal, after book printed, may be granted.

821. A cross appeal shall not under any circumstances be necessary, but if a respondent intends upon the hearing to contend that the decision should be varied, he shall with his reasons against the appeal give notice of such contention to any parties who may be affected by such contention, and such notice shall concisely state the grounds of such contention in the same manner as reasons of appeal are stated. The omission to give such notice, shall not diminish the powers conferred by Act upon the Court of Appeal, but may, in the discretion of the Court, be ground for an adjournment of the appeal, or for a special order as to costs.   App. O. 16.
Cross appeal unnecessary—proceedings in lieu of.

822. The reasons for and against the appeal shall contain a statement of the points of law intended to be argued, and the authorities relied upon. App. O. 17.
Reasons, what to contain.

823. The appeal books shall be printed on paper of good quality, on one side of the paper only, and in demy-quarto form, with small pica type leaded; and every tenth line of each page shall be numbered in the margin, the numbering to be from the top of each page and not from the beginning of the book; and the size of the books shall be 11 inches in height, and 8½ inches in width. An index showing in detail each pleading, order or entry with its date, each witness by name, each exhibit or other document with its description and date, and all other principal matters,
Appeal books, how to be printed.

shall be added ; it shall be at the beginning of the book and is not to be
arranged alphabetically, but in the order in which the matters are printed
in the book. The opinions of the Judges of the Court appealed from shall
not be printed where the same have already been issued in the regular
reports, but a reference to the same shall be given in the appeal books, and
shall be sufficient. The style of the cause in the Court below shall be used
and retained in the appeal book, and in every proceeding in the Court
of Appeal, the designation "appellant" or "respondent" being added,
e. g.,

Between A. B. (respondent)

and   PLAINTIFF.

C. D. (appellant)

DEFENDANT.

App. O. 67, 68.

Otherwise Registrar not to file case. **824.** The Registrar shall not file the case without the leave of a Judge if the preceding Rule has not been complied with. App. O. 19.

Costs when errors in press. **825.** If the press has not been carefully corrected, the Court may disallow the costs of printing, or may decline to hear the appeal, and make such order as to postponement and payment of costs as may seem just. App. O. 20.

Time for delivering appeal books.

Dismissal of appeal for non-delivery. **826.** The printed case, and the copies thereof for the use of the Court, shall be delivered to the Registrar, within thirty days after the allowance of the security, unless the time shall be extended by the Court of Appeal, or a Judge ; and in the case of neglect or omission by the appellant to comply with this Rule, the respondent may apply to a Judge upon 2 clear days' notice to the appellant for an order dismissing the appeal as for want of prosecution, and the Judge may thereupon make such order as to dismissing the appeal, or otherwise, as may appear just. App. O. 21. R. S. O. c. 38, s. 31 (2).

Appeals, how entered for hearing.

Notice of hearing. **827.** Appeals shall be entered by the Registrar upon the list for hearing at the next regular sittings of the Court which shall commence at least 8 days after the receipt by him of the printed copies ; and the appellant shall serve the respondent or such respondents as are directly affected by the appeal, with notice of hearing, at least 7 days before the first day of such sittings ; and he shall at the same time deliver to the respondent two printed books. App. O. 22.   See R. S. O. 1877, c. 38, s. 32.

Court may order parties not served to be notified. **828.** If, in the opinion of the Court, any parties not served ought to be notified, the Court may direct service to be made, and may postpone the hearing of the appeal for that purpose, upon such terms as may seem just. App. O. 23.

Default of parties at hearing—effect of. **829.** If either party neglects to appear at the proper day to support, or resist the appeal, the Court may hear the other party, and may give judgment without the intervention of the party so neglecting to appear, or may postpone the hearing upon payment of such costs as the Court shall direct. App. O. 24.

The Clerk to certify result of appeals. **830.** The decision of the Court of Appeal shall be certified by the Registrar of the Court of Appeal to the proper officer of the High Court, who shall thereupon make all proper and necessary entries thereof, and all subsequent proceedings may be taken thereupon, as if the decision had been given in the Court below. R. S. O. 1877, c. 38, s. 44.

Certificate of appeal—settlement of. **831.** Where the Registrar considers a notice of settling the certificate of the Court of Appeal to be proper, he shall appoint a time for the purpose, and two clear days' notice thereof shall be given to the unsuccessful party or parties. App. O. 31.

832. An appellant may discontinue his proceedings by giving to the *Appellants* respondent a notice headed in the Court and cause, and signed by the *may discontinue.* appellant or his solicitor, stating that he discontinues such proceedings; and thereupon the respondent shall be at once entitled to the costs of and occasioned by the proceedings in appeal, and may either sign judgment for such costs or obtain an order for their payment in the Court below, and may take all further proceedings in that Court as if no appeal had been brought. R. S. O. 1877, c. 38, s. 41.

833. A respondent may consent to the reversal of the judgment, *A respondent* order or proceeding appealed against, by giving to the appellant a notice *may consent* headed in the Court and cause, and signed by the respondent or his solici- *to a reversal of* tor, stating that he consents to the reversal of the judgment, order or *the judgment,* other proceeding, and thereupon the Court shall pronounce judgment of *etc.* reversal as of course. R. S. O. 1877, c. 38, s. 42.

834. No case shall be certified on an appeal to the Supreme Court of *Appeal to Su-* Canada, unless the proof sheets of the judgments in the Court of Appeal *preme Court.* have been submitted to the Judges thereof for correction.

835-845 inclusive)
Rule 1489 (ii) *County Court Appeals.*

835. For the purpose of avoiding unnecessary expense in appeals *Original* from the County Courts—particularly in making copies of papers—it is *papers to be* ordered that the pleadings, motions, orders, and other papers certified to *certified and* the Court of Appeal under section 41 of the Act respecting County *transmitted in* Courts, shall be the original papers filed in the County Court; and when *C. C. appeals.* the evidence has been taken by an official reporter, his transcript of the evidence used, or prepared for use, in the County Court upon the motion which is the subject of the appeal, shall be the evidence so certified.

(a) The said papers, together with the Judge's charge, and his judgment *Papers—how* or decision, and also the evidence when not taken by an official reporter, and *to be trans-* all objections and exceptions to the evidence, shall be fastened together *mitted, and* and transmitted with the Judge's certificate to the Registrar of the Court *returned.* of Appeal, who is to return them to the County Court when the appeal is disposed of.

(b) It shall not be necessary to certify or transmit the evidence, or the *Evidence,* objections or exceptions thereto, in any case in which the appeal is from *when need not* a judgment or decision upon the pleadings, or upon an action not *be certified.* founded upon the evidence. App. O. 39 a.

836. An appeal shall be set down to be heard at the first sittings of *C. C. appeals* the Court for the hearing of arguments which commences after the *when to be set* expiration of 30 days from the decision complained of. App. O. 40. *down.*

837. An appeal shall be set down for hearing, by delivering to the *C. C. appeal* Registrar of the Court of Appeal, at least 8 days before the sittings at *how set down.* which the appeal is to be heard, the certified copy of the pleadings, proceedings, evidence and other matters required by section 41 of chapter 43 of the Revised Statutes of Ontario, and ten appeal books for the use of the Judges of the Court of Appeal and the officers of the Court. App. O. 41.

838. The books shall be printed on paper of good quality, on one side *Appeal books,* of the paper only, in demy quarto-form, with small pica type, leaded, and *how printed.* every tenth line of each page shall be numbered in the margin, commencing from the top of each page and not from the beginning of the book, and a statement of the reasons of appeal shall form a part thereof. App. O. 42.

839. A full copy of the pleadings shall not be printed in the books, *Pleadings,* unless it be necessary for the proper consideration of the question raised *to be* upon the appeal, ex. gr. in questions arising on demurrer. In other cases *printed.*

it shall be sufficient to state the substance of the pleadings, in a brief form, but so as to be intelligible. App. O. 43.

Evidence not relevant, not to be printed. **840.** It shall not be necessary to print evidence which does not bear upon the question in appeal, but the books must always contain the opinion delivered by the Judge on any motion against the verdict or judgment, and his charge in case of a trial by a jury, and his note of judgment in case of a trial by himself. App. O. 44.

Exhibits, how far to be printed. **841.** Exhibits used at the trial shall not be printed in the books, unless their contents are material to the question in appeal, and then only such parts as are material. App. O. 45.

Formal proceedings not to be printed in extenso. **842.** All formal matters, such as copies of the motion papers, and rules discharging, or making rules *nisi* absolute, shall be omitted, but such reference shall be made to them including the dates thereof, as may appear necessary for giving a clear and intelligible statement of the case. App. O. 46.

Appeal book and notice of setting down, to be served on respondent 6 days before sittings. **843.** The appellant shall, at least 6 days before the sittings at which the appeal is to be heard, serve the respondent with the notice of the setting down of the appeal and with a copy of the ~~printed~~ appeal book, and of the grounds and reasons of his appeal. ~~In case the respondent is of opinion that any necessary matter has been omitted, he may at any time before the hearing leave with the Registrar a memorandum briefly referring to such omitted matter.~~ App. O. 48.

Otherwise appeal not heard. **844.** If the foregoing Rules are not complied with, the appeal shall not be heard, unless the Court, or a Judge, shall, on application made upon 2 clear days notice to the respondent, otherwise order. App. O. 50.

Non-compliance with Rules, effect of **845.** All books, as well in High Court, as County Court appeals, shall contain the date of the first proceeding in the suit or matter ; and the dates of the filing of the several pleadings shall be stated at the commencement of the copy or summary thereof. In the event of non-compliance with this Rule, the books will not be received by the Registrar, nor will the appeal be heard. App. O. 52.)

2. APPEALS FROM CHAMBERS.

Appeal to Judge. **846.** Any person affected by any order or decision of the Master in Chambers, a Local Judge or a local Master, may appeal therefrom to a Judge of the High Court in Chambers ;

(a) Such appeal may be made notwithstanding that the order or decision was in respect of a proceeding or matter as to which the Local Judge or officer aforesaid had jurisdiction only by consent ;

(b) The appeal shall be by motion, on notice served within 4 days after the decision complained of, or within such further time as may be allowed by a Judge of the High Court or by the Local Judge or officer aforesaid whose decision is complained of ;

(c) The motion shall be made within 4 days after the decision has been made which is appealed against, or within such further time as may be allowed as aforesaid ;

(d) In such case, the Deputy Registrar, Deputy Clerk of the Crown or Local Registrar, shall, on a precipe being filed in this behalf, transmit to the proper officer of the High Court of Justice all documents filed in his office and required for disposing of the appeal ; and the same shall be transmitted by mail, prepaid and registered, except where all parties interested in such documents file a consent to any other mode of transmission. The said documents shall be returned in like manner when the appeal has been disposed of ;

(e) The appeal shall be no stay of proceedings unless so ordered by a Judge of the High Court or by the Judge or officer whose decision is complained of. J. A. Rule 427.

817. Every appeal to a Divisional Court from any decision of a Judge at chambers shall be by motion, which shall be set down at latest on the day before the sittings, and shall be made at the first sittings of a Divisional Court which takes place after the decision complained of unless otherwise ordered. *See* J. A. Rule 414.

Appeal to Div. Ct.

3. APPEALS FROM MASTERS AND REFEREES.

818. Every report shall become absolute at the expiration of fourteen days from the day of filing the same, including such day, unless notice of appeal is served within that time. *See* Chy. O. 252.

Report when absolute.

819. The notice of appeal shall be a seven clear days' notice, shall set out the grounds of appeal, and shall be returnable within one month from the date of the report, n less otherwise ordered. *See* Chy. O. 642.

Notice of appeal.

850. The appeal shall be set down for argument before a Judge in Court for the day on which the motion is returnable.

Setting down.

4. APPEALS FROM TAXATION.

851. Any party who may be dissatisfied with the certificate of the taxing master, as to any item or part of an item which may have been objected to, as provided by Rules 1230 and 1231, may apply to a Judge at Chambers for an order to review the taxation as to the same item or part of an item, and the Judge may thereupon make such order as to the Judge may seem just; but the certificate of the taxing master shall be final and conclusive as to all matters which shall not have been objected to in manner aforesaid. J. A. Rule 449.

Review of taxation by judge.

852. No appeal shall lie unless a notice thereof is given within four days from the day of the date of the certificate, and is brought on for argument within nine days from the said day.

When appeal lies.

853. Such application shall be heard and determined by the Judge upon the evidence which shall have been brought in before the taxing master, and no further evidence shall be received upon the hearing thereof unless the Judge otherwise directs. J. A. Rule 450.

Evidence thereon.

854. There may be an appeal by appointment without other notice from the taxing masters in Toronto to the Master in Chambers or to the Master in Ordinary pending the taxation in all cases. J. A. Rule 544 (1).

Appeal to M. C.

5. APPEALS TO THE JUDICIAL COMMITTEE OF THE PRIVY COUNCIL.

855. The security to be given in cases of appeal to Her Majesty in Privy Council, shall be personal, and by bond to the respondent or respondents, such bond to be executed by the appellant or appellants, or one or more of them, and by two sufficient sureties, (except in special cases, as mentioned in Rule 803, in the penal sum of $2000, the condition of which bond shall be to the effect that the appellant or appellants shall and will effectually prosecute his and their appeal, and pay such costs and damages as shall be awarded in case the judgment appealed from shall be affirmed, or in part affirmed; and any application to the Court of Appeal to stay proceedings shall be made in like manner, and be upon the like terms as to security, as is provided in like cases upon appeals from the High Court to the Court of Appeal.

Security to be given on appeals to Privy Council.

Form of appeal bond.

856. The bond referred to in the foregoing Rule shall be according to the form No. 210 in the Appendix.

Affidavit of justification required from obligors.

857. In every case of appeal to Her Majesty in Council, the obligors, parties to any bond as sureties, shall justify their sufficiency by affidavit in the manner and to the same effect as is required upon appeals from the High Court to the Court of Appeal.

CHAPTER IX.

ENFORCEMENT OF JUDGMENTS AND ORDERS.

1. WRITS OF FIERI FACIAS, ETC.

Meaning of "Writ of execution," and "issuing of execution."

858. In these Rules the term "writ of execution" shall include writs of fieri facias, capias, sequestration, and attachment, and all subsequent writs that may issue for giving effect thereto. And the expression "issuing execution against any person" shall mean the issuing of any such process against his person or property as under these Rules shall be applicable to the case. J. A. Rule 344.

Writs of fi. fa., effect of.

859. Writs of *fieri facias* shall have the same force and effect as the like writs have heretofore had, and shall be executed in the same manner as the like writs have heretofore been executed. J. A. Rule 362. R. S. O. 1877, c. 66, s. 18.

Ven. ex.

860. Writs of *venditioni exponas* may be issued and executed in the same cases and in the same manner as heretofore. J. A. Rule 363.

Hab. fac. poss.

861. A writ of possession shall have the effect of a writ of assistance as well as of a writ of *habere facias possessionem.* J. A. Rule 381.

Enforcing judgment for recovery of money.

862. A judgment for the recovery by or payment to any person of money may be enforced by any of the modes by which a judgment or decree, for the payment of money, of any of the Superior Courts, might have been enforced prior to the passing of *The Ontario Judicature Act, 1881.* J. A. Rule 339.

Fi. fa.

863. Every person to whom any sum of money or any costs is payable under a judgment, shall, immediately after the time when the judgment was duly entered, be entitled to sue out one or more writ or writs of *fieri facias* to enforce payment thereof, subject nevertheless as follows :

(*a*) If the judgment is for payment within a period therein mentioned, no such writ as aforesaid shall be issued until after the expiration of such period.

(b) The Court or Judge at the time of giving judgment, or the Court or a Judge afterwards, may give leave to issue execution before, or may stay execution until any time after the expiration of such period. J. A. Rules 352, 499.

864. Any person who becomes entitled to issue a writ of execution Writs against against goods and chattels may, at or after the time of issuing the same, lands may issue a writ of execution against the lands and tenements of the person issue at same liable, and deliver the same to the sheriff to whom the writ against goods time as writs is directed, at or after the time of delivery to him of the writ against against goods. goods, and either before or after any return thereof. R. S. O. 1877, c. 66, s. 14.

865. In case any action of the proper competence of a Division Court When lands is brought in the High Court or in a County Court, no execution against not liable lands shall issue unless the amount of the judgment exceeds $40. R. S. unless the O. 1877, c. 66, s. 13. judgment exceeds $40.

866. Every order of the Court or a Judge, whether in an action, cause, Execution on or matter, may be enforced in the same manner as a judgment to the same orders. effect. J. A. Rule 357.

867. A judgment or order for the payment of money into Court For payment may be enforced by any mode by which a judgment for that purpose may into Court. be enforced, and the person having the carriage of the judgment or order for the time being, shall be deemed to be the person to receive payment for the purpose of enforcing the same. J. A. Rule 340.

868. A judgment for the recovery or for the delivery of the possession For recovery of land may be enforced by writ of possession. J. A. Rule 341. of land.

869. Where by any judgment any person therein named is directed to Writ of posses deliver up possession of any lands to some other person on or at any sion. specified time after being served with the judgment, the person prosecuting the judgment shall, without any order for that purpose, be entitled to sue out a writ of possession on filing an affidavit showing due service of the judgment and that the same has not been obeyed. J. A. Rule 380.

870. Upon judgment or order for recovery of any land and *mesne* pro- Execution for fits or rents in respect of the premises claimed and costs, there may be either land and costs. one writ or separate writs of execution for the recovery of possession, and for the *mesne* profits, rents and costs, at the election of the party entitled to recover the same. R. S. O. 1877, c. 51 s. 36.

871. The writ of assignment of dower required to be issued after a Form of writs judgment in an action for dower has been entered in favour of the plain- of assignment tiff, shall be in the form hitherto in use in Ontario. C. L. Rules, 15th of dower. February, 1862.

872. The writ of assignment of dower required to be issued under the third clause of the Dower Procedure Act, when the right of dower is acquiesced in by the owner of the estate, may be according to the form given in Form No. 201 in the Appendix. C. L. Rules, 15th February, 1862.

873. In all cases where specific goods, chattels, deeds, securities. valu- Execution for able papers, or any property other than land or money, are demanded in property other an action, and the plaintiff has judgment to recover the same or their value, than lands. the Court or a Judge shall, at the request of the plaintiff, where a recovery or delivery of the property in specie is desired, direct a writ of execution to issue on the judgment, commanding the defendant specifically to deliver up forthwith the property demanded, and in case of refusal, that the

defendant be arrested and detaine l in prison until he complies with the
terms of the writ, and also that the goods and chattels of the defendant
to double the value of the property in question be taken and kept until
Option to the the further order of the Court to ensure or enforce obedience to the writ, or
plaintiff.   that a writ of sequestration may issue ; or, at the option of the plaintiff,
               the Court or Judge may order the Sheriff to make of the defendant's
Damages,   goods the value of such property ; but the plaintiff shall, either by the
costs, etc.   same or by a separate writ or writs of execution (to be issued in the
               ordinary manner) be entitled to have made of the defendant's goods or
               lands, the damages, costs and interest in such action. R. S. O. 1877, c.
               66, s. 56. See J. A. Rules 342, 382.

Judgment re-   **874.** A judgment requiring any person to do any act other than the
quiring person payment of money, or to abstain from doing anything, may be enforced by
to do or leave writ of attachment, or by committal. J. A. Rule 343.
undone.

Judgment for   **875.** Where a judgment is to the effect that any party is entitled to
conditional   any relief subject to or upon the fulfilment of any condition or contin-
relief.   gency, the party so entitled may, upon the fulfilment of the condition or
               contingency, and demand made upon the party against whom he is
               entitled to relief, apply to the Court or a Judge for leave to issue execution
               against such party. And the Court or Judge may, if satisfied that the
               right to relief has arisen according to the terms of the judgment, order
               that execution issue accordingly, or may direct that any issue or question
               necessary for the determination of the rights of the parties be tried in any
               of the ways in which questions arising in an action may be tried. J. A.
               Rule 345.

Judgment   **876.** Where a judgment is against partners in the name of the firm,
against   execution may issue in manner following :
partners.

               (a) Against any property of the partners as such ;

               (b) Against any person who has admitted on the pleadings that he is,
                   or has been adjudged to be a partner ;

               (c) Against any person who has been served as a partner with the writ
                   of summons, and has failed to appear.

               If the party who has obtained judgment claims to be entitled to issue exe-
               cution against any other person as being a member of the firm, he may
               apply to the Court or a Judge for leave so to do ; and the Court or Judge
               may give such leave if the liability be not disputed, or if such liability be
               disputed, may order that the liability of such person be tried and deter-
               mined in any manner in which any issue or question in an action may be
               tried and determined. J. A. Rule 346.

On execution   **877.** Where any money (other than for costs) is recovered by or on
by infant,   behalf of an infant, or a person of unsound mind by his guardian, next
money to be   friend, or committee, the same shall, unless otherwise ordered, be paid
paid into   into Court subject to further order ; and no payment to the guardian,
Court.   next friend, or committee, of moneys due to such infant or person of
               unsound mind, otherwise than for the costs of any such action, shall be a
               valid discharge to the party making such payment as against the infant or
               person of unsound mind. Every writ of execution for the levying of any
               such moneys is to be ndorsed by the officer issuing the same with the
               following notice: "All moneys made under this execution, other than
               costs, are to be paid into Court by the Sheriff, as required by Rule 877."
               J. A. Rule 589.

2. ATTACHMENT AND SEQUESTRATION

Effect of   **878.** A writ of attachment against the person shall be issued under the
attachment.   same circumstances and in the same manner and shall have the same effect

as according to the practice of the Court of Chancery, prior to *The Ontario Judicature Act, 1881.* J. A. Rule 364.

879. No such writ of attachment shall be issued without the leave of the Court or a Judge, to be applied for on notice to the person against whom the attachment is to be issued. J. A. Rule 365. *Leave to issue.*

880. If a person who is ordered, otherwise than by an order of course, to do any act other than to pay money, in a limited time, refuses or neglects to obey the judgment or order, according to the exigency thereof, the party prosecuting the same shall be entitled to a writ or writs of attachment against the disobedient party. Chy. O. 288. *Attachment for non-performance of an act.*

881. In case a person is, under the preceding Rule, taken or detained in custody under a writ of attachment, without obeying the judgment or order, then upon the sheriff's return that the person has been so taken or detained, the party prosecuting the judgment or order shall be entitled, upon *precipe,* to a commission of sequestration against the estate and effects of the disobedient party. Chy. O. 289. *Upon attachment of contemnor, Sequestration may issue on precipe.*

882. If an attachment cannot be executed against the person refusing or neglecting to obey the judgment or order, by reason of his being out of the jurisdiction of the Court, or of his having absconded, or that with due diligence he cannot be found, or if in any other case the Court may think proper to dispense with a writ of attachment, an order may be granted for a commission of sequestration against the estate and effects of the disobedient person ; and it shall not be necessary for that purpose to sue out an attachment. *See* Chy. O. 290. *Where attachment cannot be executed, etc.*

883. If a person who is ordered to pay money, neglects to obey the judgment or order according to the exigency thereof, the party prosecuting the same, may, at the expiration of the time limited for the performance thereof, apply in Chambers for a writ of sequestration against the defaulting party, and upon proof of due service of a notice of the motion, unless the Court thinks proper to dispense with such service, and upon proof by affidavit of such other matters, if any, as the Court requires, the Court may order a writ of sequestration to issue. Chy. O. 291. *Sequestration may issue for default in payment of money, on application in Chambers.*

884. Commissions of sequestration are to be directed to the Sheriff, unless otherwise ordered. Chy. O. 292. *Commissions of sequestration to be directed to Sheriff.*

3. ISSUE AND FORM OF WRIT.

885. As between the original parties to a judgment, execution may issue at any time within 6 years from the recovery of the judgment. J. A. Rule 355. *Execution within 6 years.*

886. (*a*) Where 6 years have elapsed since the judgment, or the date of the order, or where any change has taken place by death or otherwise in the parties entitled or liable to execution ; *Execution by leave of Court.*

(*b*) Where a husband is entitled or liable to execution upon a judgment or order for or against his wife ;

(*c*) Where a party is entitled to execution upon a judgment of assets *in futuro ;*

The party alleging himself to be entitled to execution may apply to the Court or a Judge for leave to issue execution accordingly. And such Court or Judge, if satisfied that the party so applying is entitled to issue execution, may make an order to that effect, or may order that any issue or question necessary to determine the rights of the parties, shall be tried in any of the ways in which any question in an action may be tried. And in either case such Court or Judge may impose such terms as to costs or otherwise, as shall seem just. J. A. Rule 356.

In case of persons not parties. **887.** In cases other than those mentioned in Rule 885, any person, not being a party in an action, who obtains any order or in whose favour any order is made, shall be entitled to enforce obedience to such order by the same process as if he were a party to the action ; and any person not being a party in an action, against whom obedience to any judgment or order may be enforced, shall be liable to the same process for enforcing obedience to such judgment or order as if he were a party to the action. J. A. Rule 358.

Præcipe for writ. **888.** No writ of execution shall be issued without the party issuing it, or his solicitor, filing a *præcipe* for that purpose. The *præcipe* shall contain the title of the action, the date of the judgment, and of the order, if any, directing the execution to be issued, the names of the parties against whom, or of the firms against whose goods, the execution is to be issued ; and shall be signed by or on behalf of the solicitor of the party issuing it, or by the party issuing it if he do so in person. The forms in Part VII. of the Appendix hereto may be used, with such variations as circumstances may require. J. A. Rule 347.

Endorsement of name and address. **889.** Every writ of execution shall be indorsed with the name and place of abode or office of business of the solicitor actually suing out the same ; and when the solicitor actually suing out the writ sues out the same as agent for another solicitor, the name and place of abode of such other solicitor shall also be indorsed upon the writ ; and in case no solicitor is employed to issue the writ, then it shall be indorsed with a memorandum expressing that the same has been sued out by the plaintiff or defendant in person, as the case may be, mentioning the city, town, or other place, and also the name of the street and number of the house of such plaintiff's or defendant's residence, if any such there be. J. A. Rule 348.

Poundage etc. **890.** Upon every execution there may be levied, in addition to the sum recovered by the judgment, the poundage, fees, expenses of execution and interest upon the amount recovered. J. A. Rule 350. R. S. O. c. 66, s. 44.

Indorsements on writ. **891.** Every writ of execution for the recovery of money shall be indorsed with a direction to the sheriff, or other officer or person to whom the writ is directed, to levy the money really due and payable and sought to be recovered under the judgment, stating the amount, and also to levy interest thereon, if sought to be recovered, at the rate of 6 per cent. per annum from the time when the judgment was entered up ; provided that in cases where there is an agreement between the parties that more than 6 per cent. interest shall be secured by the judgment, then the indorsement may be accordingly to levy the amount of interest so agreed. J. A. Rule 351.

Indorsement of amounts to be paid for costs of writs. **892.** It shall be the duty of every officer issuing a writ of execution, or renewal thereof, to indorse upon the same a memorandum signed by him of the amount or amounts respectively hereinafter mentioned, which the party issuing such writ is entitled to receive for suing out such writ or renewal and placing it in the Sheriff's hands, including all attendances, indorsements, letters, &c., and for his costs of any prior, or other writs, or renewals, specifying the amount allowed for each writ or renewal ; and no sum not so indorsed is to be collected for such costs. J. A. Rule 594.

Date. **893.** Every writ of execution shall bear date of the day on which it is issued. The forms in Part XI. in the Appendix may be used, with such variations as circumstances may require. J. A. Rule 349.

Currency of writ. **894.** A writ of execution if unexecuted shall remain in force for one year only from its issue, unless renewed in the manner hereinafter provided ; but such writ may, at any time before its expiration, be renewed by the party issuing it for one year from the date of such renewal, and so on from time to time during the continuance of the renewed writ,—either by being marked in the margin with a memorandum signed by the proper officer who issued such writ, or by his successor in office, stating the date of the day, month, and year of such renewal, or by such party giving a written notice of renewal to the sheriff, signed by the party or his solicitor, and having the like memorandum ; and a writ of execution so renewed shall have effect, and be entitled to priority, according to the time of the original delivery thereof. J. A. Rule 353.

895. The production of a writ of execution, or of the notice renewing the same, purporting to be marked with the memorandum in the last preceding Rule mentioned, shewing the same to have been renewed, shall be sufficient *prima facie* evidence of its having been renewed. J. A. Rule 354. *Proof of renewal.*

896. Every writ of *capias ad satisfaciendum* shall continue in force two months from the day of the date thereof, inclusive, and no longer ; but on the expiration thereof another writ may be obtained upon a Judge's order, in the manner directed by section 9 of *The Act respecting Arrest and Imprisonment for Debt.* R. S. O. 1877, c. 66, s. 53. *Teste and date of writs of ca. sa.*

897. Writs of execution to fix bail may be tested and returnable in vacation. R. S. O. 1877, c. 66, s. 54. *Writs to fix bail.*

898. Where it is necessary to sue out process of execution against the person into any particular county in order to charge bail, the same shall continue to be necessary notwithstanding anything contained in these Rules. R. S. O. 1877, c. 66, s. 9. *It shall still be necessary to sue out execution in the proper County to charge bail.*

4. SALE UNDER WRIT.

899. Where any goods or chattels are seized in execution under a writ issued out of the High Court or out of any County Court, the Sheriff, his Deputy, or officer, who seized the same, shall, on request, deliver to the owner, his agent or servant, an inventory thereof before they are removed from the premises on which they have been so seized ; and no Sheriff or other officer shall sell any effects under a writ of execution until he has, previously thereto, given at least 8 days public notice in writing of the time and place of sale in the most public place in the Municipality where such effects have been taken in execution. R. S. O. 1877, c. 66, s. 19. *Sheriff to deliver inventory to the owner, etc.*

900. It shall be the duty of the Sheriff, in every case where goods seized by him under execution remain unsold in his hands for want of buyers, to state and specify in his return of "goods on hand," the time and place when and where such goods were offered for sale by him, and the names of at least three persons who were present at the time of such attempted sale, if so many were present, but if so many were not present, then the names of those who were present, if any, and that there were no others, and if no person was present then to state that fact. R. S. O. 1877, c. 66, s. 34. *Return where goods remain in Sheriff's hands unsold.*

900(a) Return as to goods . by reducement of certificate

901. The Sheriff shall not expose the lands for sale under a writ against lands, or sell the same within less than 12 months from the day on which the writ against the lands is delivered to him. R. S. O. 1877, c. 66, s. 14. *Lands not to be sold within a year.*

902. When a writ against lands is issued in an action against an absconding debtor in which an order for attachment has issued, the Court or a Judge may order the Sheriff to sell the lands before the expiration of the twelve months, but in like manner as in other cases. 50 V. c. 7, s. 7. *Fi. fa. lands against absconding debtor.*

903. No Sheriff, Deputy Sheriff or other officer shall sell, or expose for sale under execution, any lands or tenements in the Provisional Judicial Districts of Algoma or Thunder Bay, except between the 1st day of July and the 1st day of November. 42 V. c. 15, s. 4. *Time for Sheriff's sales in Algoma and Thunder Bay limited.*

No sale of lands until return of nulla bona. **904.** No sale shall be had under any execution against lands until after a return of *nulla bona*, in whole or in part, with respect to an execution against goods in the same action or matter by the Sheriff of the same county. R. S. O. 1887, c. 66, ss. 15, 16.

If the debt is realized under writ against goods. **905.** If the amount authorized to be made and levied under the writ against goods is made and levied thereunder, the person issuing the writ against lands shall not be entitled to the expenses thereof, or of any seizure or advertisement thereunder ; and the return to be made by the Sheriff to the writ against lands shall be to the effect that the amount has been so made and levied as aforesaid. R. S. O. 1877, c. 66, s. 17.

Notice of sale of lands in execution. **906.** Before the sale of real estate under execution against lands and tenements, the Sheriff shall publish an advertisement of sale in the *Ontario Gazette*, at least six times, specifying :

    (a) The particular property to be sold ;

    (b) The names of the plaintiff and defendant ;

    (c) The time and place of the intended sale ;

and he shall, for three months next preceding the sale, also publish such advertisement in a public newspaper of the county in which the lands lie, or shall for three months put up and continue a notice of such sale in the office of the Clerk of the Peace, or on the door of the Court House or place in which the Court of General Sessions of the Peace of the county is usually holden ; but nothing herein contained shall be taken to prevent an adjournment of the sale to a future day. R. S. O. 1877, c. 66, s. 41.

Notice in *Gazette* shall constitute incipient execution. **907.** The advertisement in the *Ontario Gazette* of any lands for sale under a writ of execution, during the currency of the writ (giving some reasonably definite description of the land in such advertisement), shall be deemed a sufficient commencement of the execution to enable the same to be completed by a sale and conveyance 'of the lands after the writ has become returnable. R. S. O. 1877, c. 66, s. 42.

5. RETURN OF WRITS, ETC.

Orders to return writs, or bring in body, to be 6 day orders. **908.** All orders against sheriffs to return writs, or to bring in the bodies of defendants, shall be returnable in 6 days, and shall be issued from the same office whence the writ was sued out. Rules T. T. 1856, 101.

Orders for return of writs, etc., to be on *præcipe*. **909.** No Judge's order shall issue for the return of any writ, or to bring in the body of the defendant, but a precipe order shall issue for that purpose, which shall be of the same force and effect as side bar rules formerly made for that purpose in Term. Rules T. T. 1856, 102.

Sheriff to file writ in office from which order to return issues. **910.** The sheriff shall file the writ in the office from which the order to return the same was issued, at the expiration of the order, or as soon after as the office shall be open, and the officer with whom it is filed shall indorse the day and hour when it was filed. Rules T. T. 1856, 103.

Arrest by sheriff before going out of office; order to bring in body. **911.** Where any sheriff, before his going out of office, arrests any defendant, and takes a bail bond and makes a return of *cepi corpus*, he shall and may, within the time allowed by law, be called upon to bring in the body by an order for that purpose, notwithstanding he may be out of office before the order is granted. Rules T. T. 1856, 105.

Deputy Clerks of the Crown and other officers may issue orders to return writs, etc. **912.** Every Deputy Clerk of the Crown and Pleas, Local or Deputy Registrar, or Clerk of the County Court, may sign and issue orders on any Sheriff to return writs issued out of the office of such Deputy Clerk, Local or Deputy Registrar, or County Court Clerk and directed to such Sheriff ; and the Sheriff shall, in case of his being served therewith, return the writs to the office from which the same issued. R. S. O. 1877, c. 66, s. 57.

913. In case a writ delivered to a sheriff for service or execution has remained in his hands 15 days, and in case he has not been delayed from returning the same by an order in writing from the party from whom he received the writ, his solicitor or agent, and in case he is afterwards directed by order of Court to return such writ, he shall not be entitled to any fees thereon unless, within 4 days after being so directed, he returns or encloses the writ by post to such party, his solicitor or agent. R. S. O. 1877, c. 66, s. 58.

Sheriff not entitled to fees on writs unless returned in 4 days after being ordered, if writ delivered 15 days before such order.

914. In case the party who delivered any writ or process to any sheriff to be executed, by himself or by his solicitor, or by the agent of such solicitor, requires, by a demand in writing, the sheriff to return the writ either to the party or to his solicitor or solicitor's agent, or to the Court from which the writ issued, (and whether such requisition is made before or after the service or other execution thereof,) the sheriff shall within 8 days, inclusive of the day of the service of the requisition, return the writ according to the terms of the requisition ; and in case the sheriff wilfully refuses or neglects to do so, he shall be liable to be ordered to return the writ, and to be further proceeded against as in other cases of contumacy. R. S. O. 1877, c. 66, s. 59.

Sheriff refusing to make return when demanded by party who delivered it to him.

Order against Sheriff.

915. In all cases where the party to the writ or process who did not deliver the same to the sheriff to be executed, is entitled, according to the practice of the Court, to call for a return of the writ or process, he may proceed in like manner to procure such return as is above provided in the case of parties who have delivered the writ or process to the sheriff for execution. R. S. O. 1877, c. 66, s. 60.

Other party entitled to return may proceed in like manner.

916. In every case in which a sheriff neglects or refuses to return any writ when so called upon, he shall be bound to pay the costs of any order taken out to compel the return, and all other costs consequent thereon, and also the costs of the previous requisition to make the return. R. S. O. 1877, c. 66, s. 61.

When Sheriff liable to costs for not returning writs.

917. In no case shall personal service on the sheriff be necessary, if it appears by affidavit that inquiry was made for him, and that he could not conveniently be found, but service shall be deemed to have been made upon the sheriff by serving the deputy sheriff if he can be conveniently found ; and if the deputy sheriff cannot conveniently be found, then service may be made upon the sheriff's clerk, or upon any bailiff of the sheriff who may for the time being be present in, or have charge of, the sheriff's office. R. S. O. 1877, c. 66, s. 64.

Personal service on Sheriff unnecessary.

918. Rules 873, 912 to 915 inclusive, 917, 919, 925 and 1233 to 1237 inclusive, shall extend and apply to coroners and elisors employed in the service or executing of the process of the High Court, or of any of the County Courts. R. S. O. 1877, c. 66, s. 65.

Certain sections to apply to Coroners and Elisors.

919. In case a writ is issued out of any Court of Record directed to a sheriff, and is delivered to him for execution, and in case the sheriff is ordered to return the same by any order of the court out of which the writ issued, and does not make the return within the time specified in the order, the plaintiff or defendant in the writ (as the case may be) may move for an order of attachment against the sheriff, and the Court or a Judge may order the sheriff to be attached, or limit a further period after which an order of attachment shall issue unless a return be made in the meantime, or may otherwise order as to him seems proper. R. S. O. 1877, c. 66, s. 66.

Attachments for non-return of writs may be issued unless further time for return granted.

920. In case the writ is not returned at the expiration of any further time limited by the order mentioned in the last preceding Rule, and in case the service of the order and the failure of the sheriff to return the writ is proved, the Court or Judge may order a writ of attachment to issue forthwith against the sheriff. R. S. O. 1877, c. 66, s. 67.

When attachment may issue.

Judge in Chambers may order issue of writs of habeas corpus. **921.** Upon the return of *"cepi corpus"* to any such attachment, any Judge having jurisdiction as aforesaid may direct the issue of a writ of *habeas corpus*, and thereupon may exercise the same powers and discretion in committing the sheriff to close custody, or in admitting him to bail, and in all other respects, as are possessed by the Court. R. S. O. 1877, c. 66, s. 68.

Such writs may be returnable on a day certain. **922.** All orders of attachment and writs of *habeas corpus* issued against a Sheriff may be returnable on a day certain to be fixed by the order of the Judge or Court ; and the return day shall not be more than 30 days from the issuing of the order ; the order when issued out of the High Court shall be made returnable before the presiding Judge in Chambers, and when issued out of any County Court, before the Judge thereof. R. S. O. 1877, c. 66, s. 69.

923. Every Deputy Sheriff, Bailiff, or other Sheriff's officer or clerk entrusted with the custody of any writ or process, or of any book, paper or document belong ng to the said Sheriff or his office, shall, upon demand upon him by such Sheriff, restore and return such writ, process, book, paper or document to the custody of the said Sheriff, and in case of any neglect or refusal to return or restore the same as aforesaid, the party so neglecting or refusing may be required by an order of any Court of Record in Ontario, or of any Ju lge of such Court, to return and restore such writ, process, book, paper or document to such Sheriff, and may be fur, ther proceeded against by attachment, as in other cases of contumacy to orders of Court. R. S. O. 1877, c. 16, s. 32.

924. If any Deputy Sheriff, Bailiff or Sheriff's officer has in his possession, custody, or control, any writ of summons, *fieri facias*, or other writ, or any bench warrant or process whatsoever, and, upon demand made by the Sheriff from who n the same was received, or his successor in office, or by any other party entitled to the possession of the same, neglects or refuses to deliver up the same, such Sheriff or his successor in office, or the party entitled to the possession of the same, may proceed before any Judge having jurisdiction in the Court out of which such writ or process issue l, to compel he production thereof ; and the order made thereupon may be enforced in the same manner as like orders f r the return of writs against Sheriffs, and with or without costs, or the motion may be refused with costs against the party applying, in the discretion of the Judge aforesaid. R. S. O. 1877, c. 16, s. 33.

6. DISCHARGE OF EXECUTION DEBTORS FROM CUSTODY.

On what authority Sheriffs may discharge debtors from custody. **925.** A written order under the hand of the solicitor in the action by whom a writ of *capias ad satisfaciendum* has been issued, shall justify the sheriff, gaoler or officer in whose custody the party is under such writ in discharging such party, unless the party for whom such solicitor professes to act has given written notice to the contrary to the said sheriff, gaoler, or officer ; but such discharge shall not be a satisfaction of the debt unless made by the authority of the creditor ; and nothing herein contained shall justify the solicitor in giving an order for discharge without the consent of his client. R. S. O. 1877, c. 66, s. 55.

7. ATTACHMENT OF DEBTS.

Application for examination of judgment debtor. **926.** Where a judgment is for the recovery by, or payment to, any person, of money, the party entitled to enforce the judgment may without an order examine the judgment debtor upon oath before a Master, or Local Master, or an Examiner, or before one of the Clerks or Deputy Clerks of the Crown, or before the Judge of the County Court of the County within which such debtor resides, or before any official referee, (or by the order of the Court or a Judge before any other person to be specially named in such order) touching his estate and effects, and as to the property and means he had when the debt or liability which was the subject of the action in which judgment has been obtained against him was incurred, and as to the property and means he still has of discharging the said judgment, and as to the disposal he has made of any property since contracting such debt or incurring such liability, and as to any and what debts are owing to him. J. A., Rule 366, R. S. O. 1877, c. 49, s. 17 ; c. 50, s. 304.

927. In case the judgment is against a body corporate, or an order for the payment of money has been obtained against a body corporate, the person entitled to enforce the judgment, or order, may in like manner examine any of the officers of such body corporate, upon oath, before the Judge of the County Court, or other officer referred to in the next preceding rule, touching the names and residences of the stockholders in said body corporate, the amount and particulars of stock held or owned by each stockholder and the amount paid thereon, also as to any and what debts are owing to the said body corporate ; and as to the estate and effects of the body corporate ; and as to the disposal made by the body corporate of any property since contracting the debt or liability, in respect of which the said judgment or order was obtained. J. A. Rule 367 ; R. S. O. 1877, c. 49, s. 19. *Application for examination of officers of corporations.*

928. Where judgment has been obtained as aforesaid, the Court or a Judge may, on the application of the party entitl d to enforce the judgment, order any clerk or employee or former clerk or employee of the judgment debtor, or any person, or the officer or officers of any corporation, to whom the d ebtor has made a transfer of his property or effects since the date when the liability or debt which was the subject of the action in which judgment was obtained was incurred, to attend at the county town of the county in which such person resides, before a Master, or an Official Referee or Examiner, or a Local Master, a Deputy Registrar of the High Court or a Deputy Clerk of the Crown, or before the Judge of the County Court of the coun'y, and to submit to be examined upon oath as to the estate and effects of the debtor, and as to the property and means he had when the debt or liability aforesaid was incurred, and as to the property or means he still has of discharging the judgment, and as to the disposal he has made of any property since contracting the debt or incurring the liability, and as to any and what debts are owing to him. The examination is to be for the purpo e of d scovery only, and no order is to be made on the evidence given on such examination. *Examination of certain persons as to a debtor's means.*

(2) Any person liable to be examined under this Rule may be compelled to attend, testify, and to produce books and documents, in the same manner and subject to the same rules of examination and the same consequences of neglecting to attend or refusing to disclose the matters in respect of which he may be examined, as in the case of a witness. 49 V. c. 16, s. 12.

929. Any person liable to be examined under any of the preceding Rules may be compelled to attend and testify, and to produce books and documents, in the same manner and subject to the same rules of examination, and the same consequences of neglecting to attend or refusing to disclose the matters in respect of which he may be examined, as in the case of a witness. J. A. Rule 368. *Compelling attendance.*

930. Any person liable to be examined under Rules 926 to 928 may be served with an appointment signed by the Judge or officer, and where the examination is to take place under an order, also with a copy of the order ; such service to be made at least 48 hours before the time appointed for the examination ; and the person to be examined be paid the same fees as a witness. J. A. Rule 369. *Service of appointment.*

Mode of conducting examination.

931. The examination shall be conducted in the same manner as in case of an oral examination of an opposite party ; and in the case of a judgment in any County Court, such County Court or the Judge or acting Judge thereof may exercise similar jurisdiction in relation to such judgment, and in like manner as might be exercised by the High Court. R. S. O. 1877, c. 50, s. 306.

Committal of debtor for non-attendance, refusal to answer, answering unsatisfactorily, etc.

932. In case such debtor does not attend as required by the said appointment, or appointment and order, as the case may be, and does not allege a sufficient excuse for not attending, or if attending, he refuses to disclose his property or his transactions respecting the same, or does not make satisfactory answers respecting the same, or if it appears from such examination that such debtor has concealed or made away with his property in order to defeat or defraud his creditors or any of them, the Court or Judge may order the debtor to be committed to the common gaol of the County in which he resides, for any term not exceeding twelve months ; or the Court or Judge may, by order, direct that a writ of *capias ad satisfaciendum* may be issued against the debtor, and a writ of *capias ad satisfaciendum* may thereupon be issued upon the judgment, or in case the debtor is at large upon bail, the Court or Judge may make an order for the debtor's being committed to close custody ; and the sheriff, on due notice of the order, shall forthwith take the debtor and commit him to close custody until he obtains an order of Court or a Judge's order for again allowing him to go out of close custody, on giving the necessary bond in that behalf, or until he is otherwise discharged in due course of law. R. S. O. 1877, c. 49, s. 18 ; c. 50, s. 305 ; J. A. Rule 369 (a).

Committal of officer of corporation in like manner.

933. In case any such officer of a corporation as aforesaid does not attend as required by the said appointment or appointment and order, and does not show a sufficient excuse for not attending, or if attending, he refuses to disclose any of the matters in respect of which he may be examined, the Court or Judge may order the officer to be committed to the common gaol of the County in which he resides, for any term not exceeding 6 months. R. S. O. 1877, c. 49, s. 19.

Judgments for payment of money or costs to be within preceding Rules.

934. Every judgment or order of the High Court and of the County Courts directing payment of money or of costs, charges or expenses, shall, so far as it relates to such money, costs, charges, or expenses, be deemed a judgment, and the person to receive payment a creditor, and the person to make payment a debtor, within the meaning of the preceding Rules. R. S. O. 1877, c. 49, s. 20.

Person having carriage of the judgment, etc., to be deemed the person to receive payment.

(a) In case a judgment or order directs the payment of money into Court, or to the credit of any cause, or otherwise than to any person, the person having the carriage of the judgment, or order, so far as relates to such payment, shall be deemed the person to receive payment within the meaning of the preceding clause of this Rule. R. S. O. 1877, c. 49, s. 20, (2).

Court or Judge may order attachment of debts.

935. The Court or a Judge may, upon the *ex parte* application of the judgment creditor, or the person entitled to enforce the judgment, either before or after the oral examination mentioned in the preceding Rules, and upon affidavit by himself or his solicitor, or some other person or persons aware of the facts respectively, stating that judgment has been recovered, and that it is still unsatisfied, and to what amount, and that any other person is indebted to the judgment debtor, and is within Ontario, order that all debts owing or accruing from such third person (hereinafter called the garnishee) to the judgment debtor, ~~and all claims and demands of the judgment debtor against the garnishee arising out of trust or con-~~

Order that garnishee appear.

~~tract, where such claims and demands could be made available under equitable execution,~~ shall be attached to answer the judgment debt ; and by the same or any subsequent order it may be ordered that the garnishee shall appear before the Court or a Judge or an officer of the Court, as the

Court or Judge shall appoint, to show cause why he should not pay the judgment creditor, or the person entitled to enforce the judgment, the . debt, claim or demand due from the garnishee to the judgment debtor, or so much thereof as may be sufficient to satisfy the judgment debt. J. A. Rule 370.

936. Service of an order that debts, claims or demands due or accruing Order for to the judgment debtor shall be attached, or notice thereof to the garnishee attachment to in such manner as the Court or Judge shall direct, shall bind such debts, bind debts claims or demands in his hands from the time of such service. J. A. from service. Rule 371.

937. If the garnishee does not forthwith pay into Court the amount Order for exe-due from him to the judgment debtor or an amount equal to the judgment cution against debt, and does not dispute the debt due or claimed to be due from him to garnishee. the judgment debtor, or if he does not appear upon notice to him, then the Court or Judge may order execution to issue, and it may issue according-ly without any previous writ or process, to levy the amount due from the garnishee, or so much thereof as may be sufficient to satisfy the judgment debt. J. A. Rule 372.

938. If the claim or demand be not due at the time of the attachment, an Execution for order may be made for payment thereof at maturity, and execution may maturing issue therefor when it matures. claims.

939. If the garnishee disputes his liability, the Court or Judge, instead Issue where of making an order that execution shall issue, may order that any issue or garnishee dis-question necessary for determining his liability be tried or determined in putes liability. any manner in which any issue or question in an action may be tried or determined. J. A. Rule 373.

940. In cases in the High Court, where the amount claim or demand When garni-claimed as due or accruing from any garnishee is within the jurisdiction shee to appear of a County or Division Court, the order to appear made under Rule 935 before County shall be for the garnishee to appear before the Judge of the County Court Judge Court of the County within which the garnishee resides, at some day and in cases in place within his County to be appointed in writing by such Judge; and High Court. written notice thereof shall be given to the garnishee at the time of the service of the order. R. S. O. 1877, c. 50, s. 311.

941. If the garnishee does not forthwith pay the amount due by him, Execution or an amount equal to the judgment debt, and does not dispute the debt from County due or claimed to be due from him to the judgment debtor, or if he does or Division not appear before the Judge named in the order at the day and place Court, if the appointed by such Judge, then such Judge, on proof of service of the garnishee does order and appointment having been made two clear days previous, may make debt. an order directing execution to issue out of the County Court or out of a Division Court, according to the amount due, and such order shall, without any previous writ or process, be sufficient authority for the Clerk of either of such Courts to issue execution for levying the amount due from such garnishee. R. S. O. 1877, c. 50, s. 312.

942. If the garnishee disputes his liability, then such Judge of the Proceedings if County Court may order that the judgment creditor shall be at liberty to he disputes proceed against the garnishee according to the usual practice of the County the debt. or Division Court, as the case may require, for the alleged debt or for the amount due to the judgment debtor if less than the judgment debt, and for costs of suit. R. S. O. 1877, c. 50, s. 315.

943. In cases in the County Courts when the amount claimed as Proceedings in due from any garnishee is within the jurisdiction of a Division Court, County Courts the order to be made under Rule 935, shall be for the garnishee to when amount appear before the Clerk of the Division Court within whose Division within the the garnishee resides, at his office, at some day to be appointed in jurisdiction of the said order by the Judge of the County Court; and the said order Courts.

shall be served on such garnishee, and if the garnishee does not forthwith pay the amount due by him or an amount equal to the judgment debt, and does not dispute the debt due or claimed to be due from him to the judgment debtor, or if he does not appear before the Division Court Clerk named in the order at his office at the day appointed by such Judge, then such Judge, on proof of the service of the order havi- g been made two clear days previous, may make an order directing execution to issue out of the Division Court of the Division in which such garnishee resides, according to the amount due, and such order shall, without any previous summons or process, be sufficient authority for the Clerk of the said Division Court to issue execution to levy the amount due from such garnishee, and the bailiff to whom such writ of execution is directed shall be thereby authorized to levy and shall levy the amount mentioned in the said execution towards satisfaction of the judgment debt, together with the costs of the proceedings to be taxed, and his own lawful fees ; but if the garnishee disputes his liability, then such Judge may order that the judgment creditor in the said County Court shall be at liberty to proceed against the garnishee, according to the practice of the said Division Court, for the alleged debt or for the amount due to the judgment debtor if less than the judgment debt, and for costs of suit.   R. S. O. 1877, c. 50, s. 316.

Order for third person to appear.   **944.** Where in proceeding to obtain an attachment of debts it is suggested by the garnishee that the debt sought to be attached belongs to some third person, or that any third person has a lien or charge upon it, the Court or Judge may order such third person to appear and state the nature and particulars of his claim upon the debt.   J. A. Rule 374.

Proceedings as to claims of third persons.   **945.** After hearing the allegations of such third person under such order, and of any other person whom by the same or any subsequent order the Court or a Judge may order to appear, or in case of such third person not appearing when ordered, the Court or Judge may order execution to issue to levy the amount due from the garnishee, or may order any issue or question to be tried or determined according to the preceding Rules, and may bar the claim of such third person, or may make such other order as the Court or Judge thinks fit, upon such terms, in all cases, with respect to the lien or charge (if any) of such third person, and to costs, as the Court or Judge thinks just and reasonable.   J. A. Rule 375.

Garnishee discharged by payment.   **946.** Payment made by or execution levied upon the garnishee under any such proceeding as aforesaid shall be a valid discharge to him as against the judgment debtor, to the amount paid or levied, although such proceeding may be set aside or the judgment reversed.   J.A. Rules 376, 500.

Attachment book to be kept by proper officer.   **947.** There shall be kept by the proper officer a debt attachment book, and in such book entries shall be made of the attachment and proceedings thereon, with names, dates, and statements of the amount recovered, and otherwise ; and copies of any entries made therein may be taken by any person upon application to the proper officer.   J. A. Rule 377.

Examination in other cases.   **948.** In case of any judgment or order other than for the recovery or payment of money, if any difficulty shall arise in or about the execution or enforcement thereof, any party interested may apply to the Court or a Judge, and the Court or Judge may make such order thereon for the attendance and examination of any party or otherwise as may be just. Eng. R. 1883, 611.

CHAPTER X.

PETITIONS OF RIGHT.

949. A petition of right may be entitled in one of the divisions of the Form of peti- High Court, and shall name the proposed place of the trial ; and such peti- tion of right. tion shall be addressed to Her Majesty in the words or to the effect of Form No. 203 in the Appendix and shall state the christian name and surname and usual place of abode of the suppliant and of his solicitor, if any, by whom the same is presented, and shall set forth with conveni- ent certainty the facts entitling the suppliant to relief, and shall be signed by such suppliant, his counsel or solicitor. R. S. O. 1877, c. 59, s. 3.

950. The said petition shall be left with the Provincial Secretary, in Petition to be order that the same may be submitted to the Lieutenant-Governor for his submitted to consideration, and in order that the Lieutenant-Governor, if he thinks fit, Lieutenant- may grant his *fiat* that right be done ; and no fee or sum of money shall Governor for be payable by the suppliant therefor. R. S. O. 1877, c. 59, s. 4.

951. Upon the Lieutenant-Governor's *fiat* being obtained, a copy of Proceedings the petition and *fiat* shall be left at the office of the Attorney-General, after fiat is with an indorsement thereon in the words or to the effect of Form No. obtained. 204 in the Appendix, praying for an answer on behalf of Her Majesty within 28 days. R. S. O. 1877, c. 59, s. 5.

952. In case the petition is presented for the recovery of any Service on real or personal property, or any right in or to the same, which has person in pos- been granted away or disposed of by or on behalf of Her Majesty or Her session of real Predecessors, a copy of the petition, allowance and fiat shall be served property. upon or left at the last or usual or last known place of abode of the person in the possession, occupation or enjoyment of the property or right, endorsed with a notice in the words or to the effect of Form No. 205 in the Appendix, requiring such person to appear thereto within 8 days, and to file his statement of defence within 14 days after the same has been so served or left as aforesaid. R. S. O. 1877, c. 59, s. 6.

953. It shall not be necessary to issue any *scire facias* or other process Appearance. to any person so served for the purpose of requiring him to appear and file his defence to the petition, but he shall, within the time so limited, enter an appearance to the same in the words or to the effect of Form No. 206 in the Appendix, and shall file his defence or demurrer to the said petition within the time specified in such notice, or within such further time as may be allowed by the Court or a Judge. R. S. O. 1877, c. 59, s. 7.

954. The time for filing a defence or demurrer to the petition, on Time for behalf of Her Majesty, shall be the said period of 28 days after the peti- pleading or tion has been left as aforesaid at the office of the said Attorney-General, demurring. or such further time as may be allowed by the Court or a Judge. R. S. O. 1877, c. 59, s. 8.

955. The petition may be answered by statement of defence or Pleadings in demurrer, or by both statement of defence and demurrer, by or in the answer to pe- name of Her Majesty's Attorney-General, on behalf of Her Majesty, and tition. by or on behalf of any other person who may be called upon to file his defence thereto, in the same manner as in an ordinary action, and without the necessity for any inquisition finding the truth of such petition or the right of the suppliant ; and any sufficient ground of defence in point of law or fact to the petition on behalf of Her Majesty, may be alleged on behalf of any other person so called on to defend. R. S. O. 1877, c. 59, s. 9.

Rules of pleading, etc. **956.** So far as the same are applicable, and except in so far as is inconsistent with these Rules, the laws and statutes in force as to pleading, evidence, trial, security for costs, amendment, arbitration, special cases, the means of procuring and taking evidence, set off, and appeal, in ordinary actions, and the rules, orders, practice and course of procedure therein for the time being, shall, unless the Court or a Judge otherwise-orders, be applicable to petitions of right. R. S. O. 1877, c. 59, s. 10.

In default of defence, etc., applicant to take petition pro confesso. **957.** In case of a failure on the behalf of Her Majesty, or of any other person duly called upon to defend in due time, at any stage of the proceedings, the suppliant shall be at liberty to apply to the Court or a Judge for an order that the petition may be taken as confessed ; and the Court or Judge may order that such petition may be taken as confessed, as against Her Majesty, or other party so making default ; and in case of default on behalf of Her Majesty, and any other person called upon as aforesaid to defend, judgment may be given by the Court in favour of the suppliant.

(*a*) Such judgment may be set aside by the Court or a Judge, upon such terms as may seem proper. R. S. O. 1877, c. 59, s. 11.

Issues to be tried by a Judge without a jury. **958.** Any issue of fact or assessment of damages to be tried or had in respect of a petition of right, shall be tried or had by a Judge without a jury. R. S. O. 1877, c. 59, s. 13.

The judgment **959.** The judgment of the Court, whether given upon demurrer, upon the pleadings, or upon default in pleading, shall be that the suppliant is or is not entitled either to the whole or to some portion of the relief sought by his petition, or that such other relief may be given, and upon such terms and conditions (if any) as the Court thinks just. R. S. O. 1877, c. 59, s. 14.

When judgment to be equivalent to *amoveas manus*. **960.** In cases in which the judgment, commonly called a judgment of *amoveas manus*, was formerly in England pronounced upon a petition of right, a judgment that the suppliant is entitled to relief, as hereinbefore provided, shall have the same effect as a judgment of *amoveas manus*. R. S. O. 1877, c. 59, s. 15.

Costs against suppliant. **961.** The costs of all proceedings under these Rules shall be in the discretion of the Court or a Judge, and shall be recovered in the same way as in ordinary actions, save when costs are ordered to be paid by Her Majesty. *New. See* R. S. O. 1877, c. 59, ss. 16, 17.

If judgment be for relief, etc., Judge to certify to Provincial Treasurer **962.** Upon any judgment or order for the payment of costs by Her Majesty, the Judge shall and may, upon application in behalf of the party entitled to costs, after the lapse of 14 days from the making, giving or affirming of the judgment, or order, certify to the Provincial Treasurer the tenor and purport of the same, in the words or to the effect of Form No. 207 in the Appendix ; and such certificate may be sent to or left at the office of the Provincial Treasurer. R. S. O. 1877, c. 59, s. 18.

963. Nothing in these Rules shall prevent a subject from proceeding by petition of right in any manner in which he might have proceeded before the 23rd day of April, 1887 ; nor shall anything in these Rules be construed as entitling a subject to proceed by petition of right in any case in which he would not be entitled so to proceed under the Acts passed by the Parliament of the United Kingdom before the said date.

CHAPTER XI.

PROCEEDINGS WITHOUT WRIT.

1. PETITIONS.

964. There shall be indorsed on every petition a notice addressed to the parties concerned, stating the time and place at which the petition is to be heard, and informing them that if they do not appear on the petition at such time and place, the Court may make such order, on the petitioner's own shewing, as shall appear just.   Chy. O. 265.

Petition to be endorsed with notice of hearing.

2. ADMINISTRATION.

965. Any person claiming to be a creditor, or a specific, pecuniary, or residuary legatee, or the next of kin, or one of the next of kin, or the heir, or a devisee interested under the will of a deceased person may apply to the Court or a Judge upon motion, without any action being instituted, or any other preliminary proceeding, for an order for the administration of the estate, real or personal, of such deceased person.   Chy. O. 467.

Creditors, legatees, next of kin, heirs or devisees, may apply on motion, in Chambers for administration.

966. The notice of motion is to be served upon all proper parties at least 14 clear days before the day named for hearing the application, and is to be in the form or to the effect set forth in Form No. 12 in the Appendix, and must be served upon the executor or administrator.   Chy. O. 468, 552, 561.

14 days' notice of motion. Form of notice.

967. Upon proof by affidavit of the due service of the notice of motion, or on the appearance in person, or by his solicitor or counsel, of the executor or administrator, and upon proof by affidavit of such other matter, if any, as the Court requires, the Court may make the usual order for the administration of the estate of the deceased, with such variations, if any, as the circumstances of the case require ; and the order so made is to have the force and effect of a judgment to the like effect made at the trial of an action between the same parties.   Chy. O. 469.

Upon proof of service of notice, or on appearance of personal representative, etc., order for administration may be granted.

968. The Court is to give any special directions touching the carriage or execution of the order, which it deems expedient ; and in case of applications for an order by two or more persons, or classes of persons, the Court may grant the same to such one or more of the claimants as it thinks fit ; and the carriage of the order may be subsequently given to any party interested, and upon such terms as the Court may direct.   Chy. O. 470.

Special directions may be given respecting order,&tc. Carriage of order may be subsequently changed.

969. An order for the administration of the estate of a deceased person may be obtained by his executor or administrator, and all the provisions of the foregoing Rules are to extend to applications by an executor or administrator.   Chy. O. 471.

Order may be obtained by personal representative.

No accounts to be ordered of realty, unless heir, or devisee served.

970. No accounts or enquiries in respect of the real estate are to be directed, unless notice of the application has been given to the heirs and dev.sees interested therein, or one or more of them. Chy. O. 472.

Accounts of realty may be directed by supplemental order.

971. After enquiries directed in respect of the personal estate, the Court may, in a proper case, after notice given to those interested in the real estate, or to one or more of them, make a supplemental order in respect of the real estate, upon such terms as the Court sees fit. Chy. O. 473.

Adult person may apply to Local Master for administration of deceased person's estate.

Notice requisite.

972. Any adult person entitled to apply, under Rules 965 or 969, for an administration order may apply to the Master in the County town of the County (other than the County of York) where the deceased person, whose estate it is desired to administer, resided at the time of his death ; and the Master may, on 14 clear days notice being given to the person or persons entitled to notice of such an application, make an order for the administration of, and proceed to administer such estate in the least expensive and most expeditious manner. Chy. O. 638.

Master to have full power to deal with realty and personalty, and dispose of costs, etc.

973. The Master shall have full power to deal with both the realty and personalty of the estate, the subject of administration, and shall dispose of the costs of the proceedings, and shall finally wind up all matters connected with the estate, without any further directions, and without any separate, interim, or interlocutory reports, or orders, except where the special circumstances of the case absolutely call therefor ; and in so doing he shall be guided by the practice in the administration of estates upon an application made in Chambers for an administration order.

Moneys realized to be paid into Court, and not paid out except on Judge's order.

974. All moneys realised from the estate shall at once be paid into Court, and no moneys shall be distributed or paid out for costs or otherwise, without an order of a judge in Chambers or the Court, and on the application for such order, the judge may review, amend, or refer back to the Master his report or order, or make such other order as he deems proper, and no order for payment out shall be made until the purchaser has consented thereto, or has been notified of the motion. Chy. O. 639.

Master to enquire as to outstanding estate.

And to compute interest on debts and legacies.

975. In taking an account of a deceased's personal estate under an order of reference, the Master is to enquire and state to the Court what, if any, of the deceased's personal estate is outstanding or undisposed of ; and is also to compute interest on the deceased's debts from the date of the judgment or order, and on legacies from the end of one year after the deceased's death, unless any other time of payment is directed by the will. Chy. O. 474.

Advertisment for creditors, form of.

976. Every advertisement for creditors affecting the estate of a deceased person, which is issued pursuant to an order, is to direct every creditor, by a time to be thereby limited, to send to such other party as the Master directs, or to his solicitor, to be named and described in the advertisement, the name and address of the creditor, and the full particulars of his claim, and a statement of his account, and the nature of the security (if any) held by him ; and such advertisement is to be in the form set out in Form No. 36 in the Appendix, with such variations as the circumstances of the case require and at the time of directing such advertisement, a time is to be fixed for adjudicating on the claims. Chy. O. 475.

Affidavit of creditor dispensed with unless required.

977. No creditor need make an affidavit. or attend in support of his claim (except to produce his security, if any,) unless he is served with a notice requiring him to do so as hereinafter provided. Chy. O. 476.

Creditors to produce securities.

978. Every creditor is to produce before the Master, the security (if any) held by him, at such time as is specified in the advertisment for that purpose, being the time appointed for adjudicating on the claims ; and every creditor, if required by notice in writing, to be given by the ex-

ecutor or administrator of the deceased, or by such other party as the And other
Master directs, in the form set forth in form No. 37 in the Appendix, is to documents, if
produce all other deeds and documents necessary to substantiate his claim notified.
before the Master, at such time as is specified in the notice.   Chy. O. 477.

979. In case a creditor neglects or refuses to comply with the next pre- Otherwise not
ceding Rule, he is not to be allowed any costs of proving his claim, unless to be allowed
the Master otherwise directs.   Chy. O. 478.   costs.

980. The executor or administrator of the deceased, or such other Creditors'
party as the Master directs, is to examine the claims sent in pursuant to claims to be
the advertisment, and is to ascertain, as far as he is able, to which of such examined.
claims the estate of the deceased is justly liable.   Chy. O. 479.

981. The executor or administrator, or one of the executors or admin- Affidavit to be
istrators, or such other party either alone or jointly with his solicitor, or made by per-
other competent person, or otherwise, as the Master directs, is, at least son examining
7 clear days before the day appointed for adjudication, to file an affi- claims.
davit which may be in the form No. 50 in the Appendix, verifying a list of When to be
the claims, the particulars of which have been sent in pursuant to the ad- filed.
vertisment, and stating to which of such claims, or parts thereof, respect- Form of.
ively, the estate of the deceased is, in the opinion of the deponent, justly
liable, and his belief that such claims, or parts thereof respectively, are
justly due, and proper to be allowed, and the reasons for such belief.
Chy. O. 480.

982. In case the Master thinks fit so to direct, the making of the affi- Time for mak-
davit referred to in the next preceding Rule, is to be postponed till after ing affidavit
the day appointed for adjudication, and is then to be subject to such may be post-
directions as the Master may give.   Chy. O. 481.   poned.

983. At the time appointed for adjudicating upon the claims, or at any Adjudication
adjournment thereof, the Master may allow any of the claims, or any part on claims by
thereof respectively, without proof by the creditors, and may direct such Master.
investigation of all or any of the claims not allowed, and require such further particulars, information, or evidence relating thereto, as he thinks fit Further evi
and may, if he so thinks fit, require any creditor to attend and prove his dence may be
claim, or any part thereof ; and the adjudication on such claims as are not required.
then allowed is to be adjourned to a time to be then fixed.   Chy. O. 482.

984. Notice is to be given by the executor or administrator, or such Notice to be
other party as the Master directs :   sent creditors.

(1) To every creditor whose claim, or any part thereof, has been allowed Where claim
without proof by the creditor, of the allowance, and the notice may be in allowed with-
the form No. 38 in the Appendix.   out proof.

(2). And to every such creditor as the Master directs to attend and Where proof
prove his claim, or such part thereof as is not allowed, by a time to be of claim
named in the notice, (which may be in the form No. 39 in the Appendix, is required.
not being less than 7 clear days after the notice, and to attend at a time
to be therein named, being the time to which the adjudication thereon
has been adjourned ; and in case any creditor does not comply with the
notice, his claim, or such part thereof as aforesaid, is to be disallowed,
unless the Master thinks fit to give further time.   Chy. O. 483.

985. A creditor who has not before sent in particulars of his claim Creditor may
pursuant to the advertisment, may do so 7 clear days previous to any day send in parti-
to which the adjudication is adjourned.   Chy. O. 484.   cularsof claim.

986. After the time fixed for the advertisment, no claim is to be re- After expiry of
ceived (except as before provided in case of an adjournment,) unless the time limited
Master thinks fit to give special leave upon application, and then upon by advertise-
such terms and conditions as to costs and otherwise as the Master directs. ment for filing
Chy. O. 485.   claims.

9

Creditors to be notified when their claims are payable out of Court.   **987.** Where an order is made for payment of money out of Court to creditors, the party whose duty it is to prosecute the order is to send each creditor, or his solicitor (if any,) a notice that the cheques may be obtained from the Accountant; and the notice may be in form No. 40 in the Appendix, and the party is, when required, to produce any papers necessary to enable the creditors to receive their cheques. Chy. O. 486.

Form of notice. Notice, how to be sent to creditors.   **988.** Every notice by these Rules, required to be given is, unless the Master otherwise directs, to be deemed sufficiently given and served if transmitted by post, prepaid, to the creditor to be served, according to the address given by the creditor in the claim sent in by him pursuant to the advertisement, or, in case the creditor has employed a solicitor, to such solicitor, according to the address given by him. Chy. O. 487.

3. PARTITION.

Adult party may apply to Local Master for partition, on motion.   **989.** Any adult person entitled to a judgment or order for the partition of an estate, may, on serving one or more of the persons entitled to a share of the estate of which partition is sought, with a 14 clear days' notice of motion, apply to the presiding Judge in Chambers, or to the Master in the County (other than the County of York) wherein the land sought to **Proceedings on judgment for partition.** be affected by the proceeding lies, for an order for the partition or sale of the premises in question; whereupon the Judge or Master may make such order for partition or sale, or such other order as may be proper, and **Infants interested must be represented by guardian ad litem.** the Master shall thereupon proceed in the least expensive and most expeditious manner, according to the practice now in force, for the partition or sale of the premises, the ascertainment of the rights of the various persons interested, the adding parties, the taxation and payment of costs, and otherwise. Provided always, that where an infant is interested in the estate, no order shall be made for partition or sale until such infant is represented by its guardian ad litem; and provided also that all moneys **Money not to be paid out without Judge's order.** realized from the estate shall at once be paid into Court, and that no moneys shall be distributed or paid out for costs or otherwise, without an order of a Judge in Chambers or the Court; and on the application for such order, the Judge may review, amend, or refer back to the Master his report or order, or make such other order as he deems proper. Chy. O. 640.

When after judgment, lands discovered in another county.   **990.** When after an order has been made under the preceding Rule lands are discovered in another county, an application may be made to a Judge of the High Court in Chambers for the partition or sale of such lands under the order formerly made, and where two or more orders have been made by Masters in different counties, an application may be made in Chambers for an order as to the conduct of the future proceedings. Chy. O. 641.

Entry of orders. At conclusion of suit papers to be forwarded to Clerk of R. & W.   **991.** The Local Masters shall enter in books kept for that purpose, all judgments, or orders, made by them, in administration and partition matters and they shall on the conclusion of the proceedings, annex together all the papers filed with them in such proceedings, and transmit the same to the Clerk of Records and Writs, who shall duly enter the same. Chy. O. 650.

4. PROPERTY OF INFANTS.

Applications to sell, etc., infants estate where made.   **992.** All applications for the sale, mortgage, lease or other disposition of an infant's estate shall be made to the Master in Chambers, and no reference in any such matter is to be directed to any Local Master, except by leave of a Judge. J. A. Rule 585.

Official Guardian to be notified.   **993.** The Official Guardian shall be duly notified of all applications under the last preceding Rule. J. A. Rule 586.

994. A petition for the sale or other disposition of the real estate of an infant, is to be intituled in the matter of the infant. Chy. O. 527. *Petition, how entitled.*

995. The petition is to be presented in the name of the infant, by his guardian, or by a person applying by the same petition to be appointed guardian as hereinafter provided. Chy. O. 528. *In whose name to be presented.*

996. The petition is to state the nature and amount of the personal property to which the infant is entitled—the necessity of resorting to the real estate—its nature, value, and the annual profits thereof. It must also state circumstances sufficient to justify the sale or other disposition of the estate, and the application of the proceeds in the manner proposed. The prayer must state specifically the relief that is desired; it must designate the lands to be disposed of, and must propose a scheme for that purpose, and for the appropriation of the proceeds. If an allowance for maintenance is desired, it must be so prayed, and a case must be stated to justify such an order, and to regulate the amount. Chy. O. 529. *What it is to state.*

997. The petition may pray for the appointment of a guardian, as well as for the disposal of the infant's estate. In that case a proper case must be made by the petition, and established by the evidence, for the appointment of the person proposed. Chy. O. 530. *Petition may pray for appointment of guardian.*

998. Upon all petitions for the sale of an infant's estate, the infant is to be produced before a Judge in Chambers, or before a Master. Chy. O. 531. *The infant to be produced to Judge or Master.*

999. When the infant is above the age of 14 years he is to be examined apart by the Judge or Master, upon the matter of the petition, as to his consent thereto ; and his examination is to be stated to have been taken under this Rule, and is to be annexed to and filed with the petition. Chy. O. 532 ; J. A. Rule 587. *Infant if over 14 years to be examined. Examination to be attached to petition.*

1000. It shall not be necessary to examine any infant under 14 years of age, in support of a petition affecting such infant's estate, unless required by a Judge ; but, unless otherwise ordered, it shall be sufficient for the officer before whom such infant shall be produced, to certify that he has been produced, and that he is under the age of 14 years. J. A. Rule 587. *Infants under 14 need not be examined.*

1001. The witnesses to verify the petition are also to be produced before the Judge, or Master, and are to be examined *viva voce* as to the matter of the petition, and the depositions so taken are to be stated to have been taken under this Rule. Chy. O. 533. *Witnesses in support of petition to be examined before Judge or Master.*

1002. The Masters of the Supreme Court may examine infants and witnesses under the preceding Rule, without special order or reference. Chy. O. 534. *Masters authorized to take examination without special order.*

1003. Upon a petition so verified, the Court or Judge may either grant the relief prayed at once, or make such order as to further evidence, or otherwise, as the circumstances of the case require. Chy. O. 535. *Court may grant relief or require further evidence.*

1004. No conveyance of the lands of infants is to be settled, until evidence is produced to the officer settling the same of the purchase money having been paid into Court, or of the payment thereof into Court having been dispensed with ; and in cases where there is to be a mortgage for part of the purchase money, until evidence is given to the said officer of such mortgage having been registered and deposited with the Accountant. J. A. Rule 506. *Conveyances of infants' lands—evidence to be produced to officer settling.*

5. DEVOLUTION OF ESTATES.

1005. Before an executor or administrator takes proceedings under *The Devolution of Estates Act*, for the sale of real estate in which infants *Notice to official guardian.*

are concerned, he shall give to the official guardian or other officer charged with the duties referred to in the 8th section of the said Act notice of the intention to sell, and shall not be entitled to any expenses incurred before giving such notice.

Application to judge. **1006.** The official guardian or other officer aforesaid, or any person interested in the real estate or in the proceeds of the sale thereof, may apply in a summary manner to a Judge in Chambers, upon notice to all parties concerned or to such persons as the Judge may direct for such direction or order touching the real estate and the proceeds thereof or the costs of the proceedings as to the Judge may seem meet.

6. SUMMARY INQUIRIES INTO FRAUDULENT CONVEYANCES.

The Court or a Judge may at the instance of any judgment creditor call on the debtor and his grantee etc., to show cause why lands conveyed by fraudulent grant should not be sold. **1007.** Where a judgment creditor or a person entitled to money under a judgment or order, alleges that the debtor or person who is to pay has made a conveyance of his lands which is void, as being made to delay, hinder or defraud creditors or a creditor, it shall not be necessary to institute an action for the purpose of setting aside such conveyance, but a motion may be made to the Court or a Judge in Chambers by the judgment creditor, calling upon the judgment debtor or person who is to pay, and the persons to whom the conveyance has been made, or who have acquired any interest thereunder, to show cause why the lands embraced therein, or a competent part thereof, should not be sold to realize the amount to be levied under the execution. R. S. O. 1877, c. 49 s. 10.

The Court or a Judge may call on a judgment debtor, etc., to show cause why his equitable interests should not be sold to pay execution. **1008.** Where any judgment creditor in an action, or a person entitled under a judgment or order as aforesaid, alleges that the debtor or person who is to pay is entitled to or has an interest in any land which under the former practice could not be sold under legal process, but could be rendered available in an action for equitable execution by sale for satisfaction of the debt, the Court or a Judge in Chambers may, upon the application of the creditor, call upon the debtor or person who is to pay, and the trustee or other person having the legal estate in the land in question, to show cause why the said land or the interest therein of the debtor or the person who is to pay, or a competent part of the said land, should not be sold to realize the amount to be levied under the execution. R. S. O. 1877, c. 49, s. 11.

Proceedings after such application. **1009.** Upon any application under either of the two preceding Rules, such proceedings shall be had, either in a summary way, or by the trial of an issue, or by inquiry before an officer of the Court, or by an action, or otherwise, as the Court or Judge may deem necessary or convenient for the purpose of ascertaining the truth of the matters in question, and whether the lands or the debtor's or other person's interest therein are liable for the satisfaction of the execution ; but if in a case in a County Court there is a dispute as to material facts, and the value of the land, or the debtor's or other person's interest therein, appears to be over $400, the Court or Judge shall direct the trial of an issue in the High Court, and may name the county in which the trial is to take place, subject to any order that the High Court or a Judge thereof may see fit to make in that behalf. R. S. O. 1877, c. 49, s. 12.

Cases in County Courts.

Application to be made to the Judge of the County in which the lands are situate in County Court cases. **1010.** In County Court cases the application under Rules 1007 and 1008 shall be made to the County Court, or to a Judge of a County Court, of the County or Union of Counties in which the lands to which the application relates are situate, unless the said Court or Judge upon the hearing of the application deems it more convenient and more conducive to the ends of justice to order, and orders, that the proceedings be had and taken in the Court or before a Judge of the Court, from which the execution issued ; in which case the Clerk of the County Court of the County in which the land lies shall transmit the papers filed with him, together with the order of transference, to the Clerk of the County Court from which the execution issued. R. S. O. 1877, c. 49, s. 13

ıg discussion followed, and the
journed after arriving at no
asion.

rty Sub-Committee.

, (Chairman), Small, Gibbs,
b-Committee of the Property
: the Beard lease, met yester-
ard asks to be relieved from
e lease compelling him to
tor. On motion of Ald. Gibbs
l to relieve Mr. Beard of his
build an elevator, on condi-
ay the rental asked by Mr.
he time the lease was made,
r foot ; failing to do this, Mr.
ut up the elevator.

Notes.

Leslie has consented to allow
Island to be made through
and has signed a document
ty harmless in the matter.
:o Incandescent Light Com-
ied for leave to lay conduits
ing streets :—Ternulay street
street, Alice street to Yonge
treet to Yonge street, both
o street from Elm to Welling-
ith sides of King street from
irch streets, both sides of Bay
ing to Queen streets, Adelaide
ay to Yonge streets, Queen
ork to Yonge streets. City
att sees no reason why tho
:ed for should not be granted.
rice cordially endorses tho
sterday's GLOBE on Municipal
Mayor says that it is the
ference of Aldermen with the
their meddling with their
h causes the trouble. THE
of making the head of each
esponsible, and to give him
ne clerks without any inter-
dermen, is, in the Mayor's
d one.
yesterday received several
ig for the vacancy caused by
ir. F. Lobb. If the writers
:ould have seen the look of
Mayor's face as he read the
ould understand that their
m. In addition to the letters
personal applications were
layor, the applicants in each
scant encouragement.
has received the following
e Secretary of the Sabbath
f Binghamton, N.Y. :—
am instructed by unanimous

1011. Where in a summary way or, upon the trial of an issue, or as the result of any inquiries under the four preceding Rules, any land, or the interest of any debtor or other person therein, is found liable to be sold, an order shall be made by the Court or Judge, declaring what land or what interest therein is liable to be sold, and directing sale thereof by the Master according to the usual practice. R. S. O. 1877, c. 49, s. 14. *If lands or interest of debtor or found liable to sale, an order to be made specifying the same.*

1012. Any notice of motion for an order under Rules 1007, 1008 or 1010, may contain a description of the land in question, and upon filing the same with the proper officer, signed by the solicitor of the applicant a certificate of *lis pendens* may be issued for registration, and in case the said motion is refused in whole or in part, a certificate for registration of the order may be issued. R. S. O. 1877, c. 49, s. 16. *Lis pendens may be registered.*

7. QUIETING TITLES.

1013. Under "*The Quieting Titles Act*" the petition for an investigation of title is not to include two or more properties dependent on separate and distinct titles ; but may include any number of lots or parcels belonging to the same person, and dependent on one and the same chain of title. Chy. O. 492. *Two or more properties held by separate titles not to be included in the same petition.*

1014. Where an application is made under section 2 of the said Act, the Clerk of Records and Writs is to attend one of the Judges with the petition for directions, before the same is referred for investigation. Chy. O. 493. *Petitions to be referred to Judge in certain cases before being referred for investigation.*

1015. A petition under the Act may, at the option of the petitioner, be referred to any of the officers of the Court at Toronto, or to any conveyancing Counsel, who may from time to time be designated by the Court for the purpose ; or to any of the following Local Masters, viz., the Masters at Barrie, Belleville, Berlin, Brampton, Brantford, Brockville, Chatham, Cobourg, Cornwall, Goderich, Guelph, Hamilton, Kingston, Lindsay, London, Ottawa, Owen Sound, Perth, Peterborough, Sandwich, Sarnia, Simcoe, Stratford, St. Catharines, Walkerton, Whitby, and Woodstock ; or to any other of the Local Masters who shall hereafter be designated. Chy. O. 494. *Petition to whom to be referred.*

1016. The Registrar of the Chancery Division is, until further order, to be the sole Inspector of Titles, in respect of petitions filed under *The Quieting Titles Act*, and sole Referee of any petitions, the proceedings under which are to be conducted in Toronto. Chy. O. 633. *Registrar to be Inspector.*

1017. To facilitate the proceedings in cases referred to the Local Masters, one or more Inspectors of Titles will be named by the Court, for the purposes, and with the powers mentioned in and provided for by the 23rd and 24th sections of the said Act ; and on the petition are to be indorsed the names of the Inspector, or one of the Inspectors, as the case may be, and of the Local Master, thus : "To be referred to the Master at   , and to Mr.   , Inspector of Titles." Chy. O. 495. *Inspector of Titles to be appointed. Indorsement on petition.*

1018. Petitions filed unindorsed with the name of a Referee, are to be referred to the Referee in Toronto, or to one of the Referees in Toronto (if more than one), in rotation or otherwise as the Court or a Judge from time to time directs ; but a petition indorsed with the name of any Referee is to be referred to him accordingly, unless the Court or a Judge otherwise directs. Chy. O. 496. *Petitions, when to be referred to Toronto Referee.*

1019. Where the petitioner desires the reference to a Local Master, the petition is to be entered with the Inspector of Titles before being filed as required by the Statute, and the Inspector is to note thereon the day of entering the same, adding to such note his own initials, and is thereupon to deliver the petition to the solicitor, or, if duly stamped, to the Registrar, to be filed. Chy. O. 497. *Petitions to be referred to Local Referees to be first entered with Inspector.*

Local Masters may confer with Inspector

1020. The Local Master shall be entitled to confer or correspond Act time to time with the Inspector of Titles, for advice and assistance from questions of practice or evidence, or other questions arising under the one or under these Rules. Chy. O. 498.

Certificate of filing of petition to be registered.

1021. The Clerk of Records and Writs is to deliver, to the party filing a petition under the Act, a certificate of the filing thereof, for registration in the proper County; and thereupon the petition is forthwith to be referred and delivered or posted by the Clerk of Records and Writs to the Referee named for that purpose. Chy. O. 499.

Papers in support of application to be delivered to Referee and examined by him.

1022. The particulars necessary, under section 7 of the Act, to support the petition are to be delivered or sent by the petitioner, or his solicitor, to the Referee, and are to be forthwith examined and considered by him. Chy. O. 500.

Evidence required as to possession.

1023. In every case of an investigation of the title to property under the said Act, the petitioner is to shew, by affidavit or otherwise, whether possession has always accompanied the title under which he claims the property, or how otherwise, or is to shew some sufficient reason for dispensing with such proof either wholly or in part. Chy. O. 501.

Where there is no contest, attendance of petitioner's solicitor dispensed with.

1024. Where there is no contest, the attendance of the petitioner, or of any solicitor on his behalf, is not to be required on the examination of the title, except where, for any special reason, the Referee directs such attendance. Chy. O. 502.

Referee to deliver requisitions and objections.

1025. If, on such examination as aforesaid, the Referee finds the proof of title defective, he is to deliver or mail to the petitioner, or to his solicitor or agent, a memorandum of such finding, stating shortly therein what the defects are, and he is therein to state as far as possible all the objections to the title. Chy. O. 503.

Advertisements to be published in Gazette and other newspapers. Notices to be posted at Court House and Post Office.

1026. When the Referee finds that a good title is shown, he is to prepare the necessary advertisement, and the same is to be published in the Official *Gazette* and in any other newspaper or newspapers in which the Referee thinks it proper to have the same inserted; and a copy of the advertisement is also to be put up on the door of the Court House of the County where the land lies, and, unless the nearest Post Office is in a city, in some conspicuous place in the Post Office which is situate nearest to the property, the title of which is under investigation; and the Referee is to endorse on the advertisement so prepared by him, the name of the newspaper or newspapers in which the same is to be published, and the number of insertions to be given therein respectively, and the period (not less than 4 weeks) for which the notice is to be continued at the Court House and Post Office respectively. Chy. O. 504.

Notices required to be served.

1027. Any notice of the application to be served or mailed under section 16 of the Act, is to be prepared by the Referee; and directions are in like manner, to be given by him as to the persons to be served with the notice, and as to the mode of serving the same. Chy. O. 505.

Inspector and Toronto Referee to confer with Judges.

1028. The Inspector, or Toronto Referee, is from time to time to confer with one of the Judges in respect of matters before such Inspector or Toronto Referee, as there shall be occasion. Chy. O. 506.

When title made out before Local Referee, he is to certify same and forward papers to Inspector.

1029. When any person has shown himself, in the opinion of a Local Master, to be entitled to a certificate or conveyance under the Act, and has published and given all the notices required, the Master is to write at the foot of the petition, and sign, a memorandum to the following effect: "I am of opinion that the petitioner is entitled to a certificate of title (or conveyance) as prayed" (or subject to the following incumbrances, &c., *as the case may be*); and is to transmit the petition (if by mail, the postage being prepaid,) with the deeds, evidence, and other papers before him in reference thereto, to the Inspector of Titles with whom the petition was entered ; and the Inspector is to examine the same carefully, and should he find any defect in the evidence of title, or in the proceedings, he is, by correspondence or otherwise, to point the same out to the petitioner, or his solicitor, or to the Master, as the case may be, in order that the defect may be remedied before a Judge is attended with the petition and papers for approval. Chy. O. 507.

Duty of Inspector.

1030. When the Inspector, or other Referee (not being a Local Master,) finds that the petitioner has shewn himself entitled to a certificate of title, or a conveyance under the Act, and has published and given all the notices required, the Inspector, or Referee, (not being a Local Master,) is to write at the foot of the petition, and sign a memorandum to the same effect as is required from a Local Master, and is to prepare the certificate of title, or conveyance, and is to engross the same in duplicate, one being on parchment or parchment paper ; and is to sign the same respectively at the foot or in the margin thereof ; and is to attend one of the Judges therewith, and with the deeds, evidence, and other papers before him in reference thereto ; and on the certificate or conveyance being signed by the Judge, the Inspector or other Referee aforesaid, as the case may be, is to procure the same to be signed by the Registrar, and registered ; and the Clerk of Records and Writs is to deliver or transmit the same when so signed or registered, to the petitioner, his solicitor, or agent, for registration in the proper County. Chy. O. 508.

When title is made out to satisfaction of Inspector or Toronto Referee, he is to certify same : and to prepare certificate of Title.

Certificate to be engrossed in duplicate.

Signed by Judge, Inspector, or Toronto Referee, and Registrar.

1031. When a certificate of title or conveyance under the Act has been granted, the Inspector or Referee may, without further order, deliver, on demand, to the party entitled thereto, or his solicitor, all deeds and other evidences of title, not including affidavits made, and evidence given in the matter of the title ; and is to take his receipt therefor. Chy. O. 509.

After certificate of title granted, Title Deeds may be delivered up without order on receipt being given.

1032. Every Inspector and other Toronto Referee is to keep a book, and to preserve therein a copy of all his letters under these Rules, and is to prepare monthly, for the information of the profession, a memorandum of points of practice decided in matters under the Act. Chy. O. 510.

Inspector or Toronto Referee to keep copies of all letters.

1033. The applicant or his solicitor is to pay, or prepay, as the case may be, all postages and other expenses of transmitting letters or papers. Chy. O. 515.

Applicant to pay all postage, etc.

1034. Petitions under section 33 of the Act are to be filed and proceeded with in the same manner (as nearly as may be) as petitions for an indefeasible title ; and the fees of officers, solicitors, and counsel, are to be the same as in respect of the like proceedings in suits. Chy. O. 516.

Proceedings under, how conducted, and fees therefor.

1035. Appeals from the Toronto Referee, Referee or Local Masters and others when they are acting under the said Act, are to be prosecuted in the same way as appeals from a Master. Chy. O. 591.

Appeals from Referee and Local Masters, under Q. T. Act.

1036. The fee of the Inspector of Titles on entering the petition with him shall be $8, and no further fee is to be paid him for correspondence, examination of the title, drawing and engrossing certificate or conveyance, or for any other matter or thing done under the petition. Chy. O. 514.

Fee payable to Inspector of Titles.

1037. The fees of solicitors and counsel, and the fees payable by stamps, for proceedings under the said Act, are respectively, to be the same as for like proceedings in suits. Chy. O. 511.

Fees to solicitors and counsel.

8. CONTROVERTED MUNICIPAL ELECTIONS.

Proceedings by motion.

Fiat to be obtained.

1038. Proceedings in the nature of *quo warranto* under the Municipal Act shall be by motion on leave obtained from the Court or a Judge. Upon the application for leave to serve a notice of motion, then upon the Court or a Judge finding sufficient ground for giving the notice, and upon such security being given as the Act requires and the sufficiency thereof being allowed, the Court or Judge shall give a *fiat* for leave to serve the notice of motion.

Notice of motion.

1039. The notice of motion shall be at least a seven clear days' notice, and the relator may either mention the return day therein or may state that the motion will be made on the eighth day after the day of service of the notice, excluding the day of service.

Notice of motion, what to contain.

1040. The relator shall, in his notice of motion, set out his name in full, his occupation, place of residence, and the interest which he has in the election, as candidate or voter, and shall also set forth specifically under distinct heads, separately numbered, all such grounds of objection as he intends to urge against the validity of the election complained against, and in favour of the validity of the election of the relator, or another or other person or persons, when he claims that he or they, or any of them, have been duly elected.

Affidavits to be filed.

1041. Before serving his notice of motion he shall file all the affidavits and material upon which he intends to move, except when *viva voce* evidence is to be taken, and in that case he shall name in his notice the witnesses whom he proposes to examine.

Hearing of motion.

1042. On the hearing of the motion the relator shall not be allowed to object to the election of the party or parties complained against, or to support the election or elections of the person or persons alleged to have been duly elected on any ground not specified in the notice of motion ; but it shall, nevertheless, be in the discretion of the Judge to entertain upon his own view of the case any substantial ground of objection to or in support of the validity of the election of either or any of the parties which may appear in the evidence before him.

Issue, when to be tried.

1043. In case a necessity shall appear for sending an issue to be tried by a jury, an order for that purpose may be made, and the issue to be tried shall be stated in the order.

Judgment.

1044. When the Judge before whom any such case shall be pending shall have determined the same an order shall be drawn up in the usual manner which shall state concisely the ground and effect of the judgment, which order may be at any time amended by the same Judge in regard to any matter of form, and the said order shall have the same force and effect as a writ of *mandamus* formerly had in the like case.

By Sec. 46. Cap. 38. (1884) -
County court judge has same jurisdiction as judge of the High Court - in cases within his county -
with right of appeal to a judge of the high court

Mr. McGreevy's connecti
d, recently resigned, forme
harges brought against th
Quebec West in the harb

masters' Salaries.

of salaries for postmaster
recommended by Postmaster
art. It is said that the com
postmasters has been dispro
nd in some classes inadequate
pointed out that for man
inaster of Montreal has bee
to the regular scale, re
00 a year, and that durin
Parliament another exceptio
the postmaster of Toronto
was also increased to $4,000
ld classification of postmaster
ve classes, as follows :—

Postage collections exceeding	Postm'ster salary.
.... $ 80,000	$2,600
.... 60,000	2,400
.... 40,000	2,200
.... 20,(0)	2,000
ss than 20,000	1,400

assification now officially re
s as follows :—

Collections exceeding	Postm'ster salary.
.... $250,000	$4,000
.... 200,000	3,750
.... 150,000	3,500
.... 100,000	3,250
.... 80,000	2,800
.... 60,000	2,400
.... 40,000	2,200
.... 20,000	2,000
css than 20,000	1,400

lteration of Pepper.

tory of the Department
ue, presided over by the chi
Thos. McFarlane, has issued
epper. Seventy-three sampl
ec, Montreal, Sherbrook
lph, Barrie, Galt and othe
analysed. Twenty-seven pe
nuine and 73 per cent. eithe
or doubtful. Mr. McFarlan
rom the results given in th
lain that at least two-thirds o
sold in Canadian towns a
some of them very grossly. I
ajority of cases these peppe
in bulk, and not labelle
nd." Legal proceedings coul
erefore, be instituted again
in question, but doing th
y tax the means at the dispos
h, owing to the great number
In the meantime, and for th
i, it is considered probable th
ay be accomplished by publisl
s of the vendors and allege
rs of the adulterated goods.

g the Capuchin Order.

, Horan of the Department
out to resign his position in tl
ffice and enter the Capuch
Horan left the Anglican Chur
ears ago and entered the Rom
minunion, connecting himse
ilica, where he was baptise
Thompson being his sponso
with St. Bridget's, the ne
lic church. He is influen
ng the Capuchin Order l
devote his life wholly to t
gion, and will be the first Can
r the order, the monastery he
st established on this side
. The Capuchins are a preac

lumo
e abc
o Cit
gent.
e sai
n elec
o sal
t Osg
ighth
ou ex
1 the
1otio1
hat E
f Tor
d an
ioth
City
under
9th d
Janua
onto,
ng th
erick
udgh
Clark
pay t
do, h
lowin
(1)
and v
occuj
corpo
mem
said
print
said
(2)
is an
occuj
corp
men
the s
self
on hl
print
said
(3)
is an
of hl
ink
of th
(4)
l1 an
of h
othe
tero
and
tho
(5)
is a1
that
and
is th
(6)
is a
that
ing

CHAPTER XII.

EXTRAORDINARY REMEDIES.

1. BAILABLE PROCEEDINGS.

(i) *Arrest.*

1045. No writ of *capias ad respondendum* shall issue in any case, but an *No ca. re. to issue.* order for arrest may be made in an action which shall have the same effect as such a writ formerly had.

1046. In case a person is to be arrested and held to special bail, the *Order for arrest.* process shall be by order of the Court or a Judge, in the words or to the effect of Form No. 155 in the Appendix, which order shall bear date on the day on which it is made, and may be delivered to the Sheriff of any County in Ontario for execution. R. S. O. 1877, c. 50, ss. 4, 30, 31.

1047. Every order for arrest shall be in force for two months from the *Orders to be in* day of the date thereof inclusive, and no longer ; but on the expiration *force two-* thereof a new order may be obtained in the manner directed by *The Act* *not renewable.* *respecting Arrest and Imprisonment for Debt.* R. S. O. 1877, c. 50, s. 29 ; J. A. Rule 9.

1048. Concurrent or duplicate orders for arrest may be issued from time *Concurrent* to time in like manner and form as the original order, and shall be in *orders may* force for the same period as such original order and no longer. R. S. O. *issue.* 1877, c. 50, s. 32.

1049. Every order, and so many copies thereof as there are persons *Copies, etc.,* intended to be arrested thereon shall be delivered with the original order *to be served.* to the Sheriff or other officer to whom the order is delivered for execution, and the plaintiff or his solicitor may direct the Sheriff or officer to arrest one or more of the defendants therein named, which direction shall be duly obeyed by the Sheriff or officer. R. S. O. 1877, c. 50, s. 33.

1050. The Sheriff or officer shall, within two months from the day of the *Sheriff to ex-* date of the order for arrest, but not afterwards, execute the same according *ecute within* to the exigency thereof, and shall upon or immediately after the execution *two months* of such order cause one copy thereof to be delivered to every person *from date.* whom he is directed to arrest, and shall exhibit the original order to each. R. S. O. 1877, c. 50, s. 34.

Defendant may apply to a Judge to be discharged from custody.

1051. Any person arrested upon any order for arrest may apply at any time after his arrest to the Court, or a Judge, for an order that he be discharged out of custody; and such Court or Judge may make such order thereon as to such Court or Judge seems fit subject to appeal; and the Judge or acting Judge of a County Court making any order to arrest,

Power of Judge.

whether in the High Court or in his own Court, shall in respect to such order, and the arrest made thereupon, possess all the powers given to a

Court may discharge or vary Judge's order.

Judge of the High Court under this Rule, and may in like manner, on application to him, order the defendant to be discharged out of custody, or make such order therein as to him seems fit; and any such order made by a County Court Judge may be discharged or varied by a Divisional Court. *See* R. S. O.1877, c. 50, s. 36.

Statement of claim when to be delivered when defendant is imprisoned for want of bail.

1052. If any defendant is taken or charged in custody upon any such order, and imprisoned for want of bail to the action, the plaintiff may, within one month after the arrest of the defendant, deliver a statement of claim in the action; otherwise the defendant shall be entitled to be discharged from the arrest or detainer, unless further time to deliver a statement of claim is given to the plaintiff by the Court or a Judge. Rules of T. T. 1856, 100; R. S. O. 1877, c. 50, s. 37.

When defendant to be charged in execution.

1053. The plaintiff shall, unless the Court or a Judge otherwise orders, cause the defendant to be charged in execution within fourteen days after the plaintiff is entitled to enter final judgment. *See* Rules T. T. 1856, 99.

Misnomer of defendant in bailable proceedings, effect of.

1054. Where the defendant is described in the order for arrest, or affidavit therefor, by initials, or by wrong name, or without a Christian name, the defendant shall not for that cause be discharged out of custody, or the bail bond be delivered up to be cancelled on motion for that purpose, if it appears to the Court that due diligence has been used to obtain knowledge of the proper name. Rules T. T. 1856, 66.

On writs from County Courts, the Sheriff to take bail from persons arrested, and assign bail bond, etc.

1055. The Sheriff to whom an order for arrest issued out of a County Court is delivered, shall take bail from any defendant arrested thereon, and if required shall assign the bail bond in like manner as in cases where like process is issued from the High Court, and such assignment shall have the same effect as if the order had issued from the High Court. R. S. O. 1877, c. 50, s. 38.

When plaintiff may sign judgment upon bail bond.

1056. In all cases where the bail bond is directed to stand as a security, the plaintiff shall be at liberty to sign judgment upon it. Rules T. T. 1856, 68.

Proceedings on bail bond may be stayed on payment of costs in one action.

1057. Proceedings on the bail bond may be stayed on payment of costs in one action, unless sufficient reason be shewn for proceeding in more. Rules T. T. 1856, 69.

Order may issue requiring Sheriff to bring body into Court.

Attachment may issue for disobedience.

1058. In case an order for returning an order for arrest expires in vacation, and the Sheriff or other officer having the return of such order, returns *cepi corpus* thereon, an order may thereupon issue requiring the Sheriff or other officer within the like number of days after the service of the order, as by the practice of the Court is prescribed with respect to orders to bring in the body, to bring the defendant into Court, by forthwith putting in and perfecting bail to the action, and if the Sheriff or other officer does not duly obey the order, an attachment shall issue for disobedience of the order, whether bail has or has not been put in and perfected in the meantime. Rules T. T. 1856, 74.

Plaintiff may not proceed against bail, pending order to bring in body.

1059. A plaintiff shall not be at liberty to proceed on the bail bond pending an order to bring in the body of the defendant. Rules T. T. 1856, 71.

1060. No order shall be drawn up for setting aside an attachment regularly obtained against a Sheriff for not bringing in the body, or for staying proceedings regularly commenced on the assignment of any bail bond, unless the application for the order, if made on the part of the original defendant, be grounded on an affidavit of merits, or if made on the part of the Sheriff, bail, or any officer of the Sheriff, be grounded on an affidavit shewing that the application is really and truly made on the part of the Sheriff, or bail, or officer of the Sheriff, as the case may be, at his or their own expense, and for his or their indemnity only, and without collusion with the original defendant. Rules T. T. 1856, 72.

Application to set aside attachment against Sheriff for not bringing in body, or to stay proceedings against bail, to be founded on affidavit of merits, etc.

1061. Whenever a plaintiff obtains an order to the Sheriff, on a return of *cepi corpus* to bring in the body, the defendant shall be at liberty to put in and perfect special bail at any time before the expiration of such order. Rules T. T. 1856, 73.

Special bail may be put in at any time before return of order to bring in body.

1062. The condition of the recognizance of special bail shall be, that, if the defendant be condemned in the action at the suit of the plaintiff, he will satisfy the costs and condemnation money, or render himself to the custody of the Sheriff of the County in which the action against such defendant has been brought, or that the cognizors will do so for him. R. S. O. 1877, c. 50, s. 40.

Condition of recognizance of bail.

1063. Upon due notice given to the plaintiff or his solicitor, and upon production of the bail-piece, and whether the defendant is detained in custody or not, bail may justify before any Judge of the Court in which the action is pending, and such justification and the opposing thereof may be by affidavit or affirmation without the attendance of the bail in open Court or before such Judge, unless specially required by such Court or Judge, and such Court or Judge may thereupon issue an order for the allowance of such bail and for the discharge of the defendant (if in custody) by a writ of *supersedeas.* R. S. O. 1877, c. 50, s. 41.

How bail may justify.

And order for allowance to issue.

(*a*) Every order of a Judge directing the discharge of a defendant out of custody, upon special bail being put in and perfected, shall also direct a *supersedeas* to issue forthwith. Rules T. T. 1856, 98.

Order for discharge of defendant out of custody.

1064. Special bail, on production of a copy of the bail-piece certified by the Officer of the Court having the custody thereof, may surrender their principal to the Sheriff of the County in which the principal is resident or found, and the Sheriff shall receive the principal into his custody and give the bail a certificate under his hand and seal of office of the surrender, for which certificate the Sheriff shall be entitled to the sum of one dollar, and any Judge of the Court in which the action is pending, upon proof of due notice to the plaintiff or his solicitor of the surrender, and upon production of the Sheriff's certificate thereof, shall order an *exoneretur* to be entered on the bail-piece, and thereupon the bail shall be discharged. R. S. O. 1877, c. 50, s. 42.

Bail may surrender their principal to the Sheriff of any County, etc.

1065. In cases where the surrender is made to any other Sheriff than the Sheriff of the County specified in the condition of the recognizance of bail, the plaintiff shall not be compelled to change the place of trial or to conduct his suit in any manner different from that in which he would have been required to conduct it had the surrender been made to such last-mentioned Sheriff. R. S. O. 1877, c. 50, s. 43.

Such surrender not to affect the place of trial.

1066. In case a person is surrendered by his bail to the Sheriff of any County other than that in which he resided or carried on business at the time, such person shall be entitled to be transferred to the gaol of his own County on prepaying the expense of his removal ; and the Sheriff in whose County he was arrested may, if he is satisfied of the facts, transfer him accordingly ; but if the Sheriff declines to act without an order of the Court or a Judge, such an order shall be made on the application of the prisoner and notice to the opposite party. R. S. O. 1877, c. 50, s. 44.

Person arrested out of his County may be transferred to it, paying the costs.

Special bail may be entered and plaintiff may proceed as upon a writ of summons. **1067.** Special bail may be put in and perfected according to the established practice. *See* R. S. O. 1877, c. 50, s. 39.

In cases in a County Court, how plaintiff to proceed. **1068.** In case (in any action in a County Court) the defendant has been surrendered by his bail into the custody of the Sheriff of a County other than that in which the action has been instituted, the plaintiff may charge the defendant in execution, and take all other necessary proceedings in like manner as if the suit had been instituted in the High Court. R.S.O. 1877, c. 50, s. 45.

Bail in C. C. **1069.** Recognizances of bail in County Courts may be proceeded upon in like manner as in the High Court. *See* R. S. O. 1877, c. 50, s. 46.

Notice of more than two bail, irregular. **1070.** Notice of more bail than two shall be deemed irregular, unless by order of the Court or a Judge. Rules T. T. 1856, 75.

Bail not to be changed without leave. **1071.** The bail of whom notice shall be given, shall not be changed without leave of the Court or a Judge. Rules T. T. 1856, 76.

Bail indemnified by solicitor of defendant cannot justify. **1072.** No person shall be permitted to justify himself as good and sufficient bail for any defendant if such person has been indemnified for so doing by the solicitor or solicitors concerned for such defendant. Rules T. T. 1856, 77.

Solicitor for either party cannot take recognizance. **1073.** No solicitor shall take any recognizance of bail in a case in which he is employed as solicitor or agent for either party. Rules T. T. 1856, 78.

Solicitor, Sheriff's Officer, or Bailiff cannot be bail, except for purpose of rendering. **1074.** If any person put in as bail to the action, except for the purpose of rendering only, be a practising solicitor, or clerk to a practising solicitor, or Sheriff's officer, bailiff, or person concerned in the execution of process, the plaintiff may treat the bail as a nullity, and sue upon the bail bond as soon as the time for putting in bail has expired, unless good bail be duly put in in the meantime. Rules T. T. 1856, 79.

Bail put in, in the country, how to be justified in Court. **1075.** When bail which has been put in, in the country, is to be justified in Court, the bail-piece with the affidavit of the due taking thereof and the affidavit of justification, shall be transmitted by the Deputy Clerk of the Crown for the County in which they have been filed to the proper office in Toronto, to be filed and produced in Court, upon the motion for allowance, on proper notice being given to such Deputy Clerk to transmit the same. Rules T. T. 1856, 80.

If notice of bail be accompanied by affidavit of justification, costs of justification how borne. **1076.** If the notice of bail is accompanied by an affidavit of each of the bail, according to the Form No. 46 in the Appendix, and the plaintiff afterwards excepts to such bail, he shall, if such bail are allowed, pay the costs of justification.

Notice of exception to bail, when to be served. **1077.** If the plaintiff does not give one day's notice of exception to the bail by whom the affidavit was made, the recognizance of the bail may be taken out of Court without other justification than the affidavit. Rules T. T. 1856, 82.

When notice of bail not accompanied by affidavit of justification, plaintiff has 20 days to except. **1078.** Where notice of bail is not accompanied by such affidavit, the plaintiff may except thereto within twenty days next after the putting in of such bail, and notice thereof given in writing to the plaintiff or his solicitor, or where special bail is put in before any commissioner, the plaintiff may except thereto within twenty days next after the bail piece is filed in the proper office, and notice thereof given as aforesaid; and no exception to bail shall be admitted after the time hereinbefore limited. Rules T. T. 1856, 83.

1079. Affidavits of justification shall be deemed insufficient, unless they state that each person justifying is worth double the amount sworn to, over and above what will pay his just debts, and over and above every other sum for which he is then bail, except when the sum sworn to exceeds $4,000, when it shall be sufficient for the bail to justify in $4,000 beyond the sum sworn to. Rules T. T. 1856, 84.

Affidavits of justification form of.

1080. It shall be sufficient in all cases if notice of justification of bail be given two days before the time of justification. Rules T. T. 1856, 85.

Two days' notice of justification is sufficient.

1081. In all cases bail to the action shall be justified, when required, within four days after exception, before a Judge at Chambers. Rules T. T. 1856, 86.

Bail to action to justify within four days after exception.

1082. Bail, though rejected, shall be allowed to render the principal with out entering into a fresh recognizance. Rules T. T. 1856, 87.

Bail, though rejected, may render their principal.

1083. Where bail to the sheriff become bail to the action, the plaintiff may except to them, though he has taken an assignment of the bail bond. Rules T. T. 1856, 70.

Plaintiff may except to bail to sheriff who become bail to an action.

1084. When the plaintiff proceeds by action on the recognizance of bail, the bail shall be at liberty to render their principal at any time within the space of 8 days next after service of process upon them, but not at any later period, and upon notice thereof given, the proceedings shall be stayed upon payment of the costs of the writ and service thereof only. Rules T. T. 1856, 88.

When action commenced against bail, they may, render their principal.

1085. Bail shall only be liable to the sum sworn to by the affidavit of debt, and the costs of suit, not exceeding in the whole the amount of their recognizance. Rules T. T. 1856, 89.

Bail, extent of liability of.

1086. To entitle bail to a stay of proceedings pending an appeal, the application must be made before the time to surrender is out. Rules T. T. 1856, 90.

Staying proceedings pending appeal.

1087. Wherever two or more notices of justification of bail have been given before the notice on which bail appear to justify, no bail shall be permitted to justify without first paying (or securing to the satisfaction of the plaintiff, his solicitor, or agent) the reasonable costs incurred by such prior notices, although the names of the parties intended to justify, or some of them, may not have been changed, and whether the bail mentioned in any such prior notice have not appeared, or have been rejected. Rules T. T. 1856, 91.

Costs of prior notices of bail.

1088. In case an order is made for arrest in an action for alimony, the amount of the bail required shall not exceed what may be considered sufficient to cover the amount of future alimony for 2 years, besides arrears and costs, but may be for less at the discretion of the Court or Judge. R. S. O. 1877, c. 40, s. 46.

Limit of bail.
alimony

(ii) *Absconding Debtors.*

1089. Every attaching order in an action against an absconding debtor shall be issued in duplicate and shall be so marked on its face, and one of the duplicates shall be delivered to the sheriff, and the other shall be used for the purpose of serving the defendant. *See* R. S. O. 1877, c. 68, s. 6.

Orders in duplicate.

1090. Every such attaching order shall be dated on the day on which it is made, and shall remain in force as long as the writ of summons is in force.

Date.

Further orders within six months,   **1091.** The plaintiff may, at any time within six months from the date of the original order of attachment, upon application to the proper officer, obtain one or more certified copy or copies of the attaching order, which may be delivered to any Sheriff other than the Sheriff to whom the original order was delivered, for the purpose of attaching the property, credits, or effects of the defendant in aid of the original order. *See* R. S. O. 1877, c. 68, s. 7.

Service.   **1092.** In actions against absconding debtors, the writ of summons and order of attachment may be served in like manner as in ordinary actions.

Plaintiff to prove claim.   **1093.** Before the plaintiff shall be entitled to sign judgment by default he shall file an affidavit, proving the amount of the debt and damages claimed by him in such action, after giving credit for all payments and claims which might be set off or lawfully claimed by the debtor at the time of making the affidavit. *See* R. S. O. 1877, c. 68, s. 9.

Defendant may be let in.   **1094.** The Court or Judge may, either before or after final judgment, let in the defendant to put in special bail and defend the action, in the same manner, and subject to the same rules and discretion, as on a like application in an ordinary action. *See* R. S. O. c. 68, s. 10.

Special bail, how put in.   **1095.** The special bail (whether put in within the time limited by the order, or within such time as the Court or a Judge directs,) shall be put in and perfected in like manner as if the defendant had been arrested for the amount sworn to on obtaining the attachment. *See* R. S. O. 1877, c. 68, s. 11.

Property to be returned.   **1096.** Upon the defendant so putting in and perfecting special bail, all his property, credits and effects attached in the action (excepting any which may have been disposed of as perishable, and then the net proceeds of the goods so disposed of,) shall be restored and paid to him, unless there be some other lawful ground for the Sheriff to withhold or detain the same. *See* R. S. O. 1877, c. 68, s. 12.

Motion against order.   **1097.** If at any time before the execution issues it appears, upon motion, that the defendant was not an absconding debtor at the time of obtaining the attaching order, such defendant shall recover his costs of defence, to be deducted from the amount of the plaintiff's claim or judgment; and the plaintiff shall be entitled only to judgment or execution for the excess, if any ; and if the taxed costs of the defendant are greater than the amount of the plaintiff's claim or judgment, then the defendant shall be entitled to an order for payment of the excess forthwith. *See* R. S. O. 1877, c. 68, s. 19.

2. REPLEVIN.

Writ of replevin abolished.   **1098.** The writ of replevin is hereby abolished. Whenever a party is entitled to replevy goods he may obtain an order therefor in an action commenced by writ of summons.

1099. An order of replevin may be obtained,

When motion for order required.   (1) On motion therefor on an affidavit by the person claiming the property, or some other person showing to the satisfaction of the Court or a Judge, the facts of the wrongful taking or detention which is complained of, as well as the value and description of the property, and that the person claiming it is the owner thereof, or is lawfully entitled to the possession thereof (as the case may be) ;

On *præcipe*.   (2) Or on *præcipe* if the person claiming the property, his servant or agent, makes an affidavit which shall be entitled and filed in the Court out of which the order is to issue, stating, (*a*) That the person claiming the property is the owner thereof, or that he is lawfully entitled to the possession thereof, (describing the property in the affidavit) ; *Affidavit to obtain order on præcipe.*

(*b*) The value thereof to the best of his belief ;

(*c*) That the property was wrongfully taken out of the possession of the claimant, or was fraudulently got out of his possession, within 2 months next before the making of the affidavit ;

(*d*) That the deponent is advised and believes that the claimant is entitled to the order ;

(*e*) And that there is good reason to apprehend that unless the order is issued without waiting for a motion, the delay would materially prejudice the just rights of the claimant in respect to the property.

(3) Or on *præcipe* (in case the property was distrained for rent or damage feasant), if the person claiming the property, his servant or agent, makes an affidavit (which shall be entitled and filed in the Court from which the order is to issue), stating, *Order may issue on præcipe if the property was distrained for rent or damage feasant.*

(*a*) That the person claiming the property is the owner thereof, or that he is lawfully entitled to the possession thereof, (describing the property in the affidavit) ;

(*b*) The value thereof to the best of his belief ;

(*c*) That the property was taken under colour of a distress for rent or damage feasant, and in such case the order shall state that the defendant has taken and unjustly detains the property, under colour of a distress for rent or damage feasant (as the case may be). R. S. O. 1877, c. 53, s. 6.

(4) Except as hereinbefore mentioned no order of replevin shall be issued.'

1100. Where a motion for an order is made, the Court or Judge may proceed on the *ex parte* application of the plaintiff, or may direct notice to be served on the defendant to show cause why the order should not issue ; and may, on the *ex parte* application, or on the return of the motion, grant or refuse the order, or direct the sheriff to take a bond in less or more than treble the value of the property, or may direct him to take and detain the property until the further order of the Court, instead of at once replevying the same to the plaintiff ; or may impose any terms or conditions in granting the order, or in refusing the same, on the return of a motion, as under all the circumstances in evidence appear just. R. S. O. 1877, c. 53, s. 7. *Discretionary power of the Court or Judge when an application for an order is made.*

1101. In case an order of replevin is issued, the defendant may at any time, or from time to time, on notice to the plaintiff, apply to the Court or a Judge, on affidavit or otherwise, to discharge, vary, or modify the order, or to stay proceedings under the order, or for any other relief, to be specified in the notice, with respect to the return, safety or sale of the property or any part thereof, or otherwise ; and the Court or Judge may make such order thereon as, under all the circumstances, best consists with justice between the parties. R. S. O. 1877, c. 53, s. 9. *Defendant may apply to discharge order.*

1102. The order shall state the description and value of the property, and shall be dated on the day on which it is made, and may be in the words or the effect of Form No 153 in the Appendix, or otherwise adapted to the circumstances of the case. R. S. O. 1877, c. 53, s. 10. *Contents of order and how to be dated.*

1103. Before the Sheriff acts on the order he shall take a bond from the plaintiff with two sufficient sureties in treble the value of the property to be replevied, as stated in the order; which bond shall be assignable to the *Sheriff, before he replevies, to take bond.*

defendant ; and the bond and assignment thereof may be in the words or
to the effect of Form No. 208 in the Appendix, the condition being varied
to correspond with the order. R. S. O.1877, c. 53, s. 11.

Replevin bond to be subject to 8 & 9 Wm. iii. c. 11, s. 8
(a) The bond shall be subject to the provisions of section 8 of chapter
11 of the Act passed by the Imperial Parliament in the 8th and 9th years
of the reign of His Majesty King William the Third. R. S. O. 1877, c.
53, s. 12.

Indemnity of defendant in replevin proceedings.
1104. Where an order of replevin is issued for any personal property
which had not been previously taken out of the plaintiff's possession, and
for which the plaintiff might formerly have brought an action of trespass
or trover, the defendant shall be entitled, if the plaintiff fails in the action
to be fully idemnified against all damages sustained by the defendant, including any extra costs which he may incur in defending the action ; and
the bond to be taken by the Sheriff or Bailiff shall be conditioned, not
only as heretofore required in that behalf but also to indemnify and save
harmless the defendant from all loss and damage which he may sustain by
reason of the seizure, and of any deterioration of the property in the
meantime, in the event of its being returned, and all costs, charges, and
expenses which the defendant may incur, including reasonable costs
not taxable between party and party.   This Rule shall not apply to cases
of distress for rent or damage-feasant.   48 V. c. 13, s. 8.

Sheriff not to serve writ till he has replevied.
1105. The Sheriff shall not serve a copy of the writ of summons or
the order until he has replevied the property, or some part of the property
therein mentioned, if he cannot replevy the whole in consequence of
the defendant having eloigned the same out of his county, or because
the same is not in the possession of the defendant, or of any person for
him. R. S. O. 1877, c. 53 s. 13.

What Sheriff shall do when the orders issues on *præcipe*.
1106. In case the order issues on *præcipe* the Sheriff shall take and
detain the property, and shall not replevy the same to the plaintiff without
the order of the Court or a Judge in that behalf ; but may, within
14 days from the time of his taking the same, re-deliver it to the
defendant, unless in the meantime the plaintiff obtains and serves on the
Sheriff an order directing a different disposition of the property ;
but this Rule shall not apply in case of a distress for rent or damage
feasant, under Rule 1099. R. S. O. 1877, c. 53, s. 14.

If property to be replevied is concealed in any house, etc. how Sheriff to act.
1107. In case the property to be replevied or any part thereof is secured
or concealed in any dwelling house or other building or enclosure of the
defendant, or of any other person holding the same for him, and in case
the Sheriff publicly demands from the owner and occupant of the premises
deliverance of the property to be replevied, and in case the same is not
delivered to him within 24 hours after such demand, he may, and
shall if necessary, break open such house, building or enclosure for
the purpose of replevying such property or any part thereof, and shall
make replevin according to the order. R. S. O. 1877, c. 53, s. 15.

If concealed about the person or premises.
1108. If the property to be replevied, or any part thereof, is concealed
either about the person or on the premises of the defendant, or of any
other person holding the same for him, and in case the Sheriff demands
from the defendant or such other person deliverance thereof, and deliverance is neglected or refused, he may, and if necessary shall, search and
examine the person and premises of the defendant or other person for the
purpose of replevying the property or any part thereof, and shall make
replevin according to the order. R. S. O. 1877, c. 53, s. 16.

When order to be returned with Schedule annexed.
What Schedule to contain.
1109. The Sheriff shall return the order on or before the tenth day
after the service thereof, and shall transmit annexed thereto,

(1.) The names of the sureties in, and the date of the bond taken from
the plaintiff, and the name or names of the witnesses thereto ;

(2.) The place of residence and additions of the sureties ;

(3.) The number, quantity, and quality of the articles of property replevied ; and in case he has replevied only a portion of the property mentioned in the order, and cannot replevy the residue by reason of the same having been eloigned 'out of his county by the defendant, or not being in the possession of the defendant, or of any other person for him, he shall state in his return the articles which he cannot replevy and the reason why not. R. S. O. 1877, c. 53, s. 17.

1110. If the Sheriff makes such a return of the property distrained, taken *If Sheriff re-* or detained, having been eloigned, as would have warranted the issuing of *turns that the* a *capias in withernam* by the law of England on the . th day of December, *property has* 1859, then upon the filing of such return, an order shall be issued on *præ-* *been eloigned,* *cipe* in the words or to the effect of Form No. 154 in the Appendix, which *order to issue.* shall have the same force and effect as a *capias in withernam* had, and before executing such order the Sheriff shall take security as provided by Rule 1103. R. S. O. 1877, c. 53, s. 18.

1111. In case the plaintiff becomes entitled to sign judgment by default, *Damages on* he shall be at liberty to sign final judgment for the sum of five dollars, *judgment by* and costs according to the proper scale, but shall not be entitled to recover *default.* a larger sum except upon an assessment before a Judge or jury, or upon filing the written consent of the defendant or his solicitor, and an affidavit verifying the signature to such consent. R. S. O. 1877, c. 53, s. 28.

3. MANDAMUS.

(i) *In Actions.*

1112. The plaintiff in any action in the High Court of Justice, except *Mandamus in* replevin or ejectment, may indorse upon the writ and copy to be *action.* served, a notice that the plaintiff intends to claim a *mandamus;* and the plaintiff may thereupon claim in the statement of claim, either together with any other demand which may be enforced in the action, or separately, a *mandamus* commanding the defendant to fulfil any duty in the fulfilment of which the plaintiff is personally interested. R. S. O. 1877, c. 52, s. 4.

1113. The plaintiff shall indorse the claim to such *mandamus* upon the *Indorsement* writ of summons, and the indorsement may be in the form given in *of writ.* No. 6 in the Appendix. *New.* See Eng. Rules 719, 720.

1114. If judgment be given for the plaintiff, the Court or Judge may by *Judgment.* the judgment command the defendant, either forthwith or on the expiration of such time and upon such terms as may appear to the Court or Judge to be just, to perform the duty in question. The Court or Judge may also extend the time for the performance of the duty. *New.* See Eng. Rule 721.

1115. No writ of *mandamus* shall hereafter be issued in an action, but *Writ abolish-* a *mandamus* shall be by judgment or order, which shall have the same *ed.* effect as a writ of *mandamus* formerly had. *New.* See Eng. Rule 722.

1116. The pleadings and other proceedings shall be the same in all *Proceedings* respects, as nearly as may be, and costs shall be recoverable by either *as in ordinary* party, as in an ordinary action. *See* R. S. O. 1877, c. 52, s. 6, *first part.* *action.*

(ii) *On Motion.*

1117. Nothing in the 5 preceding Rules contained shall take away the *Jurisdiction* jurisdiction of the High Court of Justice to grant orders of *manda-* *not to be* *mus*; nor shall any order of *mandamus* issued be invalid by reason of *affected.* the right of the prosecutor to proceed by action for *mandamus* but

10

the preceding Rules, so far as they are applicable, shall apply to the pleadings and proceedings upon a prerogative order of *mandamus* issued by the Court. R. S. O. 1877, c. 52, s. 10.

Provisions of Act of 9 Anne, c. 20, extended to all other writs of mandamus.
1118. Whereas the provisions contained in a certain Act of Parliament passed in the ninth year of the reign of Queen Anne, entitled *"An Act for rendering the proceedings upon Writs of Mandamus and information in the nature of a Quo Warranto more speedy and effectual, and for the more easy trying and determining the rights of Offices and Franchises in Corporations and Boroughs,"* relating to the writs of *mandamus* therein mentioned, have been found useful and convenient, and the same ought to be extended to the proceedings on other such writs ; it is therefore ordered that the several enactments contained in the said statute relating to the return of writs of *mandamus*, and the proceedings on such returns, and to the recovery of damages and costs, shall extend and be applicable to all orders of *mandamus*, and the proceedings thereon, except so far only as the same are varied and altered by these Rules. R. S. O. 1877, c. 52, s. 11.

Court may make orders calling on all persons having interest in the matter of the writ to show cause against issuing, etc.
1119. Whereas writs of *mandamus*, other than such as relate to the offices and franchises mentioned in or provided for by the said Act passed in the ninth year of the reign of Queen Anne, are sometimes issued to officers and other persons, commanding them to admit to offices, or to do or perform other matters in respect whereof the persons to whom such writs are directed claim no right or interest, or whose functions are merely ministerial in relation to such offices or matters ; and it may be proper tha such officers and persons should in certain cases be protected against the payment of damages or costs to which they may otherwise become liable : it is therefore ordered, that it shall be lawful for the Court to which application is made for any order of *mandamus* (other than such as relate to the said offices and franchises mentioned in or provided for by the said Act passed in the reign of Queen Anne), if such Court sees fit to so do, to hear motions calling not only upon the persons to whom such order is required to issue, but also all and every other person having or claiming any right or interest in or to the matter of such order, to show cause against the issuing of such order and payment of costs of the application ; and upon the appearance of such other person on such motion, or in default of appearance after notice given, to exercise all such powers and authorities, and to make all such orders applicable to the case as are or may be given or mentioned by or in any Act for giving relief against adverse claims upon persons having no interest in the subject of such claims. R. S. O. 1877, c. 52, s. 12

Form of return of issues joined, on demurrer, etc.
1120. The return to be made to any such order, and issues joined in fact or law upon any traverse thereof, or upon any demurrer shall be made and joined by and in the name of the person to whom such order is directed ; but nevertheless the same shall, if the Court thinks fit so to direct, be expressed to be made and joined on the behalf of such other person as may be mentioned in such rules ; and in that case such other person shall be permitted to frame the return, and to conduct the subsequent proceedings at his own expense ; and in such case, if any judgment is given for or against the party suing such order, such judgment shall be given against or for the person on whose behalf the return is expressed to be made, and such person shall have the like remedy for the recovery of costs and enforcing the judgment as the person to whom the order was directed might and would otherwise have had. R. S. O. 1877, c. 52, s. 13.

For or against whom judgment shall be given.
Costs.

Case of death, resignation or removal, of persons making the return, provided for.
1121. In case the return to any such order is, in pursuance of the authority given as aforesaid, expressed to be made on behalf of any other person as aforesaid, the further proceedings on such order shall not abate or be discontinued by the death or resignation of, or removal from office of the person having made such return, but the same shall and may be continued and carried on in the name of such person ; and if a peremptory order is awarded, the same shall and may be directed to any successor in office or right of such person. R. S. O. 1877, c. 52, s. 14.

1122. In all cases in which the person prosecuting any order of *mandamus* wishes or intends to object to the validity of any return to the same, he shall do so by way of demurrer to the same, in such and the like manner as is now practised in the High Court of Justice in ordinary actions; and thereupon the said order and return and the said demurrer shall be entered upon record in the said Court, and the like further proceedings shall be thereupon had and taken as upon a demurrer to pleadings in ordinary actions in the said Court.

Form of objections to return.

Demurrer.

(*a*) The said Court shall thereupon adjudge either that the return is valid in law, or that it is not valid in law, or that the order of *mandamus* is not valid in law ; and if they adjudge that the order is valid in law, but that the return thereto is not valid in law, then the Court shall also by the judgment award that a peremptory order of *mandamus* shall issue in that behalf, and thereupon such peremptory order of *mandamus* may be issued accordingly, at any time after 4 days from the signing of the judgment ; and it shall be lawful for the said Court, and it is hereby required, in and by its said judgment, to award costs to be paid to the party in whose favour it thereby decides, by the other party or parties. R. S. O. 1877, c. 52, s. 15.

Proceedings thereon.

Judgment.

Peremptory *mandamus* if the order be good and the return bad.

Costs.

1123. Upon application by motion for any order of *mandamus* the order may in all cases be made in the first instance, if the Court thinks fit ; and the order shall be dated on the day of its being made, and may be made returnable forthwith, but time may be allowed to return it by the Court or a Judge either with or without terms. R. S. O. 1877, c. 52, s. 16.

Order may issue in the first instance.

(iii) *Applications in Chambers.*

1124. In all cases in which the High Court of Justice has jurisdiction to issue an order of peremptory *mandamus*, application for the said order may be made upon affidavit to a Judge, upon notice of motion in the ordinary manner, to any person who may, in his judgment, be affected by the order, if made, to show cause why the same should not be made. R. S. O. 1877, c. 52, s. 17. *& tent. Re Burkfeld 12 P. R. 485*

Judge may issue order of peremptory *mandamus*.

1125. It shall be the duty of the Judge to whom the application is made, provided he is of opinion that the case is a proper one for the issue of the same to make an order of *mandamus* absolute in the first instance. R. S. O. 1877, c. 52, s. 18.

Duty of Judge

1126. The notice of motion may be served upon the person or party named therein, either personally or by substitution as may be directed by the Judge, in the same manner as a writ of summons ; and the motion may be prosecuted in Chambers upon affidavit or other evidence in the same manner as other applications in Chambers, and in case an order of *mandamus* is made, the same may be enforced by process of attachment. *New.* See R. S. O. 1877, c. 52, s. 19-23.

Service and direction of order.

1127. Upon hearing the parties who appear, or their counsel, and after service of the notice upon all proper persons, as hereinbefore provided, the Judge, if in his opinion the case is a proper one, shall make the order and shall thereby direct what is to be done and performed by the person or party to whom the writ is directed : but if, in his opinion, the application should be refused, the said motion shall be dismissed. R. S. O. 1877, c. 52, s. 24.

Order.

1128. If a mandamus granted in an action or otherwise, or a mandatory order, injunction, or judgment, for specific performance of any contract be not complied with, the Court or a Judge, besides or instead of proceedings against the disobedient party for contempt, may direct that the act required to be done may be done so far as practicable by the party by

Mandatory order, how enforced.

whom the judgment or order has been obtained, or some other person
appointed by the Court or Judge, at the cost of the disobedient party;
and upon the act being done the expenses incurred may be ascertained in
such manner as the Court or Judge may direct and execution may issue
for the amount so ascertained and costs. *New* See Eng. Rule 608 and
R. S. O. 1877, c. 52, s. 9.

Master in Chambers and Local Judges not to grant orders of mandamus. **1129.** No part of the jurisdiction by Rules 1112 to 1128, conferred
upon a Judge shall be exercised by the master in Chambers or the Local
Judges of the High Court ; and nothing in the preceding Rules contained
shall prevent any person from applying to the Court for a *mandamus*
according to the present practice. R. S. O. 1877, c. 52, ss. 1 and 26.

4. INJUNCTIONS.

Writ of injunction abolished. **1130.** No writ of injunction shall be issued in any case. An injunction
shall be by a judgment or order, and any such judgment or order shall
have the effect which a writ of injunction formerly had. J. A. Rule 401.

5. INTERIM PRESERVATION OF PROPERTY, ETC.

Order for interim preservation of property. **1131.** Where by any contract a *prima facie* case of liability is established,
and there is alleged as matter of defence a right to be relieved wholly or
partially from such liability, the Court or a Judge may make an order for
the preservation or interim custody of the subject-matter of the litigation,
or may order that the amount in dispute be brought into Court or otherwise secured. J. A. Rule 396.

Application when may be made. **1132.** An application for an order under the preceding Rule may be
made by the plaintiff at any time after his right thereto appears from the
pleadings, or, if there be no pleadings, is made to appear by affidavit or
otherwise to the satisfaction of the Court or a Judge. J. A. Rule 400.

Sale of perishable goods. **1133.** It shall be lawful for the Court or a Judge, on the application of
any party to an action, to make any order for the sale, by any person or
persons named in the order, and in such manner and on such terms as to
the Court or Judge may seem desirable, of any goods, wares, or merchan-
dise which may be of a perishable nature or likely to injure from keeping,
or which for any other just or sufficient reason it may be desirable to have
sold at once. J. A. Rule 397.

Application under rules. **1134.** An application for an order under section 53, sub-section 8, of *The
Judicature Act*, or under the three preceding Rules, may be made to the
Court or a Judge by any party. If the application be by the plaintiff for an
order under the said sub-section 8, it may be made either *ex parte* or on
notice, and if for an order under the two preceding Rules, it may be made,
after notice to the defendant, at any time after the issue of the writ
of summons, and if it be by any other party, then on notice to the
plaintiff, and at any time after appearance, by the party making the application. J. A. Rule 399.

Order for detention and inspection of property. **1135.** It shall be lawful for the Court or a Judge, upon the application
of any party to an action, and upon such terms as may seem just, to make
any order for the detention, preservation, or inspection of any prope ty,
being the subject of the action ; and for all or any of the purposes aforesaid to authorize any person or persons to enter upon or in o any land
or building in the possession of any party to such action ; and for all or
any of the purposes aforesaid to authorize any samples to be taken, or
any observation to be made or experiment to be tried, which may seem
necessary or expedient for the purpose of obtaining full information or
evidence. J. A. Rule 398.

1136. Where an action is brought to recover, or a defendant in his statement of defence seeks by way of counter-claim to recover, specific property other than land, and the party from whom such recovery is sought does not dispute the title of the party seeking to recover the same, but claims to retain the property by virtue of a lien or otherwise as security for any sum of money, the Court or a Judge, at any time after such last mentioned claim appears from the pleadings, or, if there be no pleadings, by affidavit or otherwise to the satisfaction of the Court or Judge, may order that the party claiming to recover the property be at liberty to pay into Court, to abide the event of the action, the amount of money in respect of which the lien or securi y is claimed, and such further sum (if any) for interest and costs as the Court or Judge may direct, and that upon such payment into Court being made, the property claimed be given up to the party claiming it. J. A. Rule 402.

(margin: Amount of lien claimed may be paid into Court, and property delivered up.)

6. PROHIBITION.

1137. It shall not be necessary to file a suggestion on any application for an order for prohibition. The application may be made on affidavit, subject to the general rules as to motions and evidence on motions.

(margin: Application for order of prohibition may be made on affidavit only.)

1138. No writ of prohibition shall issue in any case, but the order for prohibition shall have the same effect as a writ of prohibition formerly had.

(margin: Writ abolished.)

1139. Any such order may be discharged or varied or set aside by a Divisional Court, subject to an appeal to the Court of Appeal. R. S. O. 1877, c. 52, ss. 2 and 3.

(margin: Order may be varied.)

7. CERTIORARI.

1140. No writ of certiorari shall issue in any case, but an order may be made which shall have the same effect as a writ of certiorari formerly had.

(margin: Certiorari.)

8. INTERPLEADER.

(i) *Generally.*

1141. Relief by way of interpleader may be granted,

(margin: When relief by interpleader granted.)

(a) Where the person seeking relief (hereinafter called the applicant) is under liability for any debt, money, goods, or chattels, for or in respect of which he is, or expects to be, sued by two or more parties (herein f.er called the claimants) making adverse claim thereto :

(b) Where the applicant is a sheriff or other officer charged with the execution of process by or under the authority of the High Court, and claim is made to any money, goods, or chattels, lands or tenements, taken or intended to be taken in execution under any process, or under an attachment against an absconding debtor, or to the proceeds or value of any such goods or chattels, by any person other than the person against whom the process issued.

1142. The applicant must satisfy the Court or a Judge by affidavit, or otherwise—

(margin: Matters to be proved by applicant.)

(a) That the applicant claims no interest in the subject-matter in dispute, other than for charges or costs ; and

(b) That the applicant does not collude with any of the claimants ; and

(c) That the applicant is willing to pay or transfer the subject-matter into Court, or to dispose of it as the Court or a Judge may direct.

Adverse titles of claimants. 1143. The applicant shall not be disentitled to relief by reason only that the titles of the claimants have not a common origin but are adverse to and independent of one another.

When application to be made by defendant. 1144. Where the applicant is a defendant, application for relief may be made at any time after service of the writ of summons.

Motion by applicant. 1145. The applicant may make a motion calling on the claimants to appear and state the nature and particulars of their claims, and either to maintain or relinquish them.

Stay of action. 1146. If the application is made by a defendant in an action the Court or a Judge may stay all proceedings in the action.

Order 1147. If the claimants appear on the motion, the Court or a Judge may order either that any claimant be made a defendant in any action already commenced in respect of the subject-matter in dispute in lieu of or in addition to the applicant, or that an issue between the claimants be stated and tried, and in the latter case may direct which of the claimants is to be plaintiff, and which defendant.

Disposal of matters in summary manner. 1148. The Court or a Judge may, with the consent of both claimants or on the request of any claimant, if, having regard to the value of the subject-matter in dispute, it seems desirable so to do, dispose of the merits of their claims, and, subject to appeal, decide the same in a summary manner and on such terms as may be just.

Questions of law. 1149. Where the question is a question of law, and the facts are not in dispute, the Court or a Judge may either decide the question without directing the trial of an issue, or order that a special case be stated for the opinion of the court.

Failure of claimant to appear, or neglect to obey summons. 1150. If a claimant, having been duly served with a notice of motion calling on him to appear and maintain, or relinquish, his claim, does not appear in pursuance of the notice, or, having appeared, neglects or refuses to comply with any order made after his appearance, the Court or a Judge may make an order declaring him and all persons claiming under him for ever barred against the applicant, and persons claiming under him, but the order shall not affect the rights of the claimants as between themselves.

Order for sale of goods seized in execution. 1151. Where goods or chattels have been seized in execution by a sheriff or other officer charged with the execution of process of the High Court, and any claimant alleges that he is entitled, under a bill of sale or otherwise, to the goods or chattels by way of security for debt, the Court or a Judge may order a sale of the whole or a part thereof, and direct the application of the proceeds of the sale in such manner and upon such terms as may be just.

1152. In case a Sheriff or other officer applies to a Court or Judge for relief by interpleader proceedings, and any execution creditor declines to join in contesting the claim of the adverse claimant, the Court or Judge may direct that such creditor shall be excluded from any benefit which may be derived from the contestation of such claim 48 V. c. 13, s. 27.

Final disposition of all matters. 1153. The Court or Judge who tries the issue may finally dispose of the whole matter of the interpleader proceedings, including all costs not otherwise provided for.

1154. Where in any interpleader proceeding it is necessary or expedient *Title of order.* to make one order in several actions or matters pending in several Divisions, or before different Judges of the same Division, such order may be made by the Court or Judge before whom the interpleader proceeding may be taken, and shall be entitled in all such actions or matters ; and any such order (subject to the right of appeal) shall be binding on the parties in all such actions or matters.

1155. In case a Sheriff has more than one writ at the suit or instance of *In case of* different persons against the same property, it shall not be necessary for *several execu-* him to make a separate application on each writ, or in each action ; *be embraced* but he may make one application, and may make all the persons who are *in one applica-* execution creditors parties to said application, and the Court or Judge *tion for inter-* before whom the application is made shall take such proceedings, and *pleader.* make such order thereon and therein, as if a separate application had been made upon and in respect of each writ. R. S. O. 1877, c. 54, s. 11.

1156. In case there are writs from several Courts, including the High *Cases of exe-* Court of Justice and one or mo e County Courts or including the High *cutions from* Court and one or more Division Courts against the same goods, and *to whom ap-* whether at the suit or instance of the same plaintiff, or of different *plication to be* plaintiffs, the application for such interpleader shall be made to the High *made.* Court, or to one of the Judges thereof ; and such Court or Judge shall dispose of the whole matter, as if all of the writs against the goods had been issued from the said Court ; and in such case the County Court or Division Court shall have no cognizance of or jurisdiction whatever in the matter. R. S. O. 1877, c. 54, s. 12 ; 49 V. c. 16, s. 13.

1157. In any such case as in the next preceding two sections mentioned, *Orders as to* the High Court, or a Judge thereof, shall make such order with respect to *sale, etc., in* staying proceedings on the several writs, or with respect to directing a sale *the two last* of the goods or property in question, as may be necessary, and with *sections.* respect to the final disposition or order to be made as to the goods or the proceeds thereof, and in all other matters whatsoever, as fully as if all the writs had been issued from the said Court. R. S. O. 1877, c. 54, s. 13.

1158. In case an issue is directed to be tried for the determination of the *When an issue* adverse claim in respect of property seized or taken under an order of *is ordered, the* attachment or writ of execution, the Sheriff (or other officer) to whom *Sheriff may* such order is delivered or such writ is directed may tax the costs incurred *and serve allo-* by him in consequence of such adverse claim, and may, when taxed serve *catur on each* a copy of the certificate of the same upon each of the parties to such issue, *party, etc.* and the successful party upon the issue shall tax such costs among his costs of the cause, and upon receipt thereof shall pay over the same to such Sheriff or other officer. R. S. O. 1877, c. 54, s. 15.

1159. If after the service of such certificate the party succeeding upon the *The successful* issue neglects or refuses to tax such costs, the Sheriff or other officer may *party liable to* obtain an order that the successful party shall pay the same. R. S. O. *the Sheriff for* 1877, c. 54, s. 16. *costs.*

1160. In case of any such proceedings being compromised between the *If case com-* parties thereto, such costs of the Sheriff or other officer shall be paid by *promised,* the party, plaintiff, or defendant, by whom the execution or attachment *liable to the* was sued out. R. S. O. 1877, c. 54, s. 17. *Sheriff for his* *costs.*

1161. In case, after the seizure of any property under attachment or in *If goods seized* execution, an issue is directed, and the property seized remains, pending *remain in the* the trial of the issue, in the custody of the Sheriff or other officer who *Sheriff's cus-* seized the same, the Court from which the writ or order of attachment *Court may* issued, or any Judge thereof may make an order for the payment to the *award remune-* Sheriff or other officer of such sum for his trouble in and about the *ration.* custody of the property as the Court or Judge deems reasonable ; and the Sheriff or other officer shall have a lien upon the property for payment of the same in the event of the issue being decided against the claimant and only to the extent to which such issue shall be so decided. R. S. O. 1877, c. 54, s. 18 ; 49 V. c. 16, s. 13

(ii) *Interpleader in County Courts.*

In what County Court the proceedings in interpleader shall be had.

1162. In case any claim is made to any goods or chattels taken or intended to be taken under an attachment against an absconding debtor or in execution, under any process issued out of any County Court, or to the p oceeds or value thereof, all the proceedings shall be had and taken in the County Court of the county or union of counties in which such goods or chattels are so taken or intended to be taken, or before the Judge of such Court notwithstanding that there are writs from two or more County Courts against the same go ds, and whether at the suit or instance of the same plaintiff or different plaintiffs; or the said Court or Judge in any such case, if it appears more convenient and more conducive to the ends of justice so to do, may order that the said proceedings be had and taken in the County Court from which such proce s issued, or before the Judge of such Court. R. S. O.1877, c. 54, s. 22. 49 V. c. 16, s. 13.

When issue may be tried in County Court.

1163. —(1) Where the amount claimed under or by virtue of an execution, or of an attachment against an absco ding debtor in the heriff's or other officer's hands, issued out of the High Court or under executions or attachments in the Sheriff's or other officer's hands, issued out of different County Courts, or out of one or more County Courts, or one or more Division Courts, does not exceed the sum of $400, exclusive of interest and Sheriff's or other officer's costs, or when the goods seized are not, in the opinion of the Judge, or other person making the order, of the value of more than $400, the order directing an issue to be tried may direct that the issue shall be drawn up and tried in the County Court o the county in which the issue would, under the provisions of the preceding Rule be tried, and in such case the issue shall be drawn up, filed and tried in the County Court, and all subsequent proceedings therein, up to and i clusive of judgment and execution, shall be had and taken in the County Court which shall have jurisdiction in the premises as fully as though the writ of execution or attachment had issued out of a County Court.

(2) When an application is made for an order, under this Rule upon the ground that the goods seized are not of the value of more than $400, a list of the goods and of the value placed upon them shall be set out in the affidavit or affidavits, upon which the application is based. 44 V. c. 7, s. 1 ; 49 V. c. 16, s. 42.

(3) The Judge making the order shall have the like powers as are provided in Rule 1157 with regard to the proceedings therein mentioned. 49 V. c. 16, s. 42 (*a*).

Order for costs to be made by judge of County Court.

1164. The proceedings for and relating to the order for costs, and for obtaining money out of Court, when the same has been paid into Court by the Sheriff, and for such other purposes as may be necessary, may, in the cases provided for in the preceding Rule, be made to the Judge of the County Court who tried the issue, and he shall have power and authority to make such order in the premises as a Judge has heretofore had in such cases, but the application for such order may be made as now in the original cause. 44 V. c. 7, s. 2.

Costs of proceedings in County Court.

1165. In respect of all such proceedings as shall be had in the County Court, the costs and disbursements shall be taxed upon the County Court scale. 44 V. c. 7, s. 3.

Appeal given to parties dissatisfied in interpleader cases in County Courts.

1166. Any party who is dissatisfied with the decision of the Judge of a County Court upon any question of law or fact arising in the course of interpleader proceedings, may appeal from such decision to the Court of Appeal, and sections 40 to 52 inclusive of *The County Courts' Act* shall extend and apply to and shall regulate and govern the manner of prosecuting and determining such appeal. R. S. O. 1877, c. 54, s. 23.

(iii) *Interpleader by Bailees and Carriers.*

1167. —(1) Any common carrier or other bailee of goods and chattels, Bailee or carrier may in whether under a special contract or otherwise howsoever upon whom any terplead on claim is made to any goods or chattels in the possession of such carrier or certain bailee by any one or more claimants, whether such claims have or have affidavit. not a common origin, may either before or at any time after action is brought by any such claimants respecting the said goods, upon affidavit showing how the said goods and chattels came to his possession, the nature and extent of any lien which the said carrier or bailee has' upon the said goods and chattels for services rendered and money advanced thereon, if any such claim exists, and the value or supposed value thereof, also showing, who said claimants respectively are, and the nature (as far as said carrier or bailee knows) of the claims respectively made to said goods, and that he the said carrier or bailee has good reason to believe, and does believe, that if he delivers such goods to either of the claimants he will be sued by the other or others of them, and that he does not collude with any or either of the parties claiming possession of said goods and chattels, apply to any Judge of 'the High Court of Justice, or, where the value of the goods does not exceed $200, to any Judge of a County Court of the county within which such goods are at the time of the application, by motion calling upon all the parties respectively claiming the said goods and chattels, to appear and state the nature and particulars of their respective claims, and to maintain or relinquish the same.

(2) The Judge in disposing of said application, shall have and exercise all the powers given to a Judge in interpleader matters. R. S. O. 1877, c. 54, s. 24.

1168. In case any such claimant, being duly served with notice of the said When and motion does not appear to maintain or relinquish his claim or right, or refuses how claimant to comply with any order made after appearance, the said Judge may declare served may be him barred from making or prosecuting his claim against the said carrier barred. or bailee, saving the right or claim of such party against the person or party to whom, under said order, said goods. or the proceeds thereof, may be delivered ; and the said Judge may make such order between the parties to the said application as may seem just. R. S. O. 1877, c. 54, s. 25.

1169. It shall not be necessary, in order to entitle any such carrier or The Court bailee to relief by way of interpleader, that he should abandon any lawful may provide lien he may have upon the goods and chattels the subject of such applica- for satisfaction tion ; and in disposing of said application, the Judge, in case of any such of lien of lien, may make such order respecting the satisfaction or payment thereof, bailee and as to the relief asked and sought thereby, and as to the costs of the parties and the payment thereof, as the right and justice of the case may require. R. S. O. 1877. c. 54. s. 26.

CHAPTER XIII.

COSTS.

1. GENERAL RULES.

To be in discretion of Court.
Saving as to trustee, etc.
Of issues tried before jury.

1170. Subject to the provisions of *The Judicature Act*, the costs of and incident to all proceedings in the High Court shall be in the discretion of the Court, but nothing herein contained shall deprive a trustee, mortgagee, or other person of any right to costs out of a particular estate or fund to which he would be entitled according to the rules hitherto acted upon in Courts of Equity : Provided, that where any action or issue is tried by a jury, the costs shall follow the event, unless, upon application made at the trial, for good cause shown, the Judge before whom the action or issue is tried or the Court otherwise orders. J. A. Rule 428.

(*a*) Costs of proceedings before judicial officers, unless otherwise disposed of, shall be in their discretion, subject to appeal. *See* Chy. O. 225, 585.

Where one of several plaintiffs fails.

1171. When several plaintiffs have been joined, and some or one of them only have or has been found entitled to relief the defendant, though unsuccessful, shall be entitled to his costs occasioned by so joining any person or persons who has or have not been found e titled to relief, unless the Court in disposing of the costs of the action otherwise orders. J. A. Rule 89, *part.*

In Inferior Court actions brought in High Courts.

1172. In case an action of the proper competence of a County Court is brought in the High Court, or in case an action of the proper competence of a Division Court is brought in the High Court, or in a County Court, and is tried by jury, and the Judge or Court makes no order respecting the costs, the plaintiff shall recover only County Court costs, or Division Court costs, as the case may be, and the defendant shall be entitled to tax his costs of suit as between solicitor and client, and so much thereof as exceeds the taxable costs of defence which would have been incurred in the County Court or Division Court, shall, on entering judgment, be set off and allowed by the Taxing Officer against the plaintiff's County Court or Division Court costs to be taxed, or against the costs to be taxed and the amount of the verdict if it be necessary, and if the amount of costs so set off exceeds the amount of the plaintiff's verdict and taxed costs, the defendant shall be entitled to execution for the excess against the plaintiff. See R. S. O. 1877, c. 50, s. 347, and J. A. Rule 512, *first part.*

The "event" in such case.

(*a*) The event shall in such case be to recover costs according to such scale, subject to such rights of set off as to costs, as are herein mentioned. J. A. Rule 512, *last part.*

Costs in cases within competence of Division Court brought in County Court.

1173. The plaintiff in any action which is of the proper competence of a Division Court but is brought in a County Court shall not be entitled to full County Court costs, if judgment is recovered in such action by default for want of an appearance or defence, or on the ground only of a commission for the taking of evidence out of the Province having been issued therein or necessary, whether judgment be recovered by default or otherwise. R. S. O. 1877, c. 50, s. 349.

which judgment is entered without trial, or the | Costs in
dge, or order as to the costs, and where the | actions *prima*
a facie, appears to be within the jurisdiction of | *facie* within
ng officer shall not tax full costs of the High | the jurisdic-
fidavit to his satisfaction that the action was | tion of inferior
. ; and if properly within the jurisdiction of the | Courts when
, then the taxation shall be on the scale of fees | judgment
c 511. 48 V. c. 13, s. 22. | entered with-
 | out trial, how
 | to be taxed.

till after non-appearance to a writ not specially | Non-appear-
rs of his claim under Rule 707, he shall not be | ance, subse-
he statement of the particulars of his claim, | quent particu-
is satisfied that there was good reason for not | lars.
t, so as to render unnecessary filing and serving
les 74, 497.

ctions are brought on one bond, recognizance, | Where several
change, or other instrument, or where several | actions on
the maker and endorser of a note, or against the | bonds etc.
er of a bill of exchange, there shall be collected
ndant the costs taxed in one action only at the
d the actual disbursements only in the other
otherwise orders ; but this provision shall not
 costs in the progress of an action. R. S. O.

tion of parties or of officers of corpora- | Costs of pre-
han at the trial of an action, shall be | liminary ex-
Judge in adjusting the costs of the | amination.
party inquire, or cause inquiry to be
made such examination ; and if it is *New rule*
the taxing officer, as the case may be,
unreasonably, vexatiously, or at un- *29ᵗ Sept 1844*
ed by the examination shall be borne
ault. The taxing officer may make
J. A. Rule 220.

e, or officer exercising jurisdiction in | Sum in gross
eems it proper to award costs to either party, | may be
direct payment of a sum in gross in lieu of | allowed.
himself or the officer who settles the order, and
ch sum in gross is to be paid. See Chy. O.

guardian or other guardian of an infant, lunatic, | Costs of
, is entitled to costs, or against any party to an | guardian.
Court or Judge may order the successful adult
costs and add them to his own.

pplication for an attachment of debts, and of any | Costs of
or incidental to, such application, including | attaching
r other person liable to examination, shall be | debts.
t or a Judge. See J. A. Rule 378.

of one defendant ought to be paid by another | Costs may be
rder payment to be made by the one defendant | ordered to be
is not to be necessary to order payment through | paid by one
 | defendant to
 | another.

oceedings where a High Court case is tried in | Costs of H. C.
Court case in the High Court, shall be the | case in C. C.
the Court in which the action was brought.

Costs of short-hand notes, to be costs in the cause.

1183. The disbursements incurred in any cause, matter or proceeding in obtaining copies of the evidence for the purpose of moving against a judgment or for a new trial, shall, unless the Court otherwise orders, be costs in the cause to the party obtaining and paying for the same. C. L. Rules 10th March, 1876, 3.

Taxing officer to allow reasonable sum for short-hand writer in cases not provided for.

1184. In cases not otherwise provided for, the Taxing Officer may in any cause, matter, or other proceeding, allow a reasonable sum for the expense of a short-hand writer, on the certificate of the Judge before whom the examination of any wi ness or witnesses in any such cause, matter, or other proceeding takes place. C. L. Rules 10th March, 1876, 7.

Application for interim costs, when it may be made.

1185. No application for costs, in an alimony action, is to be made until the time for delivering the defence has expired, and no costs shall be ordered to be paid *de d e in d·em* by the defendant beyond the amount of the cash disbursements actually and properly made by the plaintiff's solicitor. R. S. O. 1877, c. 40, s. 47 ; Chy. O. 489.

Nor any costs by defendant beyond disbursements where plaintiff fails.

1186. In case the plaintiff in an alimony action fails to obtain a judgment for alimony, no costs beyond the amount of the cash disbursements actually and properly made by the plaintiff's solicitor, shall be ordered to be paid by the defendant. R.S. O. 1877, c. 40, s. 48.

Commission to be allowed in lieu of taxed costs in administration and partition.

1187. In all actions or proceedings instituted for administration, or partition, or administration and partition, unless otherwise ordered by the Court or a Judge, instead of the costs being allowed according to the tariff, each person properly represented by a solicitor, and entitled to costs out of the estate.—other than creditors not parties to the action or proceeding—shall be entitled to his actual disbursements in the action or proceeding, not including counsel fees, and there shall be allowed for the other costs of the suit payable out of the estate, a commission on the amount realized, or on the value of the property partitioned in the action or proceeding, which commission shall be apportioned amongst the persons entitled to costs, as the Judge or Master thinks proper. Such commission shall be as follows :

On sums not exceeding $500........................ 20 per cent.
for every additional $100 up to $1,500.............. 5 " "
for every additional $100 up to $4,000............. 3 " "
for every additional $1,000 up to $10,000........... 2½ " "
for every additional $1,000............................... 1 " "

and such remuneration shall be in lieu of all fees, whether between "party and party," "as between solicitor and client," or "between solicitor and client." Chy. O. 643.

Costs of actions unnecessarily prosecuted may be disallowed.
Party insisting on being represented by a different solicitor to pay costs occasioned thereby.

1188. When two or more actions or proceedings are instituted for administration, or partition, or sale, the Judge may, in his discretion, disallow all or any of the costs of any action or proceeding which in his opinion has been unnecessarily prosecuted ; where any one of the parties, constituting a class formed by a Master for representation in his office by one solicitor, insists on being represented by a different solicitor, such party is personally to pay the costs of his own solicitor of and relating to the proceedings before the Master, with respect to which such nomination has been made, and all such further costs as are occasioned to any of the parties by his being represented by a different solicitor from the solicitor so nominated. Chy. O. 218, and 644.

Costs of not admitting.

1189. When anything in the course of an action or reference which ought to have been admitted, has not been admitted, the party who neglected or refused to make the admission may be ordered to pay the costs occasioned by his neglect or refusal. See Chy. O. 234. J. A. Rule 163.

Notice to admit.

1190. No costs of proving a document shall be allowed unless a notice to admit has been given under Rule 617, except when the omission to give the notice is a saving of expense.

1191. The costs of an application to extend the time for taking any *Costs of application for proceeding shall, in the absence of an order by the Court or a Judge extension of directing by whom they are to be paid, be in the discretion of the taxing time.* officer. J. A. Rule 463.

1192. In actions in the High Court of Justice no reference or examina- *Certain refer-* tion for the purpose of discovery, or examination of a judgment debtor, *ences or ex-* on which fees may be payable otherwise than in law stamps, shall be taken *aminations* before the Judge of the County Court, or local Judge of the High Court, *before officer* or Local Master being also a Judge of the County Court, by whom the *ordering same.* order or appointment for such reference or examination has been made.

(a) References in administration and partition matters under these Rules, and other like references in mortgage actions are excepted from the operation of this Rule. J. A. Rule 549.

1193. Where a petition in any action or matter is served, and noticeis *Tender of* given to the party served that in case of his appearance in Court his costs *costs, on* will be objected to, and accompanied by a tender of costs for perusing the *service of* same, the amount to be tendered shall be $5. The party making the *petition.* payment shall be allowed the same in his costs, provided the service was proper, but not otherwise ; but this Rule is without prejudice to the rights of either party to costs, or to object to costs where no such tender is made, or where the Court or Judge shall consider the party entitled, notwithstanding such notice or tender, to appear in Court. J. A. Rule 434.

1194. Where any party appears upon any application or proceeding in *Unnecessary* Court or at Chambers in which he is not interested, or upon which, *appearance in* according to the practice of the Court, he ought not to attend, he is not *Court or at* to be allowed any costs of such appearance, unless the Court or Judge *Chambers.* shall expressly direct such costs to be allowed. J. A. Rule 437.

1195. The Court or Judge may, at the hearing of any action or matter, or *Disallowance* upon any appeal, application or proceeding in any action or matter in Court *of costs of* or at Chambers, and whether the same is objected to or not, direct the costs *unnecessary* of any writ, pleading, petition affidavit, evidence, notice to cross-examine *proceedings.* witnesses, account, statement, or other proceeding, or any part thereof, which is improper, unnecessary, or contains unnecessary matter, or is of unnecessary length, to be disallowed ; or may direct the taxing officer to look into the same and to disallow the costs thereof, or of such part thereof, as he shall find to be improper, unnecessary, or to contain unnecessary matter, or to be of unnecessary length. In such case the party whose costs are so disallowed shall pay the costs occasioned to the other parties by such unnecessary proceeding, matter, or length ; and in any case where such question shall not have been raised before and dealt with by the Court or a Judge, the taxing officer may look into the same (and, as to evidence, although the same may be entered as read in any judgment or order) for the purpose aforesaid, and thereupon the same consequences shall ensue as if he had been specially directed to do so. *See* Chy. O. 71. J. A. Rule 435; App. O. 10.

1196. No allowance is to be made for any order for production or any *Costs of* notice or inspection under any of the Rules relating to production and *inspection of* inspection of documents unless it is shewn to the satisfaction of the taxing *documents.* officer that there were good and sufficient reasons for taking the order, giving the notice, or making the inspection. J. A. Rule 230.

· 2. TAXATION.

1197. Where costs are awarded to be paid, it shall be competent to a *Taxing Offi-* taxing officer to tax the same, without an express reference to him for *cers may tax* that purpose. Chy. O. 316. *costs without express reference.*

No bill of costs exceeding $30 to be taxed by Registrars, etc.

1198. No bill of costs where the amount claimed exceeds $30 is to be taxed by the Registrars, the Master in Ordinary, the Master in Chambers or Clerk in Chambers, but every bill exceeding that sum is in Toronto to be taxed by one of the Taxing officers, notwithstanding anything to the contrary contained in the order for taxation. Chy. O. 310.

One day's notice of taxation sufficient.

1199. One day's notice of taxing costs, together with a copy of the bill of costs and affidavit of increase, if any, shall be given by the solicitor of the party whose costs are to be taxed to the other party or his solicitor in all cases where a notice to tax is necessary. Rules T. T. 1856, 48.

Notice of taxation unnecessary when defendant has not appeared.

1200. Notice of taxing costs shall not be necessary in any case where the defendant has not appeared in person, or by his solicitor or guardian. Rules T. T. 1856, 50.

Parties to attend taxations.

1201. The taxing officer shall have authority to arrange and direct what parties are to attend before him on the taxation of costs to be borne by a fund or estate, and to disallow the costs of any party whose attendance the officer shall in his discretion consider unnecessary in consequence of the interest of the party in the fund or estate being small or remote, or sufficiently protected by other parties interested. J. A. Rule 440.

Defendants' improperly severing are to be allowed but one set of costs without special order.

1202. Where two or more defendants defend by different solicitors under circumstances that by the law of the Court, entitle them to but one set of costs, the taxing officer, without any special order from the Court, is to allow but one set of costs ; and if two or more defendants defending by the same solicitor separate unnecessarily in their defences, or otherwise, the taxing officer is, without any special order of the Court, to allow but one defence and set of costs   Chy. O. 315.

Neglect to bring in or tax costs.

1203. Where any party entitled to costs refuses or neglects to bring in his costs for taxation, or to procure the same to be taxed, and thereby prejudices any other party, the taxing officer shall be at liberty to certify the costs of the other parties, and certify such refusal or neglect, or may allow such party refusing or neglecting a nominal or other sum for such costs, so as to prevent any other party being prejudiced by such refusal or neglect. J. A. Rule 441.

Set-off of costs.

1204. In any case in which a party entitled to receive costs is liable to pay costs to any other party, the taxing officer may tax the costs such party is so liable to pay, and may adjust the same by way of deduction or set off, or may, if he thinks fit, delay the allowance of the costs such party is entitled to receive until he has paid or tendered the costs he is liable to pay ; or the officer may allow or certify the costs to be paid, and the . same may be recovered by the party entitled thereto in the same manner as costs ordered to be paid may be recovered. J. A. Rule 436.

Set-off of damages and costs not to prejudice solicitor's lien.

1205. No set-off of damages or costs between parties shall be allowed to the prejudice of the solicitor's lien for costs in the particular action against which the set-off is sought ; provided, nevertheless, that interlocutory costs in the same action awarded to the adverse party may be deducted. Rules T. T. 1856, 52.

Costs may be taxed on an award, though time for moving not elapsed.

1206. Costs may be taxed on an award, although the time for appealing from or moving against the award has not elapsed. Rules T. T. 1856, 142.

Revision of certain costs.

1207. All bills of costs or disbursements in actions brought for the administration of an estate, or for partition, or for the foreclosure, redemption or sale of mortgaged premises, and all bills in other actions where the amount is to be paid out of an estate or out of a fund in Court, or in which any infant, lunatic, or person of unsound mind is interested, (or which shall be payable out of any estate in which any infant, lunatic, or person of unsound mind, is interested,) are to be revised by one of the taxing officers of the Supreme Court at Toronto, before the amount thereof is inserted in any certificate, report, order, or judgment. J. A. Rules 439 and 593.

1208. The Local Master or other local officer is forthwith, after taxing any such bill of costs, to transmit the same by mail to Toronto, addressed to the proper taxing officer, and he is to allow int he bill the postage for the transmission and return of the bill, and shall prepay the same; and is to allow in the bill the sum of one dollar as a fee for the revision of the bill by the taxing officer at Toronto, and a law stamp for that sum, with postage stamps for the postage, is to be paid at the time of taxation by the party procuring the bill to be taxed; and the Local Master or other officer is to transmit with the bill to the taxing officer at Toronto, the law stamp, and the necessary stamps for postage on the return of the bill to the Local Master or other officer. Chy. O. 311. *Revision of taxations by local officers.*

1209. The taxing officer at Toronto, upon receiving the bill of costs is to examine the same, and to mark in the margin such sums (if any) as may appear to him to have been improperly allowed, or to be questionable; and he is to revise the taxation either *ex parte*, or upon notice to the Toronto agent (if any) of the solicitor whose bill is in question, as in his discretion he may see fit; but notifying such agent (if any) in all cases where the taxation is not clearly erroneous, or where the amount in question is so large as in the judgment of the taxing officer, to make such notification proper. Such notification may be by appointment mailed to the address of the agent (if any). If upon the revision the sums dis allowed shall amount to one-twentieth of the amount allowed upon taxation, the taxing officer is to add to the amount taxed off, the amount of postages, and the sum of one dollar aforesaid, and is thereupon to re-transmit the bill so revised to the Local Master or other officer. Chy. O. 312. *Duty of taxing Officer on receipt of bill for revision.*

1210. In any such case no sum is to be inserted in the report of a Local Master or other officer as taxed and allowed for costs, until such revision by a taxing officer; but in a case of urgency a writ of execution may issue to levy debt or costs, or both, upon the order of a Judge, subject to the future revision by the taxing officer. Chy. O. 313. *No sum to be inserted for costs in report, until after revision.*

1211. Pending a revision, judgment may be entered and execution issued, unless the Court or a Judge otherwise orders; and in case of an execution being so issued, if the amount taxed is reduced on revision, the party entitled to the costs shall forthwith give notice of the reduction and of the amount thereof to the Sheriff or other officer in whose hands the execution had been placed; and the amount struck off on the revision shall be deducted from the amount indorsed on the execution. J. A. Rule 439 (d). *But execution in cases of urgency may issue.*

1212. No mileage shall be taxed or allowed for the service of any writ, paper or proceeding, without an affidavit being made and produced to the proper taxing officer, stating the sum actually disbursed and paid for such mileage, and the name of the party to whom such payment has been made; and, except in cases provided for in Rule 254, no fees shall be allowed for the mileage or service of writs ot summons unless served, and sworn in the affidavit of service to have been served, by the Sheriff, his Deputy or Bailiff, being a literate person (or by a Coroner when the Sheriff is a party to the action), nor unless a return of the Sheriff or Coroner (as the case may be) is indorsed thereon. R. S. O. 1877, c. 50, s. 335; Rule T. T. 1856, 160. *Mileage not allowed on service of mesne process unless served by Sheriff.*

Affidavits of increase, to be made by solicitor, or his clerk having management of cause, or the client.

Form of

Allowance for maps, &c.

1213. All affidavits of increase must be made by the solicitor in the cause, or some clerk having the management thereof, or by the client. They must set forth the sums paid to counsel, naming them, and for what service, the names of witnesses, their places of abode, the places at which they were subpœnaed, and the distance which each such witness was necessarily obliged to travel in order to attend the trial, that every such witness was necessary and material for the client in the cause, that they did attend, and that they did not attend as witnesses in any other cause (or otherwise, as the case may be). The number of days which each witness was necessarily absent from home in order to attend such trial must also be accurately stated. If a solicitor attends as a witness, it must be stated whether or not he attended at the place of trial as solicitor or witness in any other cause, and whether or not he had any other business there. The day on which the trial occurred should be stated. If maps or plans were used at the trial, the necessity for them must be shown in the affidavit, or no allowance will be made for them ; the sum paid for them must also be set forth, and that they were prepared or procured with a view to the trial of the cause. The taxing officer is authorized in such case to make a reasonable allowance for maps and plans. **Rules T. T. 1856, 165.**

Taxations between party and party.

1214. As to costs to be paid or borne by another party, no costs are to be allowed which do not appear to the taxing officer to have been necessary or proper for the attainment of justice or defending the rights of the party, or which appear to the taxing officer to have been incurred through over-caution, negligence, or mistake, or merely at the desire of the party. **J. A. Rule 442.**

Costs of unnecessary proceedings not to be taxed

Exception in case of taxation between solicitor and his client, when costs incurred at client's request, after notice that proceeding unnecessary.

1215. If upon the taxation of costs it should appear to the officer taxing the same that any proceedings have been taken unnecessarily, and which were not calculated to advance the interests of the party on whose behalf the same were taken, it shall be the duty of the officer to disallow the costs of such proceedings, as well on the taxation of costs between solicitor and client, as on a taxation between party and party, unless the officer shall be of opinion that such proceedings were taken by the solicitor because they were in his judgment, reasonably exercised, conducive to the interest of his client. It shall not be the duty of the officer, on a taxation of costs between a solicitor and his client, to disallow to the solicitor his costs of such proceedings where it is made to appear that such proceedings were taken by the desire of the client, after being informed by his solicitor that the same were unnecessary, and not calculated to advance the interests of the client. **Chy. O. 306.**

Certain costs taxable between party and party as would be allowed as between solicitor and client.

1216. Where costs are to be taxed as between party and party, the officer taxing the same may allow to the party entitled to receive such costs, the like costs as are taxable where costs are directed to be taxed as between solicitor and client, in respect of the following matters :

1. Advising with counsel on the pleadings, evidence, and other proceedings in the cause ;
2. Procuring counsel to settle such pleadings and petitions as may appear to have been proper to be settled by counsel ;
3. Procuring and attending consultations of counsel ;
4. The amendment of pleadings ;
5. On proceedings in the Master's office.
6. Supplying counsel with copies of, or extracts from, necessary documents. **Chy. O. 307.**

Tariff of costs.

1217. The table of costs set forth in the Tariff A. appended to these Rules shall be that according to which all costs in civil actions in the High Court and in the County Courts shall be allowed and taxed, and no other fees, costs or charges than therein set down shall be allowed in respect of the matters thereby provided for.

1218. The fees and disbursements payable in stamps or otherwise upon Tariff of disproceedings in the High Court and the Court of Appeal shall henceforward be those enumerated in the Tariff B annexed hereto. *New.*

bursements.

1219. The fees and disbursements mentioned in the 2nd or "Lower Lower scale. ...nd B, shall be the amounts taxable in ...there enumerated in all actions where ...the following cases :—

...d seeking, an account of the dealings Partnership. dissolved or expired, the joint stock or ...;

...mortgagee, whose mortgage has been Mortgage writing, or a judgment creditor, or a su ts for fore- ...y for a debt, seeking foreclosure or sale, closure or sale. ...ty, where the sum claimed as due does

...deem any legal or equitable mortgage, Redemption. ...ng to redeem the same, when the sum ...xceed $200 ;

" (4) By any person seeking equitable relief for, or by reason of any Equitable matter whatsoever, where the subject matter involved does not exceed relief. the sum of $200."

1220. The practice of any Court, whose jurisdiction is vested in the Application of High Court of Justice or Court of Appeal, relating to costs, and to the former practice. allowance of the fees of solicitors, and to the taxation of costs, existing prior to *The Ontario Judicature Act, 1881*, shall, in so far as they are not inconsistent with the Act and the Rules of Court remain, in force and be applicable to costs of the same or analogous proceedings, and to the allowance of the fees of solicitors of the Supreme Court and the taxation of costs in the High Court of Justice and Court of Appeal. J. A. Rule 445.

1221. The solicitor or party instituting any action or proceeding, in Certificate to respect of which he claims to pay the fees of Court, according to the tariff be filed on referred to in Rule 1219, is to file with the officer in whose office appearance instituting is required to be entered, a certificate in the form No. 211 in the Appen- action where dix, of which certificate the said officer is, at the request of any solicitor or lower scale party acting in person in the suit or matter, to mark a copy. Chy. O. 554. cable.

tariff is appli-

1222. On production of a copy of the certificate, the officers of the On production Court are to receive and file all papers and t ke all necessary proceedings of copy of upon payment by stamps, or otherwise, as the case may be, of the proper certificate fees, according to the said tariff. Chy. O. 555.

lower scale fees to be charged.

1223. In every case certified for the said tariff in which it may happen Where costs that the solicitor becomes entitled to charge and be allowed according to on higher scale the ordinary tariff, the deficiency of the fees of Court is to be made good. afterwards Chy. O. 556.

given.

1224. In any case in which the fees of Court have been paid, according Where fees to the ordinary tariff, and in which it may happen that the solicitor have be n paid becomes entitled to charge and be allowed his own fees, only according to according to the lower tariff, the excess of fees of Court so paid may be allowed upon higher scale, the taxation of costs, if the circumstances of the case, in the judgment of allowed. the taxing officer, justify such allowance. Chy. O. 557.

excess may be

1225. Where a seal is under the 126th section of the Judicature Act, No fee for impressed on any document which before the passing of *The Ontario* seal when *Judicature Act, 1881*, did not require to be sealed, the fee of fifty cents impressed on mentioned in the 155th section of " *The Judicature Act*," shall not be documents not payable on such document. J. A. Rule 503.

formerly requiring to be sealed.

Solicitor and client taxation.

1226. When a client or other person is entitled to the delivery of a solicitor's bill of fees, charges and disbursements, or a copy thereof, the bill or a copy thereof, as the case may be, is to be delivered within fourteen days from the service of the order.

(a) The bill delivered shall be referred to the proper master for taxation, and on the refe rence the solicitor is to give credit for all sums of money by him received from or on account of the client, and is to refund what, if anything, he may on such taxation appear to have been overpaid ;

(b) The Master is to tax the costs of the reference and certify what shall be found due to or from either party in respect of the bill and demand and of the cost of the reference, to be paid according to the event of the taxation pursuant to the statute ;

(c) The solicitor is not to commence or prosecute any action touching the demand pending the reference without leave of the Court or a Judge ;

(d) The amount certified to be due shall be paid forthwith after confirmation of the certificate by filing, as in the case of a master's report, by the party liable to pay such amount ;

(e) Upon payment by the said client or other person of what (if anything) may appear to be due to the solicitor, the solicitor (if required) is to deliver to the said client or other person, or as he may direct, all deeds, books, papers, and writings in the said solicitor's possession, custody, or power, belonging to the said client ;

(f) The order shall be read as if it contained the above particulars, and shall not set forth the same, but may contain any variations therefrom, and any other directions which the Court or Judge shall see fit to make. *See* J. A. Rule 443.

What order presumed to contain.

1227. When a solicitor's bill has been delivered, the order of reference shall be presumed to contain clauses (a) to (e) inclusive of Rule 1226, whether obtained by the solicitor, client or other person liable to pay the same.

Order of course to issue on præcipe.

1228. The order, when grantable of course, shall be issued on præcipe. J. A. Rule 444.

Taxation of third party

1229. When a party not principally liable to pay a bill applies for delivery of a copy thereof for the purpose of a reference, or for taxation of a bill delivered, and it appears that by reason of the conduct of the party principally liable, he is precluded from taxing the same, but is nevertheless entitled to an account by the party principally liable, it shall not be necessary for the party so applying to bring an action for an account, but the Court or Judge may, in a summary manner, refer a bi l already deli ered for taxation, or may order delivery of a copy of the bill, and refer the same for taxation, and may add such parties not already notified as may be necessary to do complete justice to all parties.

(a) The rights of the parties are to be adjusted by reference to the pro. visions of Rule 1226 as far as they are applicable, having regard to the relations of the parties to the application and reference.

Objection to taxation.

1230. Any party who may be dissatisfied with the allowance or disallowance by the taxing officer, in any bill of costs taxed by him, of the whole or any part of any item or items, may, at any time before the certificate is signed, deliver to the other party interested therein, and carry in before the taxing officer, an objection in writing to such allowance or disallowance, specifying therein by a list, in a short and concise form, the item or items, or parts or part thereof, objected to, and may thereupon apply to the taxing officer to review the taxation in respect of the same. J. A. Rule 447.

1231. Upon such application the taxing officer shall reconsider and review his taxation upon such objections, and he may, if he thinks fit, receive further evidence in respect thereof, and, if so required by either party, he shall state either in his certificate of taxation or by reference to such objections, the grounds and reasons of his decision thereon, and any special facts or circumstances relating thereto. J. A. Rule 448.

Review of taxation by taxing officer. *Ru Rule p57*

.3. SHERIFF'S FEES.

1232. The fees and allowances set forth in the tariff C appended to these Rules shall be taken and received by sheriffs and coroners in civil proceedings in lieu of all fees to which they have been heretofore entitled under the tariffs heretofore in force. See tariff, 2 Feb. 1874.

Sheriffs fees.

1233. In case a part only is made by the Sheriff on, or by force of any execution against goods and chattels, the Sheriff shall be entitled, besides his fees and expenses of execution, to poundage only upon the amount so made by him, whatever be the sum endorsed upon the writ, and in case the personal estate, except chattels real, of the defendant is seized or advertised on or under an execution, but not sold by reason of satisfaction having been otherwise obtained, or from some other cause, and no money is actually made by the Sheriff on or by force of such execution, the Sheriff shall be entitled to the fees and expenses of execution and poundage only on the value of the property seized not exceeding the amount endorsed on the writ, or such less sum as the Court or a Judge may deem reasonable. R. S. O. 1877, c. 66, s. 45.

In what cases Sheriff entitled to poundage.

1234. In cases of writs of execution upon the same judgment to several counties, wherein the personal estate of the judgment debtor or debtors has been seized or advertised, but not sold, by reason of satisfaction having been obtained under and by virtue of a writ in some other county, and no money has been actually made on the execution, the Sheriff shall not be entitled to poundage, but to mileage and fees only for the services actually rendered and performed by him, and the Court or a Judge, may allow him a reasonable charge for such services, in case no special fee therefor is assigned in any table of costs. R. S. O. 1877, c. 66, s. 46.

When Sheriff entitled to mileage and fees only.

1235. In case any person liable on an execution is dissatisfied as to the amount of poundage, fees, and expenses of execution claimed by a Sheriff, he may, before or after payment thereof, and upon notice to the Sheriff, apply to the Court or a Judge, and if, upon a statement of the facts, the Court or Judge is of opinion that the amount is unreasonable, notwithstanding that it is according to the tariff, the same shall be reduced or ordered to be refunded upon such terms as to costs or otherwise, as the Court or Judge may think fit to impose. R. S. O. 1877, c. 66, s. 47.

If party dissatisfied he may apply to the Court, who may reduce the amount.

1236. Upon the settlement of an execution, either in whole or in part, by payment, levy or otherwise, the Sheriff or officer claiming any fees, poundage, incidental expenses or remuneration, which have not been taxed, shall, upon being required by either plaintiff or defendant, or the solicitor of either party, and on payment or tender of the expenses of such taxation, and the further sum of 25 cents for the copy of his bill in detail (which he shall be bound to render) have his fees, poundage, incidental expenses or remuneration, as the case may be, taxed by one of the Taxing officers of the Supreme Court, in the County of York, and in other counties by the proper Taxing officer of the county wherein such sheriff keeps his office. R. S. O. 1877, c. 66, s. 48; 49 V. c. 16, s. 17.

Taxing Sheriff's costs.

Costs not to be collected till taxed.   **1237.** No sheriff shall without taxation collect any fees, costs, poundage or incidental expenses, after having been required to have the same taxed ; and upon tender of the amount taxed, no fees, costs, poundage or incidental expenses in respect of proceedings subsequently taken shall be allowed to any sheriff. R. S. O. 1877, c. 66, s. 49.

How to be taxed and taxation certified.   **1238.** It shall be the duty of the taxing officer to tax the bills of costs presented to him for taxation, as herein required, upon payment or tender of his fees, and to give, when requested, a certificate of such taxation and the amount thereof. R. S. O. 1877, c. 66, s. 50.

Duty of taxing officer.   **1239.** It shall be the duty of the taxing officer, upon proof of notice of the time and place of the taxation having been duly served upon the sheriff, deputy sheriff, or other officer charged with the execution of the writ, to examine the bills presented to him for taxation, as herein required, whether such taxation is opposed or not, and to be satisfied that the items charged in such bill are correct and legal, and to strike out all charges for services which, in his opinion, were not necessary to be performed. R. S. O. 1877, c. 66, s. 51.

Revision of taxation.   **1240.** Either party dissatisfied with the taxation may appeal therefrom as in ordinary cases. R. S. O. 1877, c. 66, s. 52.

Costs etc.   **1241.** The Court or a Judge may, in or for the purposes of any interpleader proceedings, make all such orders as to costs and all other matters as may be just and reasonable.

4. SECURITY FOR COSTS.

Security for costs, order for. *after entering an appearance*   **1242.** Where it appears, by the writ of summons, notice, or other proceeding by which an action or matter is instituted, or by an indorsement thereon, that the plaintiff resides out of Ontario, the defendant shall be entitled on præcipe to an order requiring the plaintiff within 4 weeks from the service of the order to give security in $400 for the defendant's costs of the action staying all further proceedings in the meantime, and directing that in default of such security being given the action be dismissed with costs against such defendant, unless the Court or Judge upon special application for that purpose shall otherwise order. J. A. Rule 431

Additional cases in which the defendant may obtain security for costs. *amended Rule 1498*   **1243.** In addition to any cases in which a defendant in any action, may by any law or by the practice of the Courts, be entitled to obtain security for costs from a plaintiff, security for costs may be granted to the defendant or applicant in any action or proceeding in which it is made to appear satisfactorily to the Court or a Judge, that the plaintiff has brought a former action or proceeding for the same cause, which is pending either in Ontario or in any other country, or that he has judgment or order passed against him in such action or proceeding, with costs, and that such costs have not been paid ; and such Court or Judge may thereupon make such rule or order staying proceedings until such security is given as to the Court or Judge seems meet. R. S. O. c. 40, s. 97 ; c. 50, s. 70.

Persons suing for penalties may be ordered to give security for costs; in what cases and on what application.   **1244.** In any action in which the plaintiff sues as an informer, or seeks to recover any penalty given to any informer or person who sues for the same as aforesaid, under any statute or law in which any penalty is given to any person who sues for the same, either for his sole benefit, for the benefit of the Crown. or partly for his benefit and partly for the benefit of the Crown,—the person so sued, or his agent, or solicitor, m y apply to the Court in which the action was instituted or is pending, or a judge thereof, for security for costs, upon an affidavit made by the defendant applying, showing that the action is brought to recover a penalty, and that in the belief of the deponent, the plaintiff or inform r is not possessed of property sufficient to answer the costs of the action n case a verdict is given or judgment rendered in favour of the defendant, and that he (the said defendant) has a good defence to the action upon the merits, as he is advised and believes ; and the Court or Judge may make an order that the plaintiff or informer in the action shall give security for the costs to be incurred in the action, in the same manner and in accordance with the practice in cases where a plaintiff resides out of the Province, and the order shall be a stay of the proceedings in the case, until the proper security is given as aforesaid. R. S. O. c. 50, s. 71.

1245. In any action or matter in which security for costs is required, the security shall be of such amount and be given at such time or times and in such manner and form, as the Court or a Judge shall direct. J. A. Rule 429.

Amount of security for costs.

1246. Where a defendant in any action is entitled to obtain security for costs from a plaintiff, the Court or Judge may require the plaintiff to furnish the security within a time to be limited in any order for such security, or by any subsequent order.

Time for giving security for costs may be limited.

(a) If the plaintiff fails without sufficient excuse to comply with such order, he shall be liable to have his action dismissed as for want of prosecution, with costs, and the Court or Judge may make an order accordingly. 42 V. c. 15, s. 2.

1247. Where a bond is to be given as security for costs, it shall unless the Court or a Judge otherwise directs, be given to the party or persons requiring the security, and not to an officer of the Court. J. A. Rule 430.

Security for costs where given by bond.

See Rule 1378 —

1248. Whenever a party is under an obligation to give a bond as security for costs, he may, without special order, pay into Court a sum of money not less than half the penalty of the bond required, and the same when so paid in shall stand as security in lieu of the bond required.

Money may be paid into Court.

1249. The party so paying in money shall when paying the same in state the purpose for which it is so paid in, and shall forthwith serve a notice upon the opposite party specifying the fact and purpose of such payment.

Notice to be served.

1250. The amount of security may be increased or diminished from time to time by the Court or a Judge.

Amount may be varied.

1251. Where an action is brought by a foreign plaintiff liable to give security for costs, who indorses his writ of summons with particulars of his claim in such a manner that, upon motion under Rule 739, an order allowing him to sign judgment might be made, he may, on being served with an order for security for costs, pay into Court the sum of $50, as a partial compliance with such order, and thereupon he shall be at liberty to proceed with a motion for judgment under Rule 739, but the order for security shall, nevertheless, in all other respects, have its full operation and effect.

Security on motion for judgment.

1252. If upon such a motion the plaintiff is allowed to sign judgment for any portion of his claim, he may sign judgment and issue execution therefor, but shall not take any other proceedings until the order for security shall have been fully complied with.

Judgment for part.

CHAPTER XIV.

COUNTY COURTS.

All writs to be under the seal of the Courts, and tested,etc.   **1253.** All writs issued in the County Courts shall be issued by the Clerk and shall be under the seal thereof, and shall be tested in the name of the Judge thereof: or in the case of the death of such Judge, then in the name of the Junior or acting Judge in the County Court for the time being. R. S. O. 1877, c. 50, ss. 6, 8.

Subpœnas.   **1254.** The several County Courts may issue writs of *subpœna ad testifican dum*, to enforce the attendance of any witnesses resident within Ontario and also writs of *subpœna duces tecum*, to enforce the attendance of and the production of deeds and papers by any such witnesses and may proceed against persons who, having been duly served with a *subpœna*, disregard or disobey the same, with the same powers, in like manner and by the same mode of proceeding as belongs to and is practised in the High Court. R. S. O. 1877, c. 62, s. 16.

Judges may sit at any time.   **1255.** Subject to Rules of Court, the Judges of the County Court shall have power to sit and act at any time for the transaction of any part of the business of such Courts, or for the discharge of any duty which by any statute or otherwise was formerly required to be discharged out of or during term. J. A. Rule 488.

Costs where action fails for want of jurisdiction.   **1256.** In all actions or other proceedings brought in any County or Division Court in Ontario, in which the plaintiff fails to recover judgment by reason of such Court having no jurisdiction over the subject matter thereof, the said County Court, or the Judge presiding in the said Division Court, as the case may be, shall have jurisdiction over the costs of such action, suit or other proceeding, and may order by and to whom the same shall be paid, and the recovery of the costs so ordered to be paid may be enforced by the same remedies as the costs in actions, suits or proceedings within the proper competence of the said Courts respectively are recoverable. J. A. Rule 489.

Procedure in County Courts   **1257.** The pleadings, practice and procedure in actions in the High Court of Justice shall apply and extend to actions in the County Courts. J. A. Rule 490.

Motions against judgments.   **1258.** In actions in the County Courts motions against judgments and for new trials shall be disposed of upon the like grounds and principles as in the High Court. See R. S. O. 1877, c. 50, s. 292.

Notice of motion.   **1259.** Every motion against a judgment or for a new trial shall be a two clear days' notice, and the motion shall be set down at least one clear day before the first day of the sittings for which the notice is given unless otherwise ordered. See R. S. O. 1877, c. 50, s. 293.

Change of place of trial in County Court.   **1260.** In all actions brought in a County Court the Judge of the County Court where the proceedings are commenced, or the Master in Chambers, or one of the Judges of the High Court sitting at Chambers may change the place of trial according to the practice now in force in the High Court; and in the event of an order being obtained for that purpose, the Clerk of the County Court where the action was commenced shall forthwith transmit all papers in the action to the Clerk of the County Court to which the place of trial is changed, and all subsequent proceedings shall be entitled in such last mentioned Court, and carried on in such last mentioned County as if the proceedings had originally been commenced in such last mentioned Court. R. S. O. 1877, c. 50, s. 155.

1261. Every County Court Clerk shall keep his office open for the transaction of business on every day except on holidays, and except as hereinafter provided from the hour of 10 in the forenoon, to the hour of 3 in the afternoon. On and between the 1st day of July and the 31st day of August, and on and between the 24th day of December and the 6th day of January, every such Clerk shall keep his office open for the transaction of business, from 10 in the forenoon until noon ; and during the Statutory Sittings of the Court, such Clerk shall keep his office open as aforesaid, on and between the said dates until 4 in the afternoon. J. A. Rule 534. *Office hours of Clerks of County Courts*

1262. Money to be paid into the County Court, or Surrogate Court of the County Clerk, by any person, shall be paid into some incorporated bank designated for this purpose. from time to time, by order of the Lieutenant-Governor in Council ; or where there is no such bank, t en into some incorporated bank in which public money of the Province is then being deposi ed, and which has be n appointed for this purpose by any General Rule or Order made in the same manner as other General Rules or Orders of the said Courts respectively are by law directed to be made ; or if no bank has been so appointed, then into any bank in which public money of the Province is then being deposited. *Payment of money into Court.*

(2) The money shall be so paid in to the credit of the cause or matter in which the payment is made, with the privity of the Clerk or Registrar (as the case may be) of the Court, and in no other manner ; and such money shall only be withdrawn on the order of the Court or a Judge thereof, with the privity of the Clerk or Registrar of the Court. *Procedure.* *Withdrawal.*

(3) Where money is so paid in under a plea of payment into Court, the Clerk, on the production of the receipt of the bank for the money or other satisfactory proof of such payment, shall sign a receipt for the amount in the margin of the pleading. *Plea of payment into Court.*

1263. The Clerk and Registrar of said Courts shall each keep a book or books containing an account of all money so paid into their respective Courts, and of the withdrawal thereof ; and shall prepare in the month of January in every year a stat ment of all moneys so paid in and withdrawn respectively, and a statement of the condition of the various accounts upon the thirty-first day of the preceding December, and shall transmit to the Provincial Secreta y and to the Judge or each of the Judges of such Courts, a copy of such state ent, wit a decl ration hereto annexed made before a Justice of the Peace or Commissioner for taking affidavits, in the form No. 217 in the Appendix. *Clerk or Registrar to keep books and render statements.*

1264. The book or books so to be kept shall be open for inspection within office hours ; and the Clerk or Registrar shall give a certificate of t e state of any account or an extract therefrom at the desire of any party interested, or his attorney or s licitor on paym nt to the Clerk or Registrar of the sum of twenty cents for such inspection or certificate and the sum of ten cents per folio for such extract. R. S. O. 1877, c. 42, s. 25. *Books to be open for inspection.* *Fees for extracts, etc.*

SCHEDULE

Of Rules and Orders not Repealed.

Description of Rule or Order.	Extent to which Unrepealed.
Rules of the Courts of Queen's Bench and Common Pleas of 7th Feb., 1876. (Crown cases reserved.)	The whole.
Orders of the Court of Chancery. (Election Court Rule.)	Order 618.
Rules of the Supreme Court of Judicature.	Rules 493 and 494 referring to proceedings pending at the time of passing the *Judicature Act*; 538 referring to selection of *rota* Judges for trial of election petitions; and 605 referring to Fees in Surrogate Courts and fees of Clerks of the Peace.
Rules relating to controverted elections of members of the House of Commons, passed 13th Feb., 1875.	The whole.
Rules of the Court of Appeal relating to controverted elections of members of the Legislative Assembly of Ontario.	The whole.

APPENDIX

TO THE FOREGOING RULES.

FORMS·

PART I.

FORMS OF WRITS OF SUMMONS, AND NOTICE IN LIEU OF SUMMONS.

No. 1.

General Form of Writ of Summons.

In the High Court of Justice.

——Division.
Between *A.B.*, Plaintiff,
and
C.D. and *E.F.*, Defendants.

VICTORIA, by the Grace of God, &c.

To *C.D.* of   in the county of   and *E.F.* of

We command you, That within ten days after the service of this writ on you, inclusive of the day of such service, you cause an appearance to be entered for you in an action at the suit of *A.B.*; and take notice that in default of your so doing the plaintiff may proceed therein, and judgment may be given in your absence. Witness, the Honourable   President of our High Court of Justice at   in the year of Our Lord 18   .

Memorandum to be subscribed on the writ.

N.B.—This writ is to be served within *12* calendar months from the date thereof, or if renewed, within *12* calendar months from the date of such renewal, including the day of such date, and not afterwards.

The defendant [*or* defendants] may appear hereto by entering an appearance [*or* appearances] either personally or by solicitor at the [   ] office at

Indorsements to be made on the writ.

The plaintiff's claim is for, &c.

Where the writ is to be specially indorsed add :—The following are the particulars :— (*Giving them See Part II. post*)

This writ was issued by *E.F.*, of   solicitor for the said plaintiff, who resides at   or, this writ was issued by the plaintiff in person who resides at   [*mention the city, town, or township, and also the name of the street and number of the house of the plaintiff's residence, if any, or in case of a township, the number of the lot and concession.*]

Also the Indorsement No. 5.

Indorsement to be made on the writ after service thereof.

This writ was served by *X.Y.* on *C.D.* [the defendant *or* one of the defendants], on *Monday*, the   day of   , 18   .

(Signed)   *X.Y.*

No. 2.

Writ for service out of Ontario.

In the High Court of Justice. ——Division.

Between *A.B.*, Plaintiff,
and
C.D. and *E.F.* Defendants.

VICTORIA, by the Grace of God, &c.

To *C.D.*, of

We command you, *C. D.*, that within [*here insert the number of days directed by Rule 88, or as the case may be*] after the service, on you, of this writ [*or notice of this writ and of the plaintiff's statement of claim delivered herewith, inclusive of the day of such service. you cause an appearance to be entered for you in an action at the suit of *A.B*, and your defence thereto, if any, to be delivered ; and take notice that in default of your so doing the plaintiff may proceed therein, and judgment may be given in your absence.

Witness, the Honourable   President, &c.

Memorandum and indorsements as in Form No. 1.

Indorsement to be made on the writ.

N.B.—This writ is to be used where the defendant or all the defendants or one or more defendant or defendants is or are out of Ontario. When the defendant to be served is not a British subject, and is not in B itish dominions, notice of the writ, and not the writ itself, is to be served upon him.

Indorsement to be made on the writ after service thereof:

This notice was served by *X.Y.*, on *G.H.*, (the defendant *or* one of the defendants) on   the   day of   18   .   •
Indorsed the   day of   18   .

(Signed)
(Address)

———

No. 3.

Notice of writ, in lieu of writ, to be given out of Ontario.

In the High Court of Justice.
——Division.

Between *A.B.* Plaintiff,
and
C.D., *E.F.*, and *G.H.*, Defendants.

To *G.H.*, of

Take notice that *A B*, of   has commenced an action against you, *G H.*, in the   Division of Her Majesty's High Court of Justice in Ontario. by writ of that Court, dated the day of   , A.D. 18   ; which writ is indorsed as follows [*copy in full the indorsements*], and you are required within [   ] days after the receipt of this notice, inclusive of the day of such receipt, to defend the said act on. by cau ing an appearance to be entered for you in the said Court to the said action, and your defence thereto, if any, to be delivered ; and in default of your so doing, the said *A.B.* may proceed therein, and judgment may be given in your absence.

You may appear to the said writ by entering an appearance personally, or by your solicitor at the [   ] office at
Dated, &c.

(Signed)   *A.B.*, of   &c.
or
X.Y., of   &c.
Solicitor for *A.B.*

N.B.—This notice is to be used when the person to be served is not a British subject, and is not in British dominions.

Indorsement to be made on the notice of the writ after service thereof:

This notice was served by *X.Y.*, on *G.H.*, (the defendant *or* one of the defendants) on   the   day of   18   .
Indorsed the   day of   18   .

(Signed)
(Address)

PART II.

INDORSEMENTS ON WRITS OF SUMMONS.

SECTION I.

No. **4.**

Money Claims where no special Indorsement under Rule 242.

The plaintiff's claim is $ for the price of goods sold.	Goods sold

This Form shall suffice whether the claim be in respect of goods sold and delivered, or of goods bargained and sold.

The plaintiff's claim is $	for money lent [and interest].	Money lent.
The plaintiff's claim is $ whereof $ is for the price of goods sold, and $ for money lent, and $ for interest.		Several demands.
The plaintiff's claim is $	for arrears of rent.	Rent.
The plaintiff's claim is $	for arrears of salary as a clerk [*or as the case may be*].	Salary, etc.
The plaintiff's claim is $	for interest upon money lent.	Interest.
The plaintiff's claim is $	for a general average contribution.	General average.
The plaintiff's claim is $	for freight and demurrage.	Freight, etc.
The plaintiff's claim is $	for lighterage.	
The plaintiff's claim is $	for market tolls and stallage.	Tolls.
The plaintiff's claim is $	for penalties under the Statute Victoria, chap. [. . .]	Penalties.
The plaintiff's claim is $ as a banker.	for money deposited with the defendant	Banker's balance.
The plaintiff's claim is $ expended] as a solicitor.	for fees for work done [and $ money	Fees, etc., as solicitors.
The plaintiff's claim is $ auctioneer, broker, &c.]	for commission as [*state character as*	Commission.
The plaintiff's claim is $	for medical attendance.	Medical attendance, etc.
The plaintiff's claim is $ policies of insurance.	for a return of premiums paid upon	Return of premium.
The plaintiff's claim is $	for the warehousing of goods.	Warehouse rent.
The plaintiff's claim is $	for the carriage of goods by railway.	Carriage of goods.
The plaintiff's claim is $	for the use and occupation of a house.	Use and occupation of house.
The plaintiff's claim is $	for the hire of [*furniture*].	Hire of goods
The plaintiff's claim is $	for work done as surveyor.	Work done.
The plaintiff's claim is $	for board and lodging.	Board and lodging.
The plaintiff's claim is $ *X.Y.*	for the board, lodging and tuition of	Schooling.
The plaintiff's claim is $ solicitor [*or* factor, *or* collector, *or, &c.*] of the plaintiff.	for money received by the defendant as	Money received.
The plaintiff's claim is $ colour of the office of	for fees received by the defendant under	Fees of office.

Money over paid.	The plaintiff's claim is $ for the return of money overcharged for the carriage of goods by railway.
	The plaintiff's claim is $ for a return of fees overcharged by the defendant as
Return of money by stakeholder.	The plaintiff's claim is $ for a return of money deposited with the defendant as stakeholder.
Money won from stakeholder.	The plaintiff's claim is $ for money entrusted to the defendant as stakeholder, and become payable to plaintiff.
Money entrusted to agent.	The plaintiff's claim is $ for a return of money entrusted to the defendant as agent to the plaintiff.
Money obtained by fraud.	The plaintiff's claim is $ for a return of money obtained from the plaintiff by fraud.
Money paid by mistake.	The plaintiff's claim is $ for a return of money paid to the defendant by mistake.
Money paid for consideration which has failed.	The plaintiff's claim is $ for a return of money paid to the defendant for [work to be done, left undone; or a bill to be taken up, not taken up, &c.]
	The plaintiff's claim is $ for a return of money paid as a deposit upon shares to be allotted.
Money paid by surety for defendant.	The plaintiff's claim is $ for money paid for the defendant as his surety.
Rent paid.	The plaintiff's claim is $ for money paid for rent due by the defendant.
Money paid on accomodation bill.	The plaintiff's claim is $ upon a bill of exchange accepted [or indorsed] for the defendant's accomodation.
Contribution by surety.	The plaintiff's claim is $ for a contribution in respect of money paid by the plaintiff as surety.
By co-debtor.	The plaintiff's claim is $ for a contribution in respect of a joint debt of the plaintiff and the defendant, paid by the plaintiff.
Money paid for calls.	The plaintiff's claim is $ for money paid for calls upon shares, against which the defendant was bound to idemnify the plaintiff.
Money payable under award.	The plaintiff's claim is $ for money payable under an award.
Life policy.	The plaintiff's claim is $ upon a policy of insurance upon the life of X Y., deceased.
Money bond.	The plaintiff's claim is $ upon a bond to secure payment of $1,000 and interest.
Foreign judgment.	The plaintiff's claim is $ upon a judgment of the Court, in the Province of Quebec.
Bill of exchange, etc.	The plaintiff's claim is $ upon a cheque drawn by the defendant.
	The plaintiff's claim is $ upon a bill of exchange accepted [or drawn or indorsed] by the defendant.
	The plaintiff's claim is $ upon a promissory note made [or indorsed] by the defendant.
	The plaintiff's claim is $ against the defendant A.B. as acceptor, and against the defendant C.D. as drawer [or indorser], of a bill of exchange.
Surety.	The plaintiff's claim is $ against the defendant as surety for the price of goods sold.
	The plaintiff's claim is $ against the defendant A.B. as principal, and against the defendant C.D. as surety for the price of goods sold [or arrears of rent, or for money lent, or for money received by the defendant A B. , as traveller for the plaintiffs, or, &c.]
Del credere agent.	The plaintiff's claim is $ against the defendant as a del credere agent for the price of goods sold [or as losses under a policy].
	The plaintiff's claim is $ for calls upon shares.

No. 5. SECTION II.

Indorsement for Costs, &c.

[*Add to the above forms*] and $ for costs ; and if the amount claimed to be paid to the plaintiff or his solicitor within 8 days [*or if the writ is to be served out of Ontario, or notice in lieu of service allowed, insert the time limited for appearance and defence*] from the service hereof, further proceedings will be stayed.

No. 6. SECTION III.

Indorsements on Writs for Damages and other Claims.

The plaintiff's claim is for damages for breach of a contract to employ Agent, etc. the plaintiff as traveller.

The plaintiff's claim is for damages for wrongful dismissal from the defendant's employment as traveller [and $ for arrears of wages].

The plaintiff's claim is for damages for the defendant's wrongfully quitting the plaintiff's employment as manager.

The plaintiff's claim is for damages for breach of duty as factor [*or, &c.*] of the plaintiff [and $ for money received as factor, &c]

The plaintiff's claim is for damages for breach of the terms of a deed of apprenticesh p of X. Y. to the defendant [*or plaintiff*].

The plaintiff's claim is for damages for non-compliance with the award Arbitration. of X. Y.

The plaintiff's claim is for damages for assault [and false imprisonment, Assault, etc. and for malicious prosecution].

The plaintiff's claim is for damages for assault and false imprisonment By husband of the plaintiff C D. and wife.

The plaintiff's claim is for damages for assault by the defendant C. D.

The plaintiff's claim is for damages for injury by the defendant's negli- Solicitor. gence as solicitor of the plaintiff.

The plaintiff's claim is for damages for negligence in the custody of Bailment. goods [and for wrongfully detaining the same].

The plaintiff's claim is for damages for negligence in the keeping of Pledge. goods pawned [and for wrongful y detaining the same.]

The plaintiff's claim is for damages for negligence in the custody of Hire. furni ure le t on hire [*or a carriage lent*], [and for wrongfully, &c.]

The plaintiff's claim is for damages for wrongfully neglecting [*or Banker.* refusing*] to pay the plaintiff's cheque.

The pl intiff's claim is for damages for breach of a contract to accept Bill. the plaintiff's drafts.

The pl intiff's claim is upon a bond conditioned not to carry on the Bond. trade of a

The plaintiff's claim is for damages for refusing to carry the plaintiff's Carrier. goods by railway.

The plaintiff's claim is for damages for refusing to carry the plaintiff by ra lway.

The plaintiff's claim is for damages for breach of duty in and about the carriage and delivery of coals by railway.

The pl intiff's claim is for damages for breach of duty in and about the carriage and delivery of machinery by sea.

The plaintiff's claim is for damages for breach of charter-party of ship Charter party. [*Mary*].

The pl intiff's claim is for wrongfully depriving plaintiff of goods, house- Damages for depriving of hold furniture, &c. goods.

Defamation.	The plaintiff's claim is for damages for libel.
	The plaintiff's claim is for damages for slander.
Distress.	The plaintiff's claim is in replevin for goods wrongfully distrained.
Replevin.	
Wrongful	The plaintiff's claim is for damages for improperly distraining.
distress.	[*This form shall be sufficient whether the distress complained of be wrongful or excessive, or irregular, and whether the claim be for damages only, or for double value*].

Fishery.	The plaintiff's claim is for damages for infringement of the plaintiff's right of fishing.
Fraud.	The plaintiff's claim is for damages for fraudulent misrepresentation on the sale of a horse [*or* a business, *or* shares, *or*, *&c.*] The plaintiff's claim is for damages for fraudulent misrepresentation of the credit of *A. B.*
Guarantee.	The plaintiff's claim is for damages for breach of a contract of guarantee for *A. B.* The plaintiff's claim is for damages for breach of a contract to indemnify the plaintiff as the defendant's agent to distrain.
Insurance.	The plaintiff's claim is for a loss under a policy upon the ship "Royal Charter," and freight or cargo [*or* for return of premiums]. [*This Form shall be sufficient whether the loss claimed be total or partial*].
Fire insurance.	The plaintiff's claim is for a loss under a policy of fire insurance upon house and furniture.
Landlord and tenant.	The plaintiff's claim is for damages for breach of a contract to insure a house. The plaintiff's claim is for damages for breach of a contract to keep a house in repair. The plaintiff's claim is for damages for breaches of covenants contained in the lease of a fa m.
Medical man.	The plaintiff's claim is for damages for injury to the plaintiff from the defendant's negligence as a medical man.
Mischievous animal.	The plaintiff's claim is for damages for injury by the defendant's dog.
Negligence.	The plaintiff's claim is for damages for injury to the plaintiff [*or*, *if by husband and wife*, to the plaintiff *C. D.*] by the negligent driving of the defendant or his servants. The plaintiff's claim is for damages for injury to the plaintiff while a passenger on the defendant's railway by the negligence of the defendant's servants. The plaintiff's claim is for damages for injury to the plaintiff at the defendant's railway station, from the defective condition of the station.
Lord Campbell's Act.	The plaintiff's claim is as executor of *A.B.* deceased, for damages for the death of the said *A. B.*, from injuries received while a passenger on the defendant's railway, by the negligence of the defendant's servants.
Promise of marriage.	The plaintiff's claim is for damages for breach of promise of marriage.
Seduction.	The plaintiff's claim is for damages for the seduction of the plaintiff's daughter.
Sale of goods.	The plaintiff's claim is for damages for breach of contract to accept and pay for goods. The plaintiff's claim is for damages for non-delivery [*or* short delivery *or* defective quality, *or* other breach of contract of sale] of cotton [*or*, *&c.*] The plaintiff's claim is for damages for breach of warranty of a horse.
Sale of land.	The plaintiff's claim is for damages for breach of a contract to sell [*or* purchase] land. The plaintiff's claim is for damages for breach of contract to let [*or* take] a house. The plaintiff's claim is for damages for breach of a contract to sell [*or* purchase] the lease, with goodwill, fixtures, and stock-in-trade of a public-house. The plaintiff's claim is for damages for breach of covenant for title [*or* for quiet enjoyment, *or*, *&c.*] in a conveyance of land.

The plaintiff's claim is for damages for wrongfully entering the plain- Trespass to
tiff's land and drawing water from his well [or cutting his grass, or pull- land.
ing down his timber, or pulling down his fences, or removing his gate, or
using his road or path, or crossing his field, or depositing sand there, or
carrying away gravel from thence, or carrying away stones from his
river].

The plaintiff's claim is for damages for wrongfully taking away the sup- Support.
port of plaintiff's land [or house or mine].

The plaintiff's claim is for damages for wrongfully obstructing a way Way.
[public highway or private way].

The plaintiff's claim is for damages for wrongfully diverting [or Watercourse,
obstructing, or polluting, or diverting water from] a watercourse. etc.

The plaintiff's claim is for damages for wrongfully discharging water
upon the plaintiff's land [or into the plaintiff's mine].

The plaintiff's claim is for damages for wrongfully obstructing the
plaintiff's use of a well.

The plaintiff's claim is for damages for the infringement of the plain- Pasture.
tiff's right of pasture.

[*This form shall be sufficient whatever the nature of the right to
pasture be.*]

The plaintiff's claim is for damages for obstructing the access of light to Light.
plaintiff's house.

The plaintiff's claim is for damages for the infringement of the plaintiff's Patent.
patent.

The plaintiff's claim is for damages for the infringement of the plaintiff's Copyright.
copyright.

The plaintiff's claim is for damages for wrongully using [or imitating] Trade mark.
the plaintiff's trade mark.

The plaintiff's claim is for damages for breach of a contract to build a Work.
ship [or to repair a house, &c.]

The plaintiff's claim is for damages for breach of a contract to employ
the plaintiff to build a ship, &c.

The plaintiff's claim is for damages to his house, trees, crops, &c., caused Nuisance.
by noxious vapours from the defendant's factory [or, &c.]

The plaintiff's claim is for damages from nuisance by noise from the
defendant's works [or, &c.]

The plaintiff's claim is for damages for loss of the plaintiff's goods in Innkeeper.
the defendant's inn.

The plaintiff's claim is for return of household furniture, or, &c., or Claim for
their value, and for damages for detaining the same. return of
goods;
damages,

The plaintiff's claim is to recover possession of a house, No.   in Ejectment.
street, in the City of Ottawa ; or of the N. E. ¼ of lot 2, in the 3rd concession of the Township of   in the county of

The plaintiff's claim is to establish his title to [*here describe property*], To establish
and to recover the rents thereof. title and
recover rents.

[*The two previous forms may be combined.*]

The plaintiff's claim is for dower out of lot number   (or de- Dower.
scribing the property otherwise with reasonable certainty). And take notice
that the plaintiff claims damages for the detention of her dower from the
       day of

Add to indorsement if a mandamus is claimed.

And for a mandamus commanding the defendant to   Mandamus.

Add to indorsement if an injunction is claimed.

And for an injunction to restrain the defendant from   Injunction.

Add to Indorsement where Claim is to land, or to establish title, or both :

And for mesne profits. Mesne profits
And for an account of rents or arrears of rent. Arrears of
rent.
And for breach of covenant for [*repairs*]. Breach of
covenant.

No. 7.　　　　　　　　　SECTION IV.

Money Claims—Special Indorsements under Rule 243.

1. The plaintiff's claim is for the price of goods sold. The following are the particulars :—
1879— 31st December.—
　Balance of account for butcher's meat to this date .　.　$142
1880—1st January to 31st of March.—
　Butcher's meat supplied .　.　.　　　　　　　.　297
　　　　　　　　　　　　　　　　　　　　　　　　　　$439
1880—1st February.—Paid.　.　　　　　　.　180

　　　　　　　　Balance due　.　.　.　.　.　$259

2. The plaintiff's claim is against the defendant *A.B.* as principal, and against the defendant *C.D.* as surety, for the price of goods sold to *A.B.* The following are the particulars :—

1881—2nd February. Guarantee by *C.D.* of the price of woollen goods to be supplied to *A.B.*

　2nd February—To goods　　　　　.　.　$225
　3rd March—To goods　.　　　　　　.　.　151
　17th March—To goods .　　　　　　.　.　27
　5th April—To goods　.　　　　　　.　.　65
　　　　　　　　　　　　　　　　　　　　$468

3. The plaintiff's claim is against the defendant, as maker of a promissory note. The following are the particulars :—
Promissory note for $1,000 dated 1st January 1879, made by defendant, payable 4 months after date.
　Principal　.　.　.　.　.　.　.　.　.　$1,000
　Interest　.　.　.　.　.　.　.　.　.

4. The plaintiff's claim is against the defendant *A.B.* as acceptor, and against the defendant *C.D.* as drawer, of a bill of exchange. The following are the particulars :—
Bill of exchange for $2,000, dated 1st January, 1880, drawn by defendant *C.D.* upon and accepted by defendant *A.B.*, payable 3 months after date.
　Principal　.　.　.　.　.　.　.　.　$2,000
　Interest　.　.　.　.　.　.　.　.　.　.

5. The plaintiff's claim is for principal and interest due upon a bond. The following are the particulars :—
Bond dated 1st January, 1879. Condition for payment of $500 on the 26th December, 1879.
　Principal due　.　.　.　.　.　.　.　.　$500
　Interest　.　.　.　.　.　.　.　.　.

6. The plaintiff's claim is for principal and interest due under a covenant. The following are the particulars :—
Deed dated　　　　　covenant to pay $3,000 and interest.
　Principal due.............................. $800
　Interest.................................

No. **8.** SECTION V.

Indorsements of Character of Parties.

The plaintiff's claim is as executor [*or* administrator] of *C.D.*, deceased, **Executor.**
for, *&c.*
The p aintiff's claim is against the defendant *A.B.*, as executor [*or*, *&c.*]
of *C.D.*, deceased, for, *&c.*
The plaintiff's claim is against the defendant *A.B.*, as executor of *X.
Y.*, deceased, and against the defendant *C.D.*, in his personal capacity,
for, *&c.*
The claim of the plaintiff is against the defendant as executrix of *C.D.*, **Against**
deceased, for **executrix.**

The plaintiff claim is as assignee in insolvency of *A.B.*, for **Assignee in**
insolvency.
The plaintiff's claim is against the defendant as assignee in insolvency
of *A.B*, for
The plaintiff's claim is as [*or* the plaintiff's claim is against the defen- **Trustees.**
dant as] trustee under the will of *A.B.* [*or* under the settlement upon the
marriage of *A.B.* and *X.Y.*, his wife].
T.e plaintiff's claim is against the defendant as heir-at-law of *A.B.*, **Heir and**
deceased. **devisee,**
The plaintiff's cla·m is against the defendant *C.D.*, as heir-at-law, and
against the defendant *E.F.*, as dev see of lands under the will of *A.B.*
The plaintiff's cla.m is as well for the Queen as for himself, for **Qui tam**
action.

No. **9.**
SECTION VI.

*Indorsements in Matters which formerly belonged to the exclusive jurisdic-
tion of Equity.*

(a) *Creditor to administer Estate.*

The plaintiff's claim is as a creditor of *X.Y.* of
deceased, to have the [real and] personal estate of the said *X.Y.*, administered. The defendant *C D.* is sued as the administrator of the said
X.Y. [and the defendants *E.F.* and *G.H.* as his co-heirs-at-law].

(b) *Legatee to administer Estate.*

The plaintiff's claim is as a legatee under the will dated the day
of 18 , of *X.Y.* deceased, to have the [real and]
personal estate of the said *X.Y.* administered. The defendant *C.D.* is
sued as the executor of the said *X.Y.* [and the defendants *E.F.* and *G.H.*
as his devisees].

(c) *Partnership account.*

The plaintiff's claim is to have an account taken of the partnership
dealings between the plaintiff and defendant [under articles o partnership dated the day of], and to
have the affairs of the partnership wound up.

(d) *By Mortgagee for sale and for immediate payment and possession.*

The plaintiff's claim is on a mortgage dated the day
of made between [*or* by deposit of title
deeds], and that the mortgage may be enforced by sale, and payment to
the plaintiff by the defendant personally of any balance. (*If order for im_*

12

mediate payment is wanted add), And take notice further that the plaintiff claims to be entitled forthwith to ex cution against the goods a d lands of you (*naming the defendant against whom this order is claimed*) to recover payment of the amount due by you.

(*If order is wanted for immediate possession add*), And take not'ce further, that the plaintiff claims to be en it!'d to an order for the immediate delivery of the mortgaged premises to him.

(e) *By Mortgagee for foreclosure and for immediate payment and possession.*

The plaintiff's claim is on a mortgage dated the   day of   made between   (*or* by deposit of title deeds), and that the mortgage may be enforced by foreclosure.

(*If order for immediate payment is wanted add*), And take notice further that the plaintiff claims to be entitled forthwith to execution against the goods and lands of you (*naming the defendant against whom this order is claimed*) to recover payment of the amount due by you.

(*If order for immediate possession is wanted add*), And take notice further that the plaintiff claims to be entitled to the immediate possession of the mortgaged premises.

(*At the end of the endorsement add*), If you desire a sale of the mortgaged premises instead of a foreclos re, and do not intend to defend the action, you must within the time allowed for appearance, file in the office within named, a notice in writing, signed by yourself or your solicitor, to the following effect :—" I desire a sale of the mortgaged premises in the plaintiff's writ of summons mentioned, or a competent part thereof, instead f a forecl su e," and you must deposit the sum of $:0 to meet the expenses of such sale.

(f)   *By Mortgagor for Redemption.*

The plaintiff's claim is to have an account taken of what, if anything, is due on a mortgage dated   and made between [*parties*], and to redeem the property comprised therein.

(g)   *Raising portions.*

The plaintiff's claim is that the sum of $, which by an indenture of settlement dated   , was provided for the portions of the younger children of   may be raised.

(h)   *Execution of Trusts.*

The plaintiff's claim is to have the trusts of an indenture dated and made between   , carried into execution.

(i)   *Cancellation or Rectification.*

The plaintiff's claim is to have a deed dated   and made between [*parties*], set aside or rectified.

(j)   *Specific Performance.*

The plaintiff's claim is for specific performance of an agreement dated the   day f   , for the sale by the plaintiff to the defendant of certain [*freehold*] hereditaments at   .

(k)   *Alimony.*

The plaintiff's claim is for alimony ; and the plaintiff demands as interim alimony until the trial of the action the monthly (*or* weekly) sum of $ to be pai I to her on the   day of each month (*or* week) at   and the interim costs to which she is entitled by the practice in that behalf.

NOTE.—*Where the plaintiff desires to register a certificate of lis pendens the indorsement on the writ of summons may contain such short description of the property as may be necessary or proper for that purpose.*

PART III.

NOTICES, &c.

No. **10.**

Notice of Motion to Court.

In the High Court of Justice.
————Division.
Between

Plaintiff,
and
Defendant.

Take notice, that the Court will be moved on behalf of   on   day
the   d iy of   18 , .   at   o'clock in the forenoon, or so soon
thereafter as counsel can be heard, that (*state the object of the intended
application*).

Dated the   day of   18 .
(S'gned)
Solicitor for the
To

No. **11.**

Notice of Motion in Chambers.

[Title, &c.]

Take notice that a motion will be made on behalf of
befo e the Master in Chambers (*or as the case may be*), at Osgoode Hall,
in the City of Toronto, on   day the   day of
18   , at   o'clock in the   noon, or so soon thereafter as
the motion can be heard, for an order for   time to, &c.   For time.

or, that   be at liberty to sign final judgment in this action for the   For final judg-
amount indorsed on the writ with interest, if any, and costs ;   ment under
Rule 739.

or, that the plaintiff be at liberty to amend the writ of summons in this   To amend
action by   writ.

or, that the   do furnish the said   with a   For particu-
statement in writing, verified bv affidavit, setting forth the names of the   lars (Partner-
persons constituting the members or co-partners of their firm, pursuant   ship).
to the Rules of the Supreme Court, Rule 317.

or, for an account in writing of the particulars of the plaintiff's claim in   For particu-
this action (with dates and items, *or as the case may be*), and that unless   lars (gen-
such particulars be delivered in four days, all further proceedings be stayed   erally).
until the delivery thereof ;

or, for an account in writing of the particulars of the injuries and expenses   For particu-
mentioned in the Statement of Claim, together with the time and place of   lars (accident).
the accident, and the particular acts of negligence complained of, and
that unless such particulars be delivered within   days, all further
proceedings be stayed until the delivery thereof ;

or, that the order of   in this action, dated the   day of   To discharge
   , 18   , be (discharged, *or* varied by, &c.), on the grounds   or vary order.
disclosed in the affidavit of   , filed in support of
this application ;

To dismiss action. *or*, that this action be dismissed with costs to be taxed and paid to the Defendant by the Plaintiff for want of prosecution, the Plaintiff not having, &c.;

For discovery of documents. *or*, that the   answer within   days, stating what documents are or have been in   possession or power relating to the matters in question in this action ;

To inspect documents. *or*, that the   be at liberty to inspect, and take copies of, or extracts from   , and that in the meantime all further proceedings be stayed ;

To examine witness before trial. *or*, that   a witness on behalf of the   be examined forthwith before   upon the usual terms ;

For Commission to examine witnesses. *or*, that the   be at liberty to issue a commission for the examination of witnesses on   behalf at   , and that the trial of this action be stayed until the return of such commission upon the usual terms ;

To refer under section 101 of the Act. *or*, that the following question   arising in this action, namely :— be referred for inquiry and report to under section 101 of the Judicature Act ;

To refer under section 102 of the Act. *or*, that the   in this action be tried by   under section 102 of the Judicature Act ;

For examination of judgment debtor as to means. *or*, that the above-named judgment debtor be orally examined as to whether any and what debts are owing to him, and do attend for that purpose before the Master in Chambers (*or as the case may be*) at such time and place as he may appoint, and that the said judgment debtor produce his books, &c., before the said Master at the time of the examination ;

For trial of action in County Court. *or*, that this action be tried before the County Court of holden on

For interpleader order (by sheriff). *or*, that the plaintiff and the claimant appear and state the nature of their respective claims to the goods and chattels seized by the above-named sheriff under the writ of *fieri facias* issued in this action and maintain or relinquish the same and abide by such order as may be made herein, and that in the meantime all further proceedings be stayed.

No. 12.

Notice of application for Administration Order or respecting the guardianship of an infant.

In the High Court of Justice,
——Division.

Between *A.B.*, plaintiff,
and
C.D., defendant.

Take notice that an application will be made to
, in Toronto, (*or to*
at his office in the city (*or town*) of, &c., *as the case may be*), on the   day of   at the hour of o'clock in the forenoon, (or if opposed, then to a Judge in Chambers so soon thereafter as a Judge shall be sitting in Chambers, for an order for

the administration of the estate, real and personal, of   by the
Court, or for any order appointing   guardian of   an
infant) ; and upon such application will be read the affidavits of
this day filed.

Dated, &c.

                    X. Y., Solicitor for

To Mr. *C. D.*

No. 13.

Notice of Entry of Appearance.

In the High Court of Justice.
——Division.

Between

                                    Plaintiff,

               and

                                 Defendant.

Take notice, that   have this day entered an appearance at   for
the defendant   to the writ of summons in this action.

The said defendant   require [*or do* not require] delivery of a statement of claim.

Dated the   day of   18 .

              (Signed)
              Solicitor for the defendant.

To

No. 14.

Notice limiting defence.

In the High Court of Justice.
——Division.

                 Between *A. B.*, plaintiff,
                      and
               C. D., and *E. F.*, defendants.

The defendant, *C. D.*, limits his defence to part only of the property
mentioned in the writ in this action, that is to say, to the north-west
quarter of the lot.

                   Yours, &c.,
                       G. H.,
         Solicitor for the said defendant *C. D.*

To

No. 15.

Notice disputing amount.

In the High Court of Justice.
——Division.

                 Between *A. B.*, plaintiff,
                      and
               C. D., defendant.

Take notice, that the defendant disputes the amount claimed by the
plaintiff (*or the defendant insists that the amount due to the plaintiff is
$*   only ; *or the defendant insists that the amount due to the plaintiff
is $*   for principal and $ for interest, since the   day of
&c., and no more, *as the case may be.*)

              (Signed)
              Solicitor for the defendant.

To

No. 16.

Notice in lieu of Statement of Claim.

In the High Court of Justice.
——Division.

Between *A.B.*, plaintiff,
and
C.D., defendant.

The particulars of the plaintiff's claim herein, and of the relief and remedy to which he claims to be entitled, appear by the indorsement upon the writ of summons.

The plaintiff proposes that this action shall be tried at

Dated, &c.

X. Y.,
Solicitor for Plaintiff.

No. 17.

Confession of Defence.

In the High Court of Justice.
——Division.

Between *A.B.*, plaintiff,
and
C.D., defendant.

The plaintiff confesses the defence stated in the   paragraph of the defendant's statement of defence [*or*, of the defendant's further statement of defence].

Dated, &c.

X. Y.,
Solicitor for Plaintiff.

No. 18.

Notice by Defendant to Third Party.

Notice filed   ' day of

In the High Court of Justice.
——Division.

Between *A.B.*, plaintiff,
and
C.D., defendant.

To Mr. *X. Y.*

Take notice that this action has been brought by the plaintiff against the defendant [as surety for *M.N.*], upon a bond conditioned for payment of $10,000 and interest to the plaintiff.

The defendant claims to be entitled to contribution from you to the extent of one-half of any sum which the plaintiff may recover against him, on the ground that you are (his co-surety under the said bond, *or*, also surety for the said *M. N.*, in respect of the said matter, under another bond made by you in favour of the said plaintiff, dated the   day of , A.D.   )].

Or [as acceptor of a bill of exchange for $2,500, dated the day of , A. D. , drawn by you upon and accepted by the defendant and payable 3 months after date.

The defendant claims to be indemnified by you against liability under the said bill, on the ground that it was accepted for your accommodation.]

Or [to recover damages for a breach of a contract for the sale and delivery to the plaintiff of 1,000 tons of coal.

The defendant claims to be indemnified by you against liability in respect of the said contract, or any breach thereof, on the ground that it was made by him on your behalf and as your agent.]

And take notice that, if you wish to dispute the plaintiff's claim in this action as against the defendant *C. D.*, you must cause an appearance to be entered for you within 8 days after service of this notice.

In default of your so appearing, you will not be entitled in any future proceeding between the defendant *C.D.* and yourself to dispute the validity of the judgment in this action whether obtained by consent or otherwise.

Dated, &c.

(Signed)   *E. T.*

Or

X. Y.,
          Solicitor for the defendant,
                    E. T.

Appearance to be entered at

No. 19.

*Indorsement on copy Defence and Counter-claim to be served on
Third Party.*

" To the within named *X. Y.*

Take notice that if you do not appear to the within counter-claim of the within-named *C. D.*, within 8 days from the service of this defence and counter-claim upon you, you will be liable to have judgment given against you in your absence.

Appearances are to be entered at

No. 20.

Indorsement on Order adding or changing parties under Rule 625.

Take notice, that if you desire to discharge this order you must apply to the Court for that purpose within 14 days after the service hereof upon you. The original statement of claim in this cause is filed in the office of the   at
(*and if the service is after a judgment directing a reference to a Master or other officer, add*) and the reference under the judgment in this matter is being prosecuted in the office of the   at

---

No. 21.

Notice of payment into Court.

In the High Court of Justice.
      ——— Division.

Between *A.B.*, plaintiff,
              and
      C.D., defendant.

Take notice that the defendant has paid into Court $ in satisfaction of the plaintiff's claim [*or* the plaintiff's claim, for, &c.]

Dated, &c.

To Mr. *X. Y.*,
      the Plaintiff's Solicitor.

                    Z.,
                    Defendant's Solicitor.

No. 22.

Acceptance of sum paid into Court.

In the High Court of Justice.
——Division.

Between *A. B.*, plaintiff,
and
C. D., defendant.

Take notice that the plaintiff accepts the sum of $ paid by you into Court in satisfaction of his claim herein (*or* of his claim for, etc.)

Dated, &c.

         X. Y.,
           Plaintiff's Solicitor.

To *Z.*,
   Defendant's Solicitor :

No. 23.

Notice to produce Documents.

In the High Court of Justice.
——Division.

Between *A.B.*, plaintiff,
and
C.D., defendant.

Take notice that the [plaintiff *or* defendant], requires you to produce for his inspection the following documents referred to in your [statement of claim, *or* defence, *or* affidavit dated the   day of   **A.D.**   ].

Dated, &c.

     [*Describe documents required.*]

         X. Y.,
           Solicitor for the

To *Z.*,
   Solicitor for

No. 24.

Notice to produce (General Form).

In the High Court of Justice.
——Division.

Between

                 Plaintiff.
and
                 Defendant.

Take notice that you are hereby required to produce and shew to the Court on the trial of this action all books, papers, letters, copies of letters, and other writings and documents in your custody, possession or power, containing any entry, memorandum, or minute relating to the matters in question in this action, and particularly

Dated, &c.

To the above named

        }   Solicitor for the above named

h   Solicitor or agent

No. **25.**

Notice to inspect Documents.

In the High Court of Justice.
—————Division.

A. B. v. C. D.

Take notice that you can inspect the documents mentioned in your notice of the   day of   A.D.   [*except the* deed *numbered*   *in that notice*] at my office on   day next the   instant, between the hours of 12 and 4 o'clock.

Or, that the [plaintiff *or* defendant] objects to giving you inspection of the documents mentioned in your notice of the   day of A.D.   on the ground that [*state the ground*] :—

Dated, &c.

X. Y.,
. Solicitor for

———

No. **26.**

Notice to admit Documents.

In the High Court of Justice.
—————Division.

A. B. v. C. D.

Take notice that the plaintiff [*or* defendant] in this cause proposes to adduce in evidence the several documents hereunder specified, and that the same may be inspected by the defendant [*or* plaintiff] his solicitor or agent at   , on   , between the hours of   ; and the defendant [*or* plaintiff] is hereby required, within 4 days from the said day, to admit that such of the said documents as are specified to be originals were respectively written, signed, or executed, as they purport respectively to have been ; that such as are specified as copies are true copies, and such documents as are stated to have been served, sent, or delivered, were so served, sent, or delivered respectively ; saving all just exceptions to the admissibility of all such documents as evidence in this cause.

X. Y.,
Solicitor for

Dated, &c.,

To *E. F.,* solicitor [*or* agent] for defendant [*or* plaintiff].
G. H., solicitor [*or* agent] for plaintiff [*or* defendant].

Here describe the documents, the manner of doing which may be as follows :]

ORIGINALS.

Description of Documents.	Dates.
Deed of covenant between *A.B.* and *C.D.* first part, and *E.F.* second part	January 1, 1878.
Indenture of lease from *A.B.* to *C.D.*	February 1, 1878.
Indenture of release between *A.B., C.D.,* first part, &c.	February 2. 1878.
Letter—defendant to plaintiff.	March 1, 1878.
Policy of Insurance on goods by ship "Isabella," on voyage from Toronto to Kingston	July 3, 1877.
Memorandum of agreement between *C.D.,* captain of said ship, and *E.F.*	August 1, 1878.
Bill of exchange for $500 at 3 months, drawn by *A.B.* on and accepted by *C.D.,* indorsed by *E.F.* and *G.H.*	May 1, 1879.

COPIES.

Description of Documents.	Dates.	Original or duplicate served, sent, or delivered, when, how and by whom.
Register of baptism of *A.B.* in the parish of *X*	January 1, 1848.	Sent by General Post February 2, 1848.
Letter—plaintiff to defendant............	February 1, 1848.	
Notice to produce papers......	March 1, 1878.	Served March 2,1878 on defendant's attorney by *E. F.*, of ——
Record of a Judgment of the Court of Queen's Bench in an action, *J.S.* and *J.N*	Trinity Term,10th Vict.	

No. 27.

Notice of Trial.

In the High Court of Justice.
———Division.

A. B. v. *C.D.*

Take notice of trial of this action [*or* the issues in this action ordered to be tried] at   for the   day of   next

X.Y., plaintiff's solicitor [*or as the case may be*].

Dated, &c.

To *Z.*, defendant's solicitor [*or as the case may be*].

No. 28.

Notice of Entry of Demurrer for Argument.

In the High Court of Justice.
———Division.

Between

Plaintiff,

and

Defendant.

Take notice, that   have this day entered for argument the demurrer of the   to the   in this action.

Dated the   day of   18   .

(Signed)
of
Solicitor for the

To

No. 29.

Notice of Discontinuance.

In the High Court of Justice.
———Division.

Between

Plaintiff,

and

Defendant.

Take notice, that the plaintiff hereby wholly discontinues this action, (*or* withdraws so much of h   claim in this action as relates to, &c.

(*If not against all the defendants add*), "As against the defendant," &c.

Dated the   day of   18   .

(Signed)
of
Solicitor for the plaintiff.

No. 30.

Notice of Cross-examination of Deponents at Trial on Affidavits.

In the High Court of Justice.
————Division.

Between

Plaintiff,

and

Defendant.

Take notice, that the   intend at the trial of this action to cross-examine the several deponents named and described in the schedule hereto on their affidavits therein specified.

And also take notice that you are hereby required to produce the said deponents for such cross-examination before the Court aforesaid.

Dated the   day of   18 .

Solicitor for the

To

THE SCHEDULE above referred to.

Name of Deponent.	Address and Description.	Date when affidavit filed.

No. 31.

Notice of Renewal of Writ of Execution.

In the High Court of Justice.
————Division.

Between

Plaintiff,

and

Defendant.

Take notice, that the writ of   issued in this action directed to the sheriff of   and bearing date the   day of   18 , has been renewed for one year from the   day of   18 .

Dated the   day of   18 .

(Signed)
Solicitor for the

To the sheriff of

No. 32.

Notice of Election that Defendant conduct Sale.

In the High Court of Justice.
————Division.

(Short Title).

To   , Defendant.

Take notice that the plaintiff elects that the sale of the mortgaged premises be conducted by you instead of by the plaintiff, and you are at liberty to withdraw the deposit made by you in this cause for the purpose if such sale.

No. 33.

Indorsement of notice of time to move to discharge order adding a party.

Rules 47, 322, &c.

To A. B., *(the person upon whom service has been directed, set out the order.)*

If you wish to apply to discharge the foregoing order, or to add to, vary, or set aside, the judgment, you must do so within fourteen days from the service hereof. *(When the order fixes a time for the further proceedings, add,)* And if you fail to attend at the time and place appointed, either in person or by your solicitor, such order will be made and proceedings taken, in your absence, as may seem just and expedient ; and you will be bound by the judgment, and the further proceedings in the cause, in the same manner as if you had been originally made a party to the action, without notice.

No. 34.

Notice to Incumbrancers served under Rule 126.

In the High Court of Justice.

——Division.

Between A. B. Plaintiff,

and

C. D. Defendant.

Whereas an action has been instituted by the above named plaintiff for the foreclosure (*or* sale) of (*or* enforcement of a lien on) certain lands, (*insert description of lands*) and I have been directed by the judgment made in this cause, and dated the day of , to inquire whether any person, other than the plaintiff, has any charge, lien, or incumbrance upon the said estate. And whereas it has been made to appear before me that you have each some lien, charge or incumbrance upon the said estate, and I have therefore appointed the day ot , at o'clock in the noon, for you to appear before me, af my Chambers at , either in person or by your solicitor, to prove your claims.

Now you are hereby required to take notice : 1st. That if you wish to apply to discharge my order making you a party, or to add to, vary, or set aside the judgment, you must do so within fourteen days after the service hereof ; and if you fail to do so, you will be bound by the judgment, and the further proceedings in this cause as if you were originally made a party to the action. 2nd. That if you fail to attend at the time and place appointed, you will be treated as disclaiming all interest in the land in question, and it will be dealt with as if you had no claim thereon, and your claim will be in fact foreclosed.

W. L., *Master.*

To

No. 35.

Appointment, served under Rule 128.

In the High Court of Justice.

——Division.

Between A. B., Plaintiff,

and

C. D., Defendant.

Having been directed by the judgment in this cause, dated the day of , to inquire whether any person other than the plaintiff has any lien, charge or incumbrance upon the lands in the pleadings mentioned

being (*insert description of lands*), I hereby appoint the   day of
next, at   o'clock in the   noon, at my Chambers at   ,
to proceed with the said inquiries.

And you are hereby required to take notice : That if you fail to attend
at the time and place appointed, you will be treated as disclaiming all
interest in the land in question, and it will be dealt with as if you had no
claim thereon, and your claim will be in fact foreclosed.

                                                    W. L., *Master.*

No. 36.

Advertisement for Creditors, under Rule 976.

Pursuant to a judgment [or an order] of the High Court of Justice,
——Division, made in [the matter of the estate of A. B., and in] a cause
S. against P. [*short title*], the creditors of A. B., late of   in the
County of   , who died in or about the month of
18 , are, on or before the   day of   18 , to send,
by post, prepaid to E. F., of   , the solicitor of the defendant C. D., the executor [or administrator] of the deceased [or as may be
directed], their Christian and surnames, addresses and description, the
full particulars of their claims, a statement of their accounts, and the
nature of the securities (if any) held by them ; or in default thereof, they
will be peremptorily excluded from the benefit of the said judgment [or
order]. Every creditor holding any security is to produce the same before
me, at my Chambers, at, &c., on the   day of   , 18 , at
o'clock in the   noon, being the time appointed for adjudication on the
claims.

Dated this   day of   , 18 .

                                                    G. H., *Master.*

No. 37.

Notice to Creditors to produce Documents, under Rule 978.

(*Short Title*).

You are hereby required to produce, in support of the claim sent in by
you, against the estate of A. B. deceased [*describe any document required*],
before me at my Chambers, at, &c., on the   day of   , 18 , at
o'clock in the   noon.

Dated this   day of   , 18 .

                    G. R., of, &c , Solicitor for the plaintiff,
                         [or, defendant, *or as may be*].
To Mr. S. T.

No. 38.

Notice to Creditor that claim allowed, under Rule 984.

(*Short Title.*)

The claim sent in by you against the estate of A. B., deceased, has been
allowed at the sum of $, [with interest thereon at $ per cent.,
per annum, from the   day of   , 18 , and $ for costs, or
as the case may be].

If part only allowed, add.—If you claim to have a larger sum allowed,
you are hereby required to prove such further claim, and you are to file
[&c., *as in Form No. 39*].

Dated this   day of   , 18 .

                    G. R., of &c., Solicitor for the plaintiff
                         [or defendant, *or as may be.*]
To Mr. P. P.

No. 39.

Notice to Creditor to prove his claim under Rule 984.

(Short Title.)

You are hereby required to prove the claim sent in by you against the estate of A. B., deceased. You are to file such affidavit as you may be advised in support of your claim, to give notice thereof to , Master [*or as the case may be*], on or before the day of , 18 ; and to attend personally, or by your solicitor, at his Chambers, on the day of , 18 , at o'clock in the noon, being the time appointed for adjudicating on the claim.

Dated this day of , 18 .

    G. R., of, &c., Solicitor for the plaintiff
     [*or defendant, or as may be.*]
To Mr. S. T.

———

No. 40.

Notice that Cheques may be received, under Rule 987.

(Short Title.)

The cheques for the amounts directed to be paid to the creditors of A. B., deceased, by an order made in this action [*or matter*] dated the day of , 18 , may be received at the Accountant's Office, in Osgoode Hall, Toronto, on and after the day of , 18 .

    G. R., of, &c., Solicitor for the plaintiff
     [*or defendant, or as may be.*]
To Mr. W. S.
 &c.

———

No. 41.

Notice of Appeal. (J. A. Sec. 71.)

In the High Court of Justice.

———Division.

Between *A. B.* (Respondent) plaintiff,
   and
  C. D. (Appellant) defendant.

Take notice that C.D., the above-named defendant, hereby appeals from the (judgment, order *or* decision) pronounced in this action (*or* matter) by the Divisional Court (*or* by the Hon. Mr. Justice)
on the day , 18 , whereby a judgment given at the trial for the defendant was set aside and a judgment directed to be entered for the plaintiff (*or as the case may require*).

———

PÁRT IV.

———

REPORTS, &c., BY MASTERS.

No. 42.

Form of Report in Administration Suit.

In the High Court of Justice.

———Division.

Between A. B. and   Plaintiffs.
    and
  C. D. and   Defendants.

Pursuant to the Order [*or* Judgment] herein made, dated the ——— day of ——— 18 , having caused an office copy thereof to be served upon [*give the names of persons served under Rule 322, and also the names of those upon whom service has been dispensed with, and the reason for dispensing with service*], I proceeded to dispose of the matters referred to me, and thereupon was attended by the solicitors for all parties interested [*or as the case may be*].

[*If a Guardian ad litem has been appointed for any of the parties, this should be so stated, and the reason why such appointment was made*].

and I find as follows :

1. The personal estate not specifically bequeathed of the testator come to the hands of the executors, and wherewith they are chargeable, amounts to the sum of $, and they have paid, or are entitled to be allowed thereout, the sum of $, leaving a balance due from them [*or " to them," as the case may be,*] of $ on that account.

[*If no personal estate, say :* No personal estate has come to the hands of the executors, nor are they chargeable with any.]

2. The creditors' claims sent in pursuant to my advertisement in that behalf (published in   issues of the newspaper called   ), and which have been allowed, are set forth in the first Schedule hereto, and amount altogether to $.

[*If no creditors, say :* No creditor has sent in a claim pursuant to my advertisement in that behalf, nor has any such claim been proved before me.]

3. The funeral expenses of the testator amounting to $ have been paid by the executors and are allowed to them in the amount of personal estate.

4. The legacies given by the testator are set forth in the second schedule hereto, and with the interest therein mentioned, remain due to the persons named [*or as the case may be.*]

5. The personal estate of the said testator outstanding or undisposed of, is set forth in the third schedule hereto.

[*In this third schedule personal estate not specifically bequeathed should be set forth separately from the other personalty outstanding or undisposed of. If there is no specific bequest, it should be so stated in the body of the report.*]

6. The real estate which the said testator was seised of or entitled to, and the incumbrances (*if any*) affecting the same, are set forth in the fourth schedule hereto.

7. The rents and profits of the testator's real estate received by the said executors, or with which they are chargeable, amount to $, and they have paid, or are entitled to be allowed thereout, the sum of $, leaving a balance due from [*or to*] them of $ on that account.

[*If no rents, &c., received, say :* No rents and profits have come to the hands of the said executors, nor are they chargeable with any.]

8. I have allowed to the said executors the sum of $ as a compensation for their personal services in the management of the said estate.

The first Schedule referred to in the foregoing Report.

No.	Names of Creditors. [Distinguish any which are secured by mortgage, lien, or otherwise entitled to any priority.]	Principal.	Interest Allowed.		Costs (if any) subsequent to Judgment.	Costs of this suit.	Total.
			Rate per Cent.	Amount to date of Report.			
		$ c.		$ c.	$ c.	$ c.	$ c.

[No general form can well be framed for the other Schedules, but in all cases brevity is to be studied. Where particulars are given they should shew merely the general character of the things described; as, for instance, the Schedule of outstanding personalty may say: A number of book debts outstanding amounting in the aggregate to $; a quantity of household furniture and effects valued at $; and the like short particulars should be given in other cases. Lands should be described without setting forth metes and bounds.]

No. 43.

Conditions of Sale referred to in Rule 96.

1. No person shall advance less than $10 at any bidding under $500, nor less than $.0 at any bidding over $500, and no person shall retract his bidding.

2. The highest bidder shall be the purchaser ; and if any dispute arise as to the last or highest bidder, the property shall be put up at a former bidding.

3. The parties to the action, with the exception of the vendor, (and, *naming any parties, trustees, agents, or others, in a fiduciary situation,*) shall be at liberty to bid.

4. The purchaser shall, at the time of sale, pay down a deposit, in proportion of $10 for every $100 of the purchase money, to the vendor, or his solicitor ; and shall pay the remainder of the purchase money, on the day of   next ; and upon such payment, the purchaser shall be entitled to the conveyance, and to be let into possession ; the purchaser at the time of sale to sign an agreement for the completion of the purchase.

5. The purchaser shall have the conveyance prepared at his own expense, and tender the same for execution.

6. If the purchaser fails to comply with the conditions aforesaid, or any of them, the deposit and all other payments made thereon, shall be forfeited, and the premises may be resold ; and the deficiency, if any, by such re-sale, together with all charges attending the same, or occasioned by the defaulter, are to be made good by the defaulter.

No. 44.

Report on Sale referred to in Rule 104.

In the High Court of Justice.
——— Division.

Between *A. B.*,   Plaintiff,
                   and
        C. D.   Defendant.

Pursuant to the judgment (*or* order) of this Honourable Court, bearing date the   day of   , and made in this cause, I have, under the Rules of the Supreme Court of Judicature, in the presence of (*or*, after notice to), all parties concerned, settled an advertisement and particulars a d conditions of sale, for the sale of the lands mentioned or referred to in the said judgment (*or* order), and such advertisement having, according to my directions, been published in the (*naming the newspaper or newspapers*), once in each week for the   weeks immediately preceding the said sale (*or as the case may be*), and bills of the said sale having been also, as directed by me, published in different parts of the township (*town or city*) of   and the adjacent count·y and villages (*or as the case may be*), the said lands were offered for sale by public auction, according to my appointment, on the   day of   , by me (*or* by Mr.   of   , appointed by me for that purpose, auctioneer), and such sale was conducted in a fair, open and proper manner, when   , of   , was declared the highest bidder for, and became the purchaser of the same, at the price or sum of $, payable as follows (*set out shortly the condition of sale as to payment of the purchase money*).

All which having been proved to my satisfaction by proper and sufficient evidence, I humbly certify to this Honourable Court.

Dated

13

PART V.

AFFIDAVITS.

No. 45.

Affidavit of Service of Summons.

In the High Court of Justice.
———Division.

Between

A.B., Plaintiff,

and

C.D., Defendant.

I,   of   make oath and say
as follows :—

(1) I did on the   day of   · 18   , personally serve C.D., the
above-named defendant in this action with a true copy of the writ of summons
(*or* notice of the writ of summons) herein hereto annexed, by delivering the
same to and leaving the same with the said defendant on the day last
aforesaid at   in the county of   .

(2) Upon the said copy so served as aforesaid was indorsed at the time
of such service true copies of all the indorsements appearing upon the
said original writ of summons (*or* notice) except the indorsement hereinafter mentioned.

(3) To effect such service I necessarily travelled
miles.

(4) Subsequently, namely : upon the   day of   ,
I did indorse upon the said original writ of summons (*or* notice) the day
of the month and week of such service.

Sworn at   this   day of   18 .

Before me, &c.   .

This affidavit is filed on behalf of the

No. 46

Form of Affidavit of Justification of Bail.

In the High Court of Justice.
———Division.

Between *A.B.*, Plaintiff,
and
C.D., Defendant.   ︵

I, *B.B.*, one of the bail for the above-named defendant, make oath and
say, that I am a house-keeper, (or freeholder, *as the case may be*, residing
at (*give particular description of the place of residence*.) that I am worth
property to the amount of $ (*double the amount sworn to*) over and
above what will pay all my just debts, (*if bail in any other action add*, and
every other sum for which I am now bail,) that I am not bail for any defendant, except in this action, (*or if bail in any other action or actions, add*,
except for *C.D.*, at the suit of *E.F.*, in the (High Court of Justice ———
Division) in the sum of $, for *G.H.*, at the suit of *J.K.*, in the
in the sum of $, *specifying the several actions with the Courts in
which they are brought, and the sums in which the deponent is bail.*)
Sworn, &c., *as usual.* Rules T. T. 1856, 81.

No. 47.

Affidavit by Landlord.

In the High Court of Justice,
————Division.

Between *A.B.*, Plaintiff,
and
C.D., Defendant.

I,   of   make oath and say
as follows :—

I am in possession of the land sought to be recovered in this action by
myself (or by the said *C.D.*, my tenant, (*as the case may be*).

Sworn at   this   day of

Before me, etc.

————

No 48.

Affidavit as to Documents.

In the High Court of Justice.
————Division.

Between *A.B.*, Plaintiff,
and
C.D., Defendant.

I, the above-named defendant *C.D.*, make oath and say as follows :   ·

1. I have in my possession or power the documents relating to the
matters in question in this action set forth in the first and second parts of
the first schedule hereto.

2. I object to produce the said documents set forth in the second part
of the said first schedule hereto.

3. That [*here state upon what grounds the objection is made, and verify
the facts as far as may be.*]

4. I have had, but have not now, in my possession or power the documents relating to the matters in question in this suit set forth in the second
schedule hereto.

5. The last mentioned documents were last in my possession or power
on [*state when*].

6. That [*here state what has become of the last mentioned documents, and
in whose possession they now are*].

7. According to the best of my knowledge, information and belief, I
have not now, and never had in my possession, custody or power. or in
the possession, custody, or power of my solicitors or agents, solicitor or
agent, or in the possession, custody, or power of any other persons or
person on my behalf, any deed, account, book of account, voucher,
receipt, letter, memorandum, paper, or writing, or any copy of or extract
from any such document; or any other document whatsoever, relating to
the matters in question in this action or any of them, or wherein any
entry has been made relative to such matters, or any of them, other than
and except the documents set forth in the said first and second schedules
hereto, and the pleadings and other proceedings in the action.

No. 49.

Affidavit on production when made by an officer of a Corporation.

In the High Court of Justice.
– ——Division.

Between *A.B.*, Plaintiff,
and
C.D., Defendant.

I, of , make oath and say as follows :—

1. I am the *(here state the name of the office held by the deponent in the service of the Company on whose behalf he makes the affidavit)*, and as such, have knowledge of all documents which are, or have been, in the custody or possession of the said (Company;, relating to the matters in question in this action.

2. I am cognizant of the matters in question in this action.

3. The said defendants have in their possession or power, the documents relating to the matters in question in this action, set forth in the first and second parts of the first schedule hereto.

4. The said defendants object to produce the said documents set forth in the second part of the said first schedule hereto.

5. That *(here state on what grounds the objection is made, and verify the facts as far as may be)*.

6. The said defendants have had, but have not now, in their possession or power, the documents relating to the matters in question in this action, set forth in the second schedule hereto.

7. The last mentioned documents were last in the possession or power of the said defendants on *(state when)*.

8. That *(here state what has become of the last mentioned documents, and in whose possession they now are)*.

9. According to the best of my knowledge, information, and belief, the said defendants have not now, and never had, in their possession, custody, or power, or in the possession, custody, or power of myself, or of any of its solicitors or agents, or of any person or persons whomsoever, on its behalf any *(proceed as in last form.)*

———

No. 50.

Affidavit of Executor or Administrator as to claims, under Rule 981.

In the High Court of Justice,
———Division.

Between *A. B.*, plaintiff,
and
C. D., defendant.

We, *A. B.*, of, etc., the above named plaintiff [*or* defendant, *or as may be*], the executors [*or* administrators], of C. D., late of , in the County of , deceased, and *E. F.*, of, etc., solicitor, severally make oath, and say as follows :—

I, the said *E. F.*, [solicitor] for myself say as follows :—

1. I have, in the paper writing now produced and shewn to me, and marked A, set forth a list of all the claims the particulars of which have

been sent in to me by 'persons claiming to be creditors of the said *C. D.*, deceased, pursuant to the advertisement issued in that behalf, dated day of , 18 .

And I, the said A. B., for myself, say as follows :

2. I have examined the several claims mentioned in the paper writing now produced and shown to me, and marked A, and I have compared the same with the books, accounts, and documents of the said *C. D.*, [*or as may be, and state any other inquiries or investigations made*], in order to ascertain, as far as I am able, to which of such claims the estate of the said C. D. is justly liable.

3. From such examination [*and state any other reasons*], I am of opinion, and verily believe, that the estate of the said *C.D.* is justly liable to the amounts set forth in the sixth column of the first part of the said paper writing marked A ; and to the best of my knowledge and belief, such several amounts are justly due from the estate of the said *C. D.*, and proper to be allowed to the respective claimants named in the said schedule.

I am of opinion that the estate of the said *C. D.* is not justly liable to the claims set forth in the second part of the said paper writing marked A, and the same ought not to be allowed without proof by the respective claimants, [*or*, I am not able to state whether the estate of the said *C. D.*, is justly liable to the claims set forth in the second part of the said paper writing marked A, or whether such claims, or any parts thereof, are proper to be allowed without further evidence].

Sworn, etc.

Exhibit referred to in the above Affidavit.

(*Short Title.*)

List of claims the particulars of which have been sent in to *E. F.*, the solicitor of the plaintiff, [*or*, defendant, *or as may be*], by persons claiming to be creditors of *C. D*, deceased, pursuant to the advertisement issued in that behalf, dated the day of , 18 .

This paper writing, marked A, was produced and shewn to and is the same as is referred to in his affidavit, sworn before me this day of , 18 .

W. B., etc.

First Part.—Claims proper to be allowed without further evidence.

Serial No.	Name of Claimants.	Addresses and Descriptions.	Nature of Claim.	Amount claimed.	Amount proper to be allowed.
					$ c.

Second Part.—Claims which ought to be proved by the Claimants.

Serial No.	Names of Claimants.	Addresses and Description.	Nature of Claim.	Amount claimed.
				$. c.

No. 51

Affidavit in support of Garnishee Order.

In the High Court of Justice.

—— Division.

Between

Judgment Creditor,

and

Judgment Debtor.

I,   of   the above-named judgment creditor [or solicitor for the above-named judgment creditor] make oath and say as follows :—

1. By a judgment of the Court given in this action, and dated the day of   18 , it was·adjudged that I [or the above-named judgment creditor] should recover against the above-named judgment debtor the sum of $, and costs to be taxed, and the said costs were by a taxing officer's certificate dated the   day of   18 , allowed at $

2. The said   still remains unsatisfied‿to the extent of   and interest amounting to $

3.   *Name, address and description of garnishee)* is indebted to the judgment debtor   in the sum of $ or thereabouts.

4. The said *(insert name of garnishee)* is within the jurisdiction of thi Court.

Sworn at   the   day of   18 .

Before me

This affidavit is filed on behalf of the

No. 52

Affidavit on Interpleader.

In the High Court of Justice.

——- - Division.

Between

Plaintiff,

and

Defendant.

I,   of   the defendant in the above action, make oath and say as follows :—

1. The writ of summons herein was issued on the   day of   18 , and was served on me on the   day of   18 . I have not yet delivered a statement of defence herein.

2. The action is brought to recover   . The said   (is *or* are) in my possession, but I claim no interest therein.

3. The right to the said subject-matter of this action has been and is claimed *(if claim in writing make the writing an exhibit)* by one who *(state expectation of suit or that he has already sued)*.

4. I do not in any manner collude with the said   or with the above-named plaintiff, but I am ready to bring into Court or to pay or dispose of the said   in such manner as the Court may order or direct.

Sworn at   the   day of   18   .

Before me

This affidavit is filed on behalf of the   •

PART VI.

PLEADINGS.

No. 53.

In the High Court of Justice,   Account
——— Division   stated.

Writ issued 3rd. September 18   .

Between *A. B.*, Plaintiff,
and
E. F., Defendant.

Statement of Claim.

1. Between the 1st of January and the 28th of February, 1879, the Claim. plaintiff supplied to the defendant various articles of drapery ; and payments on account were from time to time made by the defendant.

2. On the 28th of February, 1879, a balance remained due to the plaintiff of $325, and an account was on that day sent by the plaintiff to the defendant showing that balance.

3. On the 1st of March following, defendant paid the plaintiff by cheque $32 on account of the same. The residue of the said balance, amounting to $293, has never been paid.

The plaintiff claims $

The plaintiff proposes that this action should be tried at Whitby.

Delivered the   day of   18   by
X. Y., of   Plaintiff's Solicitor.

No. 54.

In the High Court of Justice,   Administra-
———— Division.   tion of an
                                         Intestate's
Writ issued 22nd December, 18   .   Estate.
In the matter of the estate of *A. B.*, deceased.

Between *E. F.*, Plaintiff,
and
G. H., Defendant.

Statement of Claim.

1. *A. B.*, of *K.*, in the County of *L.*, died on the 1st July, 1880, in- Claim. testate. The defendant, *G. H.*, is the administrator of *A. B.*

2. *A. B.* died entitled to lands in the said county for an estate of fee simple, and also to some other real estate and to personal estate. The defendant has entered into possession of the real estate of *A. B.*, and received the rents thereof.

3. *A. B.* was never married ; he had one brother only, who pre-deceased him without having been married, and two sisters only, both of whom also pre-deceased him, namely *M. N.* and *P. Q.* The plaintiff is the only child of *M. N.*, and the defendant is the only child of *P. Q.*

The plaintiff claims— .

1. To have the real and personal estate of *A. B.*, administered in this Court, and for that purpose to have all proper directions given and accounts taken. .

2. To have a receiver appointed of the rents of his real estate.

·3 Such further or other relief as the nature of the case may require.

The plaintiff proposes that this action should be tried at London.

Delivered the   day of   18   by
. *X. Y.* of   Plaintiff's Solicitor.

No. 55.

In the High Court of Justice.
——Division.

In the matter of the estate of *A. B.*, deceased.

Between *E. F.*, Plaintiff,
and
G. H., Defendant.

Statement of Defence.

Defence.   1. The plaintiff is an illegitimate child of *M. N.* She was never married. The Defendant admits the other allegations contained in the 1st and 3rd paragraphs of the plaintiff's statement of claim.

2. The intestate was not entitled to any real estate at his death.

3. The personal estate of *A. B.* was not sufficient for the payment of his debts, and has all been applied in payment of his funeral and testamentary expenses, and part of his debts.

Delivered the   day of   18   by
X. Y., of   Defendant's Solicitor.

No. 56.

Administration of a Testator's estate.   In the High Court of Justice.
——Division.

Writ issued 22nd December, 18   .
In the matter of the estate of *A. B.*, deceased.

Between *E. F.*, Plaintiff,
. and
G. H., Defendant.   ,

Statement of Claim.

Claim.   1. *A. B.*, of *K.*, in the county of *L.*, duly made his last will, dated the 1st day of March, 1873, whereby he appointed the defendant and *M. N.* (who died in the testator's lifetime), executors thereof, and devised and bequeathed his real and personal estate to and to the use of his executors in trust, to pay the rents and income thereof to the plaintiff for his life ; and after his decease, and in default of his having a son who should attain 21, or a daughter who should attain that age, or marry, upon trust as to his real estate for the person who would be the testator's heir at-law, and as to his personal estate for the persons who would be the testator's next of kin, if he had died intestate at the time of the death of the plaintiff, and such failure of his issue as aforesaid.

2. The testator died on the 1st day of July, 1880, and his will was proved by the defendant, on the 4th of October, 1880. The plaintiff has not been married.

3. The testator was at his death entitled to real and personal estate ; the defendant entered into the receipt of the rents of the real estate and got in the personal estate ; he has sold some part of the estate.

The plaintiff claims—

1. To have the real and personal estate of *A. B.*, administered in this Court, and for that purpose to have all proper directions given and accounts taken.

2. Such further or other relief as the nature of the case may require.

The plaintiff proposes that this action should be tried at Napanee.

Delivered the   day of   18   by
X. Y., of   Plaintiff's Solicitor.

No. 57.

In the High Court of Justice.
——Division.

In the matter of the estate of *A. B.*, deceased.

Between *E. F.*, Plaintiff,
and
G. H., Defendant.

Statement of Defence.

1. *A. B's* will contained a charge of debts ; he died insolvent ; he was entitled at his death to some real estate which the defendant sold, and which produced the net sum of $22,500, and the testator had some personal estate which the defendant got in and which produced the net sum of $5,400. **Defence.**

2. The defendant applied the whole of the said sums and the sum of $84, which the defendant received from rents of the real estate, in the payment of the funeral and testamentary expenses and debts of the testator.

3. The Defendant made up his accounts and sent a copy thereof to the plaintiff on the 10th of January, 1880, and offered the plaintiff free access to the vouchers, to verify such accounts, but he declined to avail himself of the defendant's offer.

4. The defendant admits the allegations in the 1st and 2nd paragraphs of the plaintiff's statement of claim.

5. The Defendant submits that the plaintiff ought to pay the costs of this action.

Delivered the   day of   18   by
X. Y., of   Defendant's Solicitor.

No. 58.

Action against Del credere Agents.

Agent.　　In the High Court of Justice.
————Division.

Writ issued 23rd August, 18

Between *A. B.* and Company, Plaintiffs,
and
E. F. and Company, Defendants.

Statement of Claim.

Claim.　　1. The plaintiffs are manufacturers of artificial manures, carrying on business at   , in the county of

2. The defendants are commission agents, carrying on business in Toronto.

3. In the early part of the year   , the plaintiffs commenced, and down to the   18   , continued to consign to the defendants, as their agents, large quantities of their manures for sale, and the defendants sold the same and received the price thereof and accounted to the plaintiffs therefor.

4. No express agreement has ever been entered into between the plaintiffs and the defendants with respect to the terms of the defendants employment as agents. The defendants have always charged the plaintiffs a commission at   per cent. on all sales effected by them, which is the rate of commission ordinarily charged by all del credere agents in the said trade. And the defendants, in fact, always accounted to the plaintiffs for the price, whether they received the same from the purchaser or not.

5. The plaintiffs contend that the defendants are liable to them as del credere agents, but if not so liable are, under the circumstances hereinafter mentioned, liable as ordinary agents.

6. On the   , the plaintiffs consigned to the defendants for sale a large quantity of goods, including   tons of

7. On or about the   , the defendants sold   tons of part of such goods to one *G. H.*, for $, at three months' credit, and delivered the same to him.

8. *G. H.* was not, at that time, in good credit and was in insolvent circumstances, and the defendants might, by ordinary care and diligence, have ascertained the fact.

9. *G. H.* did not pay for the said goods, but before the expiration of the said three months for which credit had been given, the estate of the said *G. H.* was placed in liquidation under the Insolvency Acts then in force ; and the plaintiffs have never received the said sum of $ or any part thereof.

The plaintiff's claim :

1. Damages to the amount of $

2. Such further or other relief as the nature of the case may require.

The plaintiffs propose that this action should be tried at Hamilton.

Delivered the   day of   18   by
X. Y., of   Plaintiff's Solicitor.

No. 59.

[Title as in claim, omitting date of issue of writ.]

Statement of Defence.

1. The defendants deny that the said commission of   per cent. **Defence.** mentioned in paragraph 4 of the claim is the rate of commission ordinarily charged by del credere agents in the said trade, and say that the same is the ordinary commis ion for agents other than del credere agents, and they deny that they ever accounted to the plaintiffs for the price of any goods, except after they had received the same from the purchasers.

2. The defendants deny that they were ever liable to the plaintiffs as del credere agents.

3. With respect to the 8th paragraph of the plaintiff's statement of claim, the defendants say that at the time of the said sale to the said *G. H.*, the said *G. H.* was a person in good credit. If the truth is that the said *G. H.* was then in insolvent circumstances, the defendants did not suspect and had not reas n to suspect the same, and could not by ordinary care or diligence have ascertained the fact.

4. The defendants admit the allegations contained in paragraph 1, 2, 3, 6, 7 and 9 of the plaintiff's statement of claim.

    Delivered the   day of   18   , by
X. Y., of   Defendants' Solicitor.

———

No. 60.

In the High Court of Justice,   **Bill of**
  ——— Division.   **exchange.**

Writ issued 23rd August, 18 .

Between *A. B.* and *C. D.*, Plaintiffs,
and
E. F. and *G. H.*, Defendants.

Statement of Claim.

1. Messrs. *M. N. & Co.*, on the   day of   drew a bill **Claim.** of exchange upon the defendants for $, payable to the order of the said Messrs. *M. N. & Co.* 3 months after date, and the defendants accepted the same.

2. Messrs. *M. N. & Co.* indorsed the bill to the plaintiffs.

[3. (*Introduced by amendment to meet the defence in the defendant's statement of defence infra*). The plaintiff gave value and consideration for the said bill in manner following, that is to say : on the day   18 , the said Messrs. *M. N. & Co.* were indebted to the plaintiff in about $ the balance of an account for goods sold from time to time by him to them. On that day they ordered of the plaintiff further goods to the value of about $ which last mentioned goods have since been delivered by him to them. And at the time of the order for such last mentioned goods it was agreed between Messrs. *M. N. & Co.* and the plaintiff, and the order was received upon the terms, that they should indorse and hand over to him the bill of exchange sued upon, together with various other securities on account of the said previous balance, and the price of the goods so ordered on that day. The said securities, including the bill sued upon, were thereupon on the same day indorsed and handed over to the plaintiff.]

4. The bill became due on the   , and the defendant has not paid it.

The plaintiffs claim :—*(state claim)*

The plaintiffs propose that this action should be tried at Kingston.

Delivered the   day of   18   , by
X. Y., of   Plaintiffs' Solicitor.

[Title.]

No. **61**.

Statement of Defence.

Defence.

1. The bill of exchange mentioned in the statement of claim was drawn and accepted under the circumstances hereinafter stated, and except as hereinafter mentioned there never was any consideration for the acceptance or payment thereof by the defendants.

2. Shortly before the acceptance of the said bill it was agreed between the said Messrs. *M. N. & Co.*, the drawers thereof, and the defendants, that the said Messrs. *M. N. & Co.* should sell and deliver to the defendants free on board ship at the port of   1 200 tons of coal during the month of   , and that the defendants should pay for the same by accepting the said Messrs. *M. N. & Co.'s* draft for $ at 6 months.

3. The said Messrs. *M. N. & Co.* accordingly drew upon the defendants, and the defendants accepted the bill of exchange now sued upon.

4. The defendants did all things which were necessary to entitle them to delivery by the said Messrs. *M. N. & Co.* of the said 1,200 tons of coals under their said contract, and the time for delivery has long since elapsed ; but the said Messrs. *M. N. & Co.* never delivered the same, or any part thereof, but have always refused to do so, whereby the consideration for the defendant's acceptance has wholly failed.

5. The plaintiffs first received the said bill, and it was first indorsed to them after it was overdue.

6. The plaintiffs never gave any value or consideration for the said bill.

7. The plaintiffs took the said bill with notice of the facts stated in the 2nd, 3rd, and 4th paragraphs hereof.

Delivered the   day of   ´18   by
X. Y., of   Defendants' Solicitor.

No. **62**. .

(Reply where plaintiff does not introduce into his statement of claim the allegations necessary by way of reply to the defence.)

[Title.]

Reply.

1. The plaintiff joins issue upon the defendant's statement of defence.

2. The plaintiff gave value and consideration for the said bill in manner following, that is to say, on the   day of   18   , the said Messrs. *M. N. & Co.* were indebted to the plaintiff in about $ the balance of an account for goods sold from time to time by him to them. On that day they ordered of the plaintiff further goods to the value of

about **℥** which last mentioned goods have since been delivered by him to them. At the time of the order for such last mentioned goods it was agreed between Messrs. *M. N. & Co.* and the plaintiff, and the order was received upon the terms, that they should indorse and hand over to him the bill of exchange sued upon, together with various other securities on account of the said previous balance, and the price of the goods so ordered on that day. The said securities including the bill sued upon, were thereupon on the same day indorsed and handed over to the plaintiff.

Delivered the   day of   18   by
X. Y., of   Plaintiff"s Solicitor.

No. **63.**

In the High Court of Justice,   Promissory
—— Division.   note.

Writ issued 3rd November, 18 .

Between *A. B.*, Plaintiff,
and
E. F., Defendant.

Statement of Claim.

1. The defendant on the   day of
made his promissory note, whereby he promised to pay to the plaintiff or Claim.
his order **℥**   3 months after date.

2. The note became due on the   day of
18 , and the defendant has not paid it.

The plaintiff claims :—

The amount of the note and interest thereon to judgment.

The plaintiff proposes that this action should be tried at Peterborough.

Delivered the   day of   18   by
X. Y., of   Plaintiff's Solicitor.

[Title.]

No. **64.**

Statement of Defence.

1. The defendant made the note sued upon under the following circum- Defence.
stances :—The plaintiff and defendant had for some years been in partnership as coal merchants, and it had been agreed between them that they
should dissolve partnership, that the plaintiff should retire from the
business, that the defendant should take over the whole of the partnership
assets and liabilities, and should pay the plaintiff the value of his share in
the assets after deducting the liabilities.

2. The plaintiff thereupon undertook to examine the partnership books,
and inquire into the state of the partnership assets and liabilities ; and he
did accordingly examine the books, and make the said inquiries, and he
thereupon represented to the defendant that the assets of the firm exceeded
$10,000, and that the liabilities of the firm were under $3,000, whereas the
fact was that the assets of the firm were less than $5,000, and the liabilities
of the firm largely exceeded the assets.

3. The misrepresentations mentioned in the last paragraph induced the
defendant to make the note now sued on, and there never was any other
consideration for the making of the note.

Delivered the   day of   18   by
X. Y., of   Defendant's Solicitor.

No. 65.

Statement of Claim.,

Action on Bill In the High Court of Justice,
of Exchange.   —— Division.

Writ issued 1st February, 18 .

Between *A. B.*, Plaintiff,
and
C. D., Defendant.

Claim.   1. The plaintiff on the   day of   188 , drew
a bill of exchange upon the defendant for $ payable 3 months
after date, and the defendant accepted the same.

2. The bill became due on   day of   188 , and the
defendant has not paid it.

3. [(*Amendment to meet defence infra.*) The defendant, who at the time
of the acceptance of the said bill was an infant within the age of 21 years,
ratified and confirmed the said acceptance after he attained full age and
before action, by a writing made and signed by him.]

The plaintiff claims :—(*State claim.*)

The plaintiff proposes that this action should be tried at Picton.

Delivered the   day of   18   by
X. Y., of   Plaintiff's Solicitor.

No. 66.

Statement of Defence.

[Title.]

At the time of making the alleged acceptance of the said bill the defendant was an infant within the age of 21 years.

Delivered the   day of   18   by
X. Y., of   Defendant's Solicitor.

No. 67.

(*Reply where plaintiff does not introduce into his statement of claim the
allegations necessary by way of reply to the defence.*

[Title.]

Reply.

The defendant *C. D.*, who at the time of the acceptance of the said bill,
was an infant within the age of 21 years, ratified and confirmed the said
acceptance after he attained full age and before action, by a writing made
and signed by him.

Delivered the   day of   18   , by
X. Y., of   Plaintiff's Solicitor.

No. 68.

In the High Court of Justice.
——Division.

Writ issued 3rd October, 18

Between *A. B.*, and *C. D.*, Plaintiffs,
and
E. F. and *G. H.*, Defendants.

Statement of Claim.

1. The plaintiffs are   merchants, factors, and commission Claim.
agents, carrying on business in Toronto.

2. The defendants are merchants and commission agents, carrying on
business at Montreal.

3. For several years prior to the   18   , the plaintiffs
had been in the habit of consigning goods to the defendants for sale, as
their agents, and the defendants had been in the habit of consigning goods
to the plaintiffs for sale, as their agents ; and each party always received
the price of the goods sold by him for the other ; and a balance was from
time to time struck between the parties, and paid.

On the   of   , the moneys so received by the
defendants for the plaintiffs, and remaining in their names, largely exceeded the moneys received by the plaintiffs for the defendants, and a
balance of $ was accordingly due to the plaintiffs from the defendants.

4. On or about the   , 18   , the plaintiffs sent to the defendants a statement of the accounts between them, shewing the said sum
as the balance due to the plaintiffs from the defendants ; and the defendants agreed to the said statement of accounts as co rect, and to the said
sum of $ as the balance due by them to the plaintiffs, and
agreed to pay interest on such balance if time were given to them.

5. The defendants requested the plaintiffs to give them three months'
time for payment of the said sum of $, and the plaintiffs agreed
to do so upon the defendants accepting the bills of exchange hereinafter
mentioned.

6. The plaintiffs thereupon on the   drew two bills
of exchange upon the defendants, one for $, and the other for
$, both payable to the order of the plaintiffs three months after
date, and the defendants accepted the bills.

The said bills became due on the   18   , and the defendants have not paid the bills, or either of them, nor the said sum of
$.

The plaintiffs claim :—

$ and interest to the date of judgment.

The plaintiffs propose that this action should be tried at Toronto.

Delivered the   day of   18   by
X. Y., of   Plaintiffs' Solicitor.

No. 69.

False im-
prisonment.

In the High Court of Justice.
————Division.

Writ issued 3rd September, 18

Between *A. B.*, Plaintiff,
and
E. F., Defendant.

Statement of Claim.

Claim.

1. The plaintiff is a journeyman painter. The defendant is a builder having his building yard, and carrying on business at Ottawa, and for six months before and up to the 22nd August, 18 ·, the plaintiff was in the defendant's employment as a journeyman painter.

2. On the said 22nd August, 18 , the plaintiff came to work as usual in the defendant's yard, at about six o'clock in the morning.

3. A few minutes after the plaintiff had so come to work the defendant's foreman, *X. Y.*, who was then in the yard, called the plaintiff to him, and accused the plaintiff of having on the previous day stolen a quantity of paint, the property of the defendant, from the yard. The plaintiff denied the charge, but *X. Y.* gave the plaintiff into the custody of a constable, whom he had previously sent for, upon a charge of stealing paint.

4. The defendant was present at the time when the plaintiff was given into custody, and authorized and assented to his being given into custody ; and in any case *X. Y.*, in giving him into custody, was acting within the scope and in the course of his employment as the defendant's foreman, and for the purposes of the defendant's business.

5. The plaintiff upon being so given into custody, was taken by the said constable a considerable distance through various streets, on foot, to the police station and he was there detained in a cell till late in the afternoon, when he was taken to the police court, and the charge against him was heard before the magistrate then sitting there, and was dismissed.

6. In consequence of being so given into custody, the plaintiff suffered annoyance and disgrace, and loss of time and wages, and loss of credit and reputation, and was thereby unable to obtain any employment or earn any wages for three months.

The plaintiff claims $ damages.

The plaintiff proposes that this action should be tried at Ottawa.

Delivered the　　　　　　　　day of　　　　　　　18　　　by
X. Y., of　　　　　　　　　Plaintiff's Solicitor.

No. 70.

[Title.]

Statement of Defence.

Defence.

1. The defendant denies that he was present at the time when the plaintiff was given into custody, or that he in any way authorized or assented to his being given into custody. And the said *X. Y.*, in giving the plaintiff into custody, did not act within the scope or in the course of his employment as the defendant's foreman, or for the purposes of the defendant's business.

2. At some time about five or six o'clock on the , being the evening before the plaintiff was given into custody, a large quantity of paint had been feloniously stolen by some person or persons from a shed upon the defendant's yard and premises.

3. At about 5.30 o'clock on the evening of the   the plaintiff, who had left off work about half an hour previously, was seen coming out of the shed when no one else was in it, although his work lay in a distant part of the yard from, and he had no business in or near the shed. He was then seen to go to the back of a stack of timber in another part of the yard. Shortly afterwards the paint was found to have been taken, and it was found concealed at the back of the stack of timber behind which the plaintiff had been seen to go.

4. On the following morning, before the plaintiff was given into custody, he was asked by *X. Y.* what he had been in th- shed and behind the stack of timber for, and he denied having been in either place. *X. Y.* had reasonable and probable cause for suspecting, and did suspect that the plaintiff was the person who had stolen the paint, and thereupon gave him into custody.

Delivered the   day of   18   by
X. Y., of   Defendant's Solicitor.

No. 71.

In the High Court of Justice.
———Division.

Writ issued 3rd September, 188   .

Between *A. B.*, Plaintiff,
and
E. F., Defendant.

Statement of Claim.

1. In or about   March, 1880, the defendant caused to be inserted Claim. in the   Newspaper an advertisement, in which he offered for sale the lease, fixtures, fittings, goodwill, and stock-in-trade of a baker's shop and business, and described the same as an increasing business, and doing twelve barrels a week. The advertisement directed application for particulars to be made to *X. Y.*

2. The plaintiff having seen the advertisement applied to *X. Y.*, who placed him in communication with the defendant, and negotiations ensued between the plaintiff and the defendant for the sale to the plaintiff of the defendant's bakery at   with the lease, fixtures, fittings, stock-in-trade, and good-will.

3. In the course of these negotiations the defendant repeatedly stated to the plaintiff that the business was a steadily increasing business, and that it was a business of more than twelve barrels a week.

4. On the 5th of April, 1880, the plaintiff, believing the said statement of the defendant to be true, agreed to purchase the said premises from the defendant, for $2,000, and paid to him a deposit of $300 in respect of the purchase.

5. On the 15th of April the purchase was completed, an assignment of the lease executed, and the balance of the purchase money paid. On the same day the plaintiff entered into possession.

6. The plaintiff soon afterwards discovered that at the time of the negotiations of the said purchase by him and of the said agreement, and of the completion thereof, the said business was and had long been a declining business ; and at each of those times, and for a long time before, it had never been a business of more than four barrels a week. And the said premises were not of the value of $2,000, or any saleable value whatever.

14

7. The defendant made the false representations hereinbefore mentioned well knowing them to be false, and fraudulently, with the intention of inducing the plaintiff to make the said purchase on the faith of them.

The plaintiff claims $ damages.

The plaintiff proposes that this action should be tried at Brockville.

Delivered the   day of   -   18   by

X. Y., of   Plaintiff's Solicitor.

No. 72.

[Title.]

Statement of Defence.

Defence.

1. The defendant says that at the time when he made the representations mentioned in the 3rd paragraph of the statement of claim and throughout the whole of the transactions between the plaintiff and defendant, and down to the completion of the purchase and the relinquishment by the defendant of the said shop and business to the plaintiff, the said business was an increasing business, and was a business of over 12 barrels a week. And the defendant denies the allegations of the 6th paragraph of the statement of claim.

2. The defendant repeatedly during the negotiations told the plaintiff that he must not act upon any statement or representation of his, but • must as er ain for himself the extent and value of the said business. And the defendant handed to the plaintiff for this purpose the whole of his books, shewing fully and truthfully all the details of the said business, and from which the nature, extent, and value thereof could be fully seen, and those books were examined for that purpose by the plaintiff, and by an accountant on his behalf. And the plaintiff made the purchase in reliance upon his own judgment, and the result of his own inquiries and investigations, and not upon any statement or representation whatever of the defendant.

3. The defendant admits the allegations of paragraphs 1, 2, 3 and 4 of the statement of claim.

Delivered the   day of   18   by

X. Y., of   ,   Defendant's Solicitor.

No. 73.

Guarantee.

In the High Court of Justice,

——Division.

Writ issued 3rd September, 188

Between *A. B.* and *C. D.*, Plaintiffs,

and

E. F. and *G. H.*, Defendants.

'*Statement of Claim.*

Claim.

1. The plaintiffs are brewers, carrying on their business at Guelph, under the firm of *X. Y. & Co.*

2. In the month of March, 1879, *M. N.* was desirous of entering into the employment of the plaintiffs' as a traveller and collector, and it was agreed between the plaintiffs and the defendants and *M. N.*, that the plaintiffs should employ *M. N.* upon the defendants entering into the guarantee hereinafter mentioned.

3. An engagement in writing was accordingly made and entered into, on or about the 30th March, 1879, between the plaintiffs and the defendant, whereby, in consideration that the plaintiffs would employ

M. N. as their collector, the defendants agreed that they would be answerable for the due accounting by *M. N.* to the plaintiffs for, and the due payment over by him to the plaintiffs of all moneys which he should receive on their behalf as their collector.

4. The plaintiffs employed *M. N.* as their collector accordingly, and he entered upon the duties of such employment, and continued therein down to the 31st September, 1880.

5. At various times between the 29th of September, and the 25th of December, 1880, *M. N.* received on behalf of the plaintiffs and as their collector, sums of money from debtors of the plaintiffs, amounting in the whole to the sum of $3,400; and of this amount *M. N.* neglected to account for or pay over to the plaintiffs sums amounting in the whole to $903, and appropriated the last-mentioned sums to his own use.

6. The defendants have not paid the last mentioned sums, or any part thereof, to the plaintiffs.

The plaintiffs claim :—*(State claim.)*

The plaintiffs propose that this action should be tried at Guelph.

Delivered the   day of   18   by
X. Y., of   Plaintiffs' Solicitor.

No. **74.**

In the High Court of Justice,   Negligence.
——Division.

Writ issued 3rd September, 188

Between *A. B.*, Plaintiff,
and
E. F., Defendant.

Statement of Claim.

1. The plaintiff is a shoemaker, carrying on business at Toronto. The Claim. defendant is a soap and candle manufacturer at the same place.

2. On the 23rd May, 1881, the plaintiff was walking eastward along the south side of King Street, in the city of Toronto, at about 3 o'clock in the afternoon. He was obliged to cross Yonge Street, which is a street running into King Street at right angles thereto. While he was crossing this street, and just before he could reach the foot pavement on the further side thereof, a two-horse van of the defendants under the charge and control of the defendant's servants, was negligently, suddenly, and without any warning, turned at a rapid and dangerous pace out of King Street into Yonge Street. The pole of the van struck the plaintiff and knocked him down, and he was much trampled by the horses.

3. By the blow and fall and trampling the plaintiff's left arm was broken, and he was bruised and injured on the side and back, as well as internally, and in consequence thereof the plaintiff was for 4 months ill and suffering, and unable to attend to his business, and incurred heavy medical and other expenses, and sustained great loss of business and profits.

The plaintiff claims $ damages.

The plaintiff proposes that this action should be tried at Lindsay.

Delivered the   day of   18   by
X. Y., of   Plaintiff's Solicitor.

No. **75.**

[Title.]

Statement of Defence.

1. The defendant denies that the van was the defendant's van, or that Defence. it was under the charge or control of the defendant's servant. The van

belonged to John Smith, of   , a carman and contractor,
employed by the defendant to carry and deliver goods for him ; and the
persons under whose charge and control the said van was were the servants
of the said John Smith.

2. The defendant denies that the van was turned' out of King Street
either negligently, suddenly, or without warning, or at a rapid or dangerous pace.

3 The defendant says that the plaintiff might and could, by the exercise
of reasonable care and diligence, have seen the van approaching him, and
avoided any collision with it.

Delivered the   day of   18   by
X. Y., of   Defendant's Solicitor.

———

Action for
Assault.

No. 76.

Statement of Claim.

In the High Court of Justice,
——Division.

Writ issued 15th March, 18 .

Between A. B., Plaintiff,
and
E. F., Defendant.

1. The plaintiff is a   carrying on business at
2. On the   day of   the defendant assaulted the
plaintiff and the plaintiff was seriously hurt and wounded, and was for a
long time in consequence of his injuries, unable to transact his business,
and incurred expense for nursing and medical attendance.

3. [(Amendment to meet defence infra) The defendant pretends that
he committed the assault complained of in his own defence ; but the facts
are that the defendant was trespassing on the plaintiff's lai d, and refused to leave though requested to do so, whereupon the plaintiff laid his
hands on the defendant in order to remove him, .using so much force and
no more than was necessary for that purpose.]

The plaintiff claims $ damages.
The plaintiff proposes that this action should be tried at Cobourg.

Delivered the   day of   18   , by
X. Y., of   Plaintiff's Solicitor.

———

No. 77.

[Title.]

Statement of Defence.

The plaintiff first assaulted the defendant who thereupon committed
the alleged assault in his own defence.

Delivered the   day of   18   , by
X. Y., of   Defendant's Solicitor.

———

No. 78.

(Reply where plaintiff does not introduce into his statement of claim the
allegations necessary by way of reply to the defence.)

[Title.]

Reply.

The defendant E. F., pretends that he committed the assault complained of in his own defence ; but the facts are that the defendant was

trespassing on the plaintiff's land and refused to leave though requested to do s , whereupon the plaintiff laid his hands on the defendant in order to remove him, using so much force and no more than was necessary for that p rpose.

Delivered the   day of   18   , by
X. Y., of   Plaintiff's Solicitor.

No. 79.

Statement of Claim.

In the High Court of Justice.
    ———— Division.

Writ issued   188 .

Between *A. B.*, Plaintiff,
     and
    ———— Defendants.

Action against Railway Company for Injuries by collision caused through negligence.

1. The defendants are carriers of passengers upon a railway from Toronto to

2. In January, 1881, the plaintiff took a ticket from Toronto to and was received by the defendants as a passenger to be by them safely carried in a train which started from Toronto for

3. Owing to the negligence of the defendants in the management of their railway, the train in which the plaintiff was travelling came into collision with an engine, at a short distance from Toronto.

4. The plaintiff was thrown from his seat by the said collision, and much injured about the head, and had his right arm broken.

5 [*The following paragraphs may be introduced by amendment to meet Defence infra.* The defendants allege that the plaintiff accepted the sum of $300 in full satisfaction of all cause of action which he might have on account of the said collision, but the facts are as follows :

6. A short time after the collision an officer of the defendants procured the plaintiff to accept the said accord and satisfaction by fraudulently representing that his injuries were of a temporary nature, and that if they should afterwards turn out to be more serious than he anticipated, he would still be able to obtain further compensation from the defendants.

7. The plaintiff, fully believing the said representations, and acting upon the faith thereof, was induced thereby to accept the said accord and satisfaction, and then accepted the same, subject to the express condition that he should not thereby exclude himself from further compensation from the defendants if his injuries should prove more serious than he then anticipated.

8 After the acceptance of the said accord and satisfaction, the injuries suffered by the plaintiff in the collision did turn out to be more serious than was anticipated at the time aforesaid, and thereupon the plaintiff commenced the present action]

The plaintiff claims $ damages.
The plaintiff proposes that this action should be tried at Toronto.

Delivered the   day of   18   , by
X Y., of   Plaintiff's Solicitor.

No. 80.

[Title.]

Statement of Defence.

1. Shortly after the collision referred to in the statement of claim, one of the officers of the defendants called upon the plaintiff for the purpose of

ascertaining from him whether he intended to make any claim against the defendants arising out of the said collision.

2 At such interview the plaintiff informed the said officer that he did intend to make a claim against the defendants arising out of the said collision ; and it was there and then agreed between the plaintiff and the said officer acting on behalf and by the authority of the defendants, that in consideration that the defendants would pay to the plaintiff a sum of $300, he, the plaintiff, would accept such sum from the defendants in full satisfaction and discharge of all cause of action which he had or might have against the said defendants on account of the said collision.

3. Thereupon the said officer, acting on behalf of the defendants, paid to the plaintiff the sum of $300; and the plaintiff received the same in full discharge of the aforesaid cause of action.

Delivered the   day of   18   , by
X. Y., of   Defendant's Solicitor.

No. 81.

(Reply where Plaintiff does not introduce into his statement of claim the allegations necessary by way of reply to the Defence.)

[Title.]

Reply.

1. The defendants allege that the plaintiff accepted the sum of $300 in full satisfaction of all cause of action which he might have on account of the said collision, but the facts are as follows :

2. A short time after the collision an officer of the defendants procured the plaintiff to accept the said accord and satisfaction by fraudulently representing that his injuries were of a temporary nature, and that if they should afterwards turn out to be more serious than he anticipated, he would still be able to obtain further compensation from the defendants.

3. The plaintiff fully believing the said representations, and acting upon the faith thereof, was induced thereby to accept the said accord and satisfaction, and then accepted the same, subject to the express condition that he should not thereby exclude himself from further compensation from the defendants if his injuries should prove more serious than he then anticipated.

4 After the acceptance of the said accord and satisfaction, the injuries suffered by the plaintiff in the collision did turn out to be more serious than was anticipated at the time aforesaid, and thereupon the plaintiff commenced the present action.

Delivered the   day of   , 18   , by
X. Y., of   Plaintiff's Solicitor.

No. 82.

Landlord and Tenant.

In the High Court of Justice.
———Division.

Writ issued 3rd September, 188 .

Between *A. B.*, Plaintiff,
and
C. D., Defendant.

Claim.

Statement of Claim.

1. On the   day of   the plaintiff, by deed, let to the defendant a house and premises, No. 52   Street, in the City of Belleville, for a term o 21 years from the day of   , at the yearly rent of $400 payable quarterly.

2. By the said deed, the defendant covenanted to keep the said house and premises in good and tenantable repair.

3 The said deed also contained a clause of re-entry, entitling the plaintiff to re-enter upon the said house and premises, in case the rent thereby reserved, whether demanded or not, should be in arrear for twenty-one days, or in case the defendant should make default in the performance of any covenant upon his part to be performed.

4. On the   , a quarter's rent became due ; and on the   , another quarter's rent became due. On the   , both had been in arrear for twenty-one days, and both are still due.

5. On the same   , the house and premises were not, and are not now, in good or tenantable repair, and it would require the expenditure of a large sum of money to reinstate the same in good and tenantable repair, and the plaintiff's reversion is much depreciated in value.

The plaintiff claims :—

1. Possession of the said house and premises.

2. $ for arrears of rent.

3. $ damages for the defendant's breach of his covenant to repair.

4. $ for occupation of the house and premises from the   , to the day of recovering possession.
The plaintiff proposes that this action should be tried at Belleville.

Delivered the   day of   18   , by
X. Y., of   Plaintiff's Solicitor.

No. 83.

In the High Court of Justice.

————— Division.

Recovery of Land.

Writ issued 4th January, 18

Between A B. Plaintiff,
and
C. D., Defendant.

Statement of Claim.

1. On the   day of   the plaintiff let to
the defendant a house, No. 62   Street, in the City of Ottawa,
as tenant from year to year, at the yearly rent of $420, payable quarterly,
the tenancy to commence on the   day of   .

Landlord and Tenant.

2. The defendant took possession of the house and continued tenant thereof until the   day of   last, when the tenancy determined by a notice duly given.

3. The defendant has disregarded the notice and still retains possession of the house.

4. [*Amendment to meet the counter-claim infra.*] (The defendant, C. D., sets up in his defence that the plaintiff agreed to give to the defendant a new lease, and the plaintiff, A. B., admits the agreement alleged in the statement of defence, but he refuses to grant to the defendant a lease, inasmuch as such agreement provided that the lease should contain a covenant by the defendant to keep the house in good repair and a power

of re-entry by the plaintiff upon breach of such covenant. and the plaintiff says that the defendant, since the agreement was made, has not kept the house in good repair, and the same is now in a dilapidated condition.)

The plaintiff claims :—

1. Possession of the house.

2. $ for mesne profits from the   . day of

The plaintiff proposes that this action should be tried at Ottawa.

Delivered the   day of   18   , by
X. Y., of   Plaintiff's Solicitor.

No. 84.

Statement of Defence and Counter-claim.

In the High Court of Justice,
——Division.

Between *A B*, Plaintiff,
and
C. D., Defendant.
(by original action,)

Defence.   The defence and counter-claim of the above-named *C. D.*

1. Before the determination of the tenancy mentioned in the statement of claim, the plaintiff *A. B.*, by writing dated the   day of   , and signed by him, agreed to grant to the defendant *C D.*, a lease of the house mentioned in the statement of claim, at the yearly rent of $450, for the term of 21 years, commencing from the   day of   , when the defendant, *C. D.'s*, tenancy from year to year determined, and the defendant has since that date been and still is in possession of the house under the said agreement.

Counter-claim.   2. By way of counter-claim the defendant claims to have the agreement specifically performed, and to have a lease granted to him accordingly.

Delivered the   day of   18   , by
X. Y., of   Defendant's Solicitor.

No. 85.

Reply where plaintiff does not introduce into his statement of claim the allegations necessary by way of reply to the defence:

[Title.]

Reply.

Reply.   The plaintiff, *A. B.*, admits the agreement stated in the defendant, *C. D 's*, statement of defence, but he refuses to grant to the defendant a lease, because such agreement provided that the lease should contain a covenant by the defendant to keep the house in good repair, and a power of re-entry by the plaintiff upon breach of such covenant, and the plaintiff says that the defendant, since the making of the said agreement, has not kept the house in good repair, and the same is now in a dilapidated condition.

Delivered the   day of   18   , by
X. Y., of   Plaintiff's Solicitor.

No. 86.

In the High Court of Justice,
————Division.

Recovery of Land.

Writ issued   18 .

Between *A. B.*, and *C. D.*, Plaintiffs,
and
E. L., Defendant.

Statement of Claim.

1. *K. L.*, late of Barrie in the County of Simcoe duly executed his last Claim. will, dated the 4th day of April, 18 , and thereby devised his lands in the ounty of Simcoe unto and to the use of the plaintiffs and their heirs, upon the trusts therein mentioned for the benefit of his daughters Margaret and Martha, and appointed the plaintiffs executors thereof.

2. *K. L.* died on the 3rd day of January 18 , and his said will was proved by the plaintiffs in the proper Surrogate Court on or about the 4th day of February, 18 .

3. *K. L.* was at the time of his death seised in fee of lot No. 1 in the 3rd concession of the township of   , and lot No. 5 in the 4th concession of the township of   , both in the County of Simcoe.

4. The defendant, soon after the death of *K. L.*, entered into possession of the said lots, and has refused to give them up to the plaintiffs.

The plaintiffs claim :—

1. Possession of the said 2 lots.

2. $ for mesne profits of the premises from the death of *K. L.* till such possession shall be given.

The plaintiffs propose that this action should be tried at Barrie.

Delivered the   day of   18   , by
X. Y., of   Plaintiffs' Solicitor.   .

————

No. 87.

In the High Court of Justice,
————Division.

Trespass to Land.

Writ issued 3rd October, 18 .

Between *A. B.*, Plaintiff,
and
E. F., Defendant.

Statement of Claim.

1. The plaintiff was on the 5th March, 18 , and still is the owner and Claim. occupier of a farm in the Township of   in the County of   , being lot No. 4 in the 7th concession of the said Township.

2. A private road, known as Highfield Lane, runs through a portion of the plaintiff's farm. It is bounded upon both sides by fields of the plaintiff's and is separated therefrom by a fence and ditch.

3. For a long time prior to the 5th March, 18 , the defendant had wrongfully claimed to use the said road for his horses, carts and waggons on the alleged ground that the same was a public highway, and the plaintiff had frequently warned him that the same was not a public highway, but the plaintiff's private road, and that the defendant must not so use it.

4. On the 5th March, 18 , the defendant came with a cart and horse, and a large number of servants and workmen, and forcibly used the road, and broke down and removed a gate which the plaintiff had caused to be placed across the same.

5. The defendant and his servants and workmen on the same occasion pulled down and damaged the plaintiff's fence and ditch upon each side of the road, and went upon the plaintiff's field beyond the fence and ditch, an l injured the crops there growing, and dug up and injured the soil of the road ; and in any case the acts mentioned in this paragraph were wholly unnecessary for the assertion of the defendant's alleged right to use, or the user of the said road as a highway.

The plaintiff claims :—

1. Damages for the wrongs complained of.

2. An order restraining the defendant from any repetition of any of the acts complained of.

3. Such further relief as the nature of the case may require.

The plaintiff proposes that this action should be tried at Woodstock.

Delivered the   day of   18   , by
X. Y., of   Plaintiff's Solicitor.

No. 88.

[Title.]

Statement of Defence.

1. The defendant says that the road was and is a public highway for horses and carriages ; and a few days before the 5th of March, 18 , the plaintiff wrongful y erected the gate across the road for the purpose of obstructing and preventing, and it did obstruct and prevent the use of the road as a highway. And the defendant on the said 5th March, 18 , caused the said gate to be removed, in order to enable him lawfully to use the road by his horses, carts and waggons as a highway.

2. The defendant denies the allegations of the 5th paragraph of the statement of claim, and says that neither he nor any of his workmen or servants did any act, or used any violence, other than was necessary to enable the plaintiff lawfully to use the highway.

Delivered the   day of   18   , by
X. Y., of   Defendant's Solicitor.

No. 89.

Form of Demurrer.

In the High Court of Justice,
——Division.

[Title.]

The defendant [plaintiff] demurs to the [plaintiff's statement of complaint *or* defendants statement of defence, *or* of set-off, *or* of counterclaim] [*or* to so much of the plaintiff's statement of complaint as claims or as alleges as a breach of contract the matters mentioned in paragraph 7, *or as the case may be*], and says that the same is bad in law on the ground that [*here state a ground of demurrer*] and on other grounds sufficient in law to sustain this demurrer.

Delivered the   day of   18   , by
X. Y., of   Plaintiff's Solicitor.

No. 90.

Special Case for the opinion of the Court.

The following case is stated for the opinion of the Court under an order of the Honorable Mr. Justice   dated the   day of   18

made pursuant to Rule 554 *(or as the case may be), (here state the material facts of the case bearing upon the question of law to be decided.)*
The question (or questions) for the opinion of the Court is (or are)
First—Whether, &c.
Second—Whether, &c.

PART VII.

PRÆCIPES.

No. **91**

Amended Summons.

[Title, etc.]

Amend in pursuance of order [or fiat] dated   the writ of summons in this action by (*set out amendments when required*).

Dated the   day of   18 .
(Signed)
(Address)
Solicitor for the

No. **92.**

Renewed Summons.

[Title, etc.]

Required in pursuance of order dated   , a renewed writ of summons in this action,

Dated the   day of   18 .
(Signed)
(Address)
Solicitor for the

No. **93.**

Entry of Appearance.

[Title, etc.]

Enter an appearance for   in this action
Dated the   day of   18 .
(Signed)
(Address)

The said defendant   require   (or do not require, *as the case may be*) a statement of claim to be delivered.

(In case the defendant wishes to dispute the amount claimed, and to make no other defence, the following may be added), The defendant disputes the amount claimed by the plaintiff, (*or* the defendant insists that the amount due to the plaintiff is $ only, *or* the defendant insists that the amount due to the plaintiff is, $ for principal and $ for interest, since the   day of   etc., and no more,) *as the case may be.*

No. 94.

Entry of Appearance in action for land limiting Defence.

[Title, etc.]

Enter an appearance for the defendant   in this action. The said defendant limits his defence to part only of the property mentioned in the writ of summons, namely, to

Dated the   day of   18   .
(Signed)
(Address)

The said defendant   require   a statement of claim to be delivered.

No. 95.

Entry of Appearance, by new defendant.

[Title, etc.]

Enter an appearance for   who has been served with an order dated the   day of   to carry on and prosecute the proceedings in this action.

Dated the   day of   18
(Signed)
(Address)

No. 96.

Entry of Appearance, by party served with notice, under Rule 329.

[Title, etc.]

Enter an appearance for   to the notice issued in this action on the   day of   18   , by the defendant   under the Rules of the Supreme Court, Rule 329.

Dated the   day of   18
(Signed)
(Address)

The said defendant   require   a statement of claim to be delivered.

No. 97.

Entry of Appearance to Counter-claim.

[Title, etc.]

Enter an appearance for   to the counter-claim of the above-named defendant in this action.

Dated the   day of   18   .
(Signed)
(Address

No. 98.

Entry for Argument Generally.

[Title, etc.]

Set down for argument the
    Dated the   , day of   18
           (Signed)
           (Address)

No. 99.

Entry of Demurrer for Argument.

[Title, etc.]

Enter for argument the demurrer of   to the   in this action.
  Dated the   day of   18 .
        (Signed)
        (Address)

No. 100.

Entry of Special Case.

[Title, etc.]

Set down for argument the special case filed in this action on the
day of , 18 ; (*or* set down the   dated the   day of
  18 , of Mr.   the   referee in this
for hearing as a special case).
    Dated the   day of   18
          (Signed)
          (Address)

No. 101.

Search.

[Title, etc.]

Search for
   Dated the   day of   18 .
          (Signed)
          (Address)
          Agent for
             Solicitor

No. 102.

Entry of Action for Trial.

[Title, etc.]

Enter this action for trial.
    Dated the   day of   18 .
         (Signed)
         (Address)

No. 103.

Commission to Examine Witnesses.

[Title, etc.]

Required in pursuance of order dated   a commission to examine
witnesses directed to
          Dated the   day of   18 .
          (Signed)
          (Address)
               Solicitor for the

No. 104.

Habeas Corpus ad Testificandum.

[Title, etc.]

Required in pursuance of order dated   a writ of habeas corpus ad
testificandum directed to the   to bring   before
          Dated the   day of   18 .
          (Signed)
          (Address)
               Solicitor for the

No. 105.

Entry of Appeal.

[Title, etc.]

Enter this appeal from the order [*or* judgment] of   in this
action dated the   day of   18 .
          (Signed)
          (Address)

No. 106.

Fieri Facias.

[Title, etc.]

Required a writ of fieri facias directed to the sheriff of   to levy
against *C. D.*   ,   the sum of $ and interest
thereon at the rate of $ per centum per annum from the
          day of   [and $ costs] to
Judgment [*or* order] dated   day of
Taxing master's certificate, dated   day of
     Dated the   day of
          (Signed)
          (Address)
               Solicitor for the [*party on whose behalf writ is to issue.*]

No. 107.

Venditioni Exponas.

[Title, etc.]

Required a writ of venditioni exponas directed to the sheriff of
to sell the goods and   of *C. D.*, taken under a writ of fieri
facias in this action tested   day of
          Dated the   day of   18
          (Signed)
          (Address)
               Solicitor for the

No. **108.**

Writ of Sequestration.

[Title, etc.]

Required a writ of sequestration against *C. D.*   for not
      at the suit of *A. B.* directed to the sheriff of
Order dated   day of

     Dated the   day of   18
          (Signed)
          (Address)
            Solicitor for the

No. **109.**

Writ of Possession.   *(Lands.)*

[Title, etc.]

Required a writ of possession directed to the sheriff of   to
deliver possession to *A. B.* of
    Judgment dated   day of

     Dated the   day of   18
          (Signed)
          (Address)
            Solicitor for the

No. **110.**

Writ of Delivery.   *(Chattels.)*

(Title, etc.)

Required a writ of delivery directed to the sheriff of   to
make delivery to *A. B.* of

     Dated the   day of   18
          (Signed)
          (Address)
            Solicitor for the

No. **111.**

Writ of Attachment.

[Title, etc.

Required in pursuance of order dated   day of
an attachment directed to the sheriff of   against *C. D.* for
not delivering to *A. B.*

     Dated the   day of   18
          (Signed)
          (Address)
            Solicitor for the

No. **112.**

Præcipe for Direction to the Bank referred to in Rule 16.

In the Court of Appeal,
       or
In the High Court of Justice,
       Division.

(Short style of cause.)

Required a direction for the Bank to receive from
$ payable into Court to the credit of this cause
under   dated   *(or as the case may be.)*
Date.

          A. B.,
            Defendant's Solicitor.
            (or as the case may be).

General order (Chy) Sch. O.

No. 113.

Præcipe for Cheque referred to in Rule 176.

In the Court of Appeal,
     or
In the High Court of Justice,
     Division.
         (Short style of cause.)

Required a Cheque for $ with $ interest thereon from
    to   *(being a period, if any, for which interest is
payable under the order or judgment, but which has not already been taken
into account and computed).* payable to   : and the following
papers are produced herewith, *(naming the Judgments, orders, reports,
etc., showing the party's right to the cheque),* thus :
Judgment, dated   .
Order,   dated   .
Report,   dated   ., etc.
Date.

          A. B.,
            Plaintiff' Solicitor.
            (or as the case may be).

General order (Chy) 356, Sch.

PART VIII.

SUBPŒNAS, ETC., FOR EXAMINATION OF WITNESSES.

No. 114.

Subpœna ad Testificandum (General Form).

In the High Court of Justice,
——Division.

     Between   Plaintiff,
             and
              Defendant.

Victoria, by the Grace of God of the United Kingdom of Great Britain
and Ireland, Queen, Defender of the Faith, to   greeting : We command you to attend before   at   on   day the   day
of   18 ,   at the hour of   in the   noon, and so from
day to day, until the above cause is tried, to give evidence on behalf of
the (plaintiff *or* Defendant.)

Witness, the Honourable   President, etc., the
day of   188 .

No. 115.

Subpœna Duces Tecum (General Form).

[Title, etc.]

Victoria, by the Grace of God of the United Kingdom of Great Britain and Ireland, Queen, Defender of the Faith, to   greeting : We command you to attend before   at   on   day the day of   18 , at the hour of   in the   noon, and so from day to day, until the above cause is tried, to give evidence on behalf of the   and also to bring with you and produce at the time and place aforesaid *(specify documents to be produced.)*

Witness, the Honourable   President, etc., the day of   188 .

No. 116.

Subpœna ad Testificandum at Assizes.

[Title, etc.]

Victoria, by the Grace of God of the United Kingdom of Great Britain and Ireland, Queen, Defender of the Faith, to   greeting : We command you to attend before our Justices assigned to take the assizes in and for the county of   to be holden at   on   day the   day of   18 , at the hour of   in the   noon, and so from day to day during the said assizes until the above cause is tried, to give evidence on behalf of the

Witness, the Honourable   President, etc., the day of   188 .

No. 117.

Suphœna Duces Tecum at Assizes.

[Title, etc.]

Victoria, by the Grace of God of the United Kingdom of Great Britain and Ireland, Queen, Defender of the Faith, to   greeting : We command you to attend before our Justices assigned to take the assizes in and for the county of   to be holden at   on   day the   . day of   18 , at the hour of   in the   noon, and so from day to day during the said assizes, until the above cause is tried, to give evidence on behalf of the   , and also to bring with you and produce at the time and place aforesaid *(specify documents to be produced.)*

Witness, the Honourable   President, etc., the day of

No. 118.

Commission to Examine Witnesses.

[Title, etc.]

Victoria, by the Grace of God of the United Kingdom of Great Britain and Ireland, Queen, Defender of the Faith, to   of commissioner named by and on behalf of the   and to of   a commissioner named by and on behalf of the greeting : Know ye that we in confidence of your prudence and fidelity

15

have appointed you and by these presents give you power and authority to examine on interrogatories and *viva voce* as hereinafter mentioned witnesses on behalf of the said   and   respectively at   before you or either of you.—And we command you as follows :

1. Both the said   and the said   shall be at liberty to examine on interrogatories, and *viva voce* on the subject matter thereof or arising out of the answers thereto, such witnesses as shall be produced on their behalf with liberty to the other party to cross-examine the said witnesses on cross interrogatories and *viva voce* on the subject matters thereof or arising out of the answers thereto, the party producing any witness for examination being at liberty to re-examine him *viva voce;* and all such additional *viva voce* questions whether on examination, cross examination, or re-examination, shall be reduced into writing, and with the answers thereto shall be returned with the said commission.

2. Not less than forty-eight hours before the examination of any witness on behalf of either of the said parties, notice in writing, signed by one of you, the commissioner of the party on whose behalf the witness is to be examined, and stating the time and place of the intended examination and the names of the witnesses to be examined, shall be given to the other party by delivering the notice to [*name and address of the person named in the order for this purpose*] (or to a grown up person there) and shall be given also to the commissioner of the other party at the address aforesaid of such commissioner or to a grown up person for him at the said last mentioned address, and if the commissioner of that party neglect to attend pursuant to the notice, then you, the commissioner of the party on whose behalf the notice is given, shall be at liberty to proceed with and take the examination of the witness or witnesses *ex parte*, and adjourn any meeting or meetings, or continue the same from day to day until all the witnesses intended to be examined by virtue of the notice have been examined, without giving any further or other notice of the subsequent meeting or meetings.

3. In the event of any witness on his examination, cross-examination, or re-examination producing any book, document, letter, paper, or writing, and refusing for good cause to be stated in his deposition to part with the original thereof, then a copy thereof, or extract therefrom, certified by the commissioners or commissioner present and acting to be a true and correct copy or extract shall be annexed to the witnesses' deposition.

4. Each witness to be examined under this commission shall be examined on oath, affirmation, or otherwise in accordance with his religion by or before the commissioners or commissioner present at the examination.

5. If any one or more of the witnesses do not understand the English language (the interrogatories, cross-interrogatories, and *viva voce* questions, if any, being previously translated into the language with which he or they is or are conversant), then the examination shall be taken in English through the medium of an interpreter or interpreters to be nominated by the commissioners or commissioner present at the examination, and to be previously sworn according to his or their several religions, by or before the said commissioners or commissioner truly to interpret the questions to be put to the witness and his answers thereto.

6. The depositions to be taken under this commission shall be subscribed by the witness or witnesses, and by the commissioners or commissioner who shall have taken the depositions.

7. The interrogatories, cross-interrogatories, and depositions, together with any documents referred to therein, or certified copies thereof or extracts therefrom, shall be sent to the   of the Supreme Court of Judicature on or before the   day of   inclosed in a cover under the seals or seal of the commissioners or commissioner.

8. Before you or any of you, in any manner act in the execution hereof you shall severally take the oath hereon indorsed on the Holy Evangelists

or otherwise in such other manner as is sanctioned by the form of your several religions and is considered by you respectively to be binding on your respective conscience s.

And we give you or any one of you authority to administer such oath to the other or others of you.

Witness, the Honourable   President, etc., the   day of in the year of our Lord one thousand eight hundred and

This writ was issued by
of
agent for
of
solicitor for the
who reside   at

Commissioners' Oath.

You shall, according to the best of your skill and knowledge, truly and faithfully, and without partiality to any or either of the parties in this cause take the examinations and depositions of all and every witness and witnesses produced and examined by virtue of the commission within written.   So help you God.

Clerk's Oath.

You shall truly, faithfully, and without partiality to any or either of the parties in this cause, take, write down, transcribe, and engross all and every the questions which shall be exhibited or put to all and every witness and witnesses, and also the depositions of all and every such witness and witnesses produced before and examined by the said commissioners named in the commission within written, as far forth as you are directed and employed by the commission to take, write down, transcribe or engross the said questions and depositions.

So help you God.

Witnesses' Oath.

You are true answer to make to all such questions as shall be asked you, without favour or affection to either party, and therein you shall speak the truth, the whole truth, and nothing but the truth.   So help you God.

Interpreter's Oath.

You shall truly and faithfully, and without partiality to any or either of the parties in this cause, and to the best of your ability, interpret and translate the oath or oaths, affirmation or affirmations which shall be administered to, and all and every the questions which shall be exhibited or put to all and every witness and witnesses produced before and examined by the commissioners named in the commission within written, as far forth as you are directed and employed by the said commissioners, to interpret and translate the same out of the English into the language of such witness or witnesses, and also in like manner to interpret and translate the respective deposit ons taken and made to such questions out of the language of such witness or witnesses into the English language.   So help you God.

Direction of interogatories, etc., when returned by the commissioners.

The   of the Supreme Court of Judicature,
                    Osgoode Hall,
                    Toronto.

No. 119.

Habeas Corpus ad Testificandum.

[Title, etc.]

Victoria, by the Grace of God, of the United Kingdom of Great Britain and Ireland Queen, Defender of the Faith, to the [keeper of our prison at] We command you that you bring   , who it is said is detained in our prison under your custody   , before   at   on day the   day of   at the hour of   in the noon, and so from day to day until the above action is tried, to give evidence on behalf of the   . And that immediately after the said   shall have so given his evidence you safely conduct him to the prison from which he shall have been brought.

Witness, the Honourable   President, etc., the   day of

This writ was issued by
solicitor for the   who reside   at

PART IX.

ORDERS.

No. 120.

Order (General Form).

In the High Court of Justice,
———Division.
[*Name of the Judge or Master*] in Chambers.

Between   Plaintiff,
                          and
                          Defendant.

Upon hearing   , and upon reading the affidavit of   filed the   day of   18   , and
It is ordered   and that the costs of this application be
Dated the   day of   18   .

No. 121.

Order for Service out of Jurisdiction.

In the High Court of Justice,
———Division.
[*Name of the Judge or Master*] in Chambers.

Between   Plaintiff,
                          and
                          Defendant.

Upon hearing   , and upon reading the affidavit of   filed the   day of   18   , and
It is ordered that the plaintiff   be at liberty to issue a writ for service out of the jurisdiction against
And it is further ordered that the time for appearance to the said writ be within   days after the service thereof, and that the costs of this application be
Dated the   day of   18

No. **122.**

Order for Substituted Service.

In the High Court of Justice,
——Division.

[*Name of the Judge or Master*] in Chambers.

Between   Plaintiff,
           and
            Defendant.

Upon hearing   , and upon reading the affidavit of   filed the   day of   18 , and
It is ordered that service of a copy of this order, and of a copy of the writ of summons in this action, by sending the same by a prepaid and registered post letter, addressed to the defendant   at   , shall be good and sufficient service of the writ.

Dated the   day of   18 .

———

No. **123.**

Order allowing Service made out of the Jurisdiction.

In the High Court of Justice,
——Division.

[*Name of the Judge or Master*] in Chambers.

Between   Plaintiff,
           and
            Defendant.

Upon hearing   , and upon reading the affidavit of   filed the   day of   18 , and
It is ordered that the service of the writ (*or* notice of the writ) made upon the defendant as shewn by the said affidavit, be allowed as good and sufficient service.

Dated the   day of   18 .

———

No. **124.**

Order for Renewal of Writ of Summons.

In the High Court of Justice,
——Division.

[*Name of the Judge or Master*] in Chambers.

Between   Plaintiff,
           and
            Defendant.

Upon hearing   , and upon reading the affidavit of   filed the   day of   18 , and
It is ordered that the writ in this action be renewed for twelve months from the date of its renewal, pursuant to the Rules of the Supreme Court.

Dated the   day of   18

No. 125.

Order for Time

In tho High Court of Justice,
——Division.

[*Name of the Judge or Master*] in Chambers.

Between   Plaintiff,
         and
                Defendant.

Upon hearing   , and upon reading the affidavit of   filed
the   day of   18   , and
It is ordered that the   shall have   time for, etc.   and that
the costs of this application be

Dated the   day of   18

No. 126.

Order under Rule 739, &c., (final judgment).

In the High Court of Justice,
——Division.

[*Name of the Judge or Master*] in Chambers.

Between   Plaintiff,
         and
                Defendant.

Upon hearing   , and upon reading the affidavit of   filed
the   day of   18   , and
It is ordered that the plaintiff may sign final judgment in this action for
the amount indorsed on the writ, with interest, if any, and costs to be
taxed, and that the costs of this application be

Dated the   day of   18

No. 127.

Order under Rule 739, &c., (leave to defend unconditionally).

In the High Court of Justice,
——Division.

[*Name of the Judge or Master*] in Chambers.

Between   Plaintiff,
         and
                Defendant.

Upon hearing   , and upon reading the affidavit of   filed
the   day of   18   , and
It is ordered that the defendant be at liberty to defend this action by
delivering a statement of defence within   days after delivery of
the plaintiff's statement of claim, and that the costs of this application be

Dated the   day of   18   .

No. 128.

Order under Rule 739, &c., (leave to defend on payment into Court).

In the High Court of Justice,
——Division.

[*Name of the Judge or Master*] in Chambers.

Between   Plaintiff,

and

Defendant.

Upon hearing   , and upon reading the affidavit of   filed the   day of   18   , and

It is ordered that if the defendant   pay into Court within a week from the date of this order the sum of $, he be at liberty to defend this action by delivering a statement of defence within   days after delivery of the plaintiff's statement of claim, but that if that sum be not so paid the plaintiff be at liberty to sign final judgment for the amount indorsed on the writ of summons, with interest, if any, and costs, and that in either event the costs of this application be

Dated the   day of   18   .

———

No. 129.

Order under Rule 738, &c., (leave to defend as to part on payment into Court, and as to residue unconditionally).

In the High Court of Justice,
——Division.

[*Name of the Judge or Master*] in Chambers.

Between   Plaintiff,

and

Defendant.

Upon hearing   , and upon reading the affidavit of   filed the   day of   18   , and

It is ordered that if the defendant pay into Court within a week from the date of this order the sum of $, he be at liberty to defend this action as to the whole of the plaintiffs claim.

And it is ordered that if that sum be not so paid the plaintiff be at liberty to sign judgment for that sum and the defendant be at liberty to defend this action as to the residue of the plaintiff's claim.

And it is ordered that in either event the statement of defence be delivered within   days after delivery of the plaintiff's statement of claim, and that the costs of this application be

Dated the   day of   18   .

———

No. 130.

Order to Amend.

In the High Court of Justice,
——Division.

[*Name of the Judge or Master*] in Chambers.

Between   Plaintiff,

and

Defendant.

Upon hearing   , and upon reading the affidavit of   filed the   day of   18   , and

It is ordered that the plaintiff be at liberty to amend the writ of summons in this action by   , and that the costs of this application be

Dated the   day of   18   .

No. 131.

Order for names of Partners.

In the High Court of Justice,
——Division.

[*Name of the Judge or Master*] in Chambers.

Between   Plaintiff,
              and
                          Defendant.

Upon hearing   , and upon reading the affidavit of   filed
the   day of   18   , and   .
It is ordered that the   ˙   furn'sh the   with a statement in
writing, verified by affidavit, setting forth the names of the persons
constituting the members or co-partners of their firm, pursuant to
Rule 317 of the Supreme Court, and that the costs of th s application be
              Dated the   day of   18   .

No. 132.

Order for Particulars (General.)

In the High Court of Justice,
——Division.

[*Name of the Judge or Master,*] in Chambers.

Between   Plaintiff,
              and
                          Defendant.

Upon hearing   , and upon reading the affidavit of   filed
the   day of   18   , and   .
It is ordered that the plaintiff deliver to the defendant   an account
in writing of the particulars of the plaintiff's claim in this action,
and that unless s ch particula s be delivered within   days from the
date of this order all further proceedings be stayed until the delivery
thereof, and that the costs of this application be   .
              Dated the   day of   18   .

No. 133.

Order for Particulars (Accident Case).

In the High Court of Justice,
——Division.

[*Name of the Judge or Master,*] in Chambers.

Between   Plaintiff,
              and
                          Defendant.

Upon hearing   , and upon reading the affidavit of   filed
the   day of   18   .
It is ordered that the plaintiff deliver to the defendant an account in
writing of the particu'ars of the injuries and expenses mentioned in the
statement of claim, together with the time and place of the accident,
and the particular acts of negligence complained of, and that unless
such particulars be delivered within   days from the date of this
order all further proceedings in this action be stayed until the delivery
thereof, and that the costs of this application be
              Dated the   day of   18   .

No. 134.

Order to Discharge or Vary Order on Application by Third Party.

In the High Court of Justice,
——Division.

[*Name of the Judge or Master,*] in Chambers.

Between   Plaintiff,
                and
                    Defendant.

Upon hearing   *   , and upon reading the affidavit of   filed
the   day of   18   , and   .
It is ordered that the order of   in this action dated the
day of   18   be discharged [*or* varied by   ], and that the
costs of this application be

Dated the   day of   18

No. 135.

Order to Dismiss for want of Prosecution.

In the High Court of Justice,
——Division.

[*Name of the Judge or Master,*] in Chambers.

Between   Plaintiff,
                and
                    Defendant

Upon hearing   , and upon reading the affidavit of   filed
the   day of   18   , and   .
It is ordered that this action be, for want of prosecution, dismissed
with costs, to be taxed and paid to the defendant by the plaintiff, and
that the costs of this application be (*costs in the cause*)

Dated the   day of   18   .

No. 136.

Order for Production.   Rule 508

In the High Court of Justice,
——Division.

[*Name of the Judge or Master,*] in Chambers.

Between   Plaintiff,
                and
                    Defendant.

Upon hearing
It is ordered that the   do, within ten days after the service of
this order, make discovery on oath of the documents which are or have
been in   possession or power relating to any matters in question
in this action and that the costs of this application be

Dated the   day of   18   .

APPENDIX.

No. 137.

Order to Produce Documents for Inspection.

In the High Court of Justice.
———Division.

[*Name of the Judge or Master*] in Chambers.

Between   Plaintiff,

and

Defendant.

Upon hearing   , and upon reading the affidavit of   filed the   day of   18 , and .
It is ordered that the   do, at all seasonable times, on reasonable notice, produce at the office of   , solicitor, situate at   the following documents, namely   and that the   be at liberty to inspect and peruse the documents so produced and to take copies and abstracts th reof and extracts therefrom, at   expense, and that in the meantime all further proceedings be stayed, and that the costs of this application be
Dated the   day of   18

No. 138.

Order for Commission to Examine Witnesses.

In the High Court of Justice.
———Division.

· [*Name of the Judge or Master,*] in Chambers.

Between   Plaintiff,

and

Defendant.

Upon hearing   and upon reading the affidavit of   filed the day of   18 , and
It is ordered as follows :

1. A commission may issue directed to   of   a commissioner named by and on behalf of the   and to   of   a commissioner named by and on behalf of the   for the examination upon interrogatories and *viva voce* of witnesses on behalf of the said   and respectively at   aforesaid before the said commissioners.

2.   days previously to the sending out of the said commission, the solicitor of the said   shall give to the solicitor of the said notice in writing of the mail or other conveyance by which the commission is to be sent out.

3. The costs of this order, and of the commission to be issued in pursuance hereof, and of the interrogatories, cross-interrogatories, and depositions to be taken thereunder, together with any document, copy, or extract and the official copies thereof, and all other costs incidental thereto, shall be
Dated the   day of   18

No. 139.

Order of Reference under S. 101 of the Judicature Act.

In the High Court of Justice.
———Division.

[*Name of the Judge*] in Chambers.

Between   -   Plaintff,

and

Defendant.

Upon hearing , and upon reading the affidavit of filed the
day of 18 , and
It is ordered that the following question arising in this action namely,
. be referred for inquiry and report to under section 101 of the
Judicature Act, and that the costs of this application be

Dated the day of 18 .

No. 140.

Order of Reference under S. 102 of the Judicature Act.

In the High Court of Justice.
——Division.

[*Name of the Judge*] in Chambers.

Between Plaintiff,
and
Defendant.

Upon hearing and upon reading the affidavit of filed
the day of 18 , and
It is ordered that the [*state whether all or some and, if so, which of the
questions are to be tried*] in this action be tried by
‡‡And it is ordered that the costs of this application be

Dated the day of 18 .

No. 141.

Order for Examination of Witnesses before Trial.

In the High Court of Justice.
——Division.

[*Name of the Judge or Master,*] in Chambers.

Between Plaintiff,
and
Defendant.

Upon hearing and upon reading the affidavit of filed
the day of 18 , and
It is ordered that a witness on behalf of the be examined
vivâ voce (on oath or affirmation) before
[*or before* esquire, special examiner], the
solicitor or agent giving to the solicitor or agent notice in
writing of the time and place where the examination is to take place.

And it is further ordered that the examination so taken be filed in the
office of , and that an office copy or copies thereof may be
read and given in evidence on the trial of this cause, saving all just exceptions, without any further proof of the absence of the said witness than
the affidavit of the solicitor or agent of the as to his belief, and
that the costs of this application be

Dated the day of 18 .

No. 142.

Garnishee Order (Attaching Debts).

In the High Court of Justice,
——Division.

[*Name of the Judge or Master*] in Chambers.

Between Judgment Creditor,
and
Judgment Debtor.
Garnishee.

claims or demands

Upon hearing   , and upon reading the affidavit of   filed
the   day of   18   and
    It is ordered that all debts owing or accruing due from the above-
named garnishee to the above-named judgment debtor be attached to
answer a judgment recovered against the said judgment debtor by the
above-named judgment creditor in the High Court of Justice on the
    day of   18   , for the sum of $, on which judgment
the said sum of $, remains due and unpaid.
    And it is further ordered that the said garnishee attend the
in Chambers (*or as the case may be*). on   day the   day of
          18   , at   o'clock in the   noon, on an applica-
tion by the said judgment creditor, that the said garnishee pay the debt,
Claim or demand due from him to the said judgment debtor, or so much thereof as may
    , be sufficient to satisfy the judgment.
    And that the costs of this application be
          Dated the   day of   18   .

No. 143.

Garnishee Order (Absolute).

In the High Court of Justice,
——Division.

[*Name of the Judge or Master*] in Chambers.

      Between   Judgment Creditor,
                              and
                                     Judgment Debtor.
                                     Garnishee.

    Upon hearing   , and upon reading the affidavit of   filed
the   day of   18   , and   .   whereby it was ordered
that all debts owing or accruing due from the above-named garnishee to
the above-named judgment debtor should be attached to answer a judgment recovered against the said judgment debtor by the above-named
judgment creditor in the High Court of Justice on the   day of
          18   , for the sum of $, on which judgment the said
sum of $ remained due and unpaid.
    It is ordered that the said garnishee do forthwith pay the said judg-
ment creditor the debt due from him to the said judgment debtor (*or so
much thereof as may be sufficient to satisfy the judgment debt*), and that
in default thereof execution may issue for the same, and that the costs
of this application be
          Dated the   day of   18

No. 144.

Order on Application to tax Solicitor's Bill of Costs.

In the High Court of Justice,
——Division.

[*Name of the Judge or Master*] in Chambers.

      In the matter of   .

                                     Gentleman,
              One of the Solicitors of the Supreme Court.
    Upon application of
    It is ordered that the above-named solicitor do deliver to the applicant a
bill of his fees, charges and disbursements and that the same when so delivered be [*or the bill of fees charges and disbursements delivered to the
applicant by the above-named solicitor (or by the above solicitor to
          as the case may be*) be] referred to the   to be taxed.
    And it is ordered that the costs of this application be
          Dated the   day of   18   .

No. 145.

Order to try Action in County Court.

In the High Court of Justice,
———Division.

[*Name of the Judge or Master*] in Chambers.

Between   Plaintiff,
          and
                  Defendant.

Upon hearing   , and upon reading the affidavit of   filed
the   day of   18 , and .
It is ordered that this action be tried before the County Court of
, and that the costs of this application be
      Dated the   day of   18 .

No. 146.

Interpleader Order, No. 1.

the High Court of Justice.
———Division.

Name of the Judge or Master,] in Chambers.

Between   Plaintiff,
          and
                  Defendant,
      and between
                  Claimant,
          and
                  Respondent.

Upon hearing   , and upon reading the affidavit of   filed
the   day of   18 , and .
It is ordered that the claimant be barred, that no action be brought
against the above-named [sheriff]   , and that the costs of this
application be
      Dated the   day of   18

No. 147.

Interpleader Order, No. 2.

In the High Court of Justice.
———Division.

[*Name of the Judge or Master,*] in Chambers.

Between   Plaintiff,
          and
                  Defendant,
          and
                  Claimant.

Upon hearing   , and upon reading the affidavit of   filed
the   day of   18 , and
It is ordered that the above-named claimant be substituted as defendant
in this action in lieu of the present defendant, and that the costs of this
application be
      Dated the   day of   18 .

No. 148.

In'erpleader Order, No. 3.

In the High Court of Justice.
——Division.

[*Name of the Judge or Master,*] in Chambers.

Between   Plaintiff,
                    and
                                           Defendant,
              and between
                                           Claimant,
and the said   execution creditor and
the sheriff of   Repondents.

Upon hearing   , and upon reading the affidavit of   filed
the   day of   18   , and

It is ordered that the said sheriff proceed to sell the goods seized by
him under the writ of fieri facias issued herein, and pay the net proceeds
of the sale, after deducting the expenses thereof, (*or as otherwise ordered*)
into Court in this cause, to abide further order herein.

And it is further ordered that the parties proceed to the trial of an
issue in the High Court of Justice, in which the said claimant (*or execution debtor*) shall be the plaintiff and the said execution creditor (*or
the claimant*) shall be the defendant, and that the question to be tried
shall be whether at the time [*insert here* delivery of the writ to the
sheriff *or* seizure by the sheriff *or* sale by the sheriff *as the case may require*]
the goods seized were the property of the claimant as against the execution creditor.

And it is further ordered that this issue be prepared and delivered by
the plaintiff therein within   from this date, and be returned by the
defendant therein within   days, and be tried at

And it is further ordered that the question of costs and all further
questions be reserved until after the trial of the said issue, and that no
action shall be brought against the said sheriff for the seizure of the said
goods.

Dated the   day of   18

———

No. 149.

Interpleader Order, No. 4.

In the High Court of Justice.
——Division.

[*Name of the Judge or Master,*] in Chambers.

Between   Plaintiff,
                    and
                                           Defendant,
              and between
                                           Claimant,
and the said   execution creditor and
the sheriff of   Respondents.

Upon hearing   , and upon reading the affidavit of   filed the
        day of   18   , and

It is ordered that upon payment of the sum of $ into Court by
the said claimant with n   from this date, or upon his giving within
the same time security to the satisfaction of
                    for the payment of the same amount by the said claimant
according to the directions of any order to be made herein, and upon
payment to the above named sheriff of the possession money from this
date, the said sheriff do withdraw from the possession of the goods seized
by him under the writ of fieri facias herein.

And it is further ordered that unless such payment be made or security given within the time aforesaid the said sheriff proceed to sell the said goods, and pay the proceeds of the sa e, after deducting the expenses thereof (*or as otherwise ordered*) and the possession money from this date, into Court in the cause, to abide further order herein.

And it is further ordered that the parties proceed to the trial of an issue in the High Court of Justice, in which the claimant (*or execution creditor*) shall be plaintiff and the execution creditor (*or claimant*) shall be defendant, and that the ques ion to be tried shall be whether at the time of [*insert here* the delivery of the writ to the sheriff *or the* seizure by the sheriff *or the* sale by the sheriff *as the case may require*] the goods seized were the property of the claimant as against the execution creditor.

And it is further ordered that this issue be prepared and delivered by the plaintiff therein within   from this date, and be returned by the defendant therein within   days, and be tried at

And it is further ordered that the question of costs and all further questions be reserved until after the trial of the said issue, and that no action shall be brought against the sheriff for the seizure of the said goods.

Dated the   day of   18   .

No 150.

Interpleader Order, No. 5.

In the High Court of Justice.
————Division.

[*Name of the Judge or Master,*] in Chambers.

Between   Plaintiff,
                         and
                                           Defendant,
                         and between
                                           Claimant,
and the said   execution creditor, and
the sheriff of
                                           Respondents.

Upon hearing   and upon reading the affidavit of   filed the day of   18   , and

It is ordered that upon payment of the sum of $ into Court by the said claimant, or upon his giving security to the satisfaction of   for the payment of the same amount by the claimant according to the directions of any order to be made herein, the above-named sheriff withdraw from th possession of the goods seized by him under the writ of fieri facias issued herein.

And it is further ordered that in the meantime, and until such payment made or security given, the sheriff continue in the possession of the goods, and the claimant pay possession money for the time he so continues, unless the claimant desires the goods to be sold by the sheriff, in which case the sheriff is to sell them and pay the proceeds of the sale, after deducting the expenses thereof (*or as otherwise ordered*) and the possession money from this date, into Court in the cause, to abide further order herein.

And it is further ordered that the parties proceed to the trial of an issue in the High Court of Justice, in which the claimant (*or execution creditor*) shall be plaintiff and the execution creditor (*or claimant*) shall be defendant, and that the question to be tried shall be whether at the time of [*insert here* the delivery of the said writ to the sheriff *or the* seizure by the sheriff *or the* sale by the sheriff *as the case may require*] the goods seized were the property of the claimant as against the execution creditor.

And it is further ordered that this issue be prepared and delivered by the plaintiff therein within   from this date, and be returned by the defendant therein within   days, and be tried at   .

And it is further ordered that the question of costs and all further questions be reserved until after the trial of the said issue, and that no action shall be brought against the sheriff for the seizure of the said goods.

Dated the   day of   18   .

No. 151.

Interpleader Order, No. 6.

In the High Court of Justice.
———Division.

[*Name of the Judge or Master,*] in Chambers.
      Between   Plaintiff,
             and
                       Defendant,
         and between
                       Claimant,
and the said   execution creditor and
the sheriff of   ●   ·Respondents.

The claimant and the execution creditor having requested and consented that the merits of the claim made by the claimant be disposed of and determined in a summary manner, now upon hearing   and upon reading the affidavit of   filed the   day of   18   , and
It is ordered that
And that the costs of this application be
                   Dated the   day of   18

No. 152.

Interpleader Order, No. 7.

In the High Court of Justice.
———Division.

[*Name of the Judge or Master,*] in Chambers.
      Between   ı   Plaintiff,
             and
                       Defendant,
         and between
                       Claimant,
and the said   execution creditor, and
the sheriff of   Respondents.

Upon hearing   , and upon reading the affidavit of   filed the   day of   18   , and
It is ordered that the above-named sheriff proceed to sell enough of the goods seized under the writ of fieri facias issued in this action to satisfy the expenses of the said sale, the rent (if any) due, the claim of the claimant, and this execution.
And it is further ordered that out of the proceeds of the said sale, (after deducting the expenses thereof, and rent, if any,) the said sheriff pay to the claimant the amount of his said claim, and to the execution creditor the amount of his execution, and the residue, if any, to the defendant.
And it is further ordered that no action be brought against the said sheriff, and that the costs of this application be
               Dated the   day of   18   .

No. 153.

Order of Replevin.

In the High Court of Justice.
———Division.

(*Name of Judge or Master*) in Chambers.
Date.
            Between *A. B.*, plaintiff,
                and
            C. D., defendant.

Upon the application of the above-named plaintiff, and upon reading the affidavit of   filed, and upon hearing

It is ordered that the Sheriff of (*here insert the name of County, United Counties, District or City*), do without delay take the security required by law and cause to be replevied to the plaintiff, his goods, chattes and personal property following, that is to say : (*here set out description of property as in the affidavit filed*), which the said plaintiff alleges to be of the value of $, and to have been taken and unjustly detained (*or unjustly detained, as the case may be*) by the defendant, C. D., in order that the said plaintiff may have his remedy in that behalf.

And it is further ordered that the said Sheriff do forthwith, after the execution of this order, make return to (*insert here the officer in whose office the appearance in the action is to be entered*) what we shall have done in the premises, and do also return this order.

No. 154.

Order of Withernam.

In the High Court of Justice.
——Division.

Between *A. B.*, plaintiff,
and
C. D., defendant.

Upon the application of the plaintiff, and it appearing by the return of the Sheriff of the   of   , to the order of replevin made herein on the   day of   , that the goods, chattels and personal property mentioned in the said order have been eloigned by the defendant, C. D., out of the bailiwick of the Sheriff of   , to places to him unknown so that he could not replevy the same to the said plaintiff.

It is ordered that the said Sheriff do forthwith take in withernam the goods, chattels and personal property of the said defendant, C. D., and his bailiwick, to the value of the goods, chattels and personal prop rty by the said defendant, C. D., before taken, and do forthwith deliver th m to the said plaintiff to be kept by him until the said def ndant, C. D., delivers the goods, chattels and personal property last aforesaid to the said plaintiff.

And it is further ordered that if the said plaintiff shall give security to the said Sheriff as provided by law for the pro ecution of the plaintiff's claims and for the return of the goods, chattels and property so to be taken in withernam as aforesaid, if the return thereof shall be adjudged then the said Sheriff do take security with two sufficient sureties from the said defendant, C. D., to answer to the said plaintiff for the taking and unjustly detaining of his goods, chattels and personal property aforesaid.

And it is further ordered that the said Sheriff do forthwith make return to (*insert here the officer in whose office the appearance in the action is to be entered*), what he shall have done in the premises, and do also return this order.

Dated

No. 155.

Order for Arrest.

In the High Court of Justice,
——Division.

(*Name of the Judge*) in Chambers.

Between   , plaintiff,
and
defendant.

Upon hearing   and upon reading the affidavit
of   filed

16

It is ordered that the Sheriff of the County (*or* United Counties *or* City) of   do forthwith arrest and take, *or* if already in custody, do detain C. D. the defendant (*or* one of the defenda ts) if he shall be found in the said County (*or* United Counties) and him safely keep until he shall have given bail in this action to the amount of $ or shall by other la vful means be discharged from custody.

And it is further ordered that a copy of this order be served by the said Sheriff on the said C. D.

And it is further ordered that the said C. D. do within ten days after his arrest under this order, cause special bail to be put in for him in this Court and in this action, and the bail piece filed in the office of (naming the office where appearance is required to be entered) conditioned that if the defendant be condemned in this action at the suit of the plaintiff, he will satisfy the costs and condemnation money or in default for his surrender to the Sheriff of the County (*or* United Counties *or* City) of (naming the County *or* United Counties *or* City having a Sheriff in which the office where the appearance is required to be entered, is situate).

Dated

No. 156.
Order of Certiorari to County Court.

In the High Court of Justice,
——Division.

(*Name of Judge*) in Chambers.

[Title, etc.]

Upon hearing   , and upon reading the affidavit of   .
It is ordered that the Judge of the County Court of the County of   do forthwith send to the Registrar of the   Division of the High Court of Justice at Toronto, the proceedings and papers in a certain action in the said County Court between   plaintiff, and defendant, with all things touching the same, together with this order, that this Court may further cause to be done thereupon what it shall see fit to be done, and no further proceedings are to be taken in said County Court in said action until further order of this Court or a Judge.

No. 157.
Order of Certiorari (General).

In the High Court of Justice,
·——Division.

(*Name of Judge*) in Chambers.

[Title, etc.]

Upon hearing   .   , and upon reading the affidavit of   .
It is ordered that   do send to the Registrar of the   Division of the High Court of Justice at Toronto, forthwith (*or* on the   day of   ) the   , with all things touching the same, as fully and entirely as they remain in   together with this order, that this Court may further cause to be done thereupon what it shall see fit to be done.

No. 158.

Prohibition.

[Title, etc.]

It appearing that the said   has [entered an action against] *C. D.* in the said Court, and that the said Court has no jurisdiction in the said [cause] or to hear and determine the said [action] by reason that [*state facts shewing want of jurisdiction*].

It is ordered that the said be   and he is hereby prohibited from further proceeding in the said [action] in the said Court.

No. 159.

Order dismissing Motion (Generally).

In the High Court of Justice.
———Division.

[*Name of the Judge or Master,*] in Chambers.

Between   Plaintiff,

and

Defendant.

Upon hearing   , and upon reading the affidavit of   filed the   day of   18   , and

It is ordered that the application of   be dismissed, (*if the dismissal is with costs add*), with costs to be taxed and paid by the to the

Dated the   day of   18   .

PART X.

FORMS OF JUDGMENTS.

No. 160.

Default of Appearance or Defence in case of Liquidated Demand.

In the High Court of Justice,
—— Division.

Between *A. B.*, Plaintiff,
and
C. D. and *E. F.*, Defendants.

The   day of   18   .

The defendants [*or* the defendant *C. D.*] not having appeared herein [*or* not having delivered any statement of defence], it is this day adjudged that the plaintiff recover against the said defendant $, and costs to be taxed.

No. 161.

Judgment in Default of Appearance or Defence where the Demand is Liquidated (Fixed Costs).

[Title, etc.]

The   day of   , 18   .

The defendant   not having (appeared to the writ of summons *or* delivered any statement of defence or demurrer) it is this day adjudged that the plaintiff recover against the said defendant $ and $ costs.

No. 162.

Judgment in Default of Appearance in action for Recovery of Land.

[Title, etc.]

The   day of   , 18   .

No appearance having been entered to the writ of summons herein, it is this day adjudged that the plaintiff recover possession of the land in the said writ mentioned.

No. 163.

Judgment in Default of Defence in action for Recovery of Land.

[Title, etc.]

The   day of   , 18   .

No statement of defence having been delivered herein, it is this day adjudged that the plaintiff recover possession of the land in the statement herein mentioned and described as

No. 164.

Judgment upon Confession by Defendant of action for recovery of Land.

[Title, etc.]

The   day of   , 18 .

The defendant C. D. having confessed this action *(or having confessed this action as to part of the said land, that is to say : state the part)* it is this day adjudged that the said plaintiff do recover possession of the land in the writ *(or statement of claim)* mentioned *(or of the said part of the said land)* with the appurtenances and costs to be taxed.

No. 165.

Judgment in Default of Defence in action for Recovery of Land with Damages.

[Title, etc.]

See Rule 725

The   day of   , 18 .

The defendant not having delivered any statement of defence, it is this day adjudged that the plaintiffs recover possession of the land in the statement of claim herein mentioned, and described as   , in the County of   , and costs to be taxed, and it is further adjudged that the plaintiffs recover against the defendant damages to be assessed.

Certificate for $, taxed costs, dated the   day of   , 18

No. 166.

Interlocutory Judgment in Default of Appearance or Defence where Demand Unliquidated.

[Title, etc.]

The   day of   , 18 .

No appearance having been entered to the writ of summons *(or no statement of defence or demurrer having been delivered by the defendant)* herein ;

It is this day adjudged that the plaintiff recover against the defendant the value of the goods *or damages, or both, as the case may be,* to be assessed.

No. 167.

Judgment after Appearance and Order under Rule 739.

[Title, etc.]

The   day of   , 18 .

The defendant having appeared to the writ of summons herein, and the plaintiff having by the order of   , dated   day of 18   , obtained leave to sign judgment under the Rule of the Supreme Court, No. 739, for *(recite order)*, it is this day adjudged that the plaintiff recover against the defendant $ and costs to be taxed.

The above costs have been taxed and allowed at $, as appears by a Taxing Officer's Certificate dated the   day of   18 .

No. 168.

udgment in Default of Appearance or Defence, after Assessment of Damages.

[Title, etc.]

The   day of   , 18   .

No appearance having been entered to the writ of summons [*or* no statement of defence or demurrer having been delivered by the defendant] herein, and the damages which the plaintiff was entitled to recover having been assessed at $, as by   dated the
        18   , appears, it is adjudged that the plaintiff recover $
and costs to be taxed.

No. 169.

Judgment after Trial by Court without Jury.
(No. 1.)

[Title, etc.]

The   day of   18   ..

This action having on the   day of   18   , been tried before
        and the said   on the   day of   18   , having ordered
that judgment be entered for the   for $
        It is this day adjudged that the   recover from the $
and costs to be taxed.

The above costs have been taxed and allowed at $, as appears by
a taxing officer's Certificate dated the   day of   18   .

No. 170.

Judgment at Trial by Judge without a Jury.
(No. 2.)

[Title, etc.]

The   day of   , 18   .

This action coming on for trial [the   day of   and]
this day, before   in the presence of counsel for the plaintiff and the defendants [*or, if some of the defendants do not appear*, for
the plaintiff and the defendant *C. D.*, no one appearing for the defendants *E. F.* and *G. H.*, although they were duly served with notice of trial
as by the affidavit of   filed the   day of   appears,]
upon hearing read the pleadings and what was alleged by counsel on both
sides, this Court doth declare, etc.

And this Court doth order and adjudge, etc.

No. 171.

Judgment after Trial by a Jury.
[Title, etc.]

The   day of   , 18   .

This action having on the 12th and 13th November, 18   , being tried
before the Honourable Mr. Justice   and a special jury of the

county of   , and the jury having found [*state findings as in Judge's or officer's certificate*], and the said Mr. Justice   having ordered that judgment be entered for the plaintiff for $ and costs of suit [*or as the case may be*]: Therefore it is adjudged that the plaintiff recover against the defendant $ and $ for his costs of suit [*or that the plaintiff recover nothing against the defendant, and that the defendant recover against the plaintiff $ for his costs of defence, or as the case may be.*]

No. 172.

Judgment after Trial before Referee.

[Title, etc.]

The   day of   , 18   .

The action having on the 27th November, 18   , been tried before *X. Y.*, Esq., an official [*or* special] referee ; and the said *X. Y.*, having found [*state substance of referee's certificate*], it is this day adjudged that

---

No. 173.

Judgment after Trial of Questions of Account by Referee.

[Title, etc.]

The   day of   18   .

The questions of account in this action having been referred to and he having found that there is due from the   to the   the sum of $ and directed that the   do pay the costs of the reference.

It is this day adjudged that the   recover against the said $ and costs to be taxed.

The above costs have been taxed and allowed at $, as appears by a taxing officer's Certificate dated the   day of   18   .

No. 174.

Judgment on Motion Generally.

[Title, etc.]

The   .   day of   18   .   (*Date of order of Court.*)

This action having on the   day of   18   come on before the Court on motion for judgment on behalf of the   , and the Court after hearing counsel for the   having ordered that   (*as in order of Court.*)

It is this day adjudged that the   recover against the the sum of $ and costs to be taxed.

The above costs have been taxed and allowed at $, as appears by a taxing officer's Certificate dated the   day of   18   .

No. 175.

Judgment in pursuance of order. (For use where leave had been given to sign judgment unless some condition should be complied with.)

[Title, etc.]

The   day of   18   .

Pursuant to the order of   dated   18   whereby it was ordered   and default having been made

It is this day adjudged that the plaintiff recover against the said defendant $ and costs to be taxed.

The above costs have been taxed and allowed at $, as appears by a taxing officer's Certificate dated the   day of   18   .

No. 176.

Judgment in pursuance of order. (*For use where leave has been given to sign judgment unless money should be paid into Court.*)

[Title, etc.]

The   day of   18   .

Pursuant to the order of   dated the   day of
·18   , whereby it was ordered that unless $ be paid into court
by the defendant within a week, the plaintiff be at liberty to sign final
judgment for the amount in lorsed on the writ of summons with interest, if
any, and costs ; and the said defendant not having paid into court the
said sum of $, as conditioned by the said order, it is this day
adjudged that the plaintiff recover against the defendant $ ̣   and
$ for costs.

Certificate for costs dated the   day of   18

No. 177.

Judgment on Certificate of Clerk of County Court.

[Title, etc.]

The   day of   18   .

This action having been ordered to be tried in the County Court of
and the Clerk of that Court having certified that the result was   ·
It is this day adjudged that   recover against $ and
costs to be taxed.   ·

The above costs have been taxed and allowed at $, as appears by
a taxing officer's Certificate dated the   day of   18   . .

No. 178.

Judgment for Defendant's Costs on Discontinuance.

[Title, etc.]

The   day of   18   .

The plaintiff having by a notice in writing dated the   day of
            18   , wholly discontinued this action, [or withdrawn his
claim in this action for *or* withdrawn so much of his claim in this action as
relates to—*or as the case may be.*]
It is this day adjudged that the defendant recover against the plaintiff
costs to be taxed.

The above costs have been taxed and allowed at $, as appears by
a taxing officer's certificate dated the   day of   18   .

No 179.

Judgment for Plaintiff's Costs after Confession of Defence.

[Title, etc.]

The   day of   18   .

The defendant in his statement of defence herein having alleged a
ground of defence which arose after the commencement of this action,

and the plaintiff having on the   day of   18 .-:3 delivered a
confession of that defence.
    It is this day adjudged that the plaintiff recover against the defendan
costs to be taxed.

    The above costs have been taxed and allowed at $, as appears by
a taxing officer's Certificate dated the   day of   18   .

No. 180.

Judgment for Costs after acceptance of Money paid into Court.

[Title, etc.]

The   day of   18   .
    The defendant having paid into court in this action the sum of $
in satisfaction of the plaintiff's claim, and the plaintiff having by his notice
dated the   day of   18   , accepted that sum in satisfaction of
his entire cause of action, and the plaintiff's costs herein having been
taxed, and the defendant not having paid the same within 48 hours after
the said taxation ;
    It is this day adjudged that the plaintiff recover against_the defendant
costs to be taxed.

    The above costs have been taxed and allowed at $, as appears by
a taxing officer's Certificate dated   day of   18   .

No. 181.

Judgment on Motion after Trial of Issue.

[Title, etc.]

The   day of   18   .   (*Date of order of Court.*)
    The (Issues *or* Questions) of fact arising in this action by the order
dated the   day of   ordered to be tried before   having
on the   day of   been tried before   , and the   having
found   . Now on motion before the Court for judgment on behalf of
the   , the Court having
    It is this day adjudged that the   recover against the   the
sum of $ and costs to be taxed.

    The above costs have been taxed and allowed at $ ·   , as appears
by a taxing officer's Certificate dated the   day of   18   .

No. 182.

Form of Judgment on Præcipe for Sale or Foreclosure WITH REFERENCE AS
TO INCUMBRANCES, *etc., and orders for Immediate Payment and Delivery
of Possession.*

[Title, etc.]

    1. Upon the application of the plaintiff under Rule No. 718, of the
Rules of the Supreme Court, and upon reading the writ of summons issued
in this action, and indorsed under Rule No. 218, [and the s atement claim
(*if any*) and statement of defence *where the facts entitling the plaintiff to
Judgment are admitted by the defence,*] and an affidavit of, etc., filed, etc.,
[*where Judgment is obtained by default of appearance or defence add* and an
affidavit of, etc., filed, etc., of service of the said writ on the defendant,

and no appearance having been entered in the said action, (or and the
defendant having made default in delivering a defence or demurrer) as by
the (books in the office of the   at   ) appears ;]

2. It is ordered that all necessary inquiries be made, accounts taken,
costs taxed, and proceedings had for redemption or sale (or redemption or
foreclosure), and that for these purposes the cause be referred t·) the
Master of this Court at

3. (Where judgment is for immediate payment add, It is further ordered
that the defendant   do forthwith after the making of the
Master's report pay to the plaintiff what shall be found due to him for
principal money, interest and costs at the date of the said report, and
upon payment of the amount due to him (where judgment is for sale add,
before the sale hereinbefore directed shall have taken place) that the
plaintiff do assign and convey the mortgaged premises, and deliver up all
documents relating thereto.)

4. (Where judgment is for immediate possession add, It is further ordered
that the defendant do forthwith deliver to the plaintiff, or to whom he
may appoint, possession of the lands and premises in question, in this
cause, or of such part thereof as may be in the possession of the said
defendant.)

No. 183.

Form of Judgment for Foreclosure or Sale, ACCOUNT TAKEN BY REGISTRAR
and Orders for Immediate Payment and Delivery of Possession.

[Title, etc.]

1. Upon the application of the plaintiff under Rule No. 718, of the
Rules of the Supreme Court, and upon reading the writ of summons issued
in this action, and indorsed under Rule No. 248. [and the statement of
claim (if any) and statement f defence *where the facts entitling the plaintiff to
Judgment are admitted by the defence*] and an affidavit of, etc., filed, etc.,
[*where Judgment is obtained by default of appearance or defence add* and an
affidavit of, etc., filed, etc., of service f the said writ n the defendant,
and no appearance having been entered in the said action, (or and the
defendant having made default in delivering a defence or demurrer) as by
the (books in the office of he   at   ) appears ;]

2. This Court finds that the subsequent interest at the rate of
per centum per annum on the sum of   principal money secured
by the indenture of mortgage in the pleadings mentioned, up to the
day of   next, being the time appointed for payment as hereinafter
mentioned, amounts to   and that the costs of the plaintiff
amount to   which said subsequent interest and costs be ng
added to the sum of   claimed by the indorsement on the writ served
on the defendant   make together the sum of

3. And upon the said defendant paying the said sum of   into the
bank   at the   between the hours of ten o'clock in the
forenoon and one o'clock in the afternoon of the   day of   next, to
the joint credit of the plaintiff and the Registrar [*where order for
payment granted insert*, or in case the plaintiff shall (*where judgment is
for sale add*, before the sale hereinafter directed shall have taken place)
recover the amount due to him under the order for payment hereinafter
contained], it is ordered that the said plaintiff do assign and convey the
mortgaged premises, and deliver up all documents relating thereto ;

4. But in default of the said defendant making such payment by the
time aforesaid, it is ordered (*where judgment is for foreclosure, after* "it is
ordered," *say* "that the said defendant do stand absolutely debarred and
foreclosed of and from all equity of redemption in and to the said premises ;" *where judgment is for sale, then after the words* "it is ordered," *say*
"that the said premises be sold, with the approbation of the Master of
this Court at   ).

5. (*If judgment is for foreclosure omit this section.*) And it is ordered that the purchasers do pay their purchase money into Court, to the credit of this cause, and that the same when so paid in be applied in payment of what has been found due to the sai t plaintiff together with subsequent interest and subsequent costs, to be computed and taxed by the said Master, and that the balance do abide the further order of the Court.

6. (*Where judgment is for immediate payment add :*) It is further ordered that the defendant   do forthwith pay to the plaintiff the sum of   being the amount due to the plaintiff at the date hereof for principal money, interest and costs.

7. (*Where judgment is for immediate possession add :*) And it is further ordered that the defendant do forthwit deliver to the plaintiff , or to whom he may appoint, possession of the mortgaged premises, or of such part thereof as may be in the possession of the said defendant .

No. **184**.

Form of Judgment for Redemption, issued by a local Master.

[Title, etc.]

1. Upon the application of the plaintiff, under Rule No. 718, of the Rules of the Supreme Court, and upon reading the writ of summons issued in this action, [and the statement claim (*if any*) and statement t f defence *where the facts entitling the plaintiff to Judgment are admitted by the defence,*] and an affidavit of, etc., filed, etc., [*where Judgment is obtained by default of appearence or defence add* and an affidavit of, etc., filed, etc., of service of the said writ on the defendant, and no appearance having been entered in the said action, (or a d the defendant having made default in delivering a defence r demurrer) as by the (books in the office of the   at   ) appears ;]

2. It is ordered that all necessary inquiries be made, accounts taken, costs taxed, and proceedings had for the redemption of the premises in question, and that for this purpose the cause be referred to the Master at   .

3. And it is ordered that upon the plaintiff paying to the defendant what shall be found due to him, or in case nothing shall be found due to the defendant then forthwith after the confirmation of the said Master's report, that the defendant do reconvey the said mortgaged premises, and deliver up all documents relating thereto.

4. It is further ordered that in case the plaintiff shall make default in payment as aforesaid of what may be found due to the defendant that the plaintiff's action do stand dismissed out of this Court, with costs to be paid by the plaintiff to the defendant forthwith after taxation thereof.

5. It is further ordered that in case nothing shall be found due from the plaintiff to the defendant that the defendant do pay the plaintiff his costs of this suit forthwith after taxation thereof, and in case any balance shall be found due from the defendant to the plaintiff that the defendant do pay such balance to the plaintiff forthwith after the confirmation of the Master's report.

No. **185**.

Form of Judgment for Administration by a Local Master.

1. Upon the application of the above-named plaintiff in the presence of the solicitor for the defendant [or no one appearing for the defendant although duly notified as by affidavit filed appears], and upon hearing read the affidavits and papers filed, and what was alleged by the solicitor for the applicant *or all* parties].

2. It is ordered that all necessary inquiries be made, accounts taken, costs taxed and proceedings had for the administration and final winding up of the personal [and real] estate of   and for the adjustment of the rights of all parties interested therein, by the Master of this Court at   .

3. And it is ordered that all balances which may be found due from the plaintiff or defendant [or any or either of them] to the said estate be, forthwith after the same shall have been ascertained as aforesaid, paid into Court to the credit of this cause, subject to the further order of the Court.

4. And it is ordered that such personal [and real] estate, or such parts thereof as the said Master may hereafter direct, be sold, as the said Master may direct, and that the purchasers do pay their purchase money into Court to the credit of this cause, subject to the order of the Court.

5. It is further ordered that the Master do execute conveyances for any infant parties who by reason of their tender years are unable to execute the same.

No. **186**.

Form of Judgment for Partition or Sale by Local Master.

1. Upon the application of the above-named plaintiff in the presence of the solicitor for the defendant [or no one appearing for the defendant although duly notified as by affidavit filed appears] and upon hearing read the affidavits and papers filed, and what was alleged by the solicitor for [the applicant or all parties.]

2. It is ordered that all necessary inquiries be made, accounts taken, costs taxed and proceedings had for the partition or sale of the lands and premises in the said affidavits mentioned, and for the adjustment of the rights of all parties interested therein, or for a partition of part and sale of the remainder of the said lands as may be most for the interest of the parties entitled to share therein [by the Master of this Court at   .]

3. And it is further ordered that the said lands, or such part thereof as the said Master shall think fit, be sold, with the approbation of the said Master, freed from the claims of such of the incumbrancers thereon (if any) whose claims were created by parties entitled to the said lands before the death of the said testator [or, intestate] as shall have consented to such sale, and subject to the claims of such of them as shall not have consented [and freed also from the dower of   as the case may be], and that the said Master   do execute the conveyances on behalf of such of the infant parties as, by reason of their tender years, are unable to execute the same, and that the purchasers do pay their purchase money into Court to the credit of this cause, subject to the order of the Court.

4. And it is further ordered that, in the event of a partition of the whole of the said land, or in the event of a partition of a part and the proceeds of the sale of the remainder being insufficient to pay the costs in full, the costs, or so much thereof as remains unpaid, be borne and paid by the said parties according to their shares and interests in the said lands [if there be any infant parties interested in the estate add] and that the proportion of the said costs payable by the infant parties respectively be, and the same is hereby declared to be, a lien on their respective shares, and that the plaintiff do pay the guardian of the infant defendants his costs of this suit and that the same be added to his own costs.

No. **187**.

Form of Judgment or Order for Administration Accounts.

This Court doth order that the following accounts and inquiries be taken and made by the Master of the Supreme Court of Judicature at   , that is to say :

1. An account of the personal estate of *A. B.*, deceased, the testator in the pleadings mentioned, come to the hands of, &c.

2. An account of the said testator's debts.

3. An account of the said testator's funeral expenses.

4. An account of the said testator's legacies.

5. An enquiry, what parts, if any, of the said testator's personal estate are outstanding or undisposed of.

(If ordered.)

And it is ordered that the following further accounts and inquiries be taken and made, that is to say :

6. An inquiry what real estate the said testator was seised of, or entitled to, at the time of his death.

7. An inquiry what incumbrances affect the said testator's real estate.

8. An account of the rents and profits of the said testator's real estate received by, &c.

(If Sale ordered.)

9. An account what is due to such of the incumbrancers as shall consent to the sale hereinafter directed in respect of their incumbrances.

10. An inquiry of what are the priorities of such last mentioned incumbrances.

And it is ordered that the testator's real estate be sold, with the approbation of———————.

And it is ordered that further directions and costs be reserved, until after the said Master shall have made his report.

PART XI.

No. 188.

WRITS OF EXECUTION, &c

Writ of Fieri Facias.

In the High Court of Justice.
——Division.

Between *A. B.*, Plaintiff,
and
C. D. and others, Defendants.

Victoria, by the Grace of God, of the United Kingdom of Great Britain and Ireland, Queen, Defender of the Faith.

To the sheriff of   greeting.

We command you that of the goods and chattels (*or* lands and tenements) of *C. D.* in your bailiwick you cause to be made the sum of $ and also interest thereon from the   day of [*Day of the judgment or order, or day on which money directed to be paid, or day from which interest is directed by the order to run, as the case may be,*] which said sum of money and interest were lately before the Justices of our High Court of Jus ice in a certain action [*or* certain actions, *as the case may be*] wherein *A. B.* is plaintiff, and *C. D.* and others are defendants [*or* in a certain matter there depending intituled "In the matter of *E F.*," *as the case may be*] by a judgment [*or* order *as the case may be*] of our said Court, bearing date the   day of adjudged [*or* ordered, *as the case may be*] to be paid by the said *C. D.* to *A. B.*, together with certain costs in the said judgment [*or* order *as the case may be*] mentioned, and which costs have been taxed and allowed (by one of the taxing masters of our said Court) at the sum of $ as appears by the certificate of the said taxing master, dated the   day   . And that of the goods and chattels (*or* lands or tenements) of the said *C. D.* in your bailiwick you further cause to be made the said sum of $ [costs] together with interest thereo from the   day of   , (*the date of the certificate of taxation. The writ must be so moulded as to follow the substance of the judgment or order*) and that you have that money and interest before our Justices aforesaid at Toronto immediately after the execution hereof, (*or, in the case of lands and tenements,* immediately after the expiration of twelve months from the day of your receipt hereof) to be paid to the said *A B.* in pursuance of the said judgment [*or* order *as the case may be*]. And in what manner you shall have executed this our writ make appear to our Justices aforesaid at Toronto immediately after the execution thereof. And have there then this writ.

Witness, the Honourable   President, etc.

The   day of   18

No. 189.

Fieri Facias on Order for Costs..

[Title, etc.]

Victoria, etc.

To the sheriff of   greeting.

We command you that of the goods and chattels of   in your bailiwick you cause to be made the sum of   for certain costs which by an order of our High Court of Justice dated the   day of 18   , were ordered to be paid by the said   to and which have been taxed and allowed at the said sum, and interest on the said sum at the rate of 6 per centum per annum from the   day of   18   , and that you have the said sum and interest before the Justices of our High Court at Toronto, immediately after the execution hereof, to be rendered to the said   . And in what manner you shall have executed this our writ make appear to us immediately after the execution hereof. And have there then this writ.

Witness, etc.

The   day of   18

Indorsements.

Levy $ and $ for costs of execution, etc., and also interest on $ at 6 per centum per annum from the   day of 18   , until payment; besides sheriff's poundage, officer's fees, costs of levying, and all other legal incidental expenses.

This writ was issued by

of

agent for

of

solicitor for the

The   is a   and resides

at

in your bailiwick.

No. 190.

Writ of Venditioni Exponas.

[Title, etc.]

Victoria, etc.

To the sheriff of   greeting.

Whereas by our writ we lately commanded you that of the goods and chattels (*making the necessary variations of this form throughout in the case of lands and tenements*) of *C. D.* [*here recite the fieri facias to the end*]. And on the   day of   you returned to our Justices in the   Division of our High Court of Justice aforesaid, that by virtue of the said writ to you directed you had taken goods and chattels of the said *C. D.* to the value of the money and interest aforesaid, which said goods and chattels remained in your hands unsold for want of buyers. Therefore, we being desirous that the said *A. B.* should be satisfied his money and interest aforesaid, command you that you expose to sale and sell, or cause to be sold, the goods and chattels of the said *C. D.*, by you in form aforesaid taken, and every part thereof, for the best price that can be gotten for the same, and have the money arising from such sale before our Justices aforesaid, at   immediately after the execution hereof, to be paid to the said *A. B.* And have there then this writ.

Witness, etc.,   , the   day of   18

No. **191.**

Writ of Possession.

[Title, etc.]

Victoria, etc.,   to the sheriff of   , greeting.
Whereas lately in our High Court of Justice, by a judgment of the
        Division of the same Court [*A. B.* recovered] *or* [*E. F.* was
ordered to deliver to *A. B.*] possess on of all that   with the
appurtenances in your bailiwick : Therefore, we command you that you
enter the same, and without delay cause the said *A. B.* to have possession of the said land and premises with the appurtenances, and that you
defend and keep him and his assigns in peaceable and quiet possession
when and as often as any interruption may or shall, from time to time,
be given or offered to them or any of them. Witness, etc.

No. **192.**

Writ of Delivery.

[Title, etc.]

Victoria, etc.,   to the sheriff of   greeting.
We command you, that without delay you cause the following
chattels, that is to say [*here enumerate the chattels recovered by the
judgment for the return of which execution has been ordered to issue*], to be
returned to *A. B.* which the said *A. B.* lately in our
recovered against *C. D.* [*or C. D.* was ordered to deliver to the said
A. B.] in an action in the   Division of our said Court.* And
we further command you, that if the said chattels cannot be found in
your bailiwick, you distrain the said *C. D.* by all his lands and chattels
in your bailiwick, so that neither the said *C. D.* nor any one for him do
lay hands on the same until the said *C. D.* render to the said *A. B.* the
said chattels ; and in what manner you shall have executed this our writ
make appear to the Justices of the   Division of our High
Court of Justice at Toronto, immediately after the execution hereof, and
have you there then this writ. Witness, etc.

No. **193.**

*The Like, but instead of a Distress until the Chattel is returned, commanding
the Sheriff to levy on the Defendant's goods the assessed Value of it.*

[*Proceed as in the preceding form until the*,* and then thus :*]

And we further command you that if the said chattels cannot be found in
your bailiwick, of the goods and chattels of the said *C. D.* in your bailiwick you cause to be made $ [*the assessed value of the chattels.*]
and in what manner you shall have executed this our writ make appear
to the Judges of the   Division of our High Court of Justice
at Toronto, immediately after the execution hereof, and have you there
then this writ. Witness, etc.

No. **194.**

Writ of Attachment.

[Title, etc.]

Victoria, etc.,   to the sheriff of   , greeting :
We command you to attach *C. D.* so as to have him before us in the
        Division of our High Court of Justice, there to answer to

us, as well touching a contempt which he it is alleged hath committed
against us, as also such other matters as shall be then and there laid to
his charge, and further to perform and abide such order as our said Court
shall make in this behalf, and hereof fail not, and bring this writ with
you. Witness, etc.

No. 195.

Writ of Capias ad Satisfaciendum on a Judgment for Plaintiff.

To the sheriff of, etc.
We command you that you take *C. D.* if he shall be found in your
bailiwick, an i him safely keep so that you may have his body before our
Justices of our High Cour of Justice   Division, at Toronto,
immediately after the execution hereof, to satisfy   ,* *(the amount
of all moneys recovered by the judgment)* which the said *A. B.* lately in our
High Court of Justice   Division, recovered against the said *C. D.*
for his damages *(or* debt and damages, *or otherwise according to the form of
action),* whereof the said *C. D.* is convicted, and have you then there this
writ. Witness, etc., *(as in usual form).*

No. 196.

Writ of Capias ad Satisfaciendum on an order for Payment of Money.

Victoria, etc., *(same as in form No. 195, to the*)* which lately in our
High Court of Justice (Division) by an
order of our said Court *(or*by* an order of the Honourable   , one
of the Justice‹ of our said High Court of Jus ice) dated the   day of
        18 , were ordered to be paid by the said *C. D.* to *A. B.,* and
have you then there this writ. Witness, etc.

No. 197.

*Writ of Capias ad Satisfaciendum on an order for Payment of
Money and Costs.*

Victoria, etc., *(same as No. 196 down to the words* 'were ordered') were
ordered to be paid by the said *C. D.* to the said *A. B.,* together with
certain costs in the said order mentioned, which said costs have been taxed
and allowed by our said Court at $, *(the amount of the allocatur or
allocaturs, if more than one)* and further to satisfy the said *A. B.* the said
last mentioned sum, and have you then there this writ. Witness, etc.

No. 198.

*Writ of Capias ad Satisfaciendum, on an order for the Payment of
Costs only.*

Victoria, etc., *(same as in No. 195 down to the word* " immediately,")
immediately after the execution hereof, to satisfy *A. B.*   for certain
costs, which, by an order of our High Court of Justice (
        Division) *or* by an order of the Honourable
one of the Justices of our High Court of Justice) dated the   day of
        18 , were ordered to be paid by the said *C. D.* to the said *A.
B.,* which said costs have been taxed and allowed by our said Court at the
said sum and have you there then this writ. Witness, etc.

17

No. 199.

Writ of Sequestration.

[Title, etc.]

Victoria, etc.,   to the sheriff of   , greeting :

Whereas lately in the   Division of our High Court of Justice in a certain action there depending, wherein *A. B.* is plaintiff and *C. D.* and others are defendants [*or*, in a certain matter there depending intituled " In the matter of *E. F.*, *as the case may be*] by a judgment [*or* order, *as the case may be*] of our said Court made in the said action [*or* matter], and bearing date the   day of   18 , it was ordered that the said *C. D.* should [pay into Court to the credit of the said action the sum of $; *or as the case may be*]. Know ye, therefore, that we have given, and by these presents do give to you full power and authority to enter upon all the lands, tenements and real estate whatsoever of the said *C. D.*, and to collect, receive and sequester in your hands, not only all the rents and profits of his said lands, tenements and real estate, but also all his goods, chattels and personal estates whatsoever ; and therefore we command you, that you do at certain proper and convenient days and hours, go to and enter upon all the lands, tenements and real estates of the said *C. D.*, and that you do collect, take and get into your hands not only the rents and profits of his said real estate, but also all his goods, chattels, and personal estate, and detain and keep the same under sequestration in your hands until the said *C. D.* shall [pay into Court, to the credit of the said action, the sum of $ *or, as the case may be*,] clear his contempt, and our said Court make other order to the contrary. Witness, etc.

No. 200.

Delivery or Assessed Value of Chattels.

[Title, etc.]

Victoria, etc.,   to the sheriff of   greeting :

We command you that without delay you cause to be returned to the following chattels, namely (*enumerate chattels recovered by judgment for there turn of which execution has been ordered to issue,*) which the said   lately (recovered against *or* was ordered to deliver to the said,) in an action in our High Court of Justice   Division.

And we further command you that if the said chattels cannot be found in your bailiwick then of the goods and chattels of the said   in your bailiwick you cause to be made (*the assessed value of the chattels*). And in what manner you shall have executed this our writ make appear to us in our said Court immediately after the execution hereof. And have there then this writ.

Witness, etc.

Indorsements.

If the chattels cannot be found in your bailiwick, levy $ the assessed value thereof, and interest thereon at 6 per ce tum per annum from the   day of   18 , until payment, besides sheriff's poundage, officers' fees, costs of levying, and all other legal incidenta expenses.

This writ was issued by
of
agent for
of
solicitor to the   who resides at

The defendant is a
and resides at
in your bailiwick.

No. **201.**

*Writ of Assignment of Dower (under R. S. O. 1887 c. 56, s. 3, where the
right of Dower is acquiesced in by the owner of the estate).*

ONTARIO,

County of   Victoria by the Grace of God, etc.,

> To the Sheriff of the County of
>   Greeting ;

Whereas, A. D., widow, who was the wife of C. D., deceased, demands
against E. F. the third part of (here describe the Estate in which dower
is claimed as in other writs of assignment of dower) as the dower of the
said A. D. of the endowment of the said C. D., heretofore her husband.
And whereas it has been made to appear to us in our High Court of Justice Queen's Bench Division (or Common Pleas Division *or as the case may
be*) in Ontario, that the said E. F. is the owner of the said real estate out
of which said dower is claimed, and that he acquiesces in the said claim
and is willing to as-ign to the said A. B. her proper dower, but that the
said A. B. and E. F. are not agreed as to the admeasurement thereof. We
therefore command you that, without delay, you do deliver the said A. B.
seisin of her third part of the said
with the appurtenances. To hold to her in severalty by metes and bounds ;
And that you do proceed in the execution of this our Writ, according to
the provisions of Chapter 56 of Revised Statutes of Ontario.

Witness, etc.

(*When the Plaintiff has married again, since the death of her late husband, under whom she claims dower, her name and description must be made
such as to suit her circumstances*).

Rules of 15th Feb., 1862.

No. **202.**

Warrant for arrest of a defaulting witness.

> Province of Ontario,   }
> County of   }

>   Between *A. B.*, Plaintiff,
>   and
>   *C. D.*, Defendant.

To *E. F.*

Whereas proof has been made before me that *H. N.* was duly subpœnaed
to give evidence on behalf of the plaintiff (*or as the case may be*), in the
cause at the sittings of the C urt of Assize (*or as the case may be*
at Toronto (*or as the case may be*, which commenced on the   day of
                        18   ) ; that the presence of the said *H. N.*, is material
o the ends of Justice ; and that the sa d *H. N.* has failed to attend in
accordance with the requirements of the subpœna.

These are therefore to command you to take the said *H. N.* and to bring
and have him before me at the said sittings, or before such other Judge as
may be presiding thereat, th re to testify what he may know concerning
the matters in question in the said cause, and that you detain him in your
custody until he shall have given his evidence. or until the sa d sittings
shall have ended, or until other order be made by the Court concerning
him.

> Given under my hand, this   day of
>   A.D. 18   , at
>   **J. J. M.**

PART XII.

No. **203**.

Petition.

In the High Court of Justice (Queen's Bench *or* Common Pleas *or* Chancery Division).

To the Queen's Most Excellent Majesty.

The humble petition of *A. B.* of   , by his Attorney, *E. F.*, of   , sheweth that (*state the facts*).

Conclusion.

Your suppliant therefore humbly prays that, etc.

The suppliant proposes that the trial of this petition shall take place at the   of   .

Dated the   day of   , A. D.

       (Signed)   *A. B.*

            or *C. D.*, Counsel for *A. B.*

            or *E. F.*, Solicitor for *A. B.*

R. S. O. 1877, c 59, sched. Form 1.

No. **204**.

The suppliant prays for a plea or answer on behalf of Her Majesty within twenty-eight days after the date hereof, or otherwise, that the petition may be taken as confessed.

R. S. O. 1877, c. 59, sched. Form 2.

No. **205**.

Notice to Appear.

To *A. B.*

, You are hereby required to appear to the within petition in Her Majesty's High Court of Justice within eight days, and to plead or answer thereto within fourteen days after the da e of service hereof.

Take notice, that if you fail to appear or plead or answer in due time, the said petition may, as against you, be ordered to be taken as confessed.

Dated, etc.

R. S. O. 1877, c. 59, sched. Form 3.

No. 206.

Appearance.

In the High Court of Justice (Queen's Bench *or* Common Pleas *or* Chancery Division).

Petition of Right.

A. B. suppliant, *vs.* The Queen.	*C. D.* appears in person. *or E. F.*, solicitor for *C. D.*,

appears for him.

(*If the appearance is in person, the address of the party appearing to be given*).

Entered the   day of   , 18

R. S. O. 1877, c. 59, sched. Form 4.

No. 207.

Certificate of Judgment for Petitioner.

To the Honourable the Treasurer of Ontario,

Petition of right of *A. B.*, in Her Majesty's High Court of Justice at Toronto.

I hereby certify that on the   day of   , A.D.   , it was by the said Court adjudged (*or* decreed *or* ordered) that the above-named suppliant was entitled to, etc.

Judge's signature.

R. S. O. 1877, c. 59, sched. Form 5.

PART XIII.
No. **208**.

Replevin Bond.

Know all men by these presents, that we, *A. B.*, (*the plaintiff*) of W. G., of   and J. S., of   are jointly and severally held and firmly bound to W. P., Esquire, Sheriff of the County of   , in the sum of   of lawful money of Canada, to be paid to the said Sheriff, or his certain attorney, executors, administrators or assigns, for which payment to be well and truly made we bind ourselves, and each and every of us in the whole, our, and each and every of our heirs, executors and administrators, firmly by these presents, sealed with our seals.

Dated this   day of   , one thousand eight hundred and

The condition of this obligation is such, that if the above bounden *A. B.* do prosecute his suit with effect and without delay against *C. D.* for the taking and unjustly detaining (*or unjustly detaining, as the case may be*) of his cattle, goods and chattels, to wit : (*here set forth the property distrained, taken or detained*), and do make a return of the said property, if a return thereof shall be adjudged, and also to pay such damages as the Defendant shall sustain by the issuing of the Writ of Replevin if the said *A. B.* fails to recover judgment in his said suit, and further do observe, keep and perform all rules and orders made by the Court in the said suit, then this obligation shall be void, or else remain in full force and virtue.

Sealed and delivered } in the presence of }

Form of Assignment.

Know all men by these presents, that I, W. P., Esquire, Sheriff of the County of   , have at the request of the within named *C. D.*, the avowant (*or person making cognizance*) in this cause, assigned over this Replevin Bond unto the said *C. D.*, pursuant to the Statutes in such case made and provided.

In witness whereof, I have hereunto set my hand and seal of office this   day of   , one thousand eight hundred and

Sealed and delivered } in the presence of }

R. S. O. 1877, c. 53, Form 2.

No. **209**.

Appeal Bond (on Appeal to Court of Appeal).

Know all men by these presents that we (*naming all the obligors with their places of residence and additions*), are jointly and severally held and firmly bound unto (*naming the obligees with their places of residence and additions*), in the penal sum of   dollars, for which payment, well and truly to be made, we bind ourselves, and each of us by himself, our, and each of our heirs, executors, and administrators, respectively, firmly by these presents.

Dated this   day of

Whereas *(the appellant)* complains that, in the giving of a certain judgment in a certain suit in Her Majesty's High Court of Justice Queen's Bench (or Chancery or Common Pleas Division, *as the case may be*), in the Province of Ontario, between (*naming the parties to the cause*) manifest error hath intervened, wherefore (*the appellant*) desires to appeal from the said judgment to the Court of Appeal.

[*Where it is desired also to give the security required by law in order to stay execution insert*, And whereas the said (*appellant*) is desirous of having the execution of the said judgment stayed pending the appeal.]

Now the condition of this obligation is such, that if (*the appellant*) do and shall effectually prosecute such appeal, and pay such costs and damages as shall be awarded, in case the judgment aforesaid to be appealed from shall be affirmed or in part affirmed, [*In order to stay execution* (*See Rule 804*) *where the judgment directs sale or del very of posses ion of property add*, and during the possession of the property in question in the said action (or *otherwise describing it*) by (*the appellant*) he shall not commit or suffer to be committed any waste on the property, and that if the judgment be affirmed, or in part affirmed, he shall pay the value of the use and occupation of the property from the time of the appeal until the delivery of possession thereof (add *in case the judgment is for the sale of the property and payment of any deficiency arising upon the sale,*. and that in case of any deficiency arising upon a sale as directed by the said judgment he shall pay the amount of the deficiency) or the part thereof as to which the judgment may be affirmed if it be affirmed only as to part, *or where the judgment directs the payment of money add*, and shall pay the amount by said judgment directed to be paid, either as a debt or for damages or costs or the part thereof as to which the judgment may be affirmed, if it be affirmed only as to part, and all damages awarded against (*the appellant on such appeal, or where the judgment directs the delivery of documents or personal property add*, and shall obey the order to be made by the Court of Appeal] then this obligation shall be void, otherwise to remain in full force.

Signed, sealed and delivered, in the presence of

Affidavit of Justification to be annexed.

In the High Court of Justice   Division.

Between *A. B.* Plaintiff,
                 v.
          C. D. Defendant.

I, E. F., of   make oath and say, that I am a resident inhabitant of Ontario, and am a householder in, (*or a freeholder in   ,*) and that I am worth the sum of   , (*the sum mentioned as the penalty, or such sum as the deponent is bound in*). over and above what will pay all my debts ; and I, J. H., of   , make oath and say, that I am a resident inhabitant of Ontario, and am a householder in (*or a freeholder in   ,*) and that I am worth the sum (*as in the former case*) of   over and above what will pay all my debts.

The above named deponents, ⎫
E. F. & J. H., were sworn, ⎬
etc., the   day of ⎪
          18   , before me. ⎭

Commissioner, etc.

No. 210.

Appeal bond (on Appeal to the Privy Council.)

Know all men by these presents, that we (*naming all the obligors, with their places of residence and additions*), are j intly and severally held and firmly bound unto (*naming the obligees, with their places of residence and additions*), in the penal sum of two thousand dollars, for which payment, well and truly t be made, we bind ourselves, and each of us by himself, our, and each of our heirs, executors, and admin strat rs, respectively, firmly, by these presents.

Dated this   day of   in the year f our Lord, 18

Whereas (*the appellant*) alleges, that in the giving of judgment in a cer tain action in Her Majesty's Court f Appeal f r Ontario, between (*the respondent*) and (*the appellant*), manifest er or hath intervened, wherefore (*the appellant*) desires to appeal fr m the said judgment t Her Majesty, in Her Majesty's Privy Council.

Now the condition of this obligation is such, that if (*the appellant*) do and sh ll effectually prosecute such appeal, and pay such costs and damages as shall be awarded, in case the judgment aforesaid to be appealed fr m shall be affirmed, or in part affirmed, then this obligati n shall be void, otherwise shall remain in full force.

PART XIV.

MISCELLANEOUS.

No. 211

Certificate of action being on Lower Scale.

(Title of cause or matter.)

I hereby certify that, to the best of my judgment and belief the Lower Scale tariff of fees is applicable to this case.

A. B. Solicitor for

Dated, etc.

No. 212.

Certificate of Taxation.

[Title, etc.]

I certify that the costs of the   have been taxed and allowed at $

Dated, etc.

No. 213.

Form of Certificate of Officer after Trial.

[Title, etc.]

I certify that this action was tried before the Honourable Mr. Justice [and a special jury of the county of   on the and   days of (October,) 188 .]

[The Jury found (*state findings*).]

(*If the Judge give instructions as to the judgment thereon, add*), And the said Judge directed, etc., [*as the case may be.*]

Dated, etc.

No. 214.

Form of Satisfaction Piece.

In the   on the   day of   A.D. 18   to wit. form of satis Fact on piece.

Satisfaction is acknowledged between   plaintiff and defendant in an action for $ and   costs. And   do hereby expressly nominate and appoint   solicitor to witness and attest execution of this acknowledgment of satisfaction.

Judgment entered on the   day of

Signed by the said   in the presence of me
of   one of the solicitors of the
Supreme Co rt of Judicature for Ontario.   And I
hereby declare myself to be solicitor for and on
behalf of said   expressly n med by   *(Signature)*
and attending at   request to inform   the above named
of the nature and effect o' this acknowledgment of   plaintiff.
satisfaction (which I accordingly did before the same
was signed by me). And I also declare that I subscribe my name hereto as such solicitor. Rules   Date.
T.T. 1856, 64.

No. 215.

Form of return of Judgments.

List of judgments entered into the office of the Deputy Clerk of the
Crown (*or* Deputy Registrar *or* Local Registrar, *as the case may be*) of the
County of   during the three months ending the
day of   18

(1) Plaintiff   Defendant.
(2) Date of entry of judgment.
(3) The amount recovered, or other relief given, exclusive of costs.
(4) The amount of costs taxed.   J. A. Rule 517.

No. 216.

Verification of Statement of Moneys in Court (Rule 161).

Verification of   I hereby solemnly declare that the annexed statement is a full and true
statement by   statement of the moneys paid into the High Court and the Court of Appeal
Accountant.   during the year 18   , and that it correctly shows the state of the various
accounts therein mentioned upon the 31s day of December last.

(Signature)   A. B.,
Accountant or Accountant's Clerk.

Subscribed and declared before me, at   , this   day of
January, 18   .

C. D.,
Commissioner for taking affidavits, or
Justice of the Peace.

R. S. O. c. 50, s. 121, (4).

No. 217.

Verification of Return of Moneys paid into C. C. or Surrogate Court.

Verification of   I hereby solemnly declare that the annexed statement is a full and true
statement by   statement of the moneys paid into the County (*or* Surrogate) Court of the
Clerk or Reg-   County of   , during the year 18   , and that it correctly shows the
istrar.   state of the various accounts therein mentioned upon the thirty-first day
of December last.

(Signature)   A. B.,
Clerk, or Registrar.

Subscribed and declared before me, at   , this
day of January, 18   .

C. D.,
Commissioner for taking affidavits, or
Justice of the Peace.

No. **218.**

FORM OF DEBT ATTACHMENT BOOK.

Name of Plaintiff.	Name of Judgment Debtor.	Amount of Judgment.	Date of Judgment.	Name of Garnishee.	Date of Order for Attachment.	Amount ordered to be paid by Garnishee.	Date of such Order.	Date of Order for Execution against Garnishee.	Date of order that Judgment Creditor may proceed against Garnishee.

Form of Debt Attachment Book under Rule 946.

in 1895

Abandoned Motion Costs

Costs of motion not set
down to opposite party
to be costs in the cause as
of course —

But the practice in 1855 seems to be
to apply to his counsel on motion
for an order —

See it in .... Exr Ind. 1776

1897

TARIFF A.

TABLE OF COSTS

IN THE

HIGH COURT OF JUSTICE AND COUNTY COURTS.

General allowance for Plaintiffs and Defendants, as well between Solicitor and Client as between Party and Party :—

	HIGHER SCALE.	LOWER SCALE AND COUNTY COURTS.
	$ c.	$ c.
1. Instructions to sue in undefended cases	3 00	2 00
2. In defended cases	4 00	3 00
3. Instructions to defend	4 00	3 00
4. Instructions for petition where no writ of summons issued	2 00	1 00
WRITS.		
5. All writs, except writs of execution, subpœnas, and concurrent, and renewed writs	2 00	1 00
6. Concurrent writ	1 50	0 75
7. Renewed writ (except writs of execution)	1 50	0 75
8. All writs if over four folios, for every folio	0 20	0 20
9. Subpœna ad testificandum	1 00	0 50
10. Subpœna duces tecum	1 25	0 75
11. All subpœnas if over four folios, additional per folio	0 15	0 15
12. Notice of writ for service in lieu of writ out of jurisdiction and copy	1 00	0 75
13. (Alias, and subsequent, writs, to be allowed as originals.)		
14. Special indorsement of writ of summons	1 00	0 75
15. Suing out any writ of execution	6 00	4 00
Renewal of any writ of execution	4 00	2 50
(In both cases, including placing same in the Sheriff's hands, all attendances, indorsements and letters in connection therewith.)		
COPY AND SERVICE OF WRITS OF SUMMONS, AND OTHER PROCESS.		
16. For copy, including copy of notices required to be indorsed, each	1 00	0 75
If over four folios, for every additional folio	0 10	0 10
17. Service of each copy of writ, if not done by the Sheriff or an officer employed by him, when taxable to solicitor on Sheriff's default	1 00	0 50
18. If served at a distance of over two miles from the nearest place of business, or office of the solicitor serving same, for each mile beyond such two miles	0 13	0 10
19. For service of writ out of jurisdiction	Such allowance a the Taxing Officer shall think fit.	Such allowance as the Taxing Officer or C C Judge shall think fit.

	HIGHER SCALE.	LOWER SCALE AND COUNTY COURTS.
TABLE OF COSTS.—*Continued.*	$ c.	$ c.

INSTRUCTIONS AFTER COMMENCEMENT OF ACTION.

20. To counsel in special matters	1 00	0 50
21. To counsel in common matters	0 50	0 25
22. For special affidavits when allowed by the taxing officer (or County Court Clerk in C. C. cases.)	1 00	0 50
23. For special affidavit on production when allowed by the taxing officer	2 00	1 00
24. For pleadings in action	1 50	1 00
25. For counter-claim, when such claim could not prior to the Ont. Jud. Act, 1881, have formed the subject of a set-off	2 00	1 00
26. For reply to such counter-claims	2 00	1 00
27. To amend any pleading when the amendment is proper	2 00	1 00
28. For confession of defence under Rule 440	2 00	1 00
29. For special case in course of action	2 00	1 00
30. For special case when no writ issued, or pleadings had, and no instructions to sue allowed	3 00	2 00
31. To add parties by order of Court or Judge	2 00	1 00
32. For brief	2 00	0 50
33. For every suggestion	1 00	1 00
34. For adding parties in consequence of marriage, death, assignment, etc.	1 00	0 50
35. For issue of fact, by consent, or Judge's order	2 00	1 00
36. To defend added parties after suggestion of death of original party, or on revivor	2 00	1 00
37. For confession of action in ejectment as to the whole, or in part	1 00	0 50
38. To strike or reduce special jury	2 00	1 00
39. For such other important step or proceeding in the suit as the taxing officer is satisfied warrants such a charge	2 00	1 00

DRAWING PLEADINGS, ETC.

40. Statement of claim	2 00	1 00
41. If above ten folios, for every folio above ten, in addition	0 20	0 15
42. Statement of defence, if five folios or under	2 00	1 00
43. If above five folios, for every folio in addition	0 20	0 20
44. Statement of defence and counter-claim, up to fifteen folios	3 00	1 50
45. For every folio over fifteen	0 20	0 15
46. Reply and other pleadings for or on behalf of plaintiff or defendant.	2 00	1 00
47. If above ten folios, for every folio in addition	0 20	0 15
48. Demurrer	2 00	1 00
49. Petition, per folio	0 20	0 15
50. Issue for trial of facts by agreement or order, for every folio	0 20	0 20
51. In special or contested actions or matters on the Higher Scale to be increased to such sum as the Taxing Officer in Toronto may think fit.		
52. Special case, per folio	0 20	0 20
53. Drawing interrogatories, or answers for any purposes required by law, per folio	0 20	0 20
54. Drawing reasons for or against appeal, per folio	0 20	0 20
55. (The above charges do not include engrossing, or copies to file or serve.)		
56. Taking cognovit and entering judgment thereon, when there has been no previous proceeding, and the true debt does not exceed $200	8 00	8 00
57. For same services when the true debt exceeds $200	12 0	10 00
58. Drawing and engrossing cognovit, and attending execution, when there have been previous proceedings	2 00	1 00

COPIES.

59. Of pleadings, brief and other documents, when no other provision is made, and copies properly allowable	0 10	0 10
60. Certified copy of pleadings, or issue, for use of Judge	1 50	0 75
61. For every folio above 15, per folio	0 10	0 10
62. Of special and common orders of Court or a Judge	0 75	0 50
63. Of special order of Court above three folios, per folio	0 20	0 10

	Higher Scale.	Lower Scale and County Courts.

TABLE OF COSTS.—*Continued.*

$ c. | $ c.

Notices, including One Copy.

	Higher Scale $ c.	Lower Scale $ c.
64. Of appearance, when duly entered and notice given on the day of appearance, but not otherwise	0 50	0 25
65. To Sheriff, to discharge prisoner out of custody	0 50	0 50
66. Notice, in action for recovery of land, to defend for part of premises; not to be allowed when defence limited by appearance	1 00	0 50
If above three folios, per folio in addition	0 20	0 15
67. Notice of claimant's or defendant's title in action for recovery of land, same fees.		
68. Notice of entry of appearance in action for recovery of land by a party not named in writ	0 50	0 25
69. Demand of particulars	0 50	0 50
70. Particulars of claim, demand, set-off, or counter claim, five folios or under	2 00	0 75
If exceeding five folios, per folio in addition	0 20	0 15
71. Notice of admission of right and denial of ouster by a joint tenant	0 50	....
If above three folios, for every folio additional	0 20	....
72. Of discontinuance and one copy	0 50	0 40
For every additional copy, per folio	0 10	0 10
73. Of disputing amount of claim	0 50	0 25
74. Of confession of action in action for recovery of land as to whole or part	0 50	0 40
75. Notice in lieu of statement of claim, and one copy	0 50	0 25
For every additional copy, per folio	0 10	0 10
76. Of trial or assessment and one copy	0 50	0 25
For every additional copy, per folio	0 10	0 10
77. Demand of residence of plaintiff	0 50	0 25
78. Demand of names of partners	0 50	0 25
79. All common notices not above specified	0 50	0 25
80. Notice to admit, and produce, if not exceeding two folios, and one copy	0 50	0 25
For every additional copy, per folio	0 10	0 10
81. For each necessary folio above two	0 20	0 20
82. Notice of setting down on motion for judgment, or on further directions and one copy	0 50	0 25
For every additional copy, per folio	0 10	0 10
83. Notice of motion in Court, or Chambers, engrossing and copy to serve, per folio	0 30	0 15
For every additional copy, per folio	0 10	0 10
84. Notice of taxation, or appointment to tax, and one copy	0 50	0 25
For every additional copy, per folio	0 10	0 10
85. For preparing, and filling up for service, in any cause or matter, each notice to creditors to prove claims, and each notice that cheque may be received, specifying the amounts to be received for principal and interest, and costs, if any—including mailing	0 25	0 25
86. Notice of filing affidavits, when required, and one copy (only one notice to be allowed for a set of affidavits filed, or which ought to be filed together)	0 50	0 25
For every additional copy, per folio	0 10	0 10
87. Notice by Defendant to third party, under Rule 329	1 00	0 50

Perusals.

	Higher Scale $ c.	Lower Scale $ c.
88. Of each of the pleadings as defined by the Judicature Act	1 00	0 50
89. Of special case by the solicitor of any party, except the one by whom it is prepared, when the case is submitted in the course of the cause	2 00	1 00
90. And in special, or contested actions, or matters, or of interrogatories, and cross-interrogatories on commission	Such sum as the Taxing Officer in Toronto thinks fit.	0 50
91. Of affidavits and exhibits of a party adverse in interest, filed or produced on any application, where perusal is necessary if 20 folios or under	1 00	0 50
On the Higher Scale per folio over 20 folios	0 05	....
(Not in any case to exceed the sum of $5.)		

	HIGHER SCALE.	LOWER SCALE AND COUNTY COURTS.
TABLE OF COSTS.—*Continued.*	$ c.	$ c.
ATTENDANCES.		
92. Necessary attendances consequent on the service of a notice to produce or admit, or an inspection of documents when produced under order including making admission, altogether.	1 00	0 50
To be increased by Taxing Officer (or County Court Clerk) in cases of special, difficult and important nature, to.	2 00	1 00
93. Attending on return of motion, in Chambers.	1 00	0 50
To be increased in the discretion of the presiding officer,or in C. C. cases of the Judge, to.	2 00	1 50
94. On consultation, or conference, with counsel, in special, difficult, and important matters, in the discretion of the Taxing Officer in Toronto (or in C. C. cases of the County Court Clerk) to....	2 00	1 00
To be increased in the discretion of the Taxing Officer as between solicitor and client, to such sum as he shall see fit, or in C. C. cases in the discretion of the C. C. Judge to, not exceeding		3 00
No special attendance to be allowed to a solicitor on proceedings on which he also appears as counsel.		
95. Solicitor attending Court on trial of cause, when not himself counsel, or partner of counsel	2 00	1 00
And in special, difficult, and important cases, each hour necessarily present at trial ..	2 00	1 00
In no case to exceed, per day	10 00	5 00
(Provided the attendance of such solicitor, and the length of time of such attendance, be duly entered at the time in the book of the Registrar, Deputy-Registrar, Deputy-Clerk of the Crown, Clerk of Assize, C. C. Clerk, or other officer of the Court present at the time, or proved by affidavit.)		
96. To hear judgment when not given on close of argument.	2 00	1 00
97. To hear judgment when cause on list for judgment, but judgment not given.	2 00	1 00
98. On taxation of costs		1 00
99. On taxation of costs, per hour	1 00	
100. On revision, per hour, when attendance required by Taxing Officer, or revision had on order...	1 00	0 50
101. On revision by County Court Judge on appeal.		0 50
102. To obtain or give undertaking to appear, when service accepted by a solicitor.	1 00	0 50
103. Attendance to file, or serve .	0 50	0 25
104. Attendance on warrant, or appointment, of Master, Registrar, Examiner, Referee, or County Court Clerk, per hour.	1 00	0 50
To be increased in the discretion of the Taxing Officer in Toronto, or, in C. C. cases, the C. C. Judge, to not exceeding per hour....	2 00	1 00
105. Attendance on Master, or Registrar (or County Court Clerk), in special matters, per hour.	1 00	0 50
106. Every other necessary attendance	0 50	0 25
107. On important points and matters, requiring the attendance of counsel, the Master, or Examiner, or Referee, Judgment Clerk, or Inspector of Titles, may certify the amount of counsel fee proper to be allowed (to be noted at the time,) for the guidance of the Taxing Officer in Toronto (or the Judge in C. C. cases,) who may allow the same in lieu of fees for attendance. On the Lower Scale not to exceed $5 ..		
108. Or on special and important points, and matters requiring the attendance of counsel, before Examiner, Referee, or County Court Clerk, the County Court Judge may, in County Court cases in lieu of the fees for attendance, allow a counsel fee when counsel attend the same, not to exceed $5.		
BRIEFS.		
109. For drawing briefs, five folios or under.	2 00	1 00
110. " " for each folio above five.	0 10	0 10
111. For drawing brief, per folio, for original and necessary matter.	0 20	0 20
112. Copy of documents, other than pleadings, per folio.	0 10	0 10
113. Copy of brief for second counsel, when fee taxed to him, per folio..	0 10	

	HIGHER SCALE.	LOWER SCALE AND COUNTY COURTS.
TABLE OF COSTS.—*Continued.*	$ c.	$ c.

COURT FEES.

114. Fees after statement of claim, or, where statement dispensed with, after filing writ, on defence, joinder of issue, trial, or argument before Courts or any other step in the cause, and on judgments, other than præcipe judgments in mortgage cases. No two fees to be allowed to either party when such proceedings are taken, or had, between the first day of any sittings of the Courts, (fixed by Rule 216, or (R. S. O. 1887, c. 47, s. 12, as the case may be), and the first day of the following sittings so fixed......................	1 00	0 50
115. Fee on certified copy of pleadings for Judge.	1 00	0 50
116. Fee on every order, or judgment to the party obtaining the same.	1 00	0 50
117. Fee on præcipe judgment in mortgage cases.......................	4 00	2 00

AFFIDAVITS.

118. Drawing affidavits, per folio	0 20	0 20
119. Engrossing same to have sworn, per folio	0 10	0 10
120. Copies of affidavits, per folio, when necessary	0 10	0 10
121. Common affidavits of service, including service by post when necessary, or of payment of mileage and of non-appearance, including copy, oath, and attendance to swear	1 00	0 75
122. The solicitor for preparing each exhibit in town or country........ .	0 10	0 10

DEFENDANTS.

123. Appearance, including attending to enter......:.............	1 00	0 50
For each additional defendant.	0 20	0 10
124. For limiting defence in action for recovery of land in appearance, besides above allowance for appearance; not to be allowed when notice of limiting defence served	1 00	0 50

JUDGMENT, RULES, OR ORDERS.

125. Drawing minutes of judgment, or order, per folio, when prepared by solicitor, under directions of Registrar, or Judgment Clerk, (or, in C. C. cases, of the C. C. Judge)...........................	0 20	0 20
126. Judgment for non-appearance on specially indorsed writs, and in action for recovery of land	1 00	0 50
127. Attending for appointment to settle or pass judgment, or order of Court, copy and service	1 30	0 50
128. When served on more than one party, the extra copies and services are to be allowed.		
129. For every hour's attendance before proper officer on settling or passing minutes	1 00	0 50
To be increased in the discretion of the officer in special and difficult cases, when the solicitor attends personally, to a sum not exceeding altogether.	5 00	2 50

LETTERS.

130. Letter to each defendant before suit, only one letter to be allowed to any defendants who are in partnership, and when subject of suit relates to the transactions of their partnership	0 50	0 25
131. Common letters, including necessary agency letters	0 50	0 25

18

	HIGHER SCALE.	LOWER SCALE AND COUNTY COURTS.
TABLE OF COSTS.—*Continued.*	$ c.	$ c.

LETTERS.—*Continued.*

132. With power to the taxing officer (or in C. C. cases the C. C. Clerk), as between solicitor and client, to increase the fee for special and important letters, to an amount not exceeding ....

133. Postages—the amount actually disbursed.

134. For correspondence during the progress of an appeal to the Court of Appeal a reasonable sum in the discretion of the Taxing Officer may be allowed not exceeding.........

SALES BY MASTER, OR AUCTIONEER, OR REAL REPRESENTATIVE IN PARTITION SUITS.

135. Drawing advertisements for the sale of real or personal estate under the direction of the Court, including all copies, except for printing...............
And for each folio over five, per folio............................
(To be increased in the discretion of the Master (or in C.C. cases the C. C. Judge) to a sum not exceeding ten dollars, when special information has been procured for the purpose of sale.)

136. Copies for printing, per folio..................................

137. Each necessary attendance on printer ....

138. Attending and making arrangements with auctioneer.......

139. Revising proof.....

140. Fee on conducting sale when held where solicitor resides.....

141. If solicitor is engaged for more than three hours, for every hour beyond that time..............

142. Fee on conducting sale elsewhere, besides all necessary travelling and hotel expenses, when solicitor attends with the approval of the Master (or real representative) previously given..............
If the sale occupies more than one day, the Master may allow him, in addition to his travelling expenses, *per diem*, a sum not exceeding twenty dollars.
The Master may also allow to one other party to the suit his fees and expenses for attending sales, if, in his opinion, it is necessary and proper that he should attend.

MISCELLANEOUS.

143. Statement of issues in Master's office, when required by the Master .
In special matters to be increased in the discretion of the Taxing Officer in Toronto.

144. For each folio over 10......

145. When it has been satisfactorily proved that proceedings have been taken by solicitors out of Court to expedite proceedings, save costs, or compromise actions, an allowance is to be made therefor in the discretion of the Taxing Officer in Toronto (or Judge of County Court in C. C. cases).

146. Drawing bill of costs as between party and party for taxation, (including engrossing and copy for Taxing Officer, or C. C. Clerk,) per folio.....

147. Copy, per folio, to serve.................................

COUNSEL FEES.

148. Fee on motion of course, or on motion in matters not special ....

149. On special *ex parte* motion or application to the Court, (only one counsel fee to be taxed) ....

No.	HIGHER SCALE	LOWER SCALE
132	2 00	1 00
134	5 00	2 00
135 (printing)	2 00	1 00
135 (per folio)	0 20	0 15
136	0 10	0 10
137	0 50	0 25
138	1 00	0 50
139	1 00	0 50
140	5 00	3 00
141	1 00	0 75
142	10 00	5 00
143	2 00	1 00
144	0 20	0 20
146	0 30	0 20
147	0 10	0 10
148	2 00	1 00
149	5 00	2 00

	Higher Scale.	Lower Scale and County Court.
TABLE OF COSTS.—*Continued.*	$ c.	$ c.

COUNSEL FEES.—*Continued.*

To be increased in the discretion of the Taxing Officer in Toronto, (or Judge of County Court in C. C. cases, who shall mark amount to be taxed on order of Court, if any, before taxation) to.........

	Higher Scale	Lower Scale
To be increased ... to be taxed on order of Court, if any, before taxation) to.........	10 00	5 00
150. Fee on argument on supporting or opposing application to the Court, or argument of demurrer, special case, or appeal.............	10 00	5 00
On Higher Scale and Lower Scale to be increased in the discretion of the Taxing Officer in Toronto. In C. C. to be increased in the discretion of the Judge, to..........	....	10 00
151. On consultations	5 00	2 00
152. Fee, with brief, on assessment............................	10 00	6 00
153. Fee, with brief, at trial.................................	10 00	10 00
To be increased by taxing officer in his discretion to a sum not exceeding $40 to senior counsel, and $20 to junior counsel, in actions of a special and important nature, Provided that the Taxing Officer in Toronto shall have power to tax increased fees, but more than one counsel fee shall not be allowed in any case not of a special and important nature; not more than two in any case, Provided that if an application to increase fees be made in the first instance to the Local Taxing Officer, and a *fiat* granted, no application shall thereafter be made to the Taxing Officer at Toronto.		
To be increased by the Taxing Officer at Toronto or the Judge (as the case may require) in actions of a special or important nature and on appeals to the Court of Appeal, (on notice to the opposite party,) to a sum not exceeding................................	....	25 00
(In C. C. cases no charge to be made by either party in connection with such application.)		
154. On argument or examination in Chambers in cases proper for the attendance of counsel and where counsel attends.	2 00	1 00
To be increased in the discretion of the Master in Chambers, or the Master in Ordinary in High Court cases.		
To be increased in the discretion of the Judge in C. C. cases to a sum not exceeding................................	....	5 00
155. On argument of appeal in the Court of Appeal, in the discretion of Taxing Officer at Toronto, ~~not exceeding $80 to the senior counsel and $50 to the junior counsel (in ordinary cases larger fees~~ than $40 to the senior counsel and $20 to the junior counsel not to be ~~allowed) in High Court cases and~~ in County Court appeals not exceeding $25.		
(Two counsel fees not to be allowed except in difficult and important cases.		
156. To attend reference to Master, C. C. Clerk, or Referee, when counsel necessary.....................................	5 00	3 00
To be increased in special and important matters requiring the attendance of counsel, in the discretion of the Taxing Officer in Toronto, (or County Court Clerk in C. C. cases, not exceeding)....	....	6 00
157. Fee on drawing, and settling, allegations in præcipe for revivor, in special cases, proper for opinion of counsel.......................	2 00	1 00
To be increased in the discretion of Taxing Officer, (or C. C. Clerk in C. C. cases,) to an amount not exceeding	5 00	2 00
158. On settling pleadings, interrogatories, special cases or petitions, and advising on evidence in contested cases, in the discretion of the Taxing Officer, (or C. C. Clerk in C. C. cases,) not exceeding.....	5 00	3 00
159. On settling the appeal case and reasons for or against appeal........	5 00	2 00
To be increased in the discretion of the Taxing Office at Toronto in special and important matters to a sum not exceeding	20 00	5 00
160. When any fee is subject to be increased, in the discretion of the Taxing Officer in Toronto, either party to the taxation may, during its progress, require that such item shall be referred by the Local Taxing Officer to the Taxing Officer in Toronto, whose decision shall be final as to that item, but this shall not prevent an appeal from such taxation. .		

(handwritten margin notes: died / 150 & / 155 (A))

	HIGHER SCALE.	LOWER SCALE AND COUNTY COURTS.
TABLE OF COSTS.—*Continued.*	$ c.	$ c.

COUNSEL FEES.- *Continued.*

161. The necessary letters and attendances incurred in obtaining the decision of the Taxing Officer in Toronto in any matters which are in his discretion shall be allowed as part of the costs of the cause.

162. The Taxing Officer in Toronto may apply to a Judge, or the Courts, on the taxation of any item which is in his discretion, or is referred to him.

163. No application shall be allowed by either solicitor, or counsel, to a Judge, or the Court, in reference to any item which is in the discretion of the Taxing Officers in Toronto, but this is not to prevent an appeal from a Taxing Officer.

164. On arbitrations, counsel fees may be allowed and taxed on the same scale and conditions, so far as possible, as those hereinbefore prescribed for counsel fees at trials.

NOTE 1.—In taxing costs between solicitor and client, the Taxing Officer or County Court Clerk, in County Court cases, may allow for services rendered not provided for by this tariff, a reasonable compensation as far as practicable analogous to its provisions.

NOTE 2.—On appeals to the Court of Appeal where the fees are not above provided for the same fees and allowances shall be taxed as are allowed for similar services in the High Court or County Court, as the case may be. App. O. 28-51.

TARIFF B.

TARIFF OF DISBURSEMENTS.

(Referred to in Rule 1218.)

The following fees and allowances shall be taken and received by the officers and persons herein mentioned in Civil Actions in the High Court and Court of Appeal and in the County Courts in lieu of all fees payable to those officers and persons under the tariffs heretofore in force in the said Courts :—

	HIGHER SCALE.	LOWER SCALE AND COUNTY COURT.
FEES TO BE PAYABLE IN STAMPS OR OTHERWISE TO OFFICERS OF THE COURTS.	$ c.	$ c.
(Inclusive of all Fees expressly imposed by Statute.)		
REGISTRAR OF COURT OF APPEAL.		
Setting down for argument (a)	4 00	0 50
On every judgment or order of the Court passed and entered (a)....	2 00	....
Certificate on discharging appeal...........	0 90	0 90
On every order in Chambers	0 50	0 50
For other services the like charges as are to be taken by the Registrars of the High Court for similar services.		
MASTER IN ORDINARY, LOCAL MASTERS. AND OFFICIAL AND SPECIAL REFEREES.		
Filing and entering judgment or order in Master's book.....	0 20	0 10
Every warrant or appointment...........................	0 50	0 10
Administering oath or taking affirmation.	0 20	0 20
Marking every exhibit......	0 20	0 10
Drawing depositions (in infancy matters only) reports or orders, per folio, to include time occupied.	0 20	0 20
Fair copy, per folio (when necessary).........................	0 10	0 10
Copy of papers given out when required, per folio	0 10	0 10
Every attendance upon any proceeding or enlargement thereof or selling property..	1 50	0 50
For each additional hour	1 50	0 50
Fee on report signed (only one to be allowed in each action or matter, on first report)......	2 00	*Nil.*
Every certificate, if not longer than two folios	0 50	0 20
For each folio over two	0 20	*Nil.*
Filing each paper, or subsequent order.................................	0 10	0 10
Taxing costs, per hour	1 00	....
Taxing costs, including attendance.......................		0 80
Making up and forwarding depositions, bills of costs and proceedings in Master's office....	0 50	0 10
Every special attendance out of office within two miles, per hour occupied by reference or sale...........	2 00	0 50
Every additional mile above two for travelling expenses..	0 20	0 10
Every attendance on application to a Master in Chambers.............	1 00	0 50
Every order in Chambers....	0 50	0 20
Searching files in office	....	0 10
Do. on Higher Scale same allowance as to Deputy Registrar.		

(a) Imposed by R. S. O. 1887 c. 44, s. 156.

	HIGHER SCALE.	LOWER SCALE AND COUNTY COURTS.
FEES TO BE PAYABLE IN STAMPS, ETC.	$ c.	$ c.

CLERK OF THE PROCESS, CLERK OF RECORDS AND WRITS, REGISTRARS, LOCAL REGISTRARS, DEPUTY REGISTRARS, DEPUTY CLERKS OF THE CROWN, CLERK IN CHAMBERS, ACCOUNTANT AND TAXING OFFICERS IN THE HIGH COURT, AND THE CLERKS OF THE COUNTY COURTS.

	HIGHER SCALE	LOWER SCALE
Every Writ	0 50	0 50
Every Concurrent, Alias, Pluries or Renewed Writ	0 50	0 40
Additional on every Writ by Statute (b)	0 50	
Every appearance entered, and filing memorandum thereof	0 20	0 15
Every appearance, each Defendant after the first	0 10	0 10
Filing every Affidavit, Writ, or other proceeding	0 10	0 10
Amending every Writ or other proceeding	0 30	0 25
Upon payment of money into Court	0 30	0 30
Upon payment of money out of Court	0 30	0 30
Passing and certifying Record (payable in cash to Deputy Clerks of the Crown, Local Registrars and Deputy Registrars not paid by salary)	1 00	0 50
Entering action for trial or assessment (including H. C. cases entered for trial at C. C.) payable in actions in the Chancery Division to the present Deputy Registrars so long as they retain office and are not paid by salary: in other cases payable to the Deputy Clerk, Local Registrar or Clerk of Assize	2 00	0 50
(The fee of $2 payable by Statute to be payable in cash to Deputy Clerks of the Crown, Local Registrars and Deputy Registrars not paid by salary. An additional fee of $5 cash to be also paid to the present Deputy Registrars so long as they retain office and are not paid by salary).		
On setting down on the paper for argument every demurrer or special case.	0 20	0 20
Additional fee payable by Statute (b)	0 30	
Setting down a cause for any other purpose	0 50	0 20
Subpœna, including filing Præcipe	0 50	0 20
Additional fee by Statute (b)	0 50	
Every Reference, Inquiry, Examination, or other special matter for every meeting not exceeding one hour	1 00	0 75
Every Reference, Inquiry, Examination, or other special matter for every additional hour or less	1 00	0 50
Fee on report made on such reference, etc.	1 00	1 00
Attending on opening Commission	1 00	0 50
Every Certificate made evidence by Law, or required by the practice, including any necessary search	0 50	0 50
Additional fee where Seal is required (b)	0 50	
Every Certificate for Registration	0 50	0 20
Additional fee for Seal of Court or office (b)	0 50	
Entering Certificate of Title or Conveyance, per folio	0 10	0 10
Every ordinary Rule or Order	0 30	0 30
Additional fee by Statute (b)	0 20	
Every Special Rule or Order, not exceeding six folios, per folio	0 20	0 20
Additional fee by Statute (b)	0 20	
Every Chamber Order	0 50	0 50
Every Interlocutory Judgment or Judgment by default	0 50	0 30
Additional fee by Statute (b)	0 60	
Every Final Judgment otherwise than Judgment by Default	0 50	0 50
Additional fee by Statute (b)	0 60	
Taxing Bill of Costs, and giving allocatur or certificate	0 70	0 80
Additional fee by Statute (b)	0 20	
Entering Order when necessary, per folio	0 10	0 10
Taking account on Præcipe Judgment	1 00	0 50
Exemplification, or office or other copy of papers or proceedings required to be given out, per folio, besides certificate and seal when required	0 10	0 10
Additional fee by Statute for Seal of Court (b)	0 50	
Examining and authenticating papers when copy prepared by Solicitor—every three folios	0 05	0 05
Every search, if within one year	0 10	0 10
Every search, if over one year and within two years	0 20	0 10
Every search, if over two years, or a general search	0 50	0 20
Every Affidavit, Affirmation, etc., taken before them	0 20	0 20

(b) Imposed by R. S. O. 1887 c. 44, s. 155, and payable in stamps.

	HIGHER SCALE.	LOWER SCALE AND COUNTY COURTS.

FEES TO BE PAYABLE IN STAMPS, ETC.—Con.

CLERK OF THE PROCESS, ETC.—Continued.

	$ c.	$ c.
Every Allowance and Justification of Bail......	0 30	....
Taking Recognizance of Bail	0 30	....
Entering Satisfaction on Record, and filing Satisfaction piece, including any necessary search	0 50	0 30
Every Commission for the Examination of Witnesses	1 00	0 50
Making up and forwarding papers, including bills of costs.	0 50	0 10
Every Commission for taking Bail and Affidavit (to be on parchment).....	2 00	....
Entering Exoneretur on Bail piece	0 30	0 20
Making up Records of Conviction, or of Acquittal, per folio	0 10	....
Entering and Docketing Judgment.....	0 50	....
For making the Entry required in the Debt Attachment Book and in Cognovit Book	0 50	0 50

CLERKS OF THE COUNTY COURTS (Additional).

Every Verdict taken, non-suit, Jury discharged, Record withdrawn, or rule or order of reference at the trial....................................	....	0 50
Drawing appointments made by the Judge	....	0 25
Attending at every special hearing before the Judge under R. S. O. 1887, c. 53, s. 1, and at taking Examination and Evidence and at Sittings in reference to the C. C. Judge from the H. C. not exceeding one hour.		0·50
Every additional hour or less......................................	....	0 50
Every appointment for taxation of costs or otherwise, made by C. C. Clerk.	....	0 10
Every meeting under R. S. O. 1887, c. 53, s. 9, not exceeding two hours..	....	2 00
For each additional hour or less (to be taxed by the C.C. Judge.).........	....	1 00
For every Jury sworn	....	1 00
Every enlargement on application o the Judge in Chambers, including search, if marked by the Clerk	....	0 15

DEPUTY REGISTRARS NOT PAID BY SALARY.

(Additional, only so long as the present officers retain office and are not paid by salary).

Marking every exhibit produced on the examination of witnesses ...	0 20	
Swearing each witness....................	0 20	
Attending on inspection of documents, produced with affidavits on production, per hour........	1 00	

SPECIAL EXAMINER.

Every appointment...........................	0 50	0 10
Administering oath or taking affirmation...........................	0 20	0 20
Marking every exhibit..	0 20	0 20
Taking depositions per hour..	1 50	0 75
Fair copy for Solicitor, per folio (when required)...	0 10	0 10
Every attendance out of office when within two miles...................	2 00	0 50
Every attendance over two miles out of office—extra per mile...........	0 20	0 10
Every certificate	0 50	0 25
Making up and forwarding answers, depositions, etc., including filing Præcipe...	0 50	0 25
For every attendance upon an appointment, when Solicitor or witnesses do not attend and examiner not previously notified	1 00	0 50

REFEREE OF TITLES.

Every Warrant or Appointment	0 30	....
Administering Oath or taking Affirmation............................ ...	0 20	....
Marking every exhibit......	0 20	....
Drawing depositions, reports or orders, per folio.............	0 20	....
One fair copy when necessary, per folio...........................	0 10	....

	HIGHER SCALE.	LOWER SCALE AND COUNTY COURTS.
FEES TO BE PAYABLE IN STAMPS, ETC.—*Con.*	$ c.	$ c.
REFEREE OF TITLES.—*Con.*		
Copy of papers given out when required, per folio......................	0 10	....
Every attendance upon a reference..............................	1 00	....
For each additional hour.....	1 00	....
Every certificate	0 50	....
Filing each paper...........................	0 10	....
Taxing costs, including attendance	1 00	....
Making up and forwarding answers and depositions	0 30	....
Every special attendance out of office within two miles	1 00	....
Every additional mile above two...............................	0 20	....
Reading affidavit, per folio..	0 02	....
Matter added, per folio....................................	0 20	....
Searching files in office	0 20	....
Every deed in the chain of title other than satisfied mortgages	0 50	....
Drawing and engrossing certificate of title, or conveyance in duplicate	4 00	....
REAL REPRESENTATIVE.		
The Real Representative acting under the Act respecting the partition and sale of Real Estate (R. S. O. 1887, c. 104) shall, in the case of proceedings.being instituted in the High Court or a County Court, be entitled to demand and receive for all services performed by him under the said Act, the same fees as nearly as may be as are allowed to Local Masters or Special Examiners for similar services. Rule of Q.B. and C.P., 6th June, 1878.		
CRIER.		
Calling every case, with or without jury	0 60	0 50
Swearing each witness, or constable	0 15	0 15
COMMISSIONERS.		
For taking every affidavit	0 20	0 20
For taking every recognizance of bail	0 50	0 50
For marking every exhibit	0 10	0 10
ALLOWANCE TO WITNESSES.		
To witnesses residing within three miles of the court house, per diem	1 00	1 00
To witnesses residing over three miles from the court house	1 25	1 25
Barristers and solicitors, physicians and surgeons, other than parties to the cause, when called upon to give evidence, in consequence of any professional service rendered by them, or to give professional opinions, per diem	4 00	4 00
Engineers, surveyors and architects, other than parties to the cause, when called upon to give evidence of any professional service rendered by them, or to give evidence depending upon their skill or judgment, per diem....................	4 00	4 00
If witnesses attend in one case only, they will be entitled to the full allowance. If they attend in more than one case, they will be entitled to a proportionate part in each cause only.		
The travelling expenses of witnesses, over three miles, shall be allowed, according to the sums reasonably and actually paid, but in no case shall exceed twenty cents per mile, one way.		
N.B.—In all applications and proceedings before the County Court Judges not relating to suits instituted in any Court of Civil Jurisdiction there shall be payable to the Clerks of the County Courts the same fees as in this Table so far as the same are applicable.		

TARIFF C.

FEES OF SHERIFFS AND CORONERS
IN CIVIL MATTERS.

(Referred to in Rule 1232.)

—	HIGHER SCALE.	LOWER SCALE AND COUNTY COURTS.
FEES PAYABLE TO SHERIFFS AND CORONERS.	$ c.	$ c.
General Matters.		
Receiving, filing, entering, and indorsing all Writs, Pleadings, Rules, Notices, or other papers, each	0 25	0 10
Return of all Process and Writs, except Subpœnas	0 50	0 25
Return of Pleadings, Rules, Notices, or other papers	0 25	0 15
Every search, not being by a party to a cause or his Solicitor	0 30	0 30
Certificate of result of such search, when required (a search for a Writ against lands of a party shall include sales under Writ against same party, and for the then last six months)	0 75	0 75
Where a certificate respecting executions against lands is required, the Sheriff, if so requested, is to include in one certificate any number of names in respect of which the certificate may be required in the same matter or investigation, but shall be entitled to the same fees as if one certificate were given for each name, provided that no greater sum than $4 shall be charged or collected in respect of such certificate. (50 V. c. 7, s. 5).		
Every Warrant to execute any Process *mesne* or final, directed to the Sheriff, when given to a Bailiff	0 75	0 50
Every Jury sworn, or Cause tried before a Judge	1 00	0 80
Every Letter written (including copy) required by party or his Solicitor respecting Writs or Process, when postage prepaid	0 50	0 30
Drawing every Affidavit when necessary and prepared by Sheriff	0 25	0 25
Service of Process and Papers.		
Service of non-bailable Process, each defendant (no fee for Affidavit of Service in such cases to be allowed, unless Service made or recognized, by Sheriff ; on Lower and County Court scales, including affidavit of service)	1 50	1 00
Serving Subpœnas, Rules, Notices, or other papers (besides mileage)	0 75	0 50
For each *additional* party served	0 50	0 25
Actual and necessary mileage from the Court House to the place where service of any Process, paper or proceeding is made, per mile	0 13	0 13
Arrest and Attachment.		
Arrest, when amount does not exceed $200	2 00	2 00
" " " $400	4 00	4 00
" " over $400	6 00	
Bail Bond or Bond to the limits	2 00	1 00
Assignment of the same	1 00	0 25
Mileage going to arrest when made, per mile	0 13	0 13
" conveying party arrested from place of arrest to the gaol, per mile	0 13	0 13
Bringing up Prisoner on attachment or *Habeas Corpus*, besides travel at 20c. per mile	1 50	1 00

	HIGHER SCALE.	LOWER SCALE AND COUNTY COURTS.

FEES PAYABLE TO SHERIFFS AND CORONERS.—*Con.*

	$ c.	$ c.
Absconding Debtors.		
Seizing estate and effects on attachment against an absconding debtor...	3 00	1 50
Valuators, each	1 00	1 00
Removing or retaining property, reasonable and necessary disbursements with, and allowances to be made by the Taxing Officer, or in the C. C. by order of the Court or a Judge.		
Drawing Bond to secure goods taken under an attachment against an absconding debtor, if prepared by Sheriff	1 50	1 50
Replevin.		
Precept or Warrant to Bailiff in Replevin	0 75	0 40
Drawing Notice for Service on Defendant in Replevin	0 75	0 40
Delivering Goods to the party obtaining the Order of Replevin	3 00	1 50
For Writ *De Retorno Habendo*	1 00	0 50
Drawing Replevin Bond	2 00	1 00
Assignment	1 00	0 25
All necessary disbursements for the possession, care and removal of property taken in Replevin.		
Juries.		
Notice of appointment for ballot of Jury	0 50	0 25
Notice to Clerk of Peace of such appointment	0 50	0 25
Fee on balloting Special Jury	5 00	2 50
Fee on striking "	2 50	1 25
Serving each Special Juror (besides mileage at 13c. per mile)	0 50	0 25
Returning Panel of Special Jurors	1 00	0 50
Keeping and checking pay list of Special Jurors' attendance, in each case.	1 00	1 00
Sales, Poundage, Etc.		
Poundage on Executions, and on attachments in the nature of Executions, where the sum made shall not exceed $1,000 (in the C. C. on the sum made)	6 per cent.	5 per cent.
Where the sum is over $1,000 and under $4,000, upon the excess over $1,000 (in addition to the poundage allowed up to $1,000)	3 per cent.	
Where the sum is $4,000 and over, upon the excess over $4,000 (in addition to the poundage allowed up to $4,000)	1½ per cent	
(Exclusive of mileage, for going to seize and sell, and of all disbursements necessarily incurred in the care and removal of property).		
Schedule taken on Execution, attachment, or other process, including copy to Defendant, not exceeding 5 folios	1 00	0 50
Each folio above 5	0 10	0 10
Drawing advertisements when required by law to be published in the official *Gazette* or other newspaper, or to be posted up in a Court House or other place, and transmitting same, in each suit	1 50	0 75
Every necessary notice of Sale of Goods (not more than 3), in each suit...	0 75	0 40
Every notice of Postponement of Sale, in each suit	0 25	0 20
The sum actually disbursed for Advertisements required by law to be inserted in the official *Gazette* or other newspaper.		
Sequestration.		
Upon seizure of estate and effects under writ of sequestration	4 00	1 00
Schedule of goods taken in execution (including copy for defendant) if not exceeding five folios	1 00	0 50
Each folio above five	0 10	0 10
Removing or retaining property, reasonable and necessary disbursements and allowances to be made by the Taxing Officer, or by order of the Court or Judge.		
(Poundage upon sequestration followed by sale and collection—as on other executions).		

	HIGHER SCALE.	LOWER SCALE AND COUNTY COURTS.

FEES PAYABLE TO SHERIFFS AND CORONERS.—Con.

	$ c.	$ c.

Writ of Possession.

Executing Writ of Possession and serving and executing Writ of Restitution, besides mileage.............................	6 00	2 00

Hab. Fac. Seisin.

Viewing Lands, and instructing Surveyors under Hab. Fac. Seisin, exclusive of mileage, per day..........	5 00	
Giving Possession, exclusive of mileage and assistance...................	5 00	
All necessary disbursements to Surveyors and others for surveying the lands and giving possession, to be allowed to the Sheriff.		

On a View by a Jury.

For travelling expenses to the Sheriff, Shewers, and Jurymen—Expenses actually paid, if reasonable.		
Fee to the Sheriff, when the distance does not exceed five miles from his office... ..	2 00	
Where such distance exceeds five miles............................	3 00	
In case he shall be necessarily absent more than one day—then for each day after the first, a further fee of	3 00	
Fee to each of Shewers—the same as to the Sheriff, calculating, &c.		
Fee to each common juryman, per diem...............................	1 00	
Fee to each special juryman, per diem...............................	2 00	
Allowance for refreshment to the Sheriff, shewers, and jurymen, common or special, each, per diem...............................	1 00	
To the Sheriff for summoning each juryman, whose residence is not more than five miles distant from the Sheriff's office.....	0 40	
And for each whose residence exceeds five miles from Sheriff's office.....	0 60	
Rules T. T., 1856, 39.		

Writ of Enquiry, Escheat, Etc.

Presiding or attendance on execution of Writ of Enquiry, or under any Writ of Escheat, or other Writ of a like nature	5 00	4 00
Summoning each Juror in such case.....	0 50	0 50
Bailiff's Fee summoning Jury, mileage per mile	0 13	0 13
Hire of Room, if actually paid, not to exceed $2 per day................		
Mileage from the Court House to the place where Writ executed, per mile..	0 13	0 13

CORONERS.

The same fees shall be taxed and allowed to Coroners for services rendered by them in the service, execution and return of process, as allowed to Sheriffs for the same services above specified.

(Signed)   JOHN H. HAGARTY, C.J.O.   (Signed)   W. PROUDFOOT, J.
   "   GEO. W. BURTON, J.A.   "   THOMAS FERGUSON, J.
   "   C. S. PATTERSON, J.A.   "   JOHN E. ROSE, J.
   "   F. OSLER, J.A.   "   THOMAS ROBERTSON, J.
   "   J. A. BOYD, C.   "   W. G. FALCONBRIDGE, J.
   "   THOMAS GALT, C.J., C.P.D.   "   W. P. R. STREET, J.
   "   J. D. ARMOUR, C.J., Q.B.D.   "   HUGH MacMAHON, J.

OF

RULES, ORDERS AND PARTS OF STATUTES

CONSOLIDATED.

RULES OF TRINITY TERM, 1856.					RULES OF TRINITY TERM, 1856.		
No. of Rule.	CONSOLIDATED.		REMARKS.	No. of Rule.	CONSOLIDATED.		REMARKS.
	Rule.	Page.			Rule.	Page.	
1			{ Sup. *See* C. R. 235, 278, 287 to 289.	38	....	....	Effete.
2			"	39	703	91	
3			Sup. *See* C.R. 283.	40			Sup. *See* C. R. 798.
4	463	63	"	41			Effete.
5			Sup. *See* C.R. 313.	42			"
6			" 324 (b)	43			"
7			Effete.	44			Sup. *See* C. R. 1170.
8			Sup. *See* C.R. 641, 642	45	794	103	
9			Sup. *See* C.R. 483, 484	46			Effete.
10			{ Sup. *See* C. R. 399, 449.	47			Sup. *See* C.R. 764, 765
11			Sup. *See* C. R. 635.	48	1199	158	
12			" 1170.	49			Effete.
13			" 1170.	50	1200	158	
14			{ Sup. J.A.195a, which is Sup. C. R. 390.	51			Sup. *See* C. R. 1170.
15			Sup. *See* C.R. 538, 540	52	1205	158	
16			Effete.	53			Effete.
17	}		Sup. *See* C. R. 540.	54			
18	}			55			{ Sup. *See* C. R. 888 to 891, 893.
19			" 653.	56			{ Sup. *See* C. R. 233, 1047.
20			Effete.	57			Effete.
21	418	57		58			
22			Effete.	59			
23			Sup. *See* C. R. 1245.	60			Effete.
24			" 641, 642, 670	61			
25			Effete.	62			
26	736	96		63			
27	734			64	787	103	
28	737	97		65	788		
29	}		{ Sup. *See* C. R. 400, 617 to 619.	66	1054	138	
30	}			67			Effete.
31	560	74		68	1056	138	
32			Effete.	69	1057		
33			{ Rescinded by Rule 1, Feb. 7, 1876.	70	1083	141	
34			Sup. *See* C. R. 661.	71	1059	138	
35			Effete.	72	1060	139	
36			Sup. *See* C. R. 654.	73	1061		
37	662	86		74	1058	138	
				75	1070	140	
				76	1071		

RULES OF TRINITY TERM, 1856.

No. of Rule	Consolidated Rule	Consolidated Page	Remarks.
77	1072		
78	1073		
79	1074		
80	1075		
81	1076		
82	1077		
83	1078		
84	1079	141	
85	1080		
86	1081		
87	1082		
88	1084		
89	1085		
90	1086		
91	1087		
92			Sup. See C.R. 704, 714
93			" 293 to 296
94			" 403, 672
95	643	84	
96	644		
97	645		
98	1063 (a)	139	
99	1053	138	
100	1052		
101	908	118	
102	909		
103	910		
104			Sup. See C.R. 879.
105	911	118	
106	443	60	
107	534	71	
108			{ Sup. See C.R. 526, 1170.
109			Sup. See C.R. 605.
110			" 606.
111			" 611.
112			" 605.
113			" 612.
114	613	81	
115			Effete.
116			do
117			do
118			Sup. See C.R. 41, 138
119			Sup. See C.R. 543.
120	See 25	5	
121 }			
122 }			Effete.
123			Effete. See C.R. 526.
124	481	65	
125 }			
126 }			Effete.
127 }			
128 }			
129 }			Effete. See C.R. 866.
130			Effete.
131	447	61	
132			{ Sup. See C.R. 279, 398, 461.
133			{ Sup. See C.R. 279, 461.
134	466	63	
135			Sup. See C.R. 480.

RULES OF TRINITY TERM, 1856.

No. of Rule	Consolidated Rule	Consolidated Page	Remarks.
136	{ 202 / 461	{ 26 / 62	
137	{ 203 / 461	{ 27 / 62	
138			{ Sup. See C. R. 241, 284, 285.
139	464	63	
140			Sup. See C. R. 879.
141	See 535	71	
142	1206	158	
143			Effete.
144	482	65	
145	9	2	
146			{ Sup. See C. R. 7, 19, 226.
147	450	61	
148	470	64	
149			Effete.
150	11	2	
151			{ Sup. See C. R. 7, 19, 226.
152	13	3	
153	14	3	
154			
155			{ Rescinded by Rule 1, Aug. 27, 1860. See C. R. 1174, 1219.
156			{ Sup. See C. R. 1170, 1174.
157			
158			{ Sup. Tariff 1881 (158, 159).
159			Effete.
160	1212	159	
161			Effete.
162			Sup. Tariff 1865.
163	561	75	
164			Sup. Tariff 1881.
165	1213	160	
166			{ Sup. See C. R. 474, 476.
167	452	61	
168			Sup. C. R. 3.
169	458	62	
170			Effete.

RULES OF PLEADING, 1856.

No. of Rule	Consolidated Rule	Consolidated Page	Remarks.
1			Sup. See C. R. 394.
2			" 394.
3			" 394.
4			" 653.
5-20			" 394.
21	418	57	
22 }			{ Sup. See C. R. 434, 656.
23 }			
24			Sup. See C. R. 1170.
25			Effete.

RULES OF 19TH FEBRUARY, 1859.

No. of Rule.	Consolidated. Rule.	Page.	Remarks.
1	....	.. ..Sup. Tariff 1881.	
2	15	3	
3	16	....	

RULES OF 27TH AUGUST, 1860.

1	....	......	Sup. *See* C. R. 1174 and Tariff A and B.
2	....	......	Rescinded by order of 23rd May, 1874. *See* C. R. 7, 19, 226.

RULES OF 14TH AND 15TH FEBRUARY, 1862.

1	....	......	Sup. Tariff, 2nd Feb. 1874.

RULES OF 15TH FEBRUARY, 1862.

1	{ 871 { 872	113	

RULES OF MAY, 1862.

			These rules are effete.

RULES OF 28TH NOVEMBER, 1863.

1-12	....	......	Rescinded by Rules of September, 1865.
13	....	......	Effete.

RULES OF 9TH SEPTEMBER, 1865.

1	....	......	Sup. J. A. Rule 529, now effete.
2	....	......	Sup. J. A. Rule 530, now effete.
3	....	......	Sup. J. A. Rule 531, now effete.

RULES OF 9TH SEPTEMBER, 1865.

No. of Rule.	Consolidated. Rule.	Page.	Remarks.
4	....	......	Effete or unnecessary
5-11	....	......	Sup. Rules of 17th Nov. 1875, 10, 11, 12. *See* C.R.220, 221, 222.
12	....	......	Sup. Rules of 1st Dec., 1875, 2.
13	....	......	Effete.

RULES OF 2ND DECEMBER, 1865.

1	....	......	Sup. Tariff, 1881.
2	....	......	Sup. *See* C. R. 388, 389, 390, 555.

RULES OF 12TH FEBRUARY, 1867.

1	....	......	Rescinded by Rules of 17th Nov., 1875, 17.
2	....	......	Effete.
3	....	......	Rescinded by Rules of 17th Nov., 1875, 17.

RULE OF 6TH JUNE, 1868.

1	....	......	Sup. R. S. O. 1877, c. 84, s. 2.

RULE OF 2ND DECEMBER, 1869.

1	....	......	Rescinded by Rules of 17th Nov., 1875, 17.

RULE OF 9TH FEBRUARY, 1870.

1	30	6	

RULES OF 9TH DECEMBER, 1871.

			Tariff Sup. by Tariff 1881.

RULES OF 7th FEBRUARY, 1872.

No. of Rule.	Consolidated.		Remarks.
	Rule.	Page.	
			Effete.

RULES OF 2nd FEBRUARY, 1874.

No. of Rule.	Consolidated.		Remarks.
	Rule.	Page.	
1	1232	163	

RULES OF 14th FEBRUARY, 1874.

			Effete.

RULES OF 23rd MAY, 1874.

1	....	......	{ Sup. *See* C. R. 7, 19, 226.

RULES OF 5th SEPTEMBER, 1874.

			Rescinded by Rule 23, 15th May, 1876.

RULES OF 22nd DECEMBER, 1874.

1 2 }	....	......	Effete.

RULES OF 17th NOVEMBER, 1875.

1 2 3 4 5 6 7 8 9 10 11 12 13	.... 220 221 222 223	.... 29 30	Effete.

RULES OF 17th NOVEMBER, 1875.

No. of Rule.	Consolidated.		Remarks.
	Rule.	Page.	
14 15 16 17	....	......	Effete.

RULES OF 1st DECEMBER, 1875.

1 2	....	......	Effete.

RULES OF 4th DECEMBER, 1875.

1 2 3 4 5 6	.... 671	.... 87	Unnecessary. { Sup. *See* C. R. 654, etc.

RULES OF 7th FEBRUARY, 1876.

1 2 3 4	....	......	Effete.

RULES OF 7th FEBRUARY, 1876.

1-7	....	......	Crown cases reserved

RULES OF 10th MARCH, 1876.

1 2 3 4 5 6 7	802 .... 1183 .... 205 206 1184	104 ...... 156 ...... 27 156	Effete.

RULES OF 15th MAY, 1876.

1-5 6	....	....	Sup. *See* C. R. 210. Sup. *See* C. R. 211.

RULES OF 15th MAY, 1876.

No. of Rule	Consolidated Rule	Page	Remarks.
7			Sup. Rules H.C.J. 7.
8			Sup. See C. R. 540.
9			" 537.
10	212	28	
11			Effete.
12- }			Part sup. J. A. Act,
21 }			s. 28, and part effete.
22			Unnecessary.
23 }			
24 }			Effete.

RULE OF 16th MAY, 1876.

1	28 (d)	6	

RULE OF Q. B., 3rd JUNE, 1876.

1			Effete.

RULE OF 21st MAY, 1877.

1	389	54	

RULE OF Q. B., JUNE, 1887.

1			Effete.

RULE OF C. P., 9th JUNE, 1877.

1			Effete.

RULE OF 6th JUNE, 1878.

1			Tariff B.

RULE OF 6th MARCH, 1880.

No. of Rule	Consolidated Rule	Page	Remarks.
1			Sup. Tariff, 1851.

RULE OF Q. B., 5th JUNE, 1880.

1			Effete.

RULE OF C. P., 5th JUNE, 1880.

1			Effete.

RULE OF 27th NOVEMBER, 1880.

1 {	220 223	29 30	

RULE OF Q. B., MICH. T. 1880.

1			Effete.

RULE OF C. P., MICH. T., 1880.

1			Effete.

MUN. ELECTION RULES.

			Sup. C.R. 1036, &c.

19

CHANCERY ORDERS.

CHANCERY ORDERS.

No. of Order	Consolidated Rule	Page	Remarks
1-7			Effete.
8			Sup. Chy. O. 648.
9			
10	}		Effete.
11	}		
12	762	100	
13	763		
14-	}		{ Abrogated by Chy. O
22-	}		{ 559.
23			
23	23 (14)	4	
24	{ 202	26	
	{ 203	27	
25	25	5	
26	See 24		
27	}		Rep. 41 V. c.8, s.5.
28	}		
29			Unnecessary.
30	See 615	81	
31			{ Rescinded by Chy O. 558.
32	775	101	
33	204	27	
34	18	3	
35	20	4	
36			{ Sup. 48 Vic. c. 13, s. 21. See C.R.41,138.
37	25	5	
38			{ Sup. See C. R. 718, 726, 765(a), 766, 768.
39			Effete.
40	242	33	
41	See 242		
42	461	62	
43	461	62	
44			Sup. C. R. 242.
45	462	62	
46			Sup. See C. R. 461.
47	252	34	
48	460	62	
49	463	63	
50	}		Sup. See C.R. 198.
51	}		
52	201	26	
53			Sup. See C.R. 324.
54			See C.R. 300, 445.
55			" 324, 444.
56			Sup. See C. R. 310.
57	319	44	
58	320		
59	321	45	
60	322		
61			Sup. See C.R. 309.
62			" 302, 303
63	307	42	
64	487	65	
65	323	45	

CHANCERY ORDERS.

No. of Order	Consolidated Rule	Page	Remarks
66			See C.R. 395, 448, 605
67			" "
68			{ Sup. See C. R. 399, 449, 605.
69	421	57	
70	422	52	
71	See 1195	157	
72			Sup. See C.R. 279.
73-			Effete.
87	}		
88			{ Rescinded by Chy. O. 623.
89			Effete.
90			{ Rescinded by Chy. O. 623.
91	See 267	36	Effete.
92	}		
93			Effete.
94			Effete.
95			{ Rescinded by Chy. O. 623.
96-	}		
104	}		Effete.
105			See C. R. 393.
106-	}		
133	}		Effete.
134-	}		
136	}		Sup. See C. R. 508.
137			See C. R. 513.
138	See 487	65	
139			{ Sup. See C. R. 488, 510.
140	See 489	66	
141	} 494		
142	}		
143			See C. R. 495.
144	} 499	67	
	} 520	70	
145	648	85	
146			Sup. See C. R. 506.
147	497	67	
148	498		
149-	}		{ Sup. See C. R. 368, et seq.
155	}		
156			{ Sup. See C. R. 617-619.
157	}		
158			Sup. See C. R. 653.
159	}		
160			Effete.
161			See C. R. 654, 663.
162			Effete.
163			{ Sup. See C. R. 663, 664, 665.
164			See C. R. 23 (16).
165			Sup. See C. R. 664.
166			Effete.

CHANCERY ORDERS.

No. of Order	Consolidated Rule	Page	Remarks
167			Unnecessary.
168			{ Effete. See C. R. 564,
169			676, 681.
169			Effete.
170			{ Effete. See R. S. O.
171			1877, c. 62, s. 4.
172			{ Effete. See R. S. O.
173			1877, c. 62, ss.18-20.
174			Effete.
175			Abrogated.
176	567	76	
177	683	88	
178	684		
179	See 685	89	
180			Sup. See C. R. 1189.
181			Unnecessary.
182	686	89	
183			Sup. See C. R. 672.
184			{ Sup. See C. R. 673,
			797.
185			Effete.
186	771	101	
187	777	102	
188	778		
189			
190			Effete.
191			
192			{ Effete. See 44 V. c. 5,
193			s. 85.
194			Effete.
195	773	101	
196	770		
197	542	72	
198			{ Sup. See C. R. 479,
			525-527.
199	467	63	
200	See 547	73	
201-207	547		
208	548		
209			Effete.
210	549	73	
211	45	8	
212	50	9	
213	52		
214			
215	53		
216	54		
217	55		
218	49 / 1188	156	
219	56	10	
220	57		
221	58 / 590	79	
222	50	10	
223	60	11	
224	61		
225	See 1178	155	
226	62	11	
227	63		
228	64		

CHANCERY ORDERS.

No. of Order	Consolidated Rule	Page	Remarks
229	65		
230	66		
231	67	11	
232	68		
233	69		
234	See 1189	156	
235			Unnecessary.
236			Sup. See C. R. 1201.
237	70	12	
238	71		
239	72		
240	73		
241	74		
242	75		
243	76		
244	46	9	
245	47		
246	48		
247	77	12	
248	78		
249	79		
250	80		
251	81	13	
252	See 848	111	Altered.
253	See 82	13	
254	83		
255	85		
256	86		
257	584	78	
258	{ 605 / 607	80 / 81	
259	609		
260	614		
261	616	82	
262			{ Sup. See C. R. 532, 533.
263	479	64	
264	479	64	
265	964	127	
266			
267			
268			} Sup. See C. R. 578.
269			
270			Sup. See C. R. 727.
271			Sup. See C. R. 744.
272			Sup. See C. R. 579.
273			{ Sup. See C. R. 646, 647, 648.
274			{ Sup. See C. R. 646, 647, 648.
275	See 1170 (a)	154	{ Sup. See C. R. 646, 647, 648.
276			{ Sup. See C. R. 646, 647, 648.
277	534	71	
278	See 116	16	
279	" 117		
280	" 118		
281	" 119		
282	" 120		
283	" 121	17	

	CHANCERY ORDERS.				CHANCERY ORDERS.		
No. of Order.	CONSOLIDATED.		REMARKS.	No. of Order.	CONSOLIDATED.		REMARKS.
	Rule.	Page.			Rule.	Page.	
284			{ Effete. *See* J. A. s. 16 (6).	359			Sup. *See* C. R. 141.
285			Effete.	360			" 142.
286	192	25		361			" 143.
287	193	26		362			" 144.
288	880	115		363			" 145, 146.
289	881			364			" 149.
290	*See* 882		Altered.	365			" 150.
291	883			366			" 151.
292	884			367	162	21	
293			Sup. *See* C. R. 879.	368			Sup. *See* C. R. 155.
294			{ Sup. *See* .C. R. 861, 868.	369			" 185.
				370			" 186.
				371			" 187.
295			{ Effete. *See* C. R. 526, 527.	372			" 188.
				373			" 156.
296	521	70		374	91	14	
297			Sup. *See* C. R. 887.	375	92		
298- 303 }			{ Rescinded by Chy.O. 616.	376	93		
				377	94		
304 305 }	1178	155		378	95		
				379	96		
306	1215	160		380	97		
307	1216			381	98		
308			Sup. *See* C. R. 1214.	382	99	15	
309	1218	161		383	100	15	
310	1198	158		384	101		
311	1208	159		385	{ 102		
312	1209				See 1178	155	
313	1210			386	{ 103	15	
314			Effete.		See 1178	155	
315	1202	158		387	104	15	
316	1197	157		388	105		
317 318 }			Effete.	389	106		
319	1181	155		390	108		
320			Sup. *See* C. R. 1170.	391	109		
321			{ Sup. *See* C. R. 1242, 1247.	392	110	16	
				393	111		
322- 328 }			{ Sup. *See* C. R. 798, 800.	394	112		
				395	113		
329			{ Abrogated by Chy. O. 559.	396	114		
				397	115		
330	782	102		398			
331	783			399	}		{ Sup. *See* C. R. 1141, etc.
332	784			400			
333	785			401	}		
334	786	103		402	453	61	
335			Sup. *See* C. R. 780.	403			Sup. *See* C. R. 395.
336	781	102		404			" 396.
337- 343 }			{ Sup. *See* C. R. 620 et seq.	405			Effete.
				406			{ Sup. *See* C. R. 473, 474, 476.
344- 351 }			{ Sup. *See* C. R. 444 et seq.	407	}		
				408	484	65	
352	166	22	Altered.	409	477	64	
353	167		Altered.	410	}		
354	170			411			Sup. *See* C. R. 480.
355			{ Abrogated by Chy. O. 559.	412			" 485.
				413			Effete.
356	176	23		414			Sup. *See* C. R.
357			{ Effete. *See* C.R. 172, 175.	415			*See* C. R. 210.
				416			{ Abrogated by Chy.O. 559. *See* C. R. 211.
358	178	23					

CHANCERY ORDERS.

No. of Order.	Consolidated Rule.	Consolidated Page.	Remarks.
417			Effete.
418			Sup. See C. R. 537.
419	758	100	
420			Abrogated.
421	}		
422	}		Sup. See C. R. 486.
423	}		
424			" 7.
425			" 8.
426	347	49	
427	304	41	
428	348	49	
429	See 349		
430	351		
431	352		
432	}		Sup. See C. R. 718.
433	}		
434	717	94	
435	718		
436	}		Effete.
437	}		
438	306	42	
439			Unnecessary.
440	305	42	
441	776	102	
442	124	17	
443	125		
444	126		
445	127		
446	128		
447	129		
448	130		
449	131	18	
450			Sup See C. R. 137.
451	353	89	
452	132	18	
453	133		
454	134		
455	354	49	
456	350		
457	355		
458	356		
459	357	50	
460	358		
461	359		
462	360		
463	361		
464	See 341	48	
465			Effete.
466			{ Sup. See C. R. 362, 363.
467	965	127	
468	966		
469	967		
470	968		
471	969		
472	970	128	
473	971		
474	975		
475	976		
476	977		

CHANCERY ORDERS.

No. of Order.	Consolidated Rule.	Consolidated Page.	Remarks.
477	978		
478	979	129	
479	980		
480	981		
481	982		
482	983		
483	984	129	
484	985		
485	986		
486	987	130	
487	988		
488			Sup. See C. R. 224
489	{ 530	71	
	{ 1185	156	
490	738	97	
491			Effete.
492	1013	133	
493	1014		
494	1015		
495	1017		
496	1018		
497	1019		
498	1020	134	
499	1021		
500	1022		
501	1023		
502	1024		
503	1025		
504	1026		
505	1027		
506	1028		
507	1029		
508	1030	135	
509	1031		
510	1032		
511	1037		
512	}		Tariff.
513	}		
514	1036	135	
515	1033		
516	1034		
517			{ Sup. Chy. O. 610. See C. R. 258, et seq.
518			Effete.
519	}		{ Sup. Chy. O. 610. See C. R. 258, 262.
520	}		
521	}		
522	337	47	
523	338		
524			Unnecessary.
525	337	47	
526	339	48	
527	994	131	
528	995		
529	996		
530	997		
531	998		
532	999		
533	1001		
534	1002		
535	1003		

CHANCERY ORDERS.

No. of Order.	Consolidated. Rule.	Consolidated. Page.	Remarks.
536			Abrogated.
537	122	17	
538			Sup. 48. V. c.13. s. 5.
539			Effete.
540	44	8	
541	207	27	
542	See 469	64	
543	" 470		
544 {	469		
	See 470		
545	471		
546			Effete.
547	454	61	
548	455	62	
549	456	62	
550			Effete.
551			Sup. See Tariff B.
552	966	127	
553	See 1219	161	
554	1221		
555	1222		
556	1223		
557	1224		
558			Sup. Chy. O. 633.
559			Effete.
560	30	6	
561	966	127	
562			Sup. See C. R. 42.
563			Effete.
564	1178	155	
565	See 33	7	
566			Sup. See C. R. 846.
567			Effete.
568			Sup. See C.R. 139,141
569			Effete.
570 }			
571			Sup. See C.R. 172, 175
572			Tariff.
573			
574 }			Sup. See C.R. 179.
575			
576			
577 }			" 180.
578			" 181.
579			" 180, 181
580			" 182.
581			" 183.
582			" 184.
583			" 189.
584	51	9	
585	See 1170 (a)	154	
586	See 1170 (a)		
587	322	45	
588	123	17	
589	87	13	

CHANCERY ORDERS.

No. of Order.	Consolidated. Rule.	Consolidated. Page.	Remarks.
590			Sup. See C.R. 210, 211
591	1035	135	
592 }			Sup. See C.R. 210, 211
593			
594	774	101	
595	25	5	
596	762	100	
597	451	61	
598–			Effete.
602 }			
603			Sup. See C. R. 544.
604–			Effete.
607 }			
608			Sup. Tariff 1881.
609			Effete.
610			
611			
612 }			Effete.
613			
614			Sup. See C.R. 757.
615			Tariff B.
616			Effete.
617 }			
618			Not consolidated.
619			Effete.
620			
621			
622 }			Effete.
623–			
628 }			
629			{ Sup. O. in C., 30th June, 1881.
630			Effete.
631			Sup. See C.R. 156.
632			See C. R. 23 (1).
633	1016	133	
634– }			Effete.
637			
638	972	128	
639 {	973		
	974		
640	989	130	
641	990		
642	See 849	111	Altered.
643	1187	156	
644	1188		
645	717	94	
646 {	717		
	718		
647			Effete.
648	718	94	
649			Effete.
650	991	130	
651			Effete.

RULES UNDER THE JUDICATURE ACT.

RULES UNDER ONTARIO JUDICATURE ACT.

No. of Rule	Consolidated Rule	Page	Remarks.
1	224	30	
2	....	....	{ Sup. See C. R. 1141, &c.
3	....	....	Unnecessary.
4	 224	....	Effete.
5	224	30	
6	See 1195	157	
7	·231	31	
8	232	....	
9	{ 233 / 1047	31 / 137	
10	444	00	
11	243	33	
12	244	....	
13	224	30	
14	....	....	See C.R. 245.
15	246	33	
16	247	....	
17	248	34	
18	240	32	
19	241	....	
20	See 230	31	
21	....	....	Sup. J. A. Rule 547.
22	224	30	
23	224	30	
24	229	31	
25	....	....	Sup. J. A. Rule 547.
26	235	31	
27	236	....	
28	237	32	
29	250	34	
30	251	....	
31	238	32	
32	239	....	
33	225	34	
34	253	....	
35	257	35	
36	{ 258 / ·262	36	
37	259	35	
38	263	36	
39	264		
40	265		
41	·266		
42	269	37	
43	....	....	Abrogated.
44	256	35	
45	....	....	C.R. 271 substituted.
46	276	38	
47	....	....	Effete.
48	274	38	
49	272	37	
50	....	....	Sup. J. A. Rule 547.
51	See 277	38	
52	282	39	
53	284		

RULES UNDER ONTARIO JUDICATURE ACT.

No. of Rule	Consolidated Rule	Page	Remarks.
54	285		
55	286		
56	287		
57	288		
58	289		
59	278	38	
60	283	39	
61	281		
62	293	40	
63	294		
64	295		
65	296		
66	297	41	
67	298		
68	290		
69	336 (a)	47	
70	......	....	Sup. C. R. 261.
71	704	92	
72	705		
73	706		
74	{ 707 / 1175	155	
75	708	93	
76	714		
77	715		
78	} 718	94	
79	}		
80	739	97	
81	......	....	Unnecessary.
82	740	97	
83	741		
84	742	98	
85	743		
86	745		
87	746		
88	747		
89	{ 300 / 1171	41 / 154	
90	445	61	
91	301	41	
92	302		
93	303		
94	308	42	
95	309		
96	313	43	
97	314	....	Altered.
98	315		
99	316		
100	317	....	Altered.
101	318	44	
102	320		
103	324	45	
104	325		
105	326		
106	327		
107	328	46	

RULES UNDER ONTARIO JUDICATURE ACT.				RULES UNDER ONTARIO JUDICATURE ACT.			
No. of Rule.	Consolidated. Rule.	Page.	Remarks.	No. of Rule.	Consolidated. Rule.	Page.	Remarks.
108	329			167	379		
109	330			168	374	52	
110	331			169	375		
111	332			170	{ 041	84	
112	333	47			{ 642		
113	....	......	Sup. C. R. 338.	171	670	87	
114	334	47		172	641	84	
115	{ 340	48		173	381	53	
	{ 346			174	382		
116	341			175	383		
117	342			176	392	54	
118	343			177	420	57	
119	344			178	423		
120	345			179	424		
121	346	......	Unnecessary.	180	425		
122	} 346			181	426	58	
123				182	427		
124	335	47		183	428		
125	394	54		184	429		
126	{ See 369	51		185	430		
	{ " 371	52		186	431		
127	373			187	432		
128	{ 399	55		188	433		
	{ See 449	61		189	384	53	
129	395	54		190	385		
130	396	55		191	386		
131	....	......	Sup. C. R. 461.	192	387		
132	397	55		193	388	54	
133	404	55		194	389		
134	405	56		195	539	72	
135	406			196	......	......	Sup. C. R. 390.
136	407			197	} See 1170	154	
137	408			198			
138	409			199	......	......	Effete.
139	410			200	See 1170	154	
140	411			201	391	54	
141	413			202	538	71	
142	414			203	646	85	
143	415			204	719	94	
144	416			205	720		
145	417	57		206	721	95	
146	401	55		207	722		
147	402			208	723		
148	403			209	724		
149	419	57		210	725		
150	398	55		211	727		
151	434	58		212	728		
152	435	59		213	729		
153	436			214	796	104	
154	437			215			
155	438			216			
156	439			217	}	......	Sup. See C.R. 632-640
157	440			218			
158	369	51		219	502	67	
159	370	52		220	1177	155	
160	371			221	507	68	
161	372			222	508		
162	....	......	Abrogated.	223	509		
163	1189	156		224	{ 488	66	
164	376	52			{ 510	69	
165	377	53		225	} 511		
166	378			226			

RULES UNDER ONTARIO JUDICATURE ACT.

No. of Rule	Consolidated Rule	Page	Remarks
227	487	65	
228	513	69	
229	514		
230	1196	157	
231	515	69	
232	516		
233	517		
234	518		
235	519	70	
236	{ 499	67	
	520	70	
	648	85	
237	522	70	
238	523		
239	506	68	
240	400	55	
241	{ 617	82	
	1190	156	
242	618	82	
243	619		
244	551	72	
245	552		
246	....		Abrogated C. R. 550.
247	553	73	
248	554	73	
249	555		
250	556		
251	557		
252	538	71	
253	558	74	
254	653	85	
255	{ 647		
	654	86	
256	655		
257	656		
258	660		
259	661		
260	660		
261	663		
262	664		
263	....		Effete.
264	665	87	
265	}		See C. R. 663, 668.
266			
267	669	87	
268	672		
269	673		
270	795	104	
271	676	88	
272	681		
273	682		
274	687	89	
275	688		
276	34	7	
277	See 36		
278	37	8	
279	38		
280	39		
281	40		
282	564	75	
283	{ 576	77	
	577		

RULES UNDER ONTARIO JUDICATURE ACT.

No. of Rule	Consolidated Rule	Page	Remarks
284	See 600	81	
285	566	75	
286	591	79	
287	592		
288	593		
289	See 594		
290	595		
291	596		
292	597		
293	598	80	
294	599		
295	600		
296	601		
297	602		
298	603		
299	....	80	Abrogated.
300	604	80	
301	568	76	
302	569		
303	570		
304	571		
305	572		
306	751	99	
307	789	103	
308	....		Abrogated.
309	}		Sup. J. A. Rule 526.
310			
311	791	103	
312	792		
313	....		Abrogated.
314	793	103	
315	748	98	
316	}		Sup. J. A. Rule 510.
317			
318	753	99	
319	754		
320	752		
321	755	92	
322			
323	757	100	
324	744	98	
325	766	101	
326	{ 764	100	
	See 765		
327	See 765 (a)		
328	768	101	
329	769		
330	797	104	
331	{ 89	13	
	97	14	
	107	15	
332	135	18	
333	362	50	
334	363		
335	136	18	
336	137		
337	....		Unnecessary.
338	780	102	
339	862	112	
340	867	113	
341	868		
342	See 873		

RULES UNDER ONTARIO JUDICATURE ACT.

No. of Rule	Consolidated Rule	Page	Remarks
343	874	114	
344	858	112	
345	875	114	
346	876		
347	888	116	
348	889		
349	893		
350	890		
351	891		
352	863	112	
353	894	116	
354	895	117	
355	885	115	
356	886		
357	866	113	
358	887	116	
359	See 782	102	
360 }			Unnecessary.
361 }			
362	859	112	
363	860		
364	878	114	
365	879	115	
366	926	120	
367	927	121	
368	929		
369	930		
369a	932	122	
370	935		
371	936	123	
372	937		
373	939		
374	944	124	
375	945		
376	946		
377	947		
378	1180	155	
379			{ Unnecessary. See J. A. Rule 341.
380	869	113	
381	861	112	
382			See C.R. 873.
383	620	82	
384	621		
385	622		
386	623		
387	624		
388	625		
389	626	83	
390	627		
391	628		
392	649	85	
393	650		
394	651		
395	652		
396	1131	148	
397	1133		
398	1135		
299	1134		
400	1132		
401	1130		
402	1136	149	

RULES UNDER ONTARIO JUDICATURE ACT.

No. of Rule	Consolidated Rule	Page	Remarks
403	90	14	
404	525	70	
405	526		Altered.
406	527	71	
407	479	64	
408	529	71	
409	531		
410	532		
411	533		
412	526	70	Altered.
413	543	72	
414	See 847	111	Altered.
415	10	2	
416	See 22	4	
417	19	3	
418	20	4	
419			Sup. J.A. Rule 517
420	30	6	
421	31	7	
422	{ See 41 / See 138	8 / 18	
423			Effete.
424			Sup. See C. R. 41.
425			Abrogated.
426	See 42	8	
427	846	110	
428	1170	154	
429	1245	165	
430	1247		
431	1242	164	
432			Tariff B.
433	457	62	
434	1193	157	
435	1195		
436	1204	158	
437	1194	157	
438	{ See 194 / See 197	26 /	
439	{ See 196 / 1207	26 / 158	
439a	1207		
439 }			
b c }			Sup. See C. R. 196.
439d	1211	159	
440	1201	158	
441	1203		
442	1214	160	
443	See 1226	162	
444	1228		
445	1220	161	
446			Unnecessary.
447	1230	162	
448	1231	163	
449	851	111	
450	853		
451	447	61	
452	448		
453			Unnecessary.
454	472	64	
455	473		
456	474		
457	476		

RULES UNDER ONTARIO JUDICATURE ACT.

No. of Rule.	Rule.	Page.	Remarks.
458	478	......	
459	......	......	Sup. J. A. Rule 550.
460	483	65	
461	484	......	
462	485	......	
463	1191	157	
464	} 605	80	
465			
466	606	81	
467	608	......	
468	611	......	
469	612	......	
470	See 614	......	
471	219	20	
472	......	......	Effete.
473	442	60	
474	444	......	
475	139	19	
476	161	21	
477	172	23	
478	175	......	
479	......	......	See J. A. Rule 519.
480	{ 216	28	
	218	29	
481	214	28	
482	215	......	
483	......	......	Unnecessary.
484	1	1	
485	458	62	
486	......	......	{ Sup. See R.S.O. 1887, c. 47, s. 12.
487	......	......	" "
488	1255	166	
489	1256	......	
490	1257	......	
491	2	1	
492	......	......	Unnecessary.
493	......	......	Not consolidated.
494	......	......	"
495	......	......	Unnecessary.
496	......	......	{ Sup. C. R. 271 substituted.
497	1175	155	
498	......	......	Abrogated.
499	863	112	
500	946	124	
501	317	43	
502	718	94	
503	1225	161	
504	177	23	
505	528	71	
506	1004	131	*
507	190	25	
508	......	......	Sup. J. A. Rule 517.
509	20	4	
510	See 798	104	
511	1174	155	
512	1172	154	
513	508	68	
514	485	65	
515	See 1219	......	
516	......	......	Effete. Amended R.

RULES UNDER ONTARIO JUDICATURE ACT.

No. of Rule.	Rule.	Page.	Remarks.
517	21	4	
518	334	47	
519	{ 117	16	
	156	20	
520	{ 718	94	
	726	95	
521	191	25	
522	800	104	
523	See 798	......	
524	{ 217	29	
	218		
525	......	......	Abrogated.
526	......	......	{ Effete. Rescinded Rules 309, 310.
527	......	......	Sup. C. R. 767, 798.
528	......	......	Abrogated.
529	......	......	"
530	......	......	"
531	......	......	"
532	486	65	
533	......	......	{ Omitted. Never confirmed by Order in Council.
534	1261	167	
535	8	2	
536	190	25	
537	7	2	
538	......	......	Election Rules.
539	......	......	{ Sup. J. A. Rule 544 (18). Tariff.
540	480	64	
541	88	13	
542	744 (a)	98	
543	......	......	Sup. J. A. Rule 549.
544	{ 854	111	
(1)			
545	{ 7	2	
	19	3	
	See 226	30	
546	{ See 277	38	
	279	......	
547	See 15	3	
548	234	31	
549	30	6	
549	1192	15f	
550	140	19	
551	141	19	
552	142		
553	143		
554	144		
555	145		
556	146		
557	147	20	
558	148		
559	149		
560	150		
561	151		
562	152		
563	153		
564	154		
565	155		
566	156		

RULES UNDER ONTARIO JUDICATURE ACT.

No. of Rule	Consolidated		Remarks.
	Rule.	Page.	
567	157	21	
568	158		
569	159		
570	160		
571	179	23	
572	180		
573	181		
574	182	24	
575	183		
576	184		
577	185		
578	186		
579	187		
580	188		
581	189		
582	544	72	
583	546		
584	{ 41	8	
	{ 138	18	
585	992	130	
586	993		
587	{ 999	131	
	{ 1000		
588	336	47	
589	877	114	
590	666	87 }	
591	667	}	Altered.
592	668	}	
593	1207	158	
594	892	116	
595	610	81	
596	393	54	
597	...		Sup. C. R. 490.
598	{ See 490	66	
	{ " 491		
	{ " 578	77	
599	" 84	13	
600	" 537	71	
601	620	82	
602	198	26	
603	199		
604	200		
605	...		Not consolidated.
606	174	23	

RULES H. C. J.

	Rule.	Page.	Remarks.
1	210	28	
2	...		Sup. C. R. 211.
3	210	28	
4	...		Sup. C. R. 211.
5	} 540	72	
6			
7	...		Abrogated.
8	779	102	
9	...		Effete.
10	...		"

APPEAL ORDERS.

ORDERS OF 8TH SEPTEMBER, 1871.

No. of Order	Consolidated.		Remarks.
	Rule.	Page.	
35	855	111	
36	856	112	
37	857		

ORDERS OF 30TH MARCH, 1878.

No. of Rule	Consolidated.		Remarks.
	Rule.	Page.	
1	...		{ Effete. Repeal of former rules.
2	806	106	
3	807		
4	808		
5	809		
6	810		
7	811		
8	812		
9	814	107	
10	1195	157	
11	816	107	
12	817		
13	818	107	
14	819		
15	820		
16	821		
17	822		
18	...		Sup. App. O. 67, 68.
19	824	108	
20	825		
21	826		
22	827		
23	828		
24	829		
25			
26	}		Unnecessary.
27			
28			
29	}		Tariff A.
30			
31	831	108	
32			
33			
34			
35	}		{ Insolvency matters. Effete.
36			
37			
38			
39			
39a	835	109	
40	836		

ORDERS OF 30th MARCH, 1878.

ORDERS OF 30th MARCH, 1878.

No. of Rule.	Consolidated.		Remarks.	No. of Rule.	Consolidated.		Remarks.
	Rule.	Page.			Rule.	Page.	
41	837			55			Vacations. Sup. *See* C. R. 486.
42	838			56	484	65	
43	839			57			Altered.
44	840	110		58			Sup. *See* C. R. 485.
45	841			59			Sup. *See* C. R. 474.
46	842			60	475	64	
47	1195	157		61			Unnecessary.
48	843	110		62			
49			Sup. C. R. 461.	63			
50	844	110		64			Sup. 48 V.c. 13,s. 20.
51			*See* Tariff.	65			
52	845	110		66			
53	208	27		67	823	107	
54	209			68			
				69	819		

STATUTES, R. S. O., 1877.

STATUTES, R. S. O., 1877.

Chap.	Sec.	Consolidated Rule	Page	Remarks
16	32	923	120	
	33	924		
38	22	585	78	
	27	804	105	
	28	805	106	
	30	803 part	105	
	31(1)	813	106	
	(2)	826	108	
	32	See 827		
	40	....		Sup. See C.R. 622.
	41	832	109	
	42	833		
39	44	830	108	
	11			
	12			
	13	....		{ Sup. See C. R. 214, 216.
	14			
	15			
	20	....		Sup. See C.R. 210.
	23	....		" 779.
	30	....		See C. R. 6.
	31	....		Sup. See C.R. 846.
	33	657	86	
	34	658		
	35	659		
	43	See 12	3	
40	48	....		Sup. See C. R. 7.
	9	....		See C. R. 30.
	21	....		Sup. See C.R. 210.
	46	1088	141	
	47	1185	156	
	48	1186		
	92	465	63	
	93	274	38	
	94	273	37	
	95	254	35	
	96	255		
	97	1243	164	
	100	565	75	
	102	630	83	
	103	....		Sup. See C.R.1219
41	12	....		Effete.
	13	26	5	
	14	27		
	15	27 (a)		
	16	28 (c)	6	
	17	29		
42	25 {	1262 / 1263 / 1264	167	
49	7	441	60	
	8	....		Sup. See C.R. 444.
	9	310	42	
	10	1007	132	
	11	1008		
	12	1009		
	13	1010		
	14	1011	133	

STATUTES, R. S. O., 1877.

Chap.	Sec.	Consolidated Rule	Page	Remarks
	15	1011		
	16	1012	133	
	17	926	120	
	18	932	122	
	19 {	927	121	
		933	122	
	20	934		
	(2)	934(a)		
	22	650(a)	85	
	33	690	89	
	34	691		
	35	692		
	36	693		
	37	694		
	38	695	90	
	39	696		
	42	697		
	43	1182	155	
50	3	....		{ Sup. See C.R. 224, 231.
	4	1046	137	
	5	226	30	
	6 {	226		
		227	31	
		1253	166	
	7	....		Sup. See C.R. 226
	8	1253	166	
	9	See 228	31	
	10	230		
	11	....		Sup. See C.R.230.
	12	....		" 279.
	13	....		Sup. See C.R. 243.
	14	See 224	30	
	15	....		Sup. See C.R. 233.
	16	....		Sup. See C.R. 240.
	17	....		Sup. See C.R. 241.
	18	....		" 246.
	19	245(2)	33	
	20	253	34	
	21	267	36	
	22	268		
	23	254	35	
	24	255		
	25	....		Sup. See C.R. 256.
	26	....		" 236.
	27	....		" 238.
	28	....		" 239.
	29	1047	137	
	30 } {	242	33	
	31 } {	1046	137	
	32	1048		
	33	1049		
	34	1050		
	35	....		Effete.
	36	1051	138	
	37	1052		
	38	1055		
	39	See 1067	140	

STATUTES, R. S. O., 1877.

Chap.	Sec.	Rule	Page	Remarks.
40	1062	139		
41	1063			
42	1064			
43	1065			
44	1066	140		
45	1068			
46	1069			
48	232	31		
49				Sup. See C.R. 271.
50				{ Sup. See C.R. 232, 271.
51				Sup. See C.R. 271.
52				" 237.
54				See C.R. 444.
55				"
56				Sup. See C.R. 250.
57	461	62		
58				Effete.
59	459	62		
60				Sup. See C.R. 281.
61				{ Sup. See C.R. 284, 285.
62				{ Sup. See C.R. 286, 287.
63				Effete.
64				Sup. See C.R. 705.
65				{ Sup. See C.R. 707, 1175.
66				
67				Sup. See C.R. 476.
68				Sup. See C.R. 275.
69				" 706.
70	1243	164		
71	1244			
73	See 414	56		
74				
75				Sup. See C.R. 324
76				Sup. See C.R. 325.
77				{ Sup. See C.R. 324, 444.
78				
79				{ Sup. See C.R. 324. 414.
80				
81				Sup. See C.R. 303,
82				" 414.
83	1170	154		
84				{ Sup. See C.R. 340 et. seq.
85				
86				Sup. See C.R. 346
87				
88				" 394
89				Effete.
90				Sup. See C.R. 406.
91				
92				Sup. See C.R. 394
93				" 369.
94				" 371.
95				" 484.
96				" 394.
97				{ Sup. See C.R. 394, 414.
99				{ Sup. See C.R. 394, 399.

STATUTES, R. S. O., 1877.

Chap.	Sec.	Rule	Page	Remarks.
100				Sup. See C.R. 371.
101				Effete.
102				Sup. See C.R. 394.
103				
104				Sup. See C.R. 394.
105				
106				{ Sup. See C.R. 304, 434-440.
107				
108				Sup. See C.R. 632.
109	171	22		
110				Sup. See C.R. 633.
111				" 635.
112				" 394.
113				Sup. See C.R. 373.
114				
115				Sup. See C.R. 394
116				
117				
118	389	54		
(2)				{ Sup. See C. R. 41, 138.
119				Sup. See C.R. 394.
120				Sup. See C.R. 423.
121				{ Sup. See C.R. 164, et seq.
123				Sup. See C.R. 415
124				
125				" 427.
126				" 414.
127				" 384.
128				" 385.
132				{ Sup. See C.R. 434, et. seq.
135				{ Sup. See C.R. 303, 414.
136				{ Sup. See C.R. 301, et. seq.
138	631	83		
141				Sup. See C.R. 399.
142	679	88		Sup. See C.R. 373.
144				
147	270	37		
148				{ Sup. See C. R. 41, 138.
149				Effete.
150				{ Sup. See C.R. 705, 719.
151	712	93		
152				Effete.
153				Sup. See C.R. 1174
154				" 653.
155	1260	166		
156	{ 487, 494	65, 66		
(2)	495			
157				{ Sup. See C. R. 41, 138.
158				
159				{ Sup. See C.R. 490, et seq.
160				
161	{ 493, 496	66		

STATUTES, R. S. O., 1877.

Chap.	Sec.	Consolidated Rule.	Page.	Remarks.
162	499	67		
163	500			
164	501			
165	504	68		
166	505			
167	......	.....		Sup. See C.R. 1177
168	702	91		
169	....	.....		{ Sup. See C.R. 507, et. seq.
170	....	.....		{ Sup. See C.R. 507, 514, et seq.
171	....	.....		Sup. See C.R. 617.
172	....	.....		" 619.
173	575	76		Altered.
174	....	.....		See C.R. 576.
175	579	77		
176	580			
177	581			
178	582	78		
179	....	.....		Sup. See C.R. 578.
180	....	.....		Sup. See C.R. 583.
185-	}			{ Sup. See C.R. 554, et. seq.
186	}			
187				Sup. See C.R.1170
188	....	.....		{ Sup. See C. R. 554 et. seq.
228 }				
229 }	....	.....		Sup. See C.R. 620
230-235	....	.....		" 622.
336 }				
237 }				
238 }	....	.....		{ Sup. See C.R. 620, 622.
239 }				
240 }				
241 }	629	83		
242 }				
244	....	.....		Sup. See C.R. 661.
245	....	.....		Effete.
246	....	.....		Sup. See C.R. 654.
247	....	.....		" 664.
248	....	.....		" 665.
249	....	.....		" 669.
250	....	.....		" 665.
251	....	.....		Effete.
257	677	88		
258	678			
259	....	.....		Sup. See C.R. 681.
260	674	87		
261	675			
262	....	.....		Sup. See C. R. 682.
270	....	.....		Sup. See C.R. 444.
271	....	.....		Sup. See C.R. 446.
272	....	.....		See C.R. 798.
273	....	.....		Sup. See C. R. 444.
274 }				
275 }	....	.....		{ Sup. See C. R. 663, 665.
276 }				
277 }				
278 }	....	.....		{ Sup. See C.R. 687, 688.
279	468	63		
280	689	89		
281	....	.....		Sup. See C. R. 219.

STATUTES, R. S. O., 1877.

Chap.	Sec.	Consolidated Rule.	Page.	Remarks.
253 }				
284 }				
285 }	....	.....		Sup. See C.R. 798.
286 }				
287 }				
288	790	103		
289	....	.....		Sup. See C. R.791.
290	799	104		Altered.
291	....	.....		{ Sup. See C. R. 1170.
292	1258	166		
293	1259			
294 }				
295 }	....	.....		Effete.
296	733	96		
297	735			
298	....	.....		Sup. See C.R. 767.
299	....	.....		{ Sup. See C. R. 767, 863.
300	....	.....		Effete.
301	....	.....		{ Sup. See C. R. 767, 798.
302 }	....	.....		{ Sup. See C. R. 21.
303 }				
304	926	120		
305	932	122		
306	931			
307 }				
308 }	....	.....		Sup. See C. R. 935.
309	....	.....		" 937.
310	....	.....		" 939
311	940	123		
312	941			
313	....	.....		{ Sup. See C. R. 944, 945.
315	942	123		
316	943	123		
317	....	.....		Sup. See C. R. 916.
321	....	.....		{ Sup. See C. R. 1180.
322	....	.....		" 885.
323- }	....	.....		{ Sup. See C. R. 886.
331 }				
332	....	.....		Effete.
333	....	.....		Sup. See C. R. 886.
335	1212	159		
336 }	....	.....		{ Sup. See C. R. 1170.
337 }				
338 }	....	.....		{ Sup. See C. R. 641, 642.
339 }				
340 }				
341 }				
342 }	....	.....		Sup. See C.R.1170.
343 }				
344 }				
347 }				
(1) }				
(2) }	....	.....		Sup. See C.R. 1172.
(3) }				
348 }				
349	1173	154		
350	1176	155		

STATUTES, R. S. O., 1877.

Chap.	Sec.	Rule	Page	Remarks.
51	351			Sup. See C. R. 1170.
	352			
	353			Sup. See C.R. 196.
	354			Sup. See C. R. 474.
	2			" 224.
	3			
	4			" 233, 238.
	5			Sup. See C.R. 243.
	6			
	7			See C. R. 252.
	8			Effete.
	9			Sup. See C. R. 277.
	10			" 293. 294.
	11			Sup. See C.R. 277, 279.
	12			Partly Sup. See C. R. 295.
	13			Sup. See C.R. 297.
	14			" 369,
	15			371, 399, 416, 449.
	16			Sup. See C.R. 381.
	17			" 384.
	18			" 416.
	19			Sup. See C.R. 423.
	20			" 714.
	(2)	716	94	
	23	653 (a)	86	
	24			Sup. See C.R. 554.
	25			Sup. See C.R. 654.
	26	698	90	
	27	699	90	
	28	700		
	31	750	99	
	32			Sup. See C.R. 672, 673.
	34			" 682, 767.
	35			
	36	870	113	
	37			Effete.
	39			
	40			
	41			
	42			
	43			Sup. See C.R. 620 et seq.
	44			
	45			
	46			
	47			
	48			
	49			
	50			" 641, 642.
	51			
	52	730	96	
	53	731		
	54	732		
	55			Sup. See C.R. 646, et seq.
	68			Sup. See C.R. 767.
	71	359	50	

STATUTES, R. S. O., 1877.

Chap.	Sec.	Rule	Page	Remarks.
52	1	1129	148	
	2	1139	149	
	3			
	4	224	30	
		1112	145	
	5			Effete.
	6	1116	145	
	7			Effete.
	8			
	9	1128	147	
	*10	1117	145	
	11	1118	146	
	12	1119		
	13	1120		
	14	1121		
	15	1122	147	
	16	1123		
	17	1124		
	18	1125		
	19			
	20			
	21	See 1126		
	22			
	23			
	24	1127		
	25			Unnecessary.
	26	1129	148	
	27			Sup. See C.R. 846.
	28			" 1170.
53	6-18			Sup. C. R. 1098-1110.
	19			Sup. See C.R. 252, et seq.
	20			
	21			Sup. See C.R. 704, et seq.
	22			Sup. See C.R. 368, et seq.
	23			Sup. See C.R. 653.
	24-27			Effete.
	28	1111	145	
	29			Sup. See C.R.1170.
54	11	1155	151	
	12	1156		
	13	1157		
	15	1158		
	16	1159		
	17	1160		
	18	1161		
	19			Effete.
	20			Sup. See C.R. 863, 866.
	21			Tariff C.
	22	1162	152	
	23	1166		
	24	1167	153	
	25	1168		
	26	1169		

STATUTES, R. S. O., 1877.

Chap.	Sec.	Consolidated Rule.	Page.	Remarks.
55	4			Sup. See C.R.1170.
	7			{ Partly Sup. See C. R. 224, 243, 244.
	8			{ Sup. See C. R. 231, 233, 240, 250,
	9,10 }	249	34	Part effete.
	11	253		
	12			Sup. See C₄R. 253.
	14	292	40	Altered.
	15	713	93	
	16			Sup. See C.R. 232.
	17			" 253.
	18,19 }			Effete.
	20	290	40	
	21	291		
	22			Sup. See C.R.1170.
	23,24,25,26,27 }			Sup. See C.R. 304.
	29			{ Effete or Sup. See C. R. 863, 1170.
	41			See C. R. 863.
58	1,2,3,4,5 }			Effete.
	6	364	50	
	7			See C. R. 364.
	8	364	50	
	9	365		
	10	366	51	
	11,12 }	367		
	13			Effete.
59	2			Unnecessary.
	3	949	125	
	4	950		
	5	951		
	6	952		
	7	953		
	8	954		
	9	955		
	10	956	126	
	11	957		
	12			See C. R. 653, 949.
	13	958		
	14	959	126	
	15	960		
	16,17 }	See 961		
	18	962		
	20			See C. R. 963.

STATUTES, R. S. O., 1877.

Chap.	Sec.	Consolidated Rule.	Page.	Remarks.
62	15	559	74	
	16	1254	166	
	18	562	75	
	19	586	78	
	20	587		
	21	588		
	22	589	79	
66	7			Effete.
	9	898	117	
	10			Sup. See C. R. 866.
	11			" 893,894.
	12			" 895
	13	865	113	
	14	{ 864, 901 }	117	
	15,16 }	904	118	
	17	905		
	18	859	112	
	19	899	117	
	34	900	117	
	41	906	118	
	42	907		
	44	890	116	
	45	1233	163	
	46	1234		
	47	1235		
	48	1236	163	
	49	1237	164	
	50	1238		
	51	1239		
	52	1240		
	53	896	117	
	54	897		
	55	925	120	
	56	873	113	
	57	912	118	
	58	913	119	
	59	914		
	60	915		
	61	916		
	62,63 }			Sup. See C.R.1170
	64	917	119	
	65	918		
	66	919		
	67	920		
	68	921	120	
	69	922		
	72 (2)			See C. R. 863.
	72 (3)			See C. R. 867.
68	6	See 1089	141	
	7	See 1091	142	
	9	See 1093	142	
	10	See 1094		
	11	See 1095		
	12	See 1096		
	19	See 1097		

41 VICT.

Chap.	Sec.	Consolidated. Rule.	Page.	Remarks.
8	7	585	78	
	8	503	67	
	9	{ 499, 520, 524 }	70	

42 VICT.

Chap.	Sec.	Consolidated. Rule.	Page.	Remarks.
15	2	1246(a)	165	
	3	574	76	
	4	903	117	
	6	....	......	Effete.
	7	....	......	Sup. See C.R. 487.

44 VICT.

Chap.	Sec.	Consolidated. Rule.	Page.	Remarks.
5	24	....	......	See C. R. 226.
	25	See 225	30	
	26	650(a)	85	
	44	749	98	
	83, 84 }	563	75	
7	1	1163	152	
	2	1164		
	3	1165		

47 VICT.

Chap.	Sec.	Consolidated. Rule.	Page.	Remarks.
14	7	275	38	
19	11	314	43	

48 VICT.

Chap.	Sec.	Consolidated. Rule.	Page.	Remarks.
13	8	1104	144	
	11	311	42	
	12	312	43	
	21	{ 41, See 138	8, 18 }	
	22	{ 196, 1174	26, 155 }	
	27	1152	150	

49 VICT.

Chap.	Sec.	Consolidated. Rule.	Page.	Remarks.
16	12	928	121	
	13	1156	151	
		{ 1161, 1162	152 }	
	17	1236	163	
	.42	1163		

50 VICT.

Chap.	Sec.	Consolidated. Rule.	Page.	Remarks.
7	7	902	117	

RULES OF COURT AFFECTING THE COMING INTO FORCE OF THE CONSOLIDATED RULES.

Whereas the Acts or parts of Acts mentioned in Schedule A of the Revised Statutes of 1887. stand repealed from and after the coming into force of the said Revised Statutes, 1887, and whereas a consolidation of all the statut ry provisions and other rules affecting practice and procedure is in preparation, but will not be ready for adoption until the first day of February next.

It is hereby ordered that all matters of practice and procedure affected by the said Acts, shall meanwhile be deemed in force as if the same were in substance repeated in this Rule.

31st December, 1887.

(Signed)　J. H. HAGARTY, C.J.O.	(Signed)　THOS. FERGUSON, J.
"　C. S. PATTERSON, J.A.	"　JOHN E. ROSE, J.
"　F. OSLER, J.A.	"　THOMAS ROBERTSON, J.
"　J. A. BOYD, C.	"　W. G. FALCONBRIDGE, J.

Whereas the new Consolidated Rules are not to go into force until the first day of March, next.

It is hereby ordered that all matters of practice and procedure affected by the Acts referred to in the Rule of 31st December, 1887, shall be deemed to be in force until the first day of March aforesaid, as if the same were in substance repeated in this Rule.

30th January, 1888.

(Signed)　JOHN H. HAGARTY, C.J.O.	(Signed)　W. PROUDFOOT, J.
"　GEO. W. BURTON, J.A.	"　THOMAS FERGUSON, J.
"　C. S. PATTERSON, J.A.	"　JOHN E. ROSE, J.
"　F. OSLER, J.A.	"　THOMAS ROBERTSON, J.
"　J. A. BOYD, C.	"　W. G. FALCO: BRIDGE, J.
"　THOMAS GALT, C.J., C.P.D.	"　W. P. R. STREET, J.
"　J. D. ARMOUR, C.J., Q.B.D.	"　HUGH MacMAHON, J.

It is hereby ordered that the new Consolidated Rules shall not go into force until the first day of April, next ; and it is further ordered that all matters of practice and procedure affected by the Acts referred to in the Rule of 31st December, 1887, shall be deemed to be in force until the first day of April aforesaid, as if the same were in substance repeated in this Rule.

Dated at Osgoode Hall, 29th February, 1888.

(Signed)　JOHN H. HAGARTY, C.J.O.	(Signed)　W. PROUDFOOT. J.
"　GEO. W. BURTON, J A.	"　THOMAS FERGUSON, J.
"　C. S. PATTERSON, J.A.	"　JOHN E. ROSE, J.
"　F. OSLER, J A.	"　THOMAS ROBERTSON, J.
"　J. A. BOYD, C.	"　W. G. FALCO BRIDGE, J.
"　THOMAS GALT, C.J., C.P.D.	"　W. P. R. STREET, J.
"　J. D. ARMOUR, C.J., Q.B.D.	"　HUGH MacMAHON, J.

INDEX

TO

CONSOLIDATED RULES.

Costs of abundoned motion for new trial 268

SHORTHAND WRITERS, 27.
  costs of. See *Costs.*
SITTINGS OF THE COURTS, 27, 28.
  court of appeal, 27.
  high court, 28.
SOLICITORS, roll of, 26.
  and agent's book, 26, 27.
SOLICITOR absent from trial, 89.
  undertaking of, to appear, 39
  change of, 63.
  attachment of, for not observing order for discovery, 70.
  or clerk must transact business personally, 2.
  may be required to explain conduct, 26.
  of judgment creditor may be served with foreclosure proceedings, 63.
  and client taxation. See *Taxation.*
SPECIAL CASE, 74.
  in interpleader issues, 150.
STATEMENT OF CLAIM, when to be delivered, 51.
  when defendant arrested, 138.
  amendment of, 57.
  notice in lieu of, 52. See *Pleadings.*
STOP ORDERS, 25, 26.
STRIKING OUT AND AMENDING PLEADINGS, 57.
  counter claim, 52.
STYLE OF CAUSE, short, when used, 61.
SUBPŒNA, 74.
  to produce record must be on order, 74.
  any number of names in, 75.
  and appointment for examination of party, 66.
SUBSTITUTED service, when made, 63.
SUMMONSES abolished, 70.
SUNDAY, when last day for doing act, 64.
SUPREME COURT, case to be certified on appeal to, 109.
SURETY may be joined with mortgagor, 41.
SURROGATE COURT fees, 168.

T.

TARIFF OF COSTS, 269.
  disbursements, 277.
  sheriffs' fees, 281.
TAXATION, appeal from, 111.
  one day's notice of, sufficient, 158.
  notice of, unnecessary, where no appearance, 158.
  who to attend, 158.
  between solicitor and client, 162.
  by third party, 162.
  objections to, 162.
  review of, before appeal, 162, 163.
  appeal from, 111, 162, 163.
  of sheriffs' costs, 163. See *Costs.*
TAXING OFFICERS, 26.
THIRD PARTY, when to be brought in, 46.

THUNDER BAY, sale under writ against land in, 117.
TIME, may be enlarged or abridged, 64, 65.
TRANSFER OF ACTIONS, 85.
TRANSMISSION OF INTEREST *pendente lite*, 82, 83.
  papers, 63, 64.
TRIAL, 85, *et seq.*
  at bar, 86.
  before referee, 7.
  notice of, 86.
  of high court case in C. C. and *vice versa*, 89.
  adjournment of, 88.
  non-appearance of defendant at, 87.
    plaintiff at, 87.
TRUSTEES, executors, etc, to represent estate, 42.

U.

UNDERTAKING OF SOLICITOR to appear, 39.

V.

VACATION, length of, 65.
  pleading in, 65.
  when not computed, 65.
  judges, 28.
VENDITIONI EXPONAS, 112.
  See *Execution.*
VENUE, local, abolished, 85.
  may be changed, 86.
  changing, in C. C., 166.
VERDICT need not be moved against separately, 104.
  motion against, 103.
VIEW BY JUDGE of property, 91, 148.

W.

WARRANT may include several appointments, 12.
  to consider may be dispensed with, 9.
  See *Bench Warrant.*
WITNESS may be examined on motion, 77.
  refusing to answer, penalty, 67.
  may be examined before any examiner on reference, 7.
  put out of court, 87.
  commission to examine, 78 *et seq.*
WRIT OF SUMMONS, 30 *et seq.*
  to be issued by clerk of process, 3.
  in rotation from several divisions, 30.
  renewal of, 32.
  service of, 34 *et seq.*
  copies of, to be sent to registrars, 3.
  quarterly returns of, 3.
  execution. See *Execution*, and titles of various writs.

Form

Affidavit of Service of
Interp Summons

.

RULES OF PRACTICE

OF

The Supreme Court of Judicature

FOR ONTARIO,

PASSED, SINCE THE COMING INTO FORCE OF

THE CONSOLIDATED RULES,

UNDER THE AUTHORITY OF THE JUDICATURE ACT OF
ONTARIO (R. S. O., Chap. 44.)

TORONTO:
WARWICK BROS. & RUTTER, PRINTERS &c., 68 AND 70 FRONT STREET W—.
1891

...tion
Judic...
...r Last.

...following...rules were m...e ...e Supreme Court of Judicature for ...io on Saturday, 29th Sept., 1894 :—

...5.—Rule 23 (17) is amended by ...ng out the word "demurrers."

...7.—Rule 509 is amended by striking "rule 329," and by substituting ...s 328 and 332 (c.)".

...8.—Rule 596 is amended by striking the word "examination" in the first ...| and by substituting "commission." ...39.—Rule 761 is amended by striking ...| "delivered" and by substituting "in ...| ...s tried." (See rule 1,352.)

...590.—Sub-section (d) of rule 1,277 is ...by amended by striking thereout ...| word "day" in the last line thereof,

1884, December 19 ; 1885
1886, December 4 ; 1887,
1888, December 20 ; 1889,
January 4 ; 1891, Januar;

SPECIAL NIGHT

The Street Railway Con
ranged for a special se
cars to-night and to-moi
the convenience of th
watch-night services an
night revellers. *Onsmur*
net.

TO-DAY'S NOMIN

The nominations for
Public School Trustees v
day, as follows :—For
City Hall, at 10 o'clock
Dingman's Hall, at 12
George Vennell, Deputy I
cer. Ward 2—Moss Park
street, at 12 o'clock ; Joh
Ward 3—Victoria Hall

RULES OF PRACTICE

OF

The Supreme Court of Judicature

FOR ONTARIO,

PASSED, SINCE THE COMING INTO FORCE OF

THE CONSOLIDATED RULES,

UNDER THE AUTHORITY OF THE JUDICATURE ACT OF ONTARIO (R. S. O., Chap. 44.)

TORONTO:
WARWICK BROS. & RUTTER, Printers, &c., &c., 68 and 70 Front St. West.
1894.

RULES OF PRACTICE

OF THE

SUPREME COURT OF JUDICATURE

Passed since the coming into Force of the
Consolidated Rules.

[9th June, 1888.]

It is hereby ordered that the Consolidated *Rules* 210, 211 and 212 shall **Rules 210·2** not come into force on the first day of September next, nor until the **suspended.** further order of this Court be passed fixing a day for the same to come into force.

And it is further ordered that until such *Rules* do come into force, all matters of practice and procedure affected thereby shall be deemed to be in force as if the same were in substance repeated in this *Rule*.

[15th December, 1888.]

671a. That Rule 671 be and the same is hereby rescinded and the follow- **Rule 671** ing substituted therefor, viz.: **amended.**

" **671.** Actions not tried or disposed of after being once entered for trial shall remain for trial subject to the provisions of Rule 670, but shall not be heard at any subsequent sittings unless and until a fresh notice of trial be given for such sittings by one of the parties. •

[13th June, 1890.]

1265. In the absence of the Clerk in Chambers, orders made by a **Orders in** Judge of the High Court in Chambers may be signed by the Assistant **Chambers,** Clerk in Chambers ; and such orders signed by the said Assistant Clerk **how to be** in Chambers shall have the same force and validity as if signed by the **signed.** Clerk in Chambers.

1266. All appeals to a Judge in Chambers from the report, certificate, **Appeals to be** order, decision or finding of any officer of the Court must be argued by **argued by** counsel. **counsel.**

1267. Rule 1262 is amended by striking out the words "the County **Rule 1262** of York " and substituting therefor the words " any county." **amended.**

[13th September, 1890.]

1268. Rule 217 is amended so as to read " The Divisional Court of the **Sittings of** Chancery Division shall hold sittings commencing on the first Thursday in **Divisional** June, the first Thursday in December and the third Thursday in Febru- **Court Chy. D.** ary in each year."

Investments of funds in court.
1269. Whereas under Rule 191 it is provided that the investment of the moneys in Court by the Toronto General Trusts Company shall be subject to the approval of the Official Guardian of the High Court of Justice for Ontario :

And whereas the said Official Guardian has expressed his desire to be relieved of the duty in question :

It is ordered, pursuant to sections 114 and 115 of the Judicature Act, that James S. Cartwright, Esquire, the Registrar of the Queen's Bench Division of the said High Court of Justice, be appointed in the place of the said Official Guardian to discharge the said duty ; and that the said the Toronto General Trusts Company is to satisfy the said Registrar of the Queen's Bench Division of the security as to value, and that he certify the same to the Court before cheques issue for each investment, and the said Company are to pay into Court to the credit of the surplus interest funds the fees heretofore paid to the said Official Guardian by the said Company in respect of said services.

Administration—infants.
1270.—972a. No order for the administration of an estate in which an infant is interested shall be made until such infant is represented by the Official Guardian of the High Court of Justice, who shall be duly notified of the intended application.

[18th February, 1892.]

Fees for payments into, and out of court.
1271.—1218a. The fee of thirty cents payable in stamps shall not be received or taken,—(a) In respect of payments into Court upon mortgages or securities held by the Accountant or,—(b) In respect of payments out of Court when the amount is ten dollars or less.

Master in Chambers, Official Referee may act as.
1272.—31a. In case of the death of the Master in Chambers any Official Referee, upon the request of a Judge of the High Court, may sit and act as Master in Chambers, and while so doing shall have all the authority, jurisdiction and powers of the said Master in Chambers.

[21st October, 1893.]

Interest on moneys in court.
1273.—146a. After the first of October, 1893, interest is to be credited upon moneys paid into Court only after the same have been in Court for fifteen days.

[4th November, 1893.]

Discretion as to costs. Rule 1170 amended.
1274. That Rule 1170 be amended by striking out the proviso and substituting therefor the following proviso after the word "equity" in the seventh line : "Provided that where any action or issue is tried by a jury the costs shall follow the event unless upon application made at the trial the judge before whom the action or issue is tried in his discretion otherwise orders."

Rule 1172 amended.
1275. That Rule 1172 be amended by striking out the words "or Court" in the fourth line thereof.

[29th December, 1893.]

1276.—Ordered, that Rules 210, 211 and 212 are hereby repealed, and the following are substituted therefor :

Weekly court.
"210. A Judge shall be at Osgoode Hall every week, except vacation, for the purpose of disposing of all business, except trials, which may be transacted by a single Judge. All applications during the week are to be made to the Judge assigned to take the weekly work.

Business.
"211. The business of the weekly sittings shall be as follows : Monday and Friday, Chambers business (motions first, appeals afterwards); Tuesday, Wednesday and Thursday, Court business.

"212. All business, except *ex parte* motions, is to be entered on a list for each Court day and to be disposed of in the order of entry, unless otherwise directed by the Judge. *Entry of actions.*

"212*a*. Lists shall be prepared by the proper officers of all Court business for each day in which the cases and matters shall be entered in the order in which the *præcipes* are filed with the officer. *Cause list.*

"212*b*. The above Rules shall come into operation on and after the 8th of January, 1894, and prior publication in the *Ontario Gazette* is hereby dispensed with."

1277.—666a. A list of non-jury cases to be tried at Toronto shall be prepared by the proper officer, upon which he shall enter all actions wherein, after close of the pleadings, notice of trial has been given by either party. *Non-jury actions in Toronto.*

Repealed Rule 1566

Each party shall be at liberty to give ten days' notice of trial in respect of such non-jury cases, and to enter the same on the trial list.

Such actions may be tried in the order in which they are entered at the current or next available sittings of the Court. [This Rule is not to apply to the sittings which are to commence on the 16th of January, 1894.]

[January 4th, 1894.]

1277. (*a*) Ordered that,

In cases of non-jury actions to be tried at Toronto notice of trial may be as follows :

amended Rule 1450

In the High Court of Justice,
——Division.

A. B. v. C. D.

Form of notice of trial.

Take notice of trial of this action [*or* the issues in this action ordered to be tried] at the city of Toronto in ten [*or* five] days after the service hereof, or as soon thereafter as the Court may be sitting for the trial of actions without a jury.

Dated, etc.

X. Y.
plaintiff's solicitor,
(*or as the case may be*).

To Z. defendant's solicitor,
(or *as the case may be*).

(*b*) After the expiration of the time mentioned in the notice of trial of an action in Toronto without a jury, either party may enter the action for trial. If both parties enter the action for trial it shall be tried in the order of the plaintiff's entry. *Entry of action.*

(*c*) The party entering the action for trial in Toronto without a jury shall at the time thereof deliver to the proper officer one copy of the whole of the pleadings in the action for the use of the Judge at the trial, such copy to be certified as a true copy by the officer having charge of the pleadings filed, and to be called the record. *Record to be left.*

(*d*) Actions to be tried in Toronto without a jury may be entered for trial before or during any sittings for the trial of actions without a jury ; but no such action shall be placed on the peremptory list for trial before the day following that on which the same is entered. *When action may be entered.*

duration 10 days

Notwithstanding the Rules passed this day, both jury and non-jury cases may be entered for trial at the sittings appointed to begin on Tuesday, 16th January, 1894, at the city of Toronto. The non-jury list shall be taken at Osgoode Hall on the 16th January, 1894, and the jury list at the Court House on the same day.

(e) Sittings of the High Court of Justice in the several county towns, or places, for the trial of criminal cases and of civil cases, with and without a jury, shall in each year hereafter, unless otherwise ordered, be held as set forth in the schedules "A" and "B" hereunder written, and the days of beginning shall be fixed by the Judges as heretofore.

SCHEDULE "A" REFERRED TO IN THE FOREGOING RULE.

Spring Assizes or Sittings.

With Jury.	Without Jury.	Commencement.
Milton (and without jury). L'Orignal (and without jury). St. Thomas. Belleville. St. Catharines. Ottawa. Owen Sound.	Cornwall. Chatham. Walkerton.	During the week beginning 5th March.
Brampton (and without jury). Cobourg. Sandwich. Goderich.	Toronto. Brockville.	During the week beginning 12th March.
Orangeville (and without jury). Peterborough. Woodstock. Sarnia.	Kingston. Barrie. Brantford.	During the week beginning 19th March.
Lindsay. Stratford. London. Pembroke (and without jury).		During the week beginning 26th March.
Cornwall. Perth (and without jury). Walkerton. Hamilton. Guelph.	Simcoe. Whitby. Owen Sound.	During the week beginning 2nd April.
Toronto (civil). Chatham.	Ottawa. St. Thomas.	During the week beginning 9th April.
Brockville. Brantford. Berlin (and without jury).	Belleville. Sandwich. Peterborough. Woodstock. Sarnia.	During the week beginning 16th April.
Kingston. Barrie. Welland (and without jury).	St. Catharines. Cobourg.	During the week beginning 23rd April.

Spring Assizes or Sittings.—Continued.

With Jury.	Without Jury.	Commencement.
Napanee (and without jury). Cayuga (and without jury). Toronto (criminal). Picton (and without jury). Simcoe.	London.	During the week beginning 30th April.
Whitby.	Guelph. Goderich. Hamilton.	During the week beginning 7th May.
	Stratford. Lindsay.	During the week beginning 14th May.

And at Sault Ste. Marie, Port Arthur, and Rat Portage, with and without a jury, on such days during the months of May and June, or in either of them, as may be appointed by the Judge assigned to take the same.

And at Bracebridge and Parry Sound, with, and without a jury, on such days during the months of July and August, or either of them, as may be appointed by the Judge, or Judges, respectively assigned to take the same.

SCHEDULE "B" REFERRED TO IN THE FOREGOING RULE.

Autumn Assizes or Sittings.

With Jury.	Without Jury.	Commencement.
Milton (and without jury). L'Orignal (and without jury). Owen Sound. St. Catharines. St. Thomas. Belleville. Ottawa.	Cornwall. Chatham. Walkerton.	During the week beginning 10th September.
Brampton (and without jury). Cobourg. Sandwich. Goderich.	Toronto. Brockville.	During the week beginning 17th September.
Orangeville (and without jury). Peterborough. Woodstock. Sarnia.	Kingston. Barrie. Brantford.	During the week beginning 24th September.

Autumn Assizes or Sittings.—Continued.

With Jury.	Without Jury.	Commencement.
Lindsay. Stratford. Pembroke (and without jury). London.		During the week begin- ning 1st October.
Cornwall. Perth (and without jury). Hamilton. Guelph. Walkerton.	Simcoe. Whitby. Owen Sound.	During the week begin- ning 8th October.
Toronto (civil). Chatham.	Ottawa. St. Thomas.	During the week begin- ning 15th October.
Brockville. Berlin (and without jury). Brantford.	Belleville. Sandwich. Sarnia. Peterborough. Woodstock.	During the week begin- ning 22nd October.
Barrie. Kingston. Welland (and without jury).	St. Catharines. Cobourg.	During the week begin- ning 29th October.
Napanee (and without jury). Cayuga (and without jury). Toronto (criminal). Picton (and without jury). Simcoe.	London.	During the week begin- ning 5th November.
Whitby.	Guelph. Goderich. Hamilton.	During the week begin- ning 12th November.
	Lindsay. Stratford.	During the week begin- ning 19th November.

And at Sault Ste. Marie, Port Arthur, and Rat Portage, with and without a jury, on such days during the months of October and November
and December, or in either or any two of them, as may be appointed by
the Judge assigned to take the same.

And the winter assizes and sittings at the cities of Toronto, with a jury,
and at Ottawa, Hamilton and London, respectively, with and without a
jury, on such days during the week in which occurs the second Monday
in January as may be appointed by the Judges respectively assigned to
take the same.

[17th February, 1894.]

y cases pending in any of the Divisions of ... be tried in Toronto, are to be entered for trial with the Clerk of Records and Writs, with whom the Record shall be left as prescribed by *Rule* 664.

Entry of non-jury actions for trial in Toronto.

Repealed Rule 1457

1279. RULE 545 is hereby amended by striking out the words "Clerk of Records and Writs" and inserting in lieu thereof the words "Clerk in Chambers."

Rule 545 amended.

Repealed Rule 1501

1280.—24a. All papers relating to proceedings in the weekly Court in all Divisions are to be filed, with the Clerk of Records and Writs, not later than the day preceding that upon which they are intended to be used.

Weekly court, papers for, where to be filed.

[24th March, 1894, and 23rd June, 1894.]
To come into force 1st September, 1894.

1281. RULE 2 is amended by adding thereto the following words :— "(a) The words ' County Court,' where they appear in the Consolidated Rules, shall include District Court."

Rule 2 amended.

282 — 1285 inclusive
repealed Rule 1560

1282. RULE 11 is hereby amended by adding thereto the following words. "and shall also sign and issue certificates of *lis pendens* under his seal of office, when required to do so on issuing the writ of summons."

Rule 11 amended.

1283. RULE 12 is hereby amended by adding thereto the words, "or supplied by him to other officers."

Rule 12 amended.

1284. RULE 15 is hereby amended by inserting after the word, "summons," the words "and *præcipes* for certificates of *lis pendens*."

Rule 15 amended.

1285. RULE 18 is hereby amended by inserting after the words "Deputy Registrars" wheresoever they occur in the said *Rule*, the words, "and Deputy Clerks of the Crown."

Rule 18 amended.

1286. RULE 28, clause (d) is hereby amended by inserting after the words "County of York," the words "or Registrar sitting personally, or by deputy." and by adding after the word "assize" in the second line, the words "or sittings of the Court."

Rule 28 amended.

MASTER IN CHAMBERS.

1287. RULE 30 is rescinded and the following substituted therefor :—

"30. The Master in Chambers, in regard to all actions and matters in the High Court, including proceedings in the nature of *quo warranto* under *The Municipal Act*, shall be, and hereby is, empowered and required to do all such things, transact all such business, and exercise all such authority and jurisdiction in respect to the same, as by virtue of any statute, or by the rules or practice of the Superior Courts, or any of them, respectively, were at the time of the passing of the Acts 33 Vict. (O.) cap. 11, 37 Vict. (O.) cap. 7 and *The Ontario Judicature Act, 1881*—or are now done, transacted, or exercised by any Judge of the said courts sitting at Chambers. save and except in respect to the matters following :—

Master in Chambers, jurisdiction of.

Matters excepted.

(1) All matters relating to criminal proceedings, or the liberty of the subject ;

Criminal matters, &c.

(2) Appeals and applications in the nature of Appeals ;

Appeals.

(3) Proceedings as to Lunatics under the Revised Statutes of Ontario, chapter 54, sections 5, 6, 7, 8, 9, 17 and 18, and chapter 44, section 140 ;

Lunacy.

Arrest.	(4) Applications to arrest ;
Petitions by trustees for advice.	(5) Petitions for advice under the Revised Statutes, chapter 110, section 34.
Custody of infants.	(6) Applications as to the custody of infants under the Revised Statutes, chapter 137, section 1 ;
Settled estates. Settlements of infants. Special cases.	(7) Applications as to leases and sales of settled estates ; to enable minors, with the approbation of the Court, to make binding settlements of their real and personal estate on marriage ; and in regard to questions submitted for the opinion of the Court in the form of special cases on the part of such persons as may by themselves, their committees, or guardians, or otherwise, concur therein ;
Administration.	(8) Opposed applications for Administration Orders ;
Infants or their estates.	(9) Opposed applications respecting the Guardianship of the person and property of Infants ;
Mandamus, and injunction.	(10) Applications for Prohibition, Mandamus or Injunction.
Partition.	(11) Proceedings as to Partition and sale of Real Estate, under the Revised Statutes, chapter 104.
Application to appeal.	(12) Extending the time for appealing to the Divisional Court, or the Court of Appeal, before, or after the time limited for that purpose has expired.
Appeals.	(13) Appeals from Judges of County Courts, or Local Masters, or in respect of any other matter which by these Rules is expressly required to be done by a Judge of the High Court.
Payment out of court.	(14) The payment of money out of Court, or dispensing with payment of money into Court, in administration and partition matters.
Granting taxed costs in lieu of commission.	(15) Making an order for taxed costs in lieu of commission under the provisions of *Rule* 1187.
Striking out jury notice.	(16) Striking out a jury notice except for irregularity.
	(17) And except (unless by consent of the parties) in respect of the following proceedings and matters, that is to say :
In certain matters jurisdiction by consent.	(a) The removal of causes from Inferior Courts, other than the removal of judgments for the purpose of having execution.
	(b) The referring of causes under the Revised Statutes, chapter 44, ss. 101, 102 ; and chapter 53, ss. 1, 2.
Review of taxation.	(c) Reviewing taxation of costs, except as provided in *Rule* 854.
Staying proceedings.	(d) Staying proceedings after verdict, or on judgment after trial or hearing before a Judge.
Rule 40 amended.	**1288.** RULE 40 is hereby amended by adding thereto the following words :
Reports of Referees.	"(a) The report of a Referee may be filed by any party forthwith after the same shall have been made, in the same manner as the report of a Master, and shall have the effect of, and be subject to all the incidents of, a report of a Master as regards confirmation, appealing therefrom, motions thereupon, and otherwise."
Jurisdiction in Chambers of Local Judges.	**1289.** RULE 41 is hereby rescinded and the following is substituted therefor :
	"41. The Judge of every County Court other than the County Court of York, shall, in all actions brought in his County, and in interpleader proceedings where the goods in respect of which interpleader is sought are situate in his County have concurrent jurisdiction with and the same

power and authority as the Master in Chambers in all proceedings now determined in Chambers at Toronto, except that the authority of such Judge shall not extend to ~~proceedings in the nature of a quo warranto under The Municipal Act, or to~~ the payment of money out of Court (except as provided by *Rule* 1164), or dispensing with payment of money into Court, in any action or matter, or to appeals from the Taxing Officers in Toronto pending taxation, or to making an order for the sale of infants' estates." 48 V. c. 13, s. 21. J. A. Rule 584.

1290. Rule 137 is amended by adding thereto the following :

Master to report age of infant beneficiaries.

"(*a*) Where, by a report, any money in Court is found to belong to infants, the Master shall require proper evidence of the age of the infants to be given before him. and shall in his report state the date of birth and age at the time of his report of each of such infants or shall certify special'y his reason for not so doing. This *Rule* shall also apply to infancy proceedings."

1291 Rule 138 is rescinded and the following substituted therefor :

Local Masters, jurisdiction of, in Chambers.

"138. Every Local Master who does not practise as a Barrister or Solicitor, and who has not taken out certificates to practise, shall, in addition to his other powers as Local Master, have in all actions brought in his County and in interpleader proceedings when the goods in respect of which the interpleader is sought are situated in his County concurrent jurisdiction with, and the same power and authority as, the Master in Chambers, in all proceedings now taken in Chambers at Toronto, except that the authority of such Local Masters shall not extend to proceedings in the nature of a *quo warranto* under *The Municipal Act*, or to payment of money out of Court, or dispensing with payment into Court, or to appeals from the Taxing Officers at Toronto pending taxation ; or to making an order for sale of infants' estates."

1292. Rule 146 is amended by striking out the words " bank interest " in the sec nd line, and by substituting therefor the words " interest allowe l by the Court."

Interest on money in Court—Rule 146 amended.

1293. Rule 163 is amended by striking out the words " Cayuga, or Sault Ste. Marie."

Rule 163 amended.

1294. Rule 165 is rescinded and the following substituted therefor :

Rule 165 amended.

" 165. Money required to be paid into Court may be paid into the Canadian Bank of Commerce, or any chartered Bank being its agent in this Province."

1295. Rule 167 is rescinded and the following substituted therefor :

Rule 167 amended— Directions to pay in.

" 167. The person applying for the direction is to leave a præcipe therefor in the form No. 112 in the Appendix, and is to leave with the officer issuing the direction the judgment or order or certified copy thereof under which the money is payable, and in case the direction is obtained elsewhere than in Toronto, he shall also leave the necessary postage for the transmission of the documents to the Accountant."

1296. Rule 168 is amended by striking out the word " forthwith " and substituting therefor the words " on the same day."

Rule 168 amended.

1297. Rule 171 is amended by striking out the words " Cayuga or Sault Ste. Marie."

Rule 171 amended.

1298. Rule 173 is amended by striking out the words " Cayuga or Sault Ste. Marie."

Rule 173 amended.

Rule 174 amended.

1299. RULE 174 is amended by striking out the words "prior to" and substituting the word "during"; and by striking out the word "twentieth" and substituting the word "thirtieth."

Rule 175 amended— Cheques, signing of.

1300. RULE 175 is amended by adding thereto the following clause :

"(a). In case of the unavoidable absence of the Accountant, or Chief Clerk in the Accountant's Office, a Judge of the High Court may authorize any other officers to sign or initial cheques in the place of the Accountant and Chief Clerk respectively.

Rule 176 amended.

1301. RULE 176 is amended by striking out the word "file" and substituting therefor the word "leave."

Rule 177 amended.

1302. RULE 177 is rescinded and the following substituted therefor :

"177. Orders dispensing with payment of money into Court or certified copies thereof are in all cases to be left with the Accountant forthwith after entry thereof.'

Rule 202 amended.

healed Rule 1428(2)

1303. RULE 202 is amended by striking out the word "enter" in the seventh line and substituting therefor the words "cause to be entered," and by striking out the word "make" in the last line and substituting therefor the words "cause to be made."

Rule 203 amended.

1304. RULE 203 is amended by striking out the word "enter" and substituting therefor the words "cause to be entered."

sealed Rules 217, by 1560 1268 amended.

Sittings of Chancery Divisional Court.

1305. RULE 217 as amended by *Rule* 1268 is rescinded and the following substituted therefor :

"217. The Divisional Court of the Chancery Division shall hold sittings commencing on the third Thursday in February, the last Monday in May and the first Thursday in December in each year."

sealed Rule 219 amended. by 1560

1306. RULE 219 is amended by adding thereto the words : *amended Rule 1430*

"Motions to vary or set aside judgments entered at the trial."

Rule 233 amended. Date and teste of writs.

1307. RULE 233 is rescinded and the following substituted therefor :

"233. Every writ shall bear date on the day on which the same is issued, and shall be tested in the name of the President of the High Court of Justice ; and every writ of summons shall require the defendant to appear thereto in ten days after service including the day of service, if the service is to be made in Ontario, except as provided by *Rule* 275 as amended."

Lost writ.

1308.—237a Where a writ, of which production is necessary, has been lost, the Court or a Judge, upon being satisfied of the loss and of the correctness of a copy thereof, may order that such copy shall be sealed and served in lieu of the original writ.

amended Rule 1439 1440

" Service of writ out of jurisdiction.

1309. RULE 271 is rescinded and the following substituted therefor :

SERVICE OUT OF THE JURISDICTION.

"271.—(1) Service out of the jurisdiction of a writ of summons or notice of a writ of summons may be allowed by the Court or a Judge whenever :—

(a) The whole subject-matter of the action is land situate within the jurisdiction (with or without rents or profits) ; or

(b) Any act, deed, will, contract, obligation, or liability affecting land or hereditaments situate within the jurisdiction is sought to be construed, rectified, set aside, or enforced in the action ; or

(c) Any relief is sought against any person domiciled or ordinarily resident within the jurisdiction ; or

(d) The action is for the administration of the personal estate of any deceased person who at the time of his death was domiciled within the jurisdiction, or for the execution (as to property situate within the jurisdiction) of the trusts of any written instrument of which the person to be served is a trustee, which ought to be executed according to the law of Ontario ; or

(e) The action is founded on any breach or alleged breach within the jurisdiction of any contract wherever made, which is to be performed within the jurisdiction or on any tort committed within the jurisdiction ; or

(f) Any injunction is sought as to anything to be done within the jurisdiction, or any nuisance within the jurisdiction is sought to be prevented or removed, whether damages are or are not also sought in respect thereof ; or

(g) Any person out of the jurisdiction is a necessary or proper party to an action properly brought against some other person duly served within the jurisdiction.

"(2) Service of any order or notice in the winding-up of a Company, may by leave of the Court or a Judge be allowed out of the jurisdiction. *Proceeding in winding-up of companies.*

"(3) Every application for leave to serve or give notice of any proceeding out of the jurisdiction shall be supported by affidavit or other evidence stating that in the belief of the deponent the applicant has a right to the relief claimed, and showing in what place or country the person to be served is or probably may be found, and whether he is a British subject or not, and the grounds upon which the application is made, and no such leave shall be granted unless it shall be made sufficiently to appear to the Court or Judge that the case is a proper one for service out of the jurisdiction under this *Rule. Application to be supported by evidence.*

"(4) Any order giving leave to effect service out of the jurisdiction of a writ, or to give notice of a writ out of the jurisdiction, shall limit a time after such service or notice for entering an appearance. In regulating the time for entering the appearance regard shall be had to the place or country where or within which the writ or summons is to be served or the notice given. *Order to fix time for appearance to writ.*

"(5) Any order giving leave to serve out of the jurisdiction a notice of motion, to which an appearance is not required to be entered, shall limit a time when the motion is to be heard, having regard to the place or country where or within which the notice of motion is to be served. *Order to fix time for hearing motion where no appearance to be entered.*

"(6) Where the defendant or respondent is neither a British subject nor in British dominions, notice of the writ or summons and not the writ or summons itself is to be given to him. Such notice shall be given to him personally, or in such other manner as the Court or a Judge may direct. *Notice in lieu of writ.*

"(7) Service out of the jurisdiction of a petition or notice of motion may be allowed by the Court or a Judge whenever the petition or notice is presented or given in an action or matter relating to the administration of the estate of a deceased person or to the execution of a trust, or, prays for an order dealing with any funds in Court. In regulating the time for hearing the petition or motion regard shall be had to the place or country where or within which the petition or notice of motion is to be served." *Service of petitions or notices of motion out of jurisdiction.*

1310. RULE 275 is rescinded and the following substituted therefor : *Rule 275 amended.*

"275. When a defendant is served within Ontario and not in Algoma, Rainy River or Thunder Bay, he shall appear within ten days, including the day of service. *Time for appearance.*

"(a) If served within Algoma, Rainy River or Thunder Bay, unless otherwise ordered under *Rule* 485, he is to have thirty days in an action for the recovery of land, and twenty days in other actions, after the service, including the day of service, except when he is served between the first day of November and the thirtieth day of June or on either of said days, in which case he shall have an additional period of ten days."

Rule 276 amended.

1311. RULE 276 is rescinded and the following substituted therefor :

" 276. When a defendant is to be served out of Ontario the writ of summons may be in the Form No. 2 in the Appendix, and the statement of claim is to be served therewith, unless the writ is specially indorsed under *Rules* 245. 246 or 248."

Unborn persons, representation of.

1312 RULE 316 is amended by adding thereto the following clause :

"(a) The Court shall have power to appoint a person to represent unborn persons under this *Rule.*"

Third party notice, where contribution or indemnity claimed.

1313. RULES 328, 329, 330, 331 and 332 are rescinded and the following substituted therefor :

" 328. Where a defendant claims to be entitled to contribution, or indemnity over against any person not a party to the action, he may, by leave of the Court or a Judge, issue a notice (hereinafter called the third party notice) to that effect, stamped with the seal with which writs of summons are sealed. A copy of such notice shall be filed with the proper officer and served on such person according to the *Rules* relating to the service of writs of summons. The notice shall state the nature and grounds of the claim, and shall, unless otherwise ordered by the Court or a Judge, be served within the time limited for delivering his defence. Such notice may be in the form or to the effect of the Form No. 88a in the Appendix hereto, with such variations as circumstances may require, and therewith shall be served a copy of the Statement of Claim, or if there be no Statement of Claim, then a copy of the writ of summons in the action.

Third party, appearance of.

Default of appearance.

Leave to appear, when necessary.

" 329. If a person not a party to the action, who is served as mentioned in *Rule* 328 (hereinafter called the third party) desires to dispute the plaintiff's claim in the action as against the defendant on whose behalf the notice has been given, or his own liability to the defendant, the third party must enter an appearance in the action within eight days from the service of the notice. In default of his so doing, he shall be deemed to admit the validity of the judgment obtained against such defendant, whether obtained by consent or otherwise, and his own liability to contribute or indemnify, as the case may be, to the extent claimed in the third party notice. Provided always that a person so served and failing to appear within the said period of eight days may apply to the Court or a Judge for leave to appear, and such leave may be given upon such terms, if any, as the Court or Judge shall think fit.

Third party, judgment against, how obtained.

" 330. Where a third party makes default in entering an appearance in the action, in case the defendant giving the notice suffer judgment by default, he shall be entitled at any time, after satisfaction of the judgment against himself, or before such satisfaction, by leave of the Court or a Judge, to enter judgment against the third party to the extent of the contribution or indemnity claimed in the third party notice ; provided that it shall be lawful for the Court or a Judge to set aside or vary such judgment upon such terms as may seem just.

Third party, judgment against, how obtained.

" 331. Where a third party makes default in entering an appearance in the action, in case the action is tried and results in favor of the plaintiff, the Judge who tries the action may, at or after the trial. direct such judgment as the nature of the case may require, for the defendant giving the notice against the third party ; provided that execution thereon be not issued without leave of the Judge, until after satisfaction by such defendant of the verdict or judgment against him. And if the action is finally decided in the plaintiff's favor, otherwise than by trial, the Court or a Judge may, on motion direct such judgment, as the nature of the case may require, to be entered for the defendant giving the notice against the third party at any time, after satisfaction by the defendant of the amount recovered by the plaintiff against him.

"332. If a third party appears pursuant to the third party notice, the defendant giving the notice may apply to the Court or a Judge for directions, and the Court or Judge, upon hearing of such application, may, if satisfied that there is a question proper to be tried as to the liability of the third party to make the contribution or indemnity claimed, in whole or in part order the question of such liabi ity, as between the third party and the defendant giving the notice, to be tried in such manner, at or after the trial of the action, as the Court or Judge may direct ; and, if not so satisfied, may direct such judgment as the nature of the case may require, to be entered in favor of the defendant giving the notice against the third party. *(Defendant notifying third party, may apply for directions.)*

"(a) The Court or a Judge upon the hearing of the application mentioned in the last-mentioned *Rule*, may, if it shall appear desirable to do so, give the third party liberty to defend the action, upon such terms as may be just, or to appear at the trial and take such part therein as may be just, and generally may order such proceedings to be taken, documents to be delivered, or amendments to be made, and give such directions as to the Court or Judge shall appear proper for having the question most conveniently determined, and as to the mode and extent in or to which the third party shall be bound or made liable by the judgment in the action. *(Order to be made on such application.)*

"(b) The Court or Judge may decide all questions of costs, as between a third party and the other parties to the action, and may order any one or more to pay the costs of any other, or others, or give such directions as to costs as the justice of the case may require. *(Costs.)*

"(c) Where a defendant claims to be entitled to contribution or indemnity against any other defendant to the action, a notice may be issued and the same procedure shall be adopted, for the determination of such questions between the defendants, as would be issued and taken against such other defendant, if such last-mentioned defendant were a third party ; but nothing herein contained shall prejudice the rights of the plaintiff against any defendant in the action." *(Claim to contribution or indemnity against a co-defendant.)*

1314. RULE 336a is amended by striking out the words "writ of summons" in the last line, and substituting therefor the word "notice." *(Rule 336a amended.)*

1315. RULE 341 is amended by adding to the first paragraph thereof, after the word "claimed," the following words : "or for specific performance, or for an injunction or receiver in respect of the said lands, or the rents and profits thereof". *(Rule 341 amended.)*

1316. RULE 363 is amended by adding thereto the following words :

"(a) In mortgage actions when it becomes necessary to fix a date for redemption after the lapse of the first period of six months, the further time allowed shall be one month." *(Rule 363 amended. New day for redemption.)*

1317. RULE 370 is amended by striking out in lines 3 and 4 the words "file a copy of the writ with a copy of the special indorsemen. thereon if not filed already and ". *(Rule 370 amended.)*

1318. RULE 371 is amended by inserting in line 2, before the word "counterclaim" the word "or," and by striking out in line 2 the words "or demurrer." *(Rule 371 amended.)*

1319. RULE 372 is amended by inserting in line 3 before the word "counterclaim" the word "or," and by striking out in lines 3 and 4 the words "or demurrer." *(Rule 372 amended.)*

Rule 374 amended.	**1320.** RULE 374 is amended by striking out in line 2 for the word "aforesaid" and substituting the words "hereinafter mentioned".
Rule 380 amended.	**1321.** RULE 380 is amended by inserting in line 1 after the word "plaintiff" the words "and other person, if any, named as a party to the counterclaim".
Rules 384-91 amended.	**1322.** RULES 384, 385, 386, 387, 388, 389, 390 and 391 are rescinded and the following substituted therefor : "384. No demurrer shall be allowed.
Demurrers abolished. Questions of law, how to be determined.	"385. Any party shall be entitled to raise by his pleading any point of law, and any point so raised shall be disposed of by the Judge who tries the cause at or after the trial, provided that by consent of the parties, or by order of the Court or a Judge on the application of either party, the same may be set down for hearing and disposed of at any time before the trial. "386. If, in the opinion of the Court or a Judge, the decision of such point of law substantially disposes of the whole action, or of any distinct cause of action, ground of defence, set-off, counterclaim or reply therein, the Court or Judge may thereupon dismiss the action or make such other order therein as may be just.
Pleading may be struck out.	"387. The Court or a Judge may order any pleading to be struck out on the ground that it discloses no reasonable cause of action or answer, and in any such case, or in case of the action being shown by the pleadings to be frivolous or vexatious, the Court or a Judge may order the action to be stayed or dismissed, or judgment to be entered accordingly as may be just."
Rule 392 amended.	**1323.** RULE 392 is amended by striking out in line 5 the words "or demurrer".
Rule 393 amended.	**1324.** RULE 393 is amended by striking out in line 2 the word "demurrer".
Rules 395, 396 amended.	**1325.** RULES 395, 396 are amended by inserting before the word "pleading," wherever it occurs in the said *Rules*, the words "writ or".
Particulars may be ordered.	**1326.** RULE 423 is amended by adding thereto the following words : "(a) A further and better statement of the nature of the claim or defence, or further and better particulars of any matter stated in any pleading, notice or written proceeding requiring particulars, may in all cases be ordered upon such terms, as to costs or otherwise, as may be deemed just."
Amendment of set-off or counter-claim.	**1327.** RULE 425 is rescinded and the following substituted therefor : "425. A defendant who has set up any set-off or counterclaim, may, on application in Chambers, be allowed to amend the same upon such terms in all respects as the Court or a Judge shall see fit."
Rule 426 amended.	**1328.** RULE 426 is amended by striking out the words "either of the last two preceding Rules," and by substituting therefor the words "*Rule* 424".
Rule 427 amended.	**1329.** RULE 427 is amended by striking out the words "or 425".
Rule 462 amended. Service, by posting up in office, when allowable.	**1330.** RULE 462 is rescinded and the following substituted therefor : "462. Where a party sues or defends in person and no address for service of such party is written or printed pursuant to the directions of *Rules* 240, 241 and 242, or where a party has ceased to have a solicitor, or where

a defendant served with a writ of summons, or notice in lieu of a writ of summons has not duly appeared thereto, all writs, notices, orders, appointments, warrants and other documents, proceedings and written communications, not requiring personal service upon the party to be affected thereby, shall, unless the Court otherwise directs, be deemed to be sufficiently served upon the party, by posting up a copy in the office in which the proceedings are being conducted. But if an address for service is written or printed as aforesaid, then all such writs, notices, orders, warrants and other documents, proceedings and written communications, shall be deemed sufficiently served upon such party if left for him at such address for service."

1331. RULE 484 is rescinded and the following substituted therefor :— Rule 481 amended.

" 484. The time of the long vacation, or of the Christmas vacation, Vacations, shall not be reckoned in the computation of the times appointed or allowed time of, when by these *Rules* for filing, amending, or delivering any pleading, or in the not to be times allowed for the following purposes, unless otherwise directed by the reckoned. Court or a Judge :

" (1) Appeals to Judge in Chambers ;

" (2) Masters' reports becoming absolute ;

" (3) Moving to discharge an order under *Rule* 622 ;

" (4) Moving to add to, vary, or set aside a judgment by any party served therewith ;

" (5) Doing any act or taking any proceeding in appealing to the Court of Appeal, except in County Court appeals."

1332. RULE 485 is amended by striking out the words "enlarging Rule 485 time" in the third line. amended.

1333. RULE 487 is amended by adding thereto the following words : Rule 487 " (a) But no such examination shall take place during the long vacation amended. unless upon the order of a Judge."

1334. RULE 488 is amended by adding thereto the following words : Rule 488. amended.

" (a) When any action is brought by an assignee of any chose in action, Assignor of the assignor of such chose in action may be examined for discovery." chose in action, examinable for discovery.

1335. RULE 502 is rescinded and the following substituted therefor :— Rule 502

" 502. In case of an examination before the trial, or otherwise than at amended. the trial of an action, if the examining party desires to have such examina- Examination may be taken tion taken in shorthand, he shall be entitled to have it so taken at the in shorthand. place of examination by the Examiner or by a shorthand writer approved by the Examiner and duly sworn by him, except where the Court or Judge sees fit to order otherwise."

1336. RULE 503 is rescinded and the following substituted therefor : Rule 503

" 503. Where an examination in a cause or proceeding in any court is amended. taken by the Examiner, shorthand writer as aforesaid, or any other duly authorized person, in shorthand, the examination may be taken down by Examinations question and answer ; and in such case it shall not be necessary for the how to be depositions to be read over to, or signed by, the person examined, unless taken in short-the Judge so directs where the examination is taken before a Judge, or in hand. other cases unless any of the parties so desires."

(a) A copy of the depositions so taken, certified by the person taking Certified copy the same as correct, and if such person be not the Examiner, also signed to have effect by the Examiner, shall for all purposes have the same effect as the of original original depositions in ordinary cases. 41 V. c. 8, s. 8. depositions.

2

Rule 512 rescinded.

1337. RULE 512 is rescinded.

Rule 537 amended.

1338. RULE 537 is amended by striking out the word "demurrers."

Rule 538 amended.

1339. RULE 538 is amended by striking out the word "demurrers," and also the words "when a married woman, infant or person of unsound mind is a party to the action, a copy of the order giving leave to enter a special case for argument shall also be produced."

Rule 539 rescinded.

1340. RULE 539 is rescinded.

Rule 540 amended. Special case, setting down.

1341. RULE 540 is rescinded and the following substituted therefor :

"540. A special case shall be set down to be heard, and notice thereof given to the opposite party six clear days before the day on which it is to be heard ; and a copy of the special case shall be left at the office of the Clerk of Records and Writs for the use of the Judge before whom the special case is to be heard, two days before the day appointed for the hearing "

amended Rule 1456

Where infants or married women interested.

(*a*) Where an order has been made under *Rule* 557 giving leave to set down for argument a special case in an action to which a married woman, infant or person of unsound mind is a party, su h order, or an office copy thereof, shall be produced when the special case is set down.

Rule 544 amended.

1342. RULE 544 is amended by adding after the word "same," the words "provided that the Judge pronouncing such order may himself sign the same."

Rule 553 amended.

1343. RULE 553 is rescinded and the following substituted therefor :

"553. An order of reference made under the Judicature Act or *Rule* 551 shall be read as if it contained the provisions in *Rule* 552, but may contain any variation therefrom or addition thereto."

Rule 566 amended.

1344. RULE 566 is amended by adding thereto the following words :

"(*a*) Such examination in the absence of any order to the contrary shall be conducted in accordance with the practice hereinbefore prescribed upon examinations for discovery in so far as the same shall be applicable."

Rule 577 amended. Cross-examination on affidavits.

1345. RULE 577 is rescinded and the following substituted therefor :

"577. Every person who makes an affidavit to be used in any action or proceeding other than on production of documents shall be liable to cross-examination thereon, and may be required to attend in the same manner, and subject to the same rules as a party to be examined in the cause, but the Court nevertheless may act upon the evidence before it at the time, and may make such order as appears necessary to meet the justice of the case."

Rule 601 amended. Evidence on commission may be taken in shorthand.

1346. RULE 601 is amended by adding thereto the following clause :

"(*a*) Provided that the Commissioner or Commissioners, if the examining party desires to take such examination taken in shorthand, may take the same in shorthand or employ a shorthand writer, approved by him or them and duly sworn, in which case the examination may be taken down by question and answer ; and it shall not be necessary for the depositions to be read over or signed by the person examined unless any of the parties so desire ; and a copy of the depositions so taken, certified by the Commissioner or Commissioners, or in case the same shall have been taken in shorthand by some person employed for the purpose as aforesaid, certified by such shorthand writer as correct and signed by the Commissioner or Commissioners, shall, for all purposes, have the same effect as the original depositions in ordinary cases."

(b) Form No. 118 is amended by inserting after clause six the following words :—

" But where the examination is taken in shorthand it is not necessary for the depositions to be read over or signed by the witness or witnesses, *unless any of the parties so desire* ; but in such case a copy of the depositions in long hand certified by the shorthand writer as correct is to be attached to the Commission and signed by the Commissioner or Commissioners who shall have taken the depositions."

1347. RULE 611 is amended by inserting after the words " Court or a Judge," the words " or officer before whom the affidavit is to be used."

1348. RULE 647 is rescinded and the following substituted therefor :

"647. If the pleadings are closed six weeks before the commencement of any sittings of the High Court for which the plaintiff might give notice of trial, and he does not give notice of trial therefor and proceed to trial pursuant to such notice, the action may be dismissed for want of prosecution."

1349. RULE 718 is rescinded and the following substituted therefor :

"718. Where the defendant does not appear, or by his statement of defence admits the execution of the mortgage and other facts, if any, entitling the plaintiff to a judgment, or where the defendant disclaims any interest in the mortgaged premises, or where no statement of defence is delivered, or where notice is filed and served disputing the amount of the plaintiff's claim only, the plaintiff is, on *præcipe* to the Registrar, or Deputy or Local Registrar, or Deputy Clerk of the Crown in whose office the appearance of the defendant was required to be entered, to be entitled to judgment including, where prayed for, the relief for which a claim may be indorsed upon the writ under *Rule* 248.

(a) The reference in such cases, when required by the practice, shall be to the Master-in-Ordinary, or a Local Master.

(b) Such a judgment may be granted, notwithstanding that the defendant has been served by publication, or otherwise, or is a corporation, provided always that where the writ has not been personally served, the claim of the plaintiff shall be duly verified by affidavit.

(c) This rule shall apply to actions for redemption, as well as to actions for foreclosure or sale.

(d) Where a notice disputing the amount of the plaintiff's claim is filed, the defendant filing the same shall be entitled to four days' notice of the taking of the account of the amount due to the plaintiff. Where no reference as to incumbrances is desired such account may be taken by the officer entering judgment ; and where a reference as to incumbrances is desired, then by the Master to whom the action is referred. The finding of the officer taking the account as to the amount due on entering judgment shall be subject to appeal to a Judge in Chambers in the manner prescribed by *Rule* 846, and such officer shall have power to direct a stay of proceedings until the time for appealing has expired.

(e) Where a reference as to incumbrances is directed in a case where a notice disputing the amount of the plaintiff's claim has been filed, the judgment shall direct that the defendant filing such notice shall have four days' notice of the taking of the account.

1350. RULE 727 is amended by striking out the words " or demurrer," and also by striking out the word " six " and by substituting therefor the word " eight."

amended **1351.** RULE 759 is rescinded and the following substituted therefor :
Rule 1479 "759. All judgments in cases tried at Toronto shall be settled when necessary by a Registrar."

Rule 761 amended. Judgments, settlement of, by local officers.

1352. RULE 761 is rescinded and the following substituted therefor :

" 761. All judgments delivered elsewhere than at Toronto, shall be settled when necessary by the Deputy Registrar, Deputy Clerk or Local Registrar, at the place of trial ; subject to the right of any party affected to apply upon notice to the other parties interested to one of the Judgment Clerks, or to the Judge, to vary the minutes."

Rule 764 amended. Court orders.

1353. RULE 764 is amended by adding thereto the following clause :

"(a) Every order pronounced by the Court shall be drawn up and signed by the Registrar, Local Registrar, Deputy Registrar, Deputy Clerk of the Crown, or the Clerk of the Weekly Court attending the Court at which the same is pronounced, provided that the Judge pronouncing such order may himself sign the same."

Rule 772 amended. Court orders, entry of.

1354. RULE 772 is rescinded and the following substituted therefor :

"772. Every judgment, and every order pronounced in Court, shall be entered at full length in a book to be kept for that purpose by the officer issuing the same.

Rule 835 amended.

1355. RULE 835 is amended by striking out the words "section 41," and by substituting therefor the words " the provisions."

Rule 843 amended. Notice of C. C. appeal.

Repealed
Rule 1560

1356. RULE 843 is rescinded and the following substituted therefor :

" 843. The applicant shall, at least six days before the sittings at which the appeal is to be heard, serve the respondent with the notice of the setting down of the appeal, and with a copy of the appeal book, and of the grounds and reasons of his appeal."

Rule 846 amended.

1357. RULE 846 is amended by striking out the figure "9" in clause (c) and substituting therefor the figures " 10."

Rule 852 amended.

1358. RULE 852 is amended by striking out the word "nine" and substituting therefor the word " ten."

Rule 863 amended.

1359. RULE 863 is amended by striking out the word " entered " and substituting therefor the word " signed."

Rule 926 amended. Examination of judgment debtors.

1360. RULE 926 is rescinded and the following substituted therefor :

" 926. Where a judgment is for the recovery by, or payment to, any person, of money or costs, the party entitled to enforce the judgment may, without an order, examine the judgment debtor upon oath before a Master, or Local Master, or an Examiner, or before one of the Registrars, Deputy Clerks of the Crown, or before the Judge of the County Court of the County within which such debtor resides, or before any official referee, (or by the order of the Court or a Judge before any other person to be specially named in such order), touching his estate and effects, and as to the property and means he had when the debt or liability which was the subject of the action in which judgment has been obtained against him was incurred, (or in the case of a judgment for costs only,—at the time of the issue of the writ of summons,) and as to the property, and means he still has of discharging the said judgment, and as to the disposal he has made of any property since contracting such debt or incuring such liability, (or in case of a judgment for costs only,—since the issue of the writ of summons,) and as to any and what debts are owing to him."

Rule 935 amended.

1361. RULE 935 is amended by striking out all the words after the word " debtor" in the ninth line down to and inclusive of the word " execution " in the twelfth line.

1362. RULE 1015 is rescinded and the following substituted therefor : Rule 1015
"1015. All petitions under the Act are to be filed in the office of the Petitions
Clerk of Records and Writs, and may, at the option of the petitioner, be under Q. T.
referred to any of the officers of the Court at Toronto, or to any convey- Act, filing of.
ancing Counsel who may from time to time be designated by the Court
for the purpose, or to any Local Master."

1363. RULE 1017 is rescinded and the following substituted therefor : Rule 1017
"1017. Petitions to be referred to any Local Master are to be indorsed Petitions
thus : ' To be referred to the Master at   and to under Q. T.
Mr.   Inspector of Titles.' "   Act, how to
be indorsed.

1364. RULE 1018 is amended by striking out the word " Referee " in Rule 1018
the fourth line, and substituting therefor the words " Local Master." amended.

1365. RULE 1019 is amended by striking out the words " or, if duly Rule 1019
stamped, to the Registrar." amended.

1366. RULE 1103 is rescinded and the following substituted therefor : Rule 1103
" 1103. Before the Sheriff acts on the order he shall take a bond from Replevin bond
the plaintiff with two sufficient sureties in such sum as may be prescribed to be taken
for that purpose by an order made under *Rule* 1100, if such an order by Sheriff.
has been made, or if no such order has been made then in treble the value
of the property to be replevied, as stated in the order ; which bond shall
be assignable to the defendant ; and the bond and assignment thereof
may be in the words or to the effect of Form No. 208 in the Appendix,
the condition being varied to correspond with the order."

1367. RULE 1110 is amended by adding thereto the following clause : Rule 1110
" (a) In case a Sheriff makes return that the whole or any part of the Where Sheriff
property has been eloigned, or that for any reason the same cannot be returns goods
replevied under the order, the plaintiff may, if he so elect, serve the writ eloigned.
of summons, and in his statement of claim, claim either an order for the
return of the goods and damages for their detention, or damages for their
conversion."

1368. RULE 1134 is amended by striking out the words "the two Rule 1134
preceding rules " in line five, and by substituting therefor the words amended.
" *Rules* 1131, 1132, 1133 or 1135."

1369. The several headings in Chapter XII, part 8, of the Consoli- Interpleader.
dated *Rules* relating to Interpleader, viz :

"(i) *Generally.*

(ii) *Interpleader in County Courts.*

(iii) *Interpleader by Bailees and Carriers* "

are hereby expunged.

(a) RULE 1162 is rescinded and the following substituted therefor :— Rule 1162
amended.
" 1162. The Consolidated *Rules*, 1141 to 1161 inclusive, in cases Interpleader
under sections (a) and (b) of Consolidated *Rule* 1141, shall, in so far as jurisdiction
it is not otherwise inconsistent with the provisions of those *Rules*, apply of C. C.
to the County Court in manner following :

(a) Where the debt, money, goods or chattels mentioned in the said
section (a) are the subject of a suit against the applicant in
the County Court, the application for interpleader may be to
the Judge of the said County Court, and where no such suit is
pending and where the debt, money, goods or chattels in ques-

t on do not exceed in value $200, the application may be to the Judge of the County Court of the County or union of Counties in which the applicant resides, or in which the money, goods or chattels is or are situate.

And in cases under section (b) of the said Consolidated *Rule* 1141 where the application is by a Sheriff or other officer in respect of a claim to any money, goods or chattels taken or intended to be taken in execution under any process issued by a County Court, or under an attachment against an absconding debtor issued out of the County Court, or to the proceeds or value of any such goods or chattels by any person other than the person against whom the process issued, such application for an interpleader order may be made to the Judge of the County Court of the County or union of Counties in which such money, goods or chattels are so taken or intended to be taken, notwithstanding that there are writs from two or more County Courts against the same goods.

(c) All subsequent proceedings shall be had and taken in the County or union of Counties where the application is made ; provided that the Judge to whom any such application is made as aforesaid, if it appears more convenient and conducive to the ends of justice so to do, may order that the subsequent proceedings be had and taken in any other County.

Rule 1163 amended. sue when iable in D.C.

1370. RULE 1163 is amended by adding thereto the following clause :

" (4) Where the amount of the execution or the value of the goods does not exceed $100, the issue may be directed to be tried in the Division Court, and thereafter all proceedings shall be carried on in said Court."

Rule 1164 amended.

1371. RULE 1164 is amended by inserting after the words "County Court," the words " or Division Court as the case may be."

Rule 1165 amended.

1372. RULE 1165 is amended by inserting after the word "Court" wheresoever it occurs, the words " or Division Court."

Rule 1196 amended. Costs of taking bond off files.

1373. RULE 1196 is amended by adding thereto the following words :

" (a) The costs of removing a bond from off the files of the Court for the purpose of bringing an action thereon, may be taxed as costs in the cause in the action brought thereon."

Rule 1130 amended. Taxation of costs.

1374. RULE 1230 is amended by adding thereto the following clause :

" (a) The taxing officer shall hold the taxation open for what, under the circumstances of the case, he may consider to be a reasonable time in order to allow such objections to be carried in before him."

Rule 1233 amended.

Sheriff's poundage where land or chattels real seized, but not sold.

1375. RULE 1233 is amended by striking out the word "defendant" and by substituting therefor the words " judgment debtor," and by adding the following words :

" (a) In case the real estate or chattels real of the judgment debtor has or have been advertised under an execution, but not sold by reason of payment or satisfaction having been otherwise obtained on, or within one month before, the day on which the property has been advertised to be sold. or any day to which such sale may be adjourned. the Sheriff shall be entitled to the fees and expenses of the execution and the poundage, only on the value of the debtor's interest in the property not exceeding the amount indorsed on the writ. or such less sum as the Court or Judge may deem reasonable."

1376. RULE 1242 is amended by inserting after the word "præcipe," Rule 1242 the words "after entering an appearance." amended.

1377. RULE 1245 is amended by adding thereto the following words : Rule 1245 "(a) A plaintiff ordinarily resident out of the jurisdiction may be amended. ordered to give security for costs, though he may be tempor- Security for arily resident within the jurisdiction." costs.

1378. RULE 1247 is amended by adding thereto the following words : Rule 1247 "(a) Upon filing a bond for security for costs with affidavits of execu- amended. tion and justification with the proper officer, either party may Bond for apply to the Court or a Judge to allow or disallow the said security for bond, and in case no application is made to disallow the same allowed. within fourteen days after notice of filing the bond is served, it shall stand allowed."

1379. These *Rules* shall come into force on the first day of September, 1894.

APPENDIX.

FORM 88a.

Third Party Notice.

In the High Court of Justice,
  Division.
Between A. B.,   Plaintiff,
                          and
      C. D.,   Defendant.
Notice filed   , 189 .

To Mr. X. Y.

Take notice that this action has been brought by the plaintiff against the defendant [as surety for M. N. upon a bond conditioned for payment of $2,000 and interest to the plaintiff.

The defendant claims to be entitled to contribution from you to the extent of one-half of any sum which the plaintiff may recover against him, on the ground that you are his co-surety under the said bond, *or,* also surety for the said M. N., in respect of the said matter, under another bond made by you in favor of the said plaintiff, dated the   day of   A.D.,   .]

Or [as acceptor of a bill of exchange for $500, dated the   day of   A.D.   , drawn by you upon and accepted by the defendant, and payable three months after date.

The plaintiff claims to be indemnified by you against liability under the said bill, on the ground that it was accepted for your accommodation.]

Or [as acceptor of a bill of exchange for $500, dated the .   day of   A.D.   drawn by you upon and accepted by the defendant, and payable three months after date.

The defendant claims to be indemnified by you against liability under the said bill, on the ground that it was accepted for your accommodation].

Or [to recover damages for a breach of a contract for the sale and delivery to the plaintiff of 1,000 tons of coal.

The defendant claims to be indemnified by you against liability in respect of the said contract, or any breach thereof, on the ground that it was made by him on your behalf and as your agent.]

And take notice that, if you wish to dispute the plaintiff's claim in this action as against the defendant *C. D.*, or your liability to the defendant *C. D.*, you must cause an appearance to be entered for you within eight days after service of this notice.

In default of your so appearing, you will be deemed to admit the validity of any judgment obtained against the defendant *C. D.*, and your own liability to contribute or indemnify to the extent herein claimed, which may be summarily enforced against you pursuant to the *Rules* of the Supreme Court, 328 to 332 inclusive as amended.

(Signed) *E. F.*

or

X. Y.,

Solicitor for the defendant, *E. F.*

Appearance to be entered at

INDEX.

3